PUBLISHER – DAMIAN A. WASSEL
EDITOR–IN–CHIEF – ADRIAN F. WASSEL
SENIOR ARTIST – NATHAN C. GOODEN
EVP DESIGN & PRODUCTION – TIM DANIEL
VP SALES & MARKETING – DAVID DISSANAYAKE
PRODUCTION MANAGER – IAN BALDESSARI
MANAGING EDITOR, WONDERBOUND – REBECCA TAYLOR
DIRECTOR, SALES & MARKETING, BOOK TRADE – SYNDEE BARWICK
ART DIRECTOR – SONJA SYNAK
SOCIAL MEDIA STRATEGY – ALEX SCOLA
DIRECTOR, EVENTS & SOCIAL COMMERCE – DAN CRARY
MANAGING EDITOR, VAULT – DER–SHING HELMER

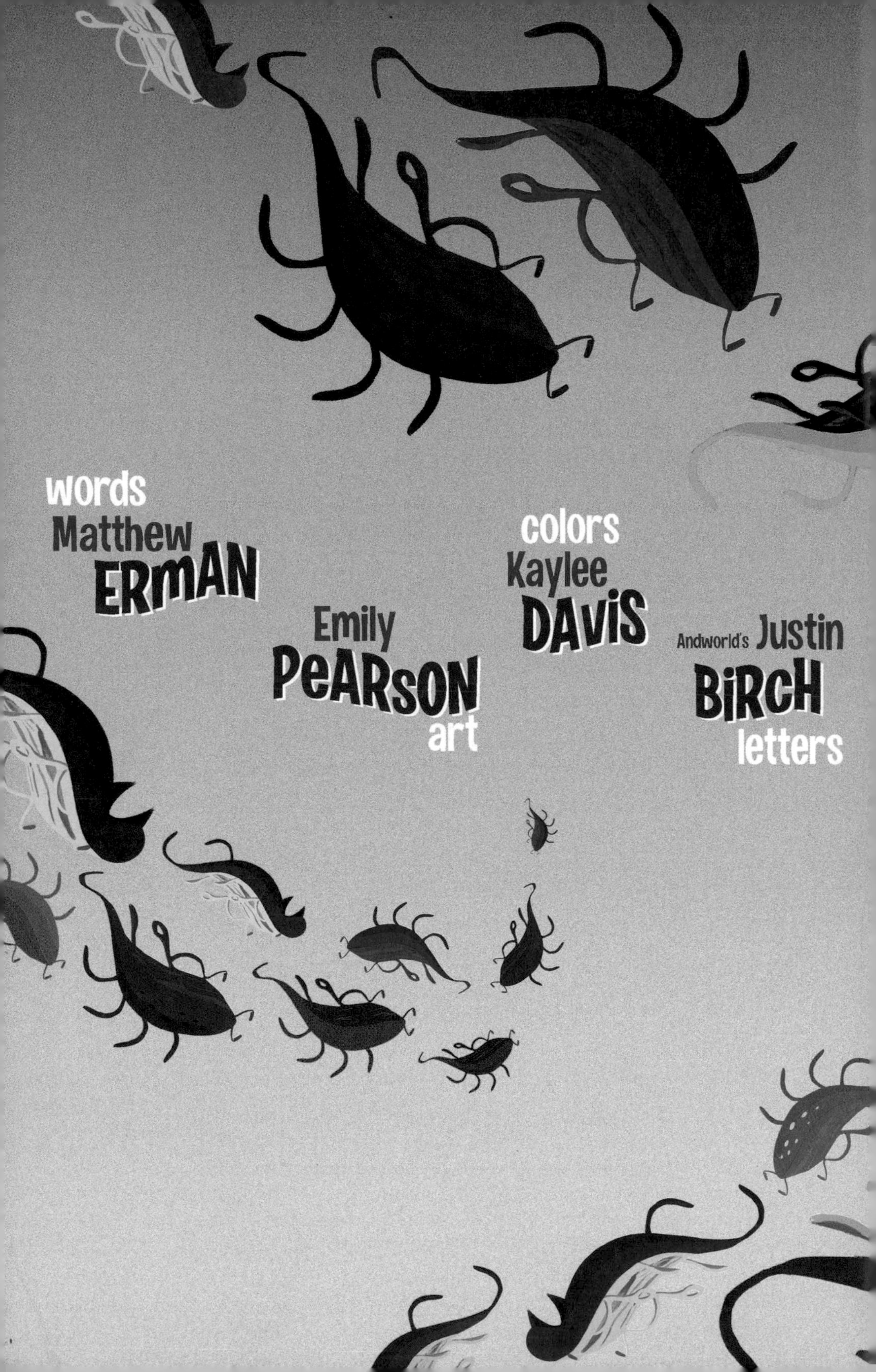

words
Matthew ERMAN

Emily PEARSON
art

colors
Kaylee DAVIS

Andworld's Justin BIRCH
letters

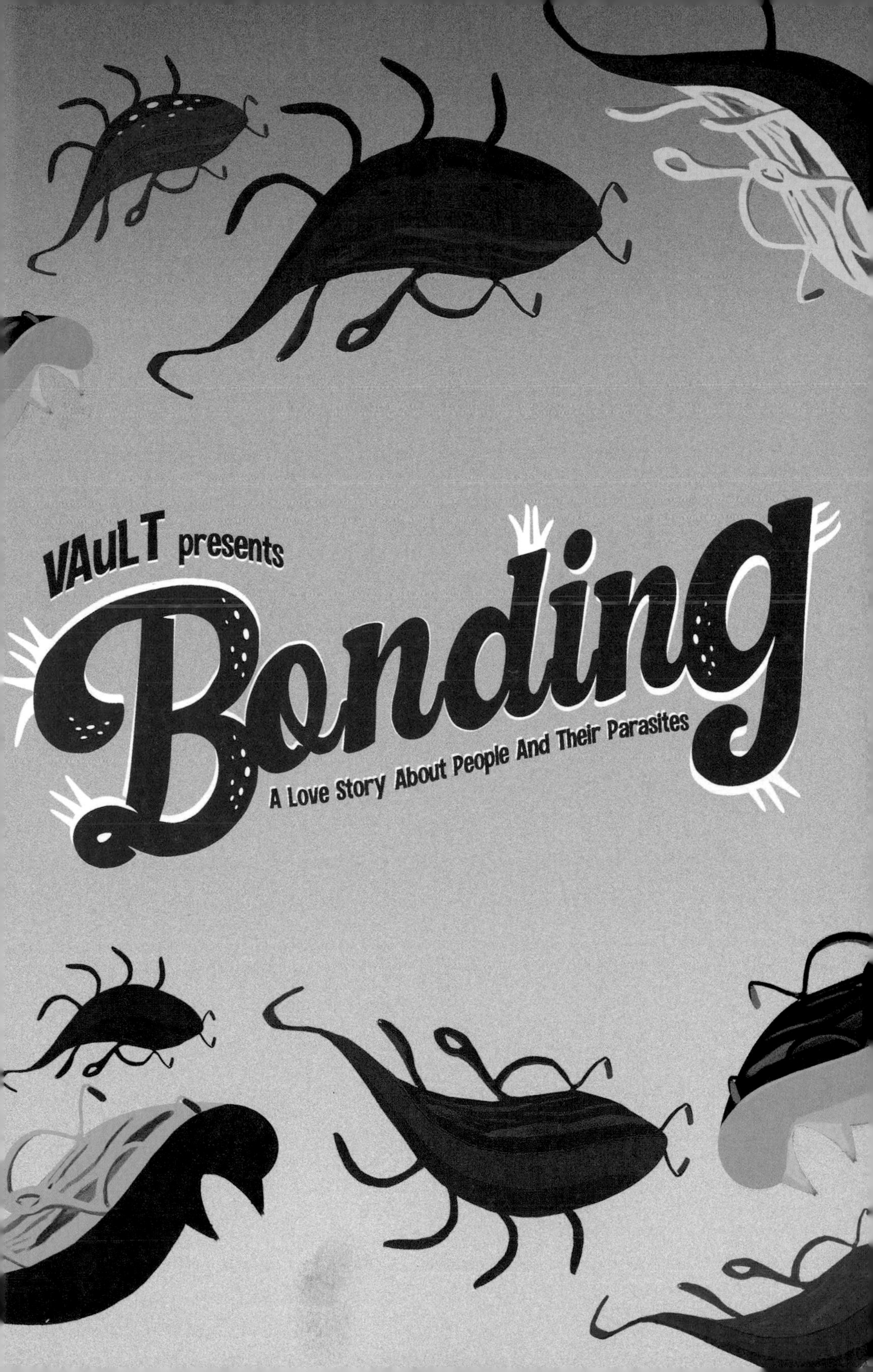
VAULT presents
Bonding
A Love Story About People And Their Parasites

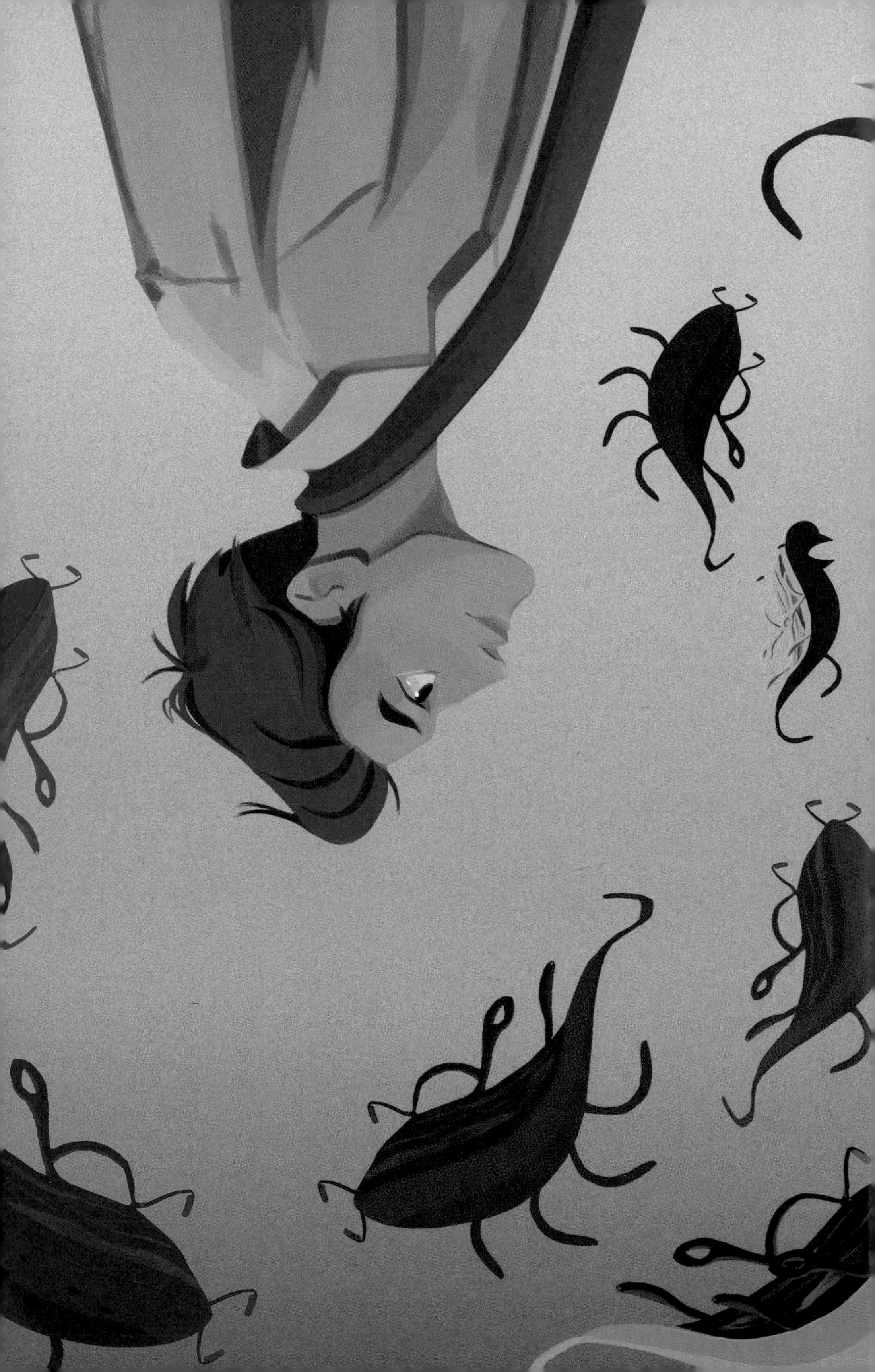

Book One
The Dependency of the Future

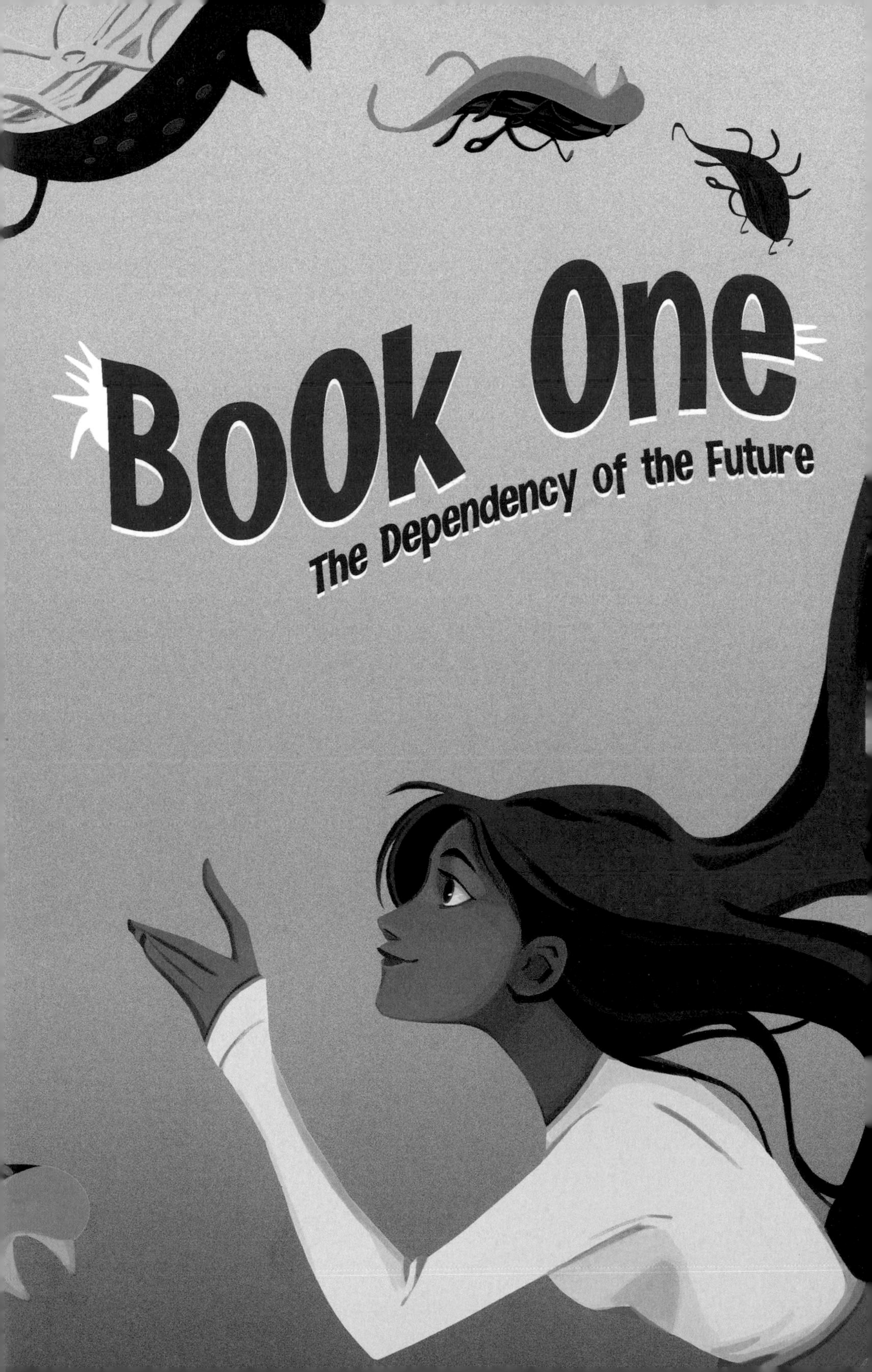

part one

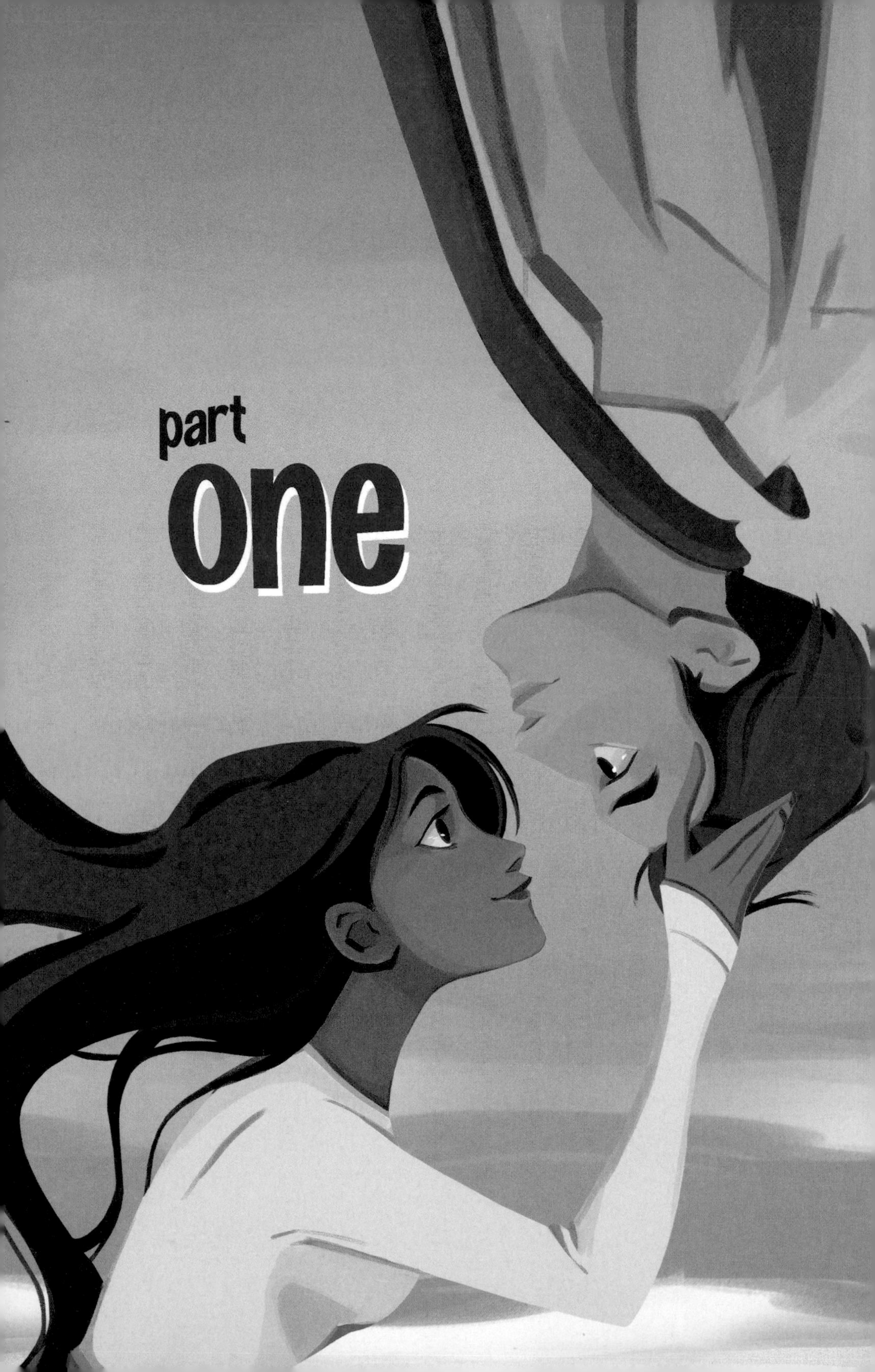

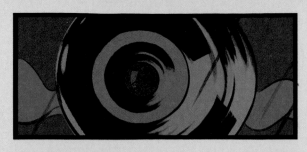

"TO BE TOTALLY CANDID...

"I HAVEN'T DONE THIS IN A *LONG* TIME.

"WELL, NOT LIKE THAT. I MEAN--*UGH.* JUST, CAN WE LEAVE IT AT THAT?"

THIS IS OUR *FIRST,* YA KNOW, SO WE DON'T NEED TO GET INTO THAT STUFF, *RIGHT?*

TABLE FOR TWO? FOLLOW ME.

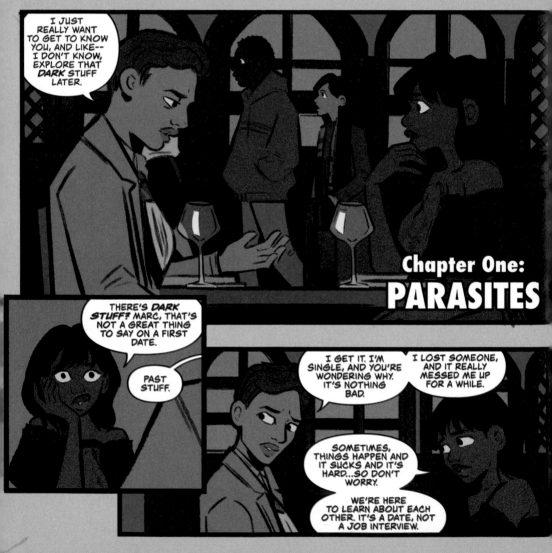

I JUST REALLY WANT TO GET TO KNOW YOU, AND LIKE-- I DON'T KNOW, EXPLORE THAT *DARK* STUFF LATER.

Chapter One:
PARASITES

THERE'S *DARK STUFF?* MARC, THAT'S NOT A GREAT THING TO SAY ON A FIRST DATE.

PAST STUFF.

I GET IT. I'M SINGLE, AND YOU'RE WONDERING WHY. IT'S NOTHING BAD.

I LOST SOMEONE, AND IT REALLY MESSED ME UP FOR A WHILE.

SOMETIMES, THINGS HAPPEN AND IT SUCKS AND IT'S HARD...SO DON'T WORRY.

WE'RE HERE TO LEARN ABOUT EACH OTHER. IT'S A DATE, NOT A JOB INTERVIEW.

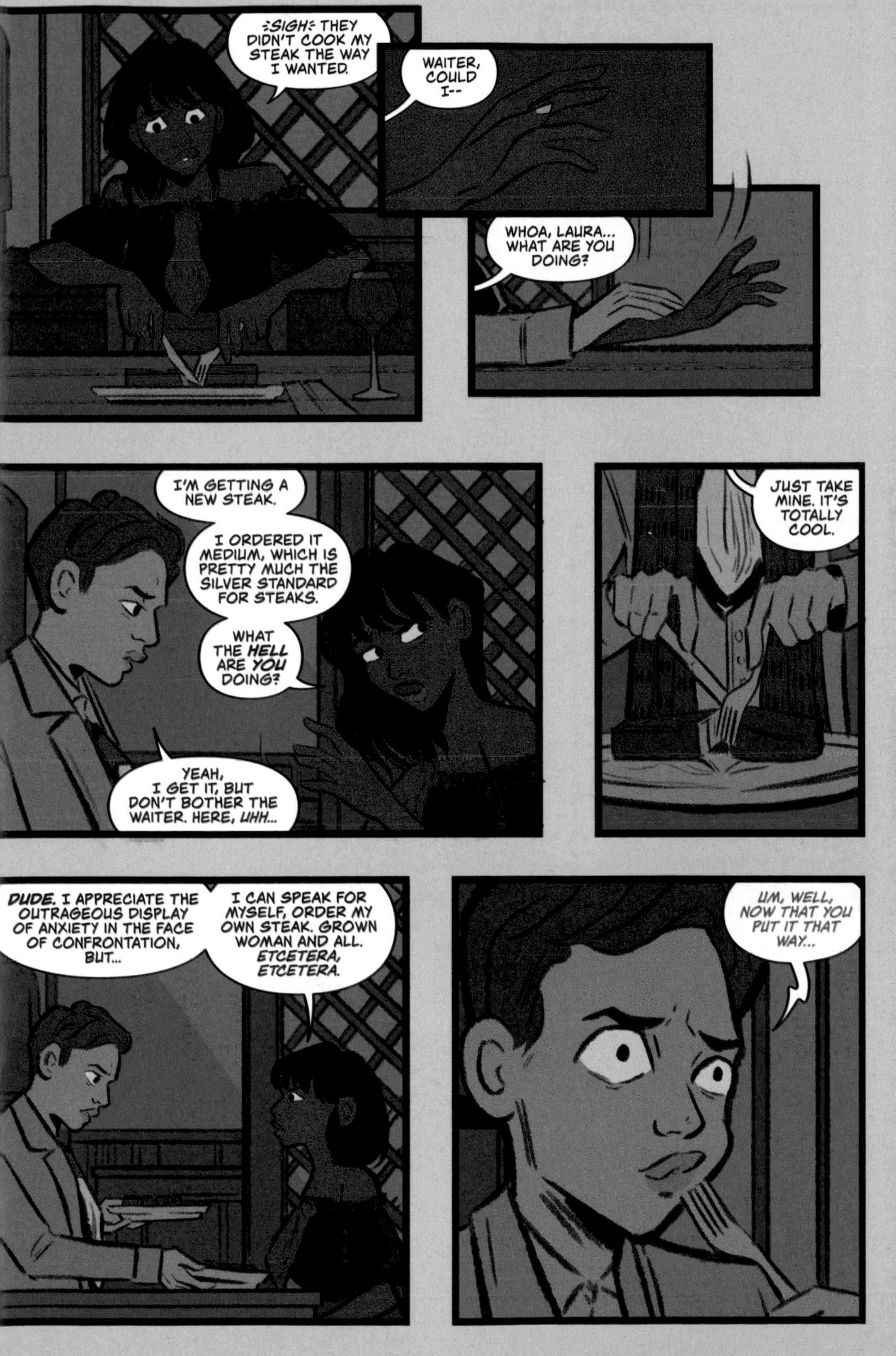

:SIGH: THEY DIDN'T COOK MY STEAK THE WAY I WANTED.
WAITER, COULD I--
WHOA, LAURA... WHAT ARE YOU DOING?
I'M GETTING A NEW STEAK.
I ORDERED IT MEDIUM, WHICH IS PRETTY MUCH THE SILVER STANDARD FOR STEAKS.
WHAT THE HELL ARE YOU DOING?
YEAH, I GET IT, BUT DON'T BOTHER THE WAITER. HERE, UHH...
JUST TAKE MINE. IT'S TOTALLY COOL.
DUDE. I APPRECIATE THE OUTRAGEOUS DISPLAY OF ANXIETY IN THE FACE OF CONFRONTATION, BUT...
I CAN SPEAK FOR MYSELF, ORDER MY OWN STEAK. GROWN WOMAN AND ALL. ETCETERA, ETCETERA.
UM, WELL, NOW THAT YOU PUT IT THAT WAY...

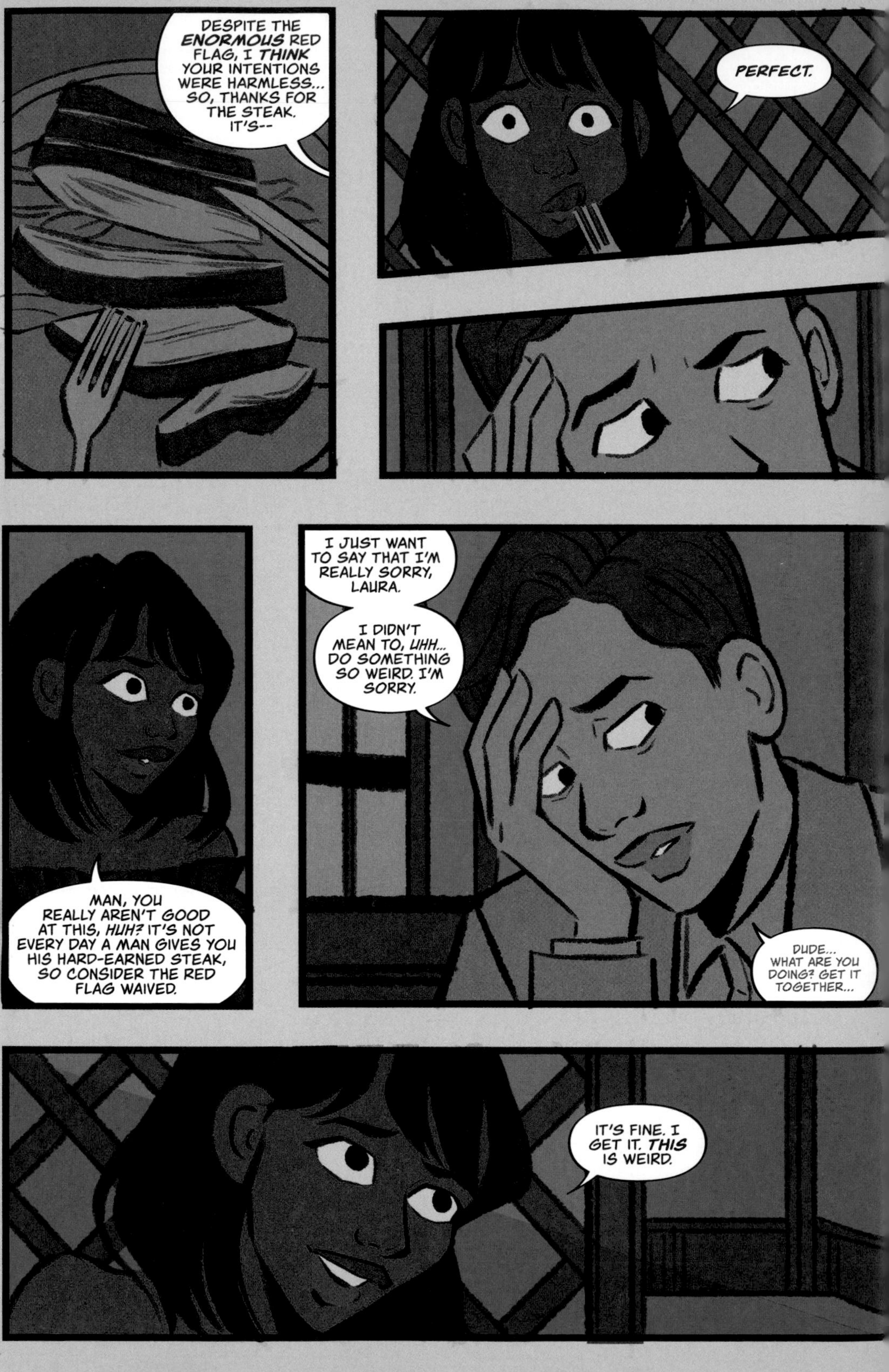
DESPITE THE ENORMOUS RED FLAG, I THINK YOUR INTENTIONS WERE HARMLESS... SO, THANKS FOR THE STEAK. IT'S--
PERFECT.
I JUST WANT TO SAY THAT I'M REALLY SORRY, LAURA.
I DIDN'T MEAN TO, UHH... DO SOMETHING SO WEIRD. I'M SORRY.
MAN, YOU REALLY AREN'T GOOD AT THIS, HUH? IT'S NOT EVERY DAY A MAN GIVES YOU HIS HARD-EARNED STEAK, SO CONSIDER THE RED FLAG WAIVED.
DUDE... WHAT ARE YOU DOING? GET IT TOGETHER...
IT'S FINE. I GET IT. THIS IS WEIRD.

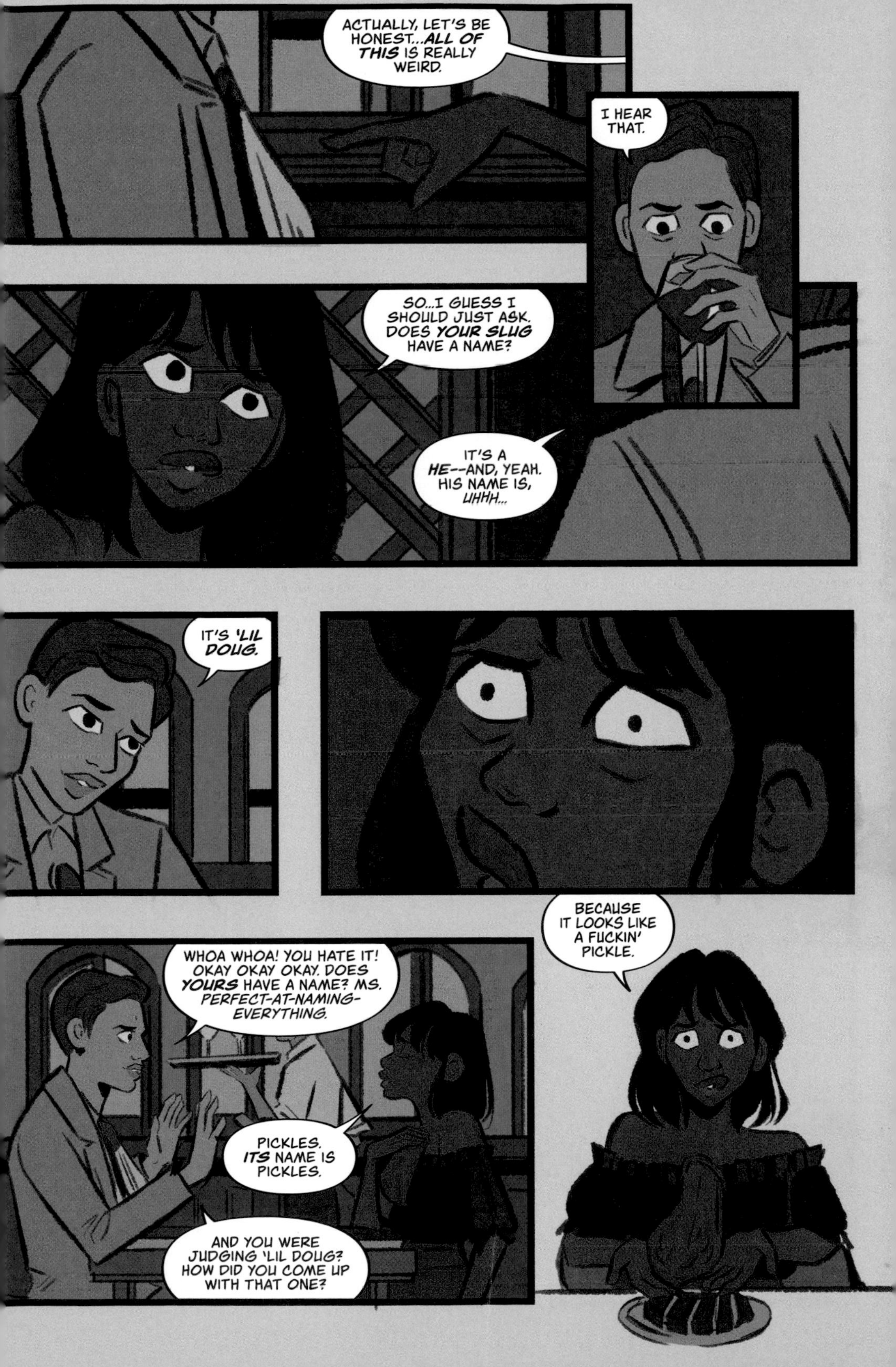
ACTUALLY, LET'S BE HONEST...ALL OF THIS IS REALLY WEIRD.
I HEAR THAT.
SO...I GUESS I SHOULD JUST ASK. DOES YOUR SLUG HAVE A NAME?
IT'S A HE--AND, YEAH. HIS NAME IS, UHHH...
IT'S 'LIL DOUG.
BECAUSE IT LOOKS LIKE A FUCKIN' PICKLE.
WHOA WHOA! YOU HATE IT! OKAY OKAY OKAY. DOES YOURS HAVE A NAME? MS. PERFECT-AT-NAMING-EVERYTHING.
PICKLES. ITS NAME IS PICKLES.
AND YOU WERE JUDGING 'LIL DOUG? HOW DID YOU COME UP WITH THAT ONE?

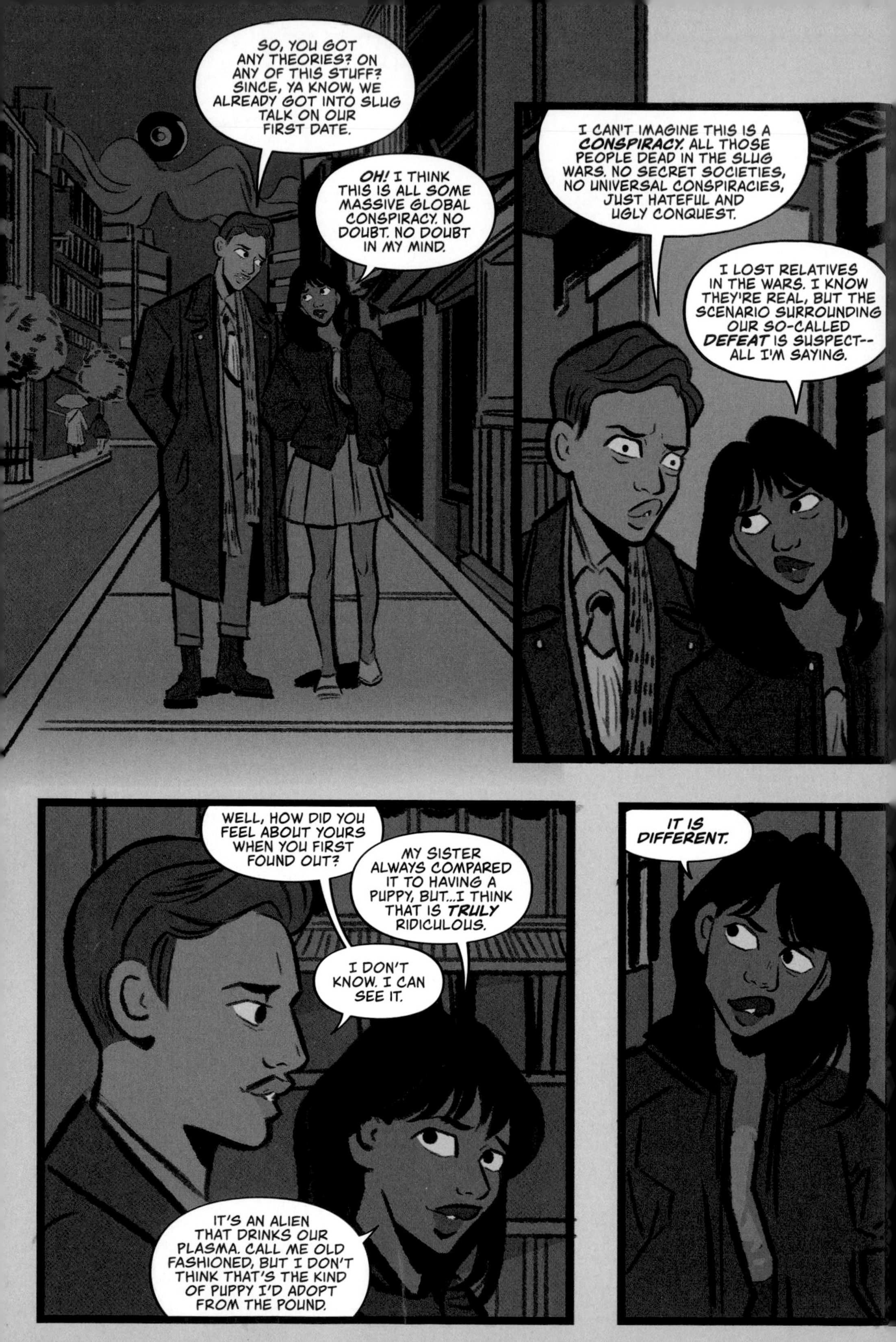

SO, YOU GOT ANY THEORIES? ON ANY OF THIS STUFF? SINCE, YA KNOW, WE ALREADY GOT INTO SLUG TALK ON OUR FIRST DATE.
OH! I THINK THIS IS ALL SOME MASSIVE GLOBAL CONSPIRACY. NO DOUBT. NO DOUBT IN MY MIND.
I CAN'T IMAGINE THIS IS A CONSPIRACY. ALL THOSE PEOPLE DEAD IN THE SLUG WARS. NO SECRET SOCIETIES, NO UNIVERSAL CONSPIRACIES, JUST HATEFUL AND UGLY CONQUEST.
I LOST RELATIVES IN THE WARS. I KNOW THEY'RE REAL, BUT THE SCENARIO SURROUNDING OUR SO-CALLED DEFEAT IS SUSPECT--ALL I'M SAYING.
WELL, HOW DID YOU FEEL ABOUT YOURS WHEN YOU FIRST FOUND OUT?
MY SISTER ALWAYS COMPARED IT TO HAVING A PUPPY, BUT...I THINK THAT IS TRULY RIDICULOUS.
I DON'T KNOW. I CAN SEE IT.
IT'S AN ALIEN THAT DRINKS OUR PLASMA. CALL ME OLD FASHIONED, BUT I DON'T THINK THAT'S THE KIND OF PUPPY I'D ADOPT FROM THE POUND.
IT IS DIFFERENT.

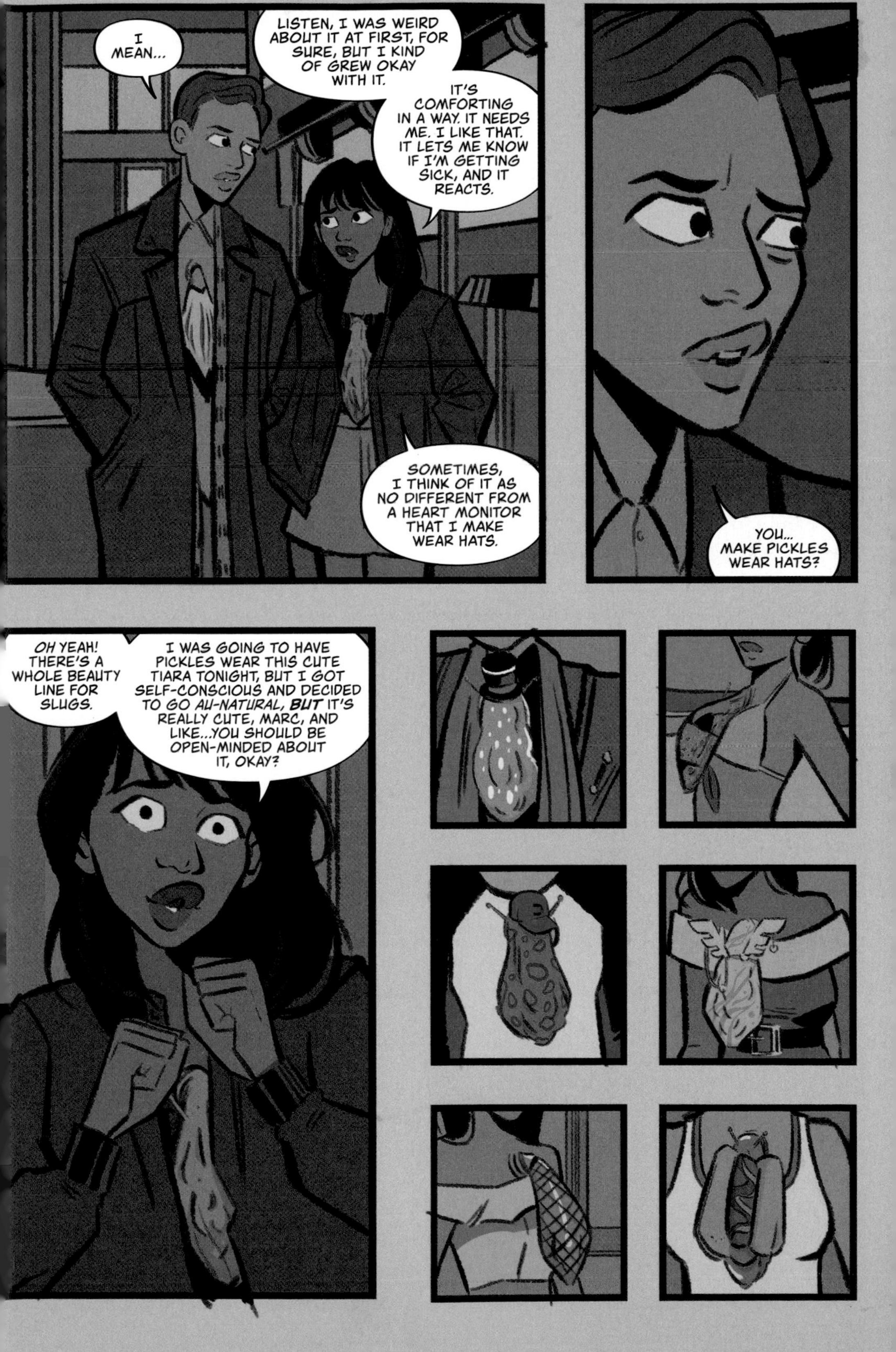
I MEAN...
LISTEN, I WAS WEIRD ABOUT IT AT FIRST, FOR SURE, BUT I KIND OF GREW OKAY WITH IT.
IT'S COMFORTING IN A WAY. IT NEEDS ME. I LIKE THAT. IT LETS ME KNOW IF I'M GETTING SICK, AND IT REACTS.
SOMETIMES, I THINK OF IT AS NO DIFFERENT FROM A HEART MONITOR THAT I MAKE WEAR HATS.
YOU... MAKE PICKLES WEAR HATS?
OH YEAH! THERE'S A WHOLE BEAUTY LINE FOR SLUGS.
I WAS GOING TO HAVE PICKLES WEAR THIS CUTE TIARA TONIGHT, BUT I GOT SELF-CONSCIOUS AND DECIDED TO GO *AU-NATURAL*, ***BUT*** IT'S REALLY CUTE, MARC, AND LIKE...YOU SHOULD BE OPEN-MINDED ABOUT IT, OKAY?

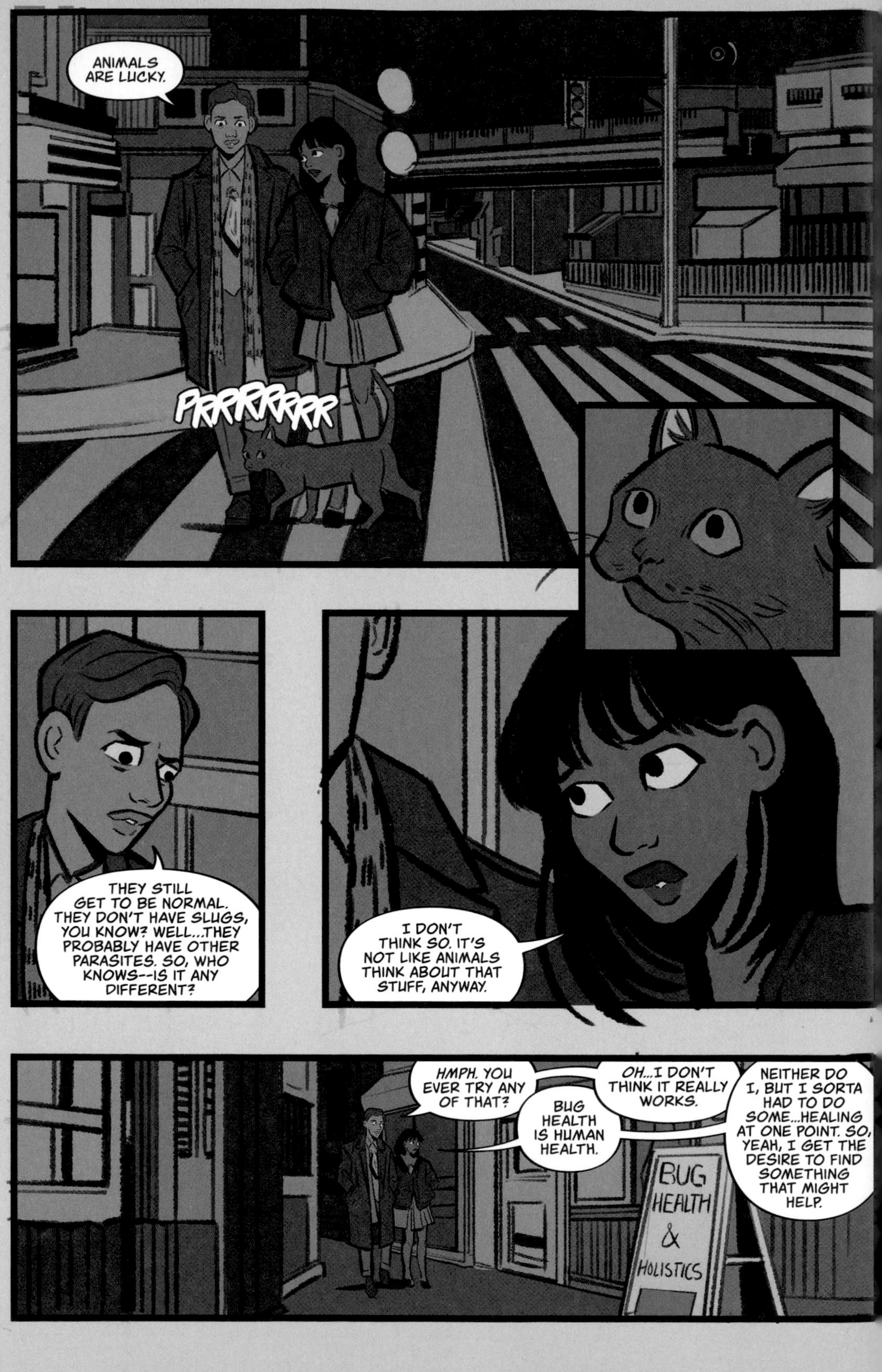
ANIMALS ARE LUCKY.
PRRRRRRR
THEY STILL GET TO BE NORMAL. THEY DON'T HAVE SLUGS, YOU KNOW? WELL...THEY PROBABLY HAVE OTHER PARASITES. SO, WHO KNOWS--IS IT ANY DIFFERENT?
I DON'T THINK SO. IT'S NOT LIKE ANIMALS THINK ABOUT THAT STUFF, ANYWAY.
HMPH. YOU EVER TRY ANY OF THAT?
BUG HEALTH IS HUMAN HEALTH.
OH...I DON'T THINK IT REALLY WORKS.
NEITHER DO I, BUT I SORTA HAD TO DO SOME...HEALING AT ONE POINT. SO, YEAH, I GET THE DESIRE TO FIND SOMETHING THAT MIGHT HELP.
BUG HEALTH & HOLISTICS

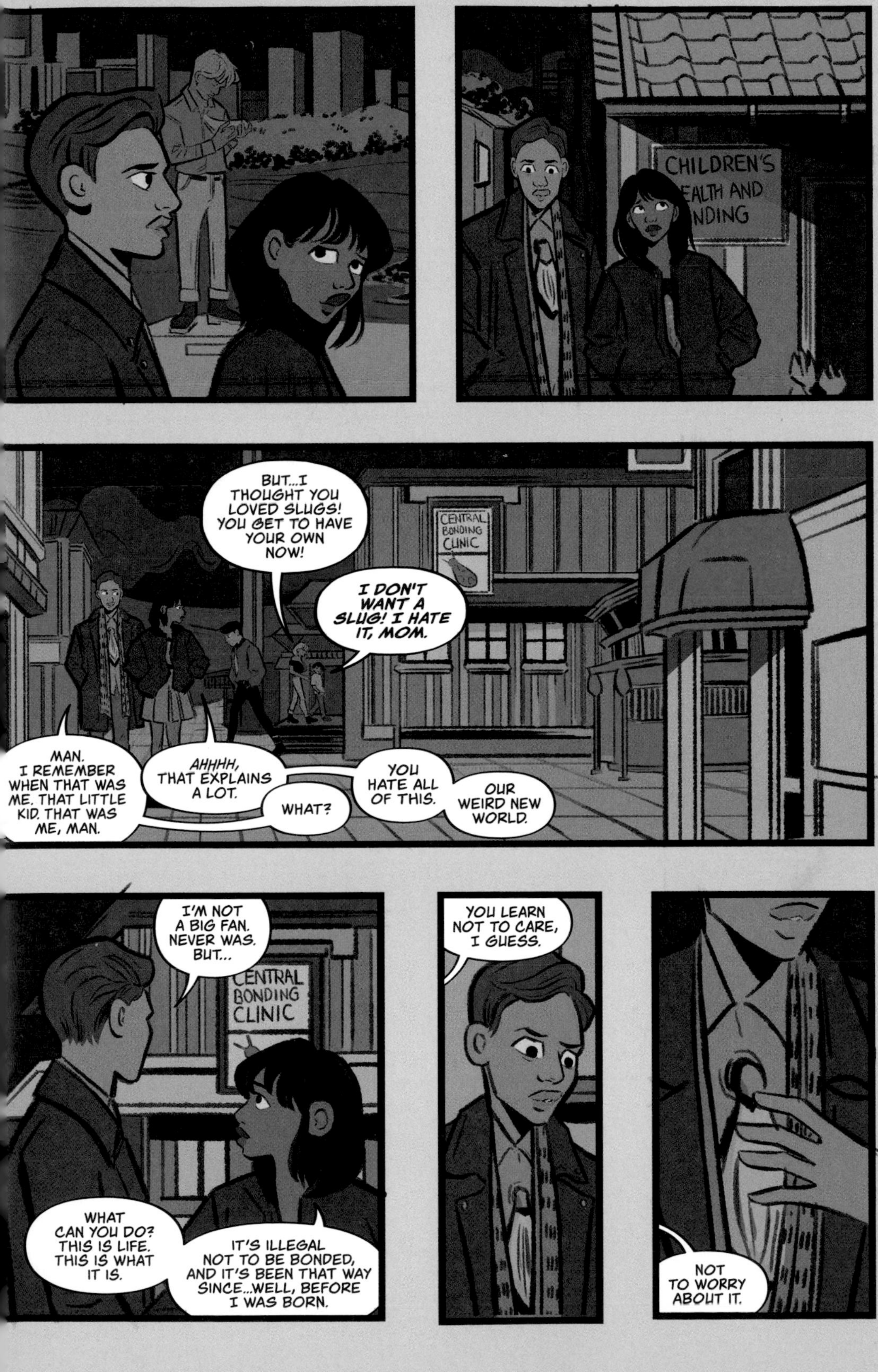
CHILDREN'S
EALTH AND
NDING
BUT...I THOUGHT YOU LOVED SLUGS! YOU GET TO HAVE YOUR OWN NOW!
CENTRAL BONDING CLINIC
I DON'T WANT A SLUG! I HATE IT, MOM.
MAN. I REMEMBER WHEN THAT WAS ME. THAT LITTLE KID. THAT WAS ME, MAN.
AHHHH, THAT EXPLAINS A LOT.
WHAT?
YOU HATE ALL OF THIS.
OUR WEIRD NEW WORLD.
I'M NOT A BIG FAN. NEVER WAS. BUT...
CENTRAL BONDING CLINIC
WHAT CAN YOU DO? THIS IS LIFE. THIS IS WHAT IT IS.
IT'S ILLEGAL NOT TO BE BONDED, AND IT'S BEEN THAT WAY SINCE...WELL, BEFORE I WAS BORN.
YOU LEARN NOT TO CARE, I GUESS.
NOT TO WORRY ABOUT IT.

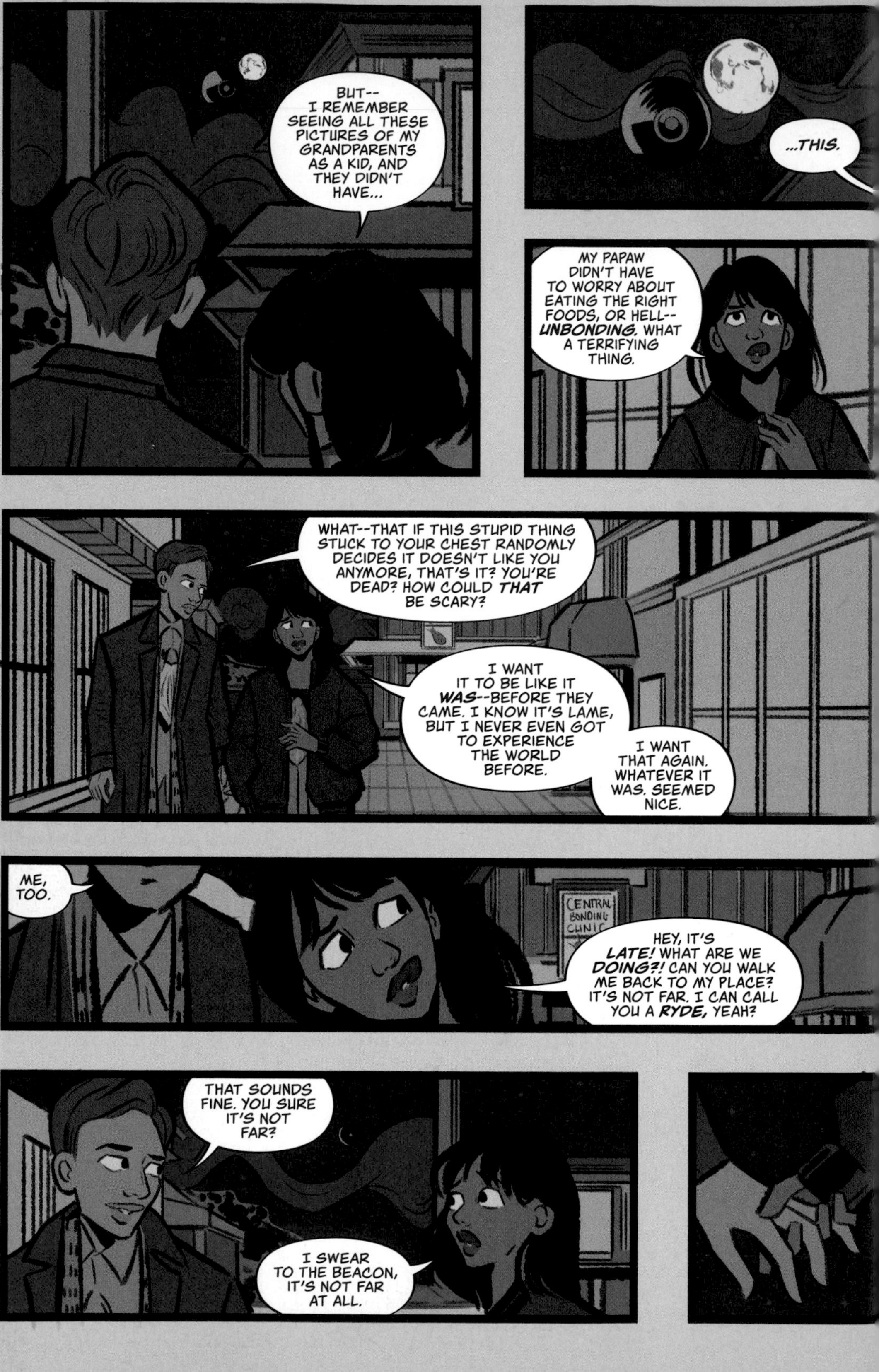
BUT-- I REMEMBER SEEING ALL THESE PICTURES OF MY GRANDPARENTS AS A KID, AND THEY DIDN'T HAVE...
...THIS.
MY PAPAW DIDN'T HAVE TO WORRY ABOUT EATING THE RIGHT FOODS, OR HELL-- UNBONDING. WHAT A TERRIFYING THING.
WHAT--THAT IF THIS STUPID THING STUCK TO YOUR CHEST RANDOMLY DECIDES IT DOESN'T LIKE YOU ANYMORE, THAT'S IT? YOU'RE DEAD? HOW COULD THAT BE SCARY?
I WANT IT TO BE LIKE IT WAS--BEFORE THEY CAME. I KNOW IT'S LAME, BUT I NEVER EVEN GOT TO EXPERIENCE THE WORLD BEFORE.
I WANT THAT AGAIN. WHATEVER IT WAS. SEEMED NICE.
ME, TOO.
CENTRAL BONDING CLINIC
HEY, IT'S LATE! WHAT ARE WE DOING?! CAN YOU WALK ME BACK TO MY PLACE? IT'S NOT FAR. I CAN CALL YOU A RYDE, YEAH?
THAT SOUNDS FINE. YOU SURE IT'S NOT FAR?
I SWEAR TO THE BEACON, IT'S NOT FAR AT ALL.

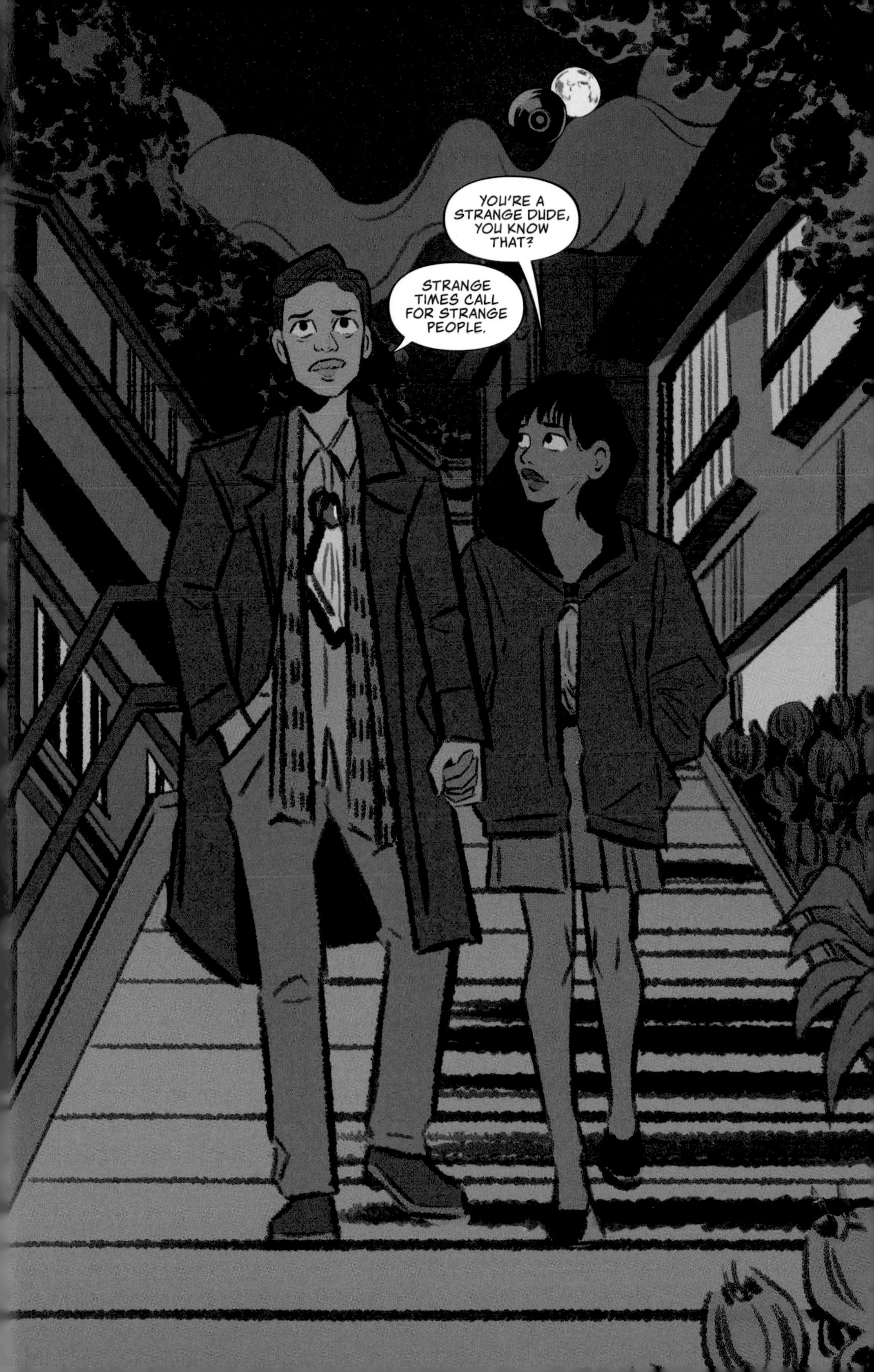
YOU'RE A STRANGE DUDE, YOU KNOW THAT?
STRANGE TIMES CALL FOR STRANGE PEOPLE.

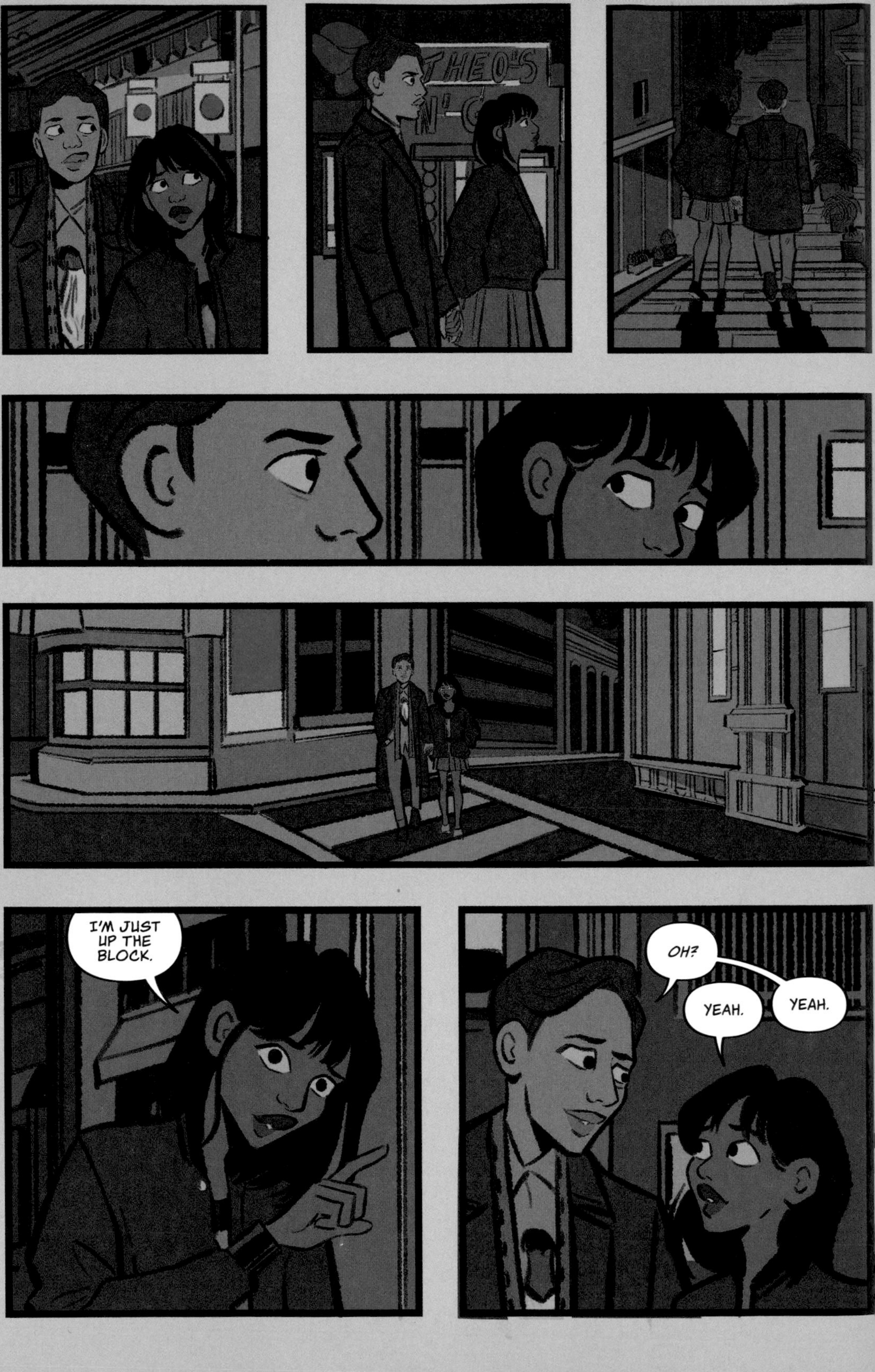
THEO'S
I'M JUST UP THE BLOCK.
OH?
YEAH.
YEAH.

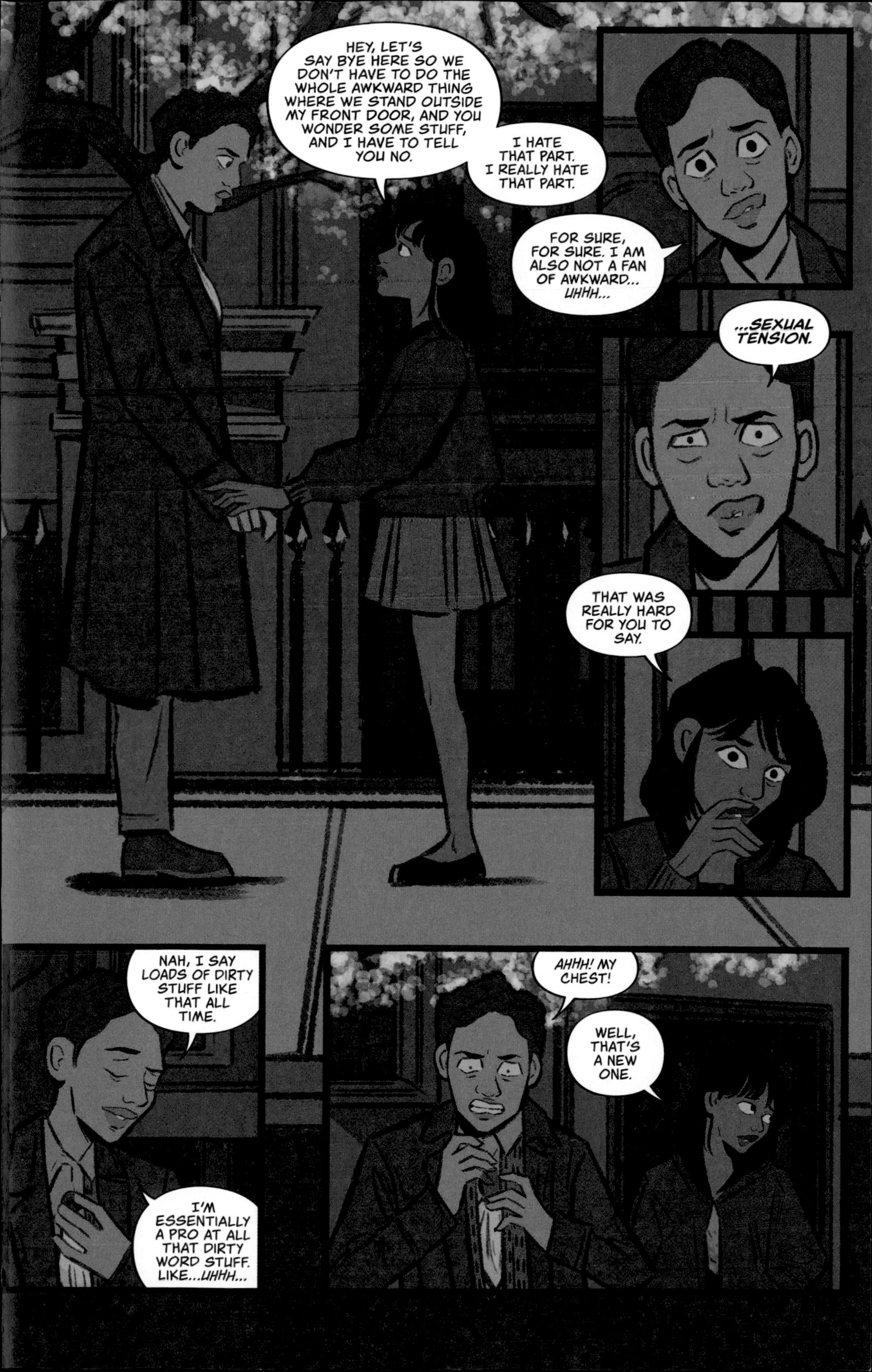
HEY, LET'S SAY BYE HERE SO WE DON'T HAVE TO DO THE WHOLE AWKWARD THING WHERE WE STAND OUTSIDE MY FRONT DOOR, AND YOU WONDER SOME STUFF, AND I HAVE TO TELL YOU NO.
I HATE THAT PART. I REALLY HATE THAT PART.
FOR SURE, FOR SURE. I AM ALSO NOT A FAN OF AWKWARD... UHHH...
...SEXUAL TENSION.
THAT WAS REALLY HARD FOR YOU TO SAY.
NAH, I SAY LOADS OF DIRTY STUFF LIKE THAT ALL TIME.
I'M ESSENTIALLY A PRO AT ALL THAT DIRTY WORD STUFF. LIKE...UHHH...
AHHH! MY CHEST!
WELL, THAT'S A NEW ONE.

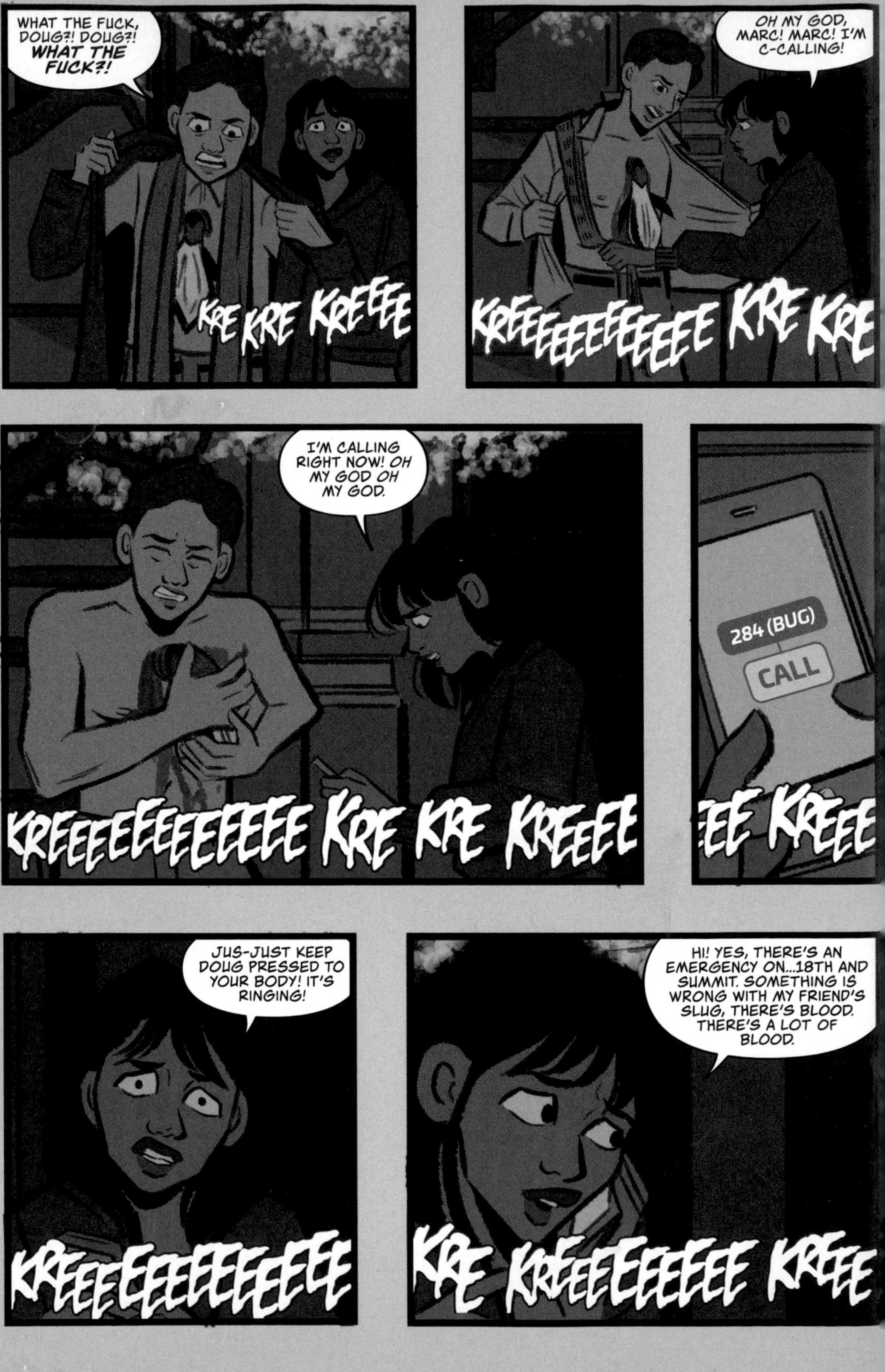
WHAT THE FUCK, DOUG?! DOUG?! WHAT THE FUCK?!
KRE KRE KREEEE
OH MY GOD, MARC! MARC! I'M C-CALLING!
KREEEEEEEEEEEE KRE KRE
I'M CALLING RIGHT NOW! OH MY GOD OH MY GOD.
KREEEEEEEEEEEE KRE KRE KREEEE
284 (BUG)
CALL
EE KREEE
JUS-JUST KEEP DOUG PRESSED TO YOUR BODY! IT'S RINGING!
KREEEEEEEEEEEEEE
HI! YES, THERE'S AN EMERGENCY ON...18TH AND SUMMIT. SOMETHING IS WRONG WITH MY FRIEND'S SLUG, THERE'S BLOOD. THERE'S A LOT OF BLOOD.
KRE KREEEEEEEEEE KREEE

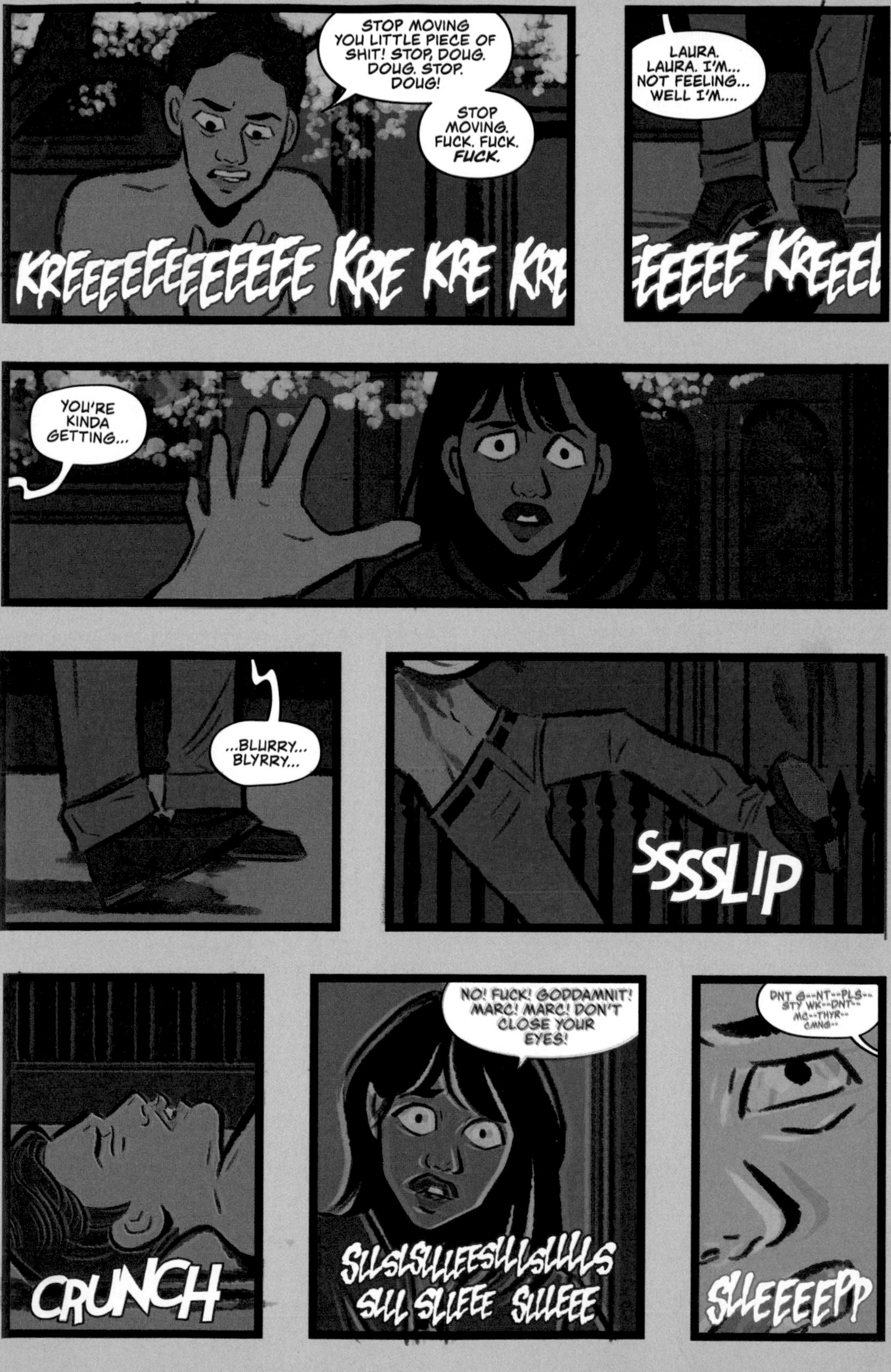
STOP MOVING YOU LITTLE PIECE OF SHIT! STOP, DOUG. DOUG. STOP. DOUG!
STOP MOVING. FUCK. FUCK. FUCK.
KREEEEEEEEEEEEE KRE KRE KRE
LAURA. LAURA. I'M... NOT FEELING... WELL I'M....
EEEEEE KREEEE
YOU'RE KINDA GETTING...
...BLURRY... BLYRRY...
SSSSLIP
CRUNCH
NO! FUCK! GODDAMNIT! MARC! MARC! DON'T CLOSE YOUR EYES!
SLLSLSLLLEESLLLSLLLLS SLLL SLLEEE SLLEEE
DNT G--NT--PLS-- STY WK--DNT-- MC--THYR-- CMNG--
SLLEEEEPP

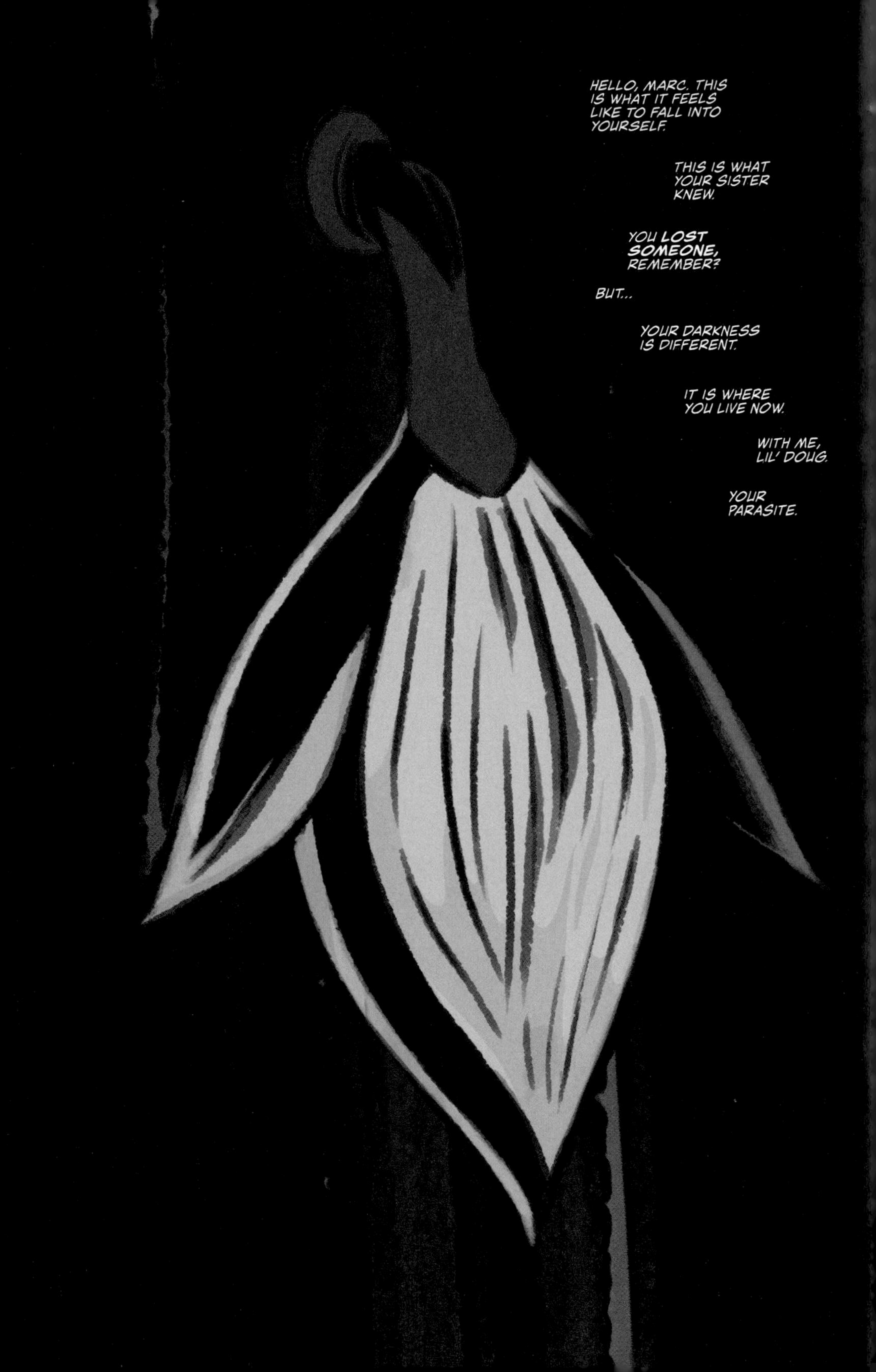

HELLO, MARC. THIS IS WHAT IT FEELS LIKE TO FALL INTO YOURSELF.
THIS IS WHAT YOUR SISTER KNEW.
YOU **LOST SOMEONE,** REMEMBER?
BUT...
YOUR DARKNESS IS DIFFERENT.
IT IS WHERE YOU LIVE NOW.
WITH ME, LIL' DOUG.
YOUR PARASITE.

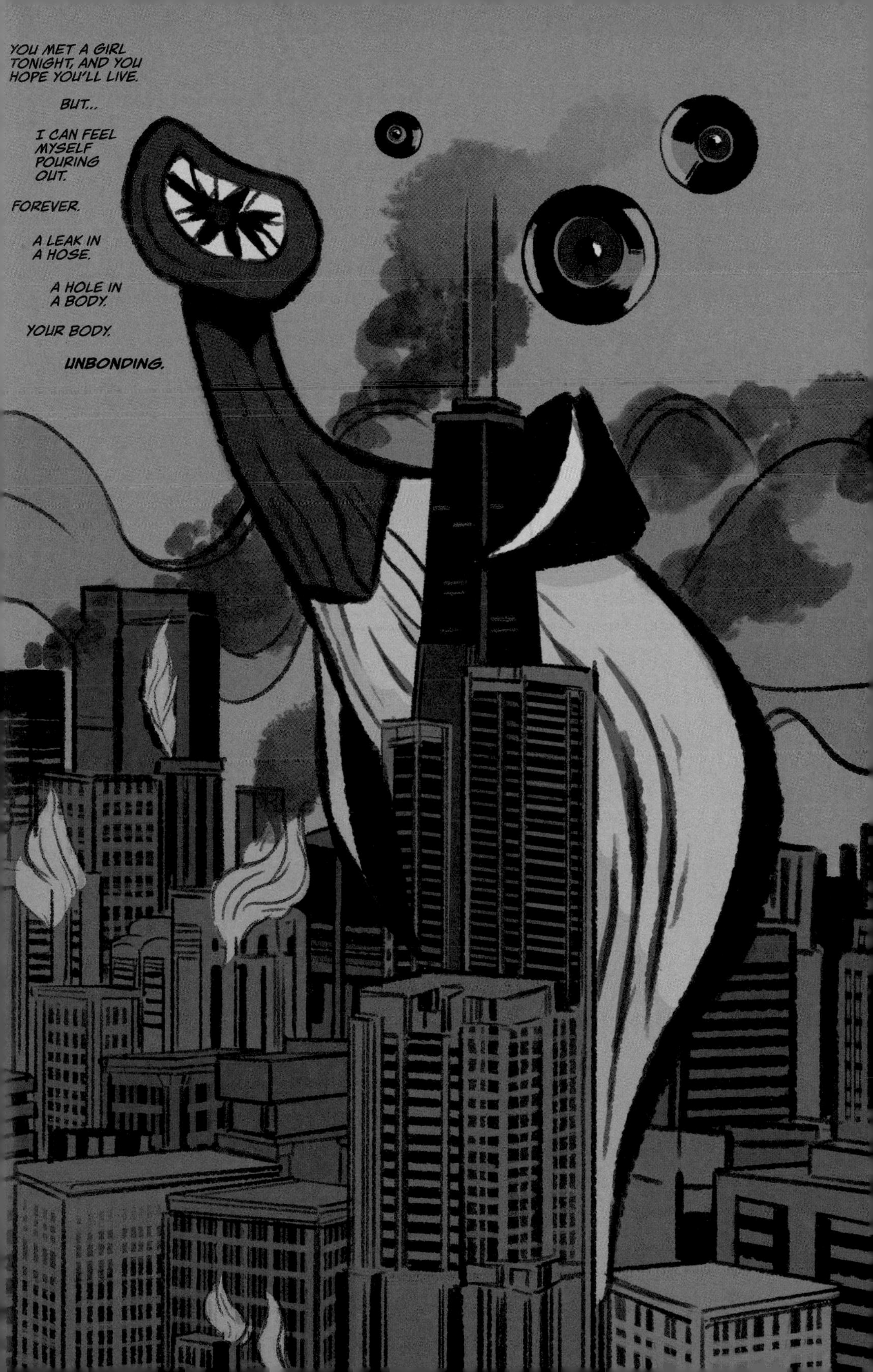
YOU MET A GIRL TONIGHT, AND YOU HOPE YOU'LL LIVE.
BUT...
I CAN FEEL MYSELF POURING OUT.
FOREVER.
A LEAK IN A HOSE.
A HOLE IN A BODY.
YOUR BODY.
UNBONDING.

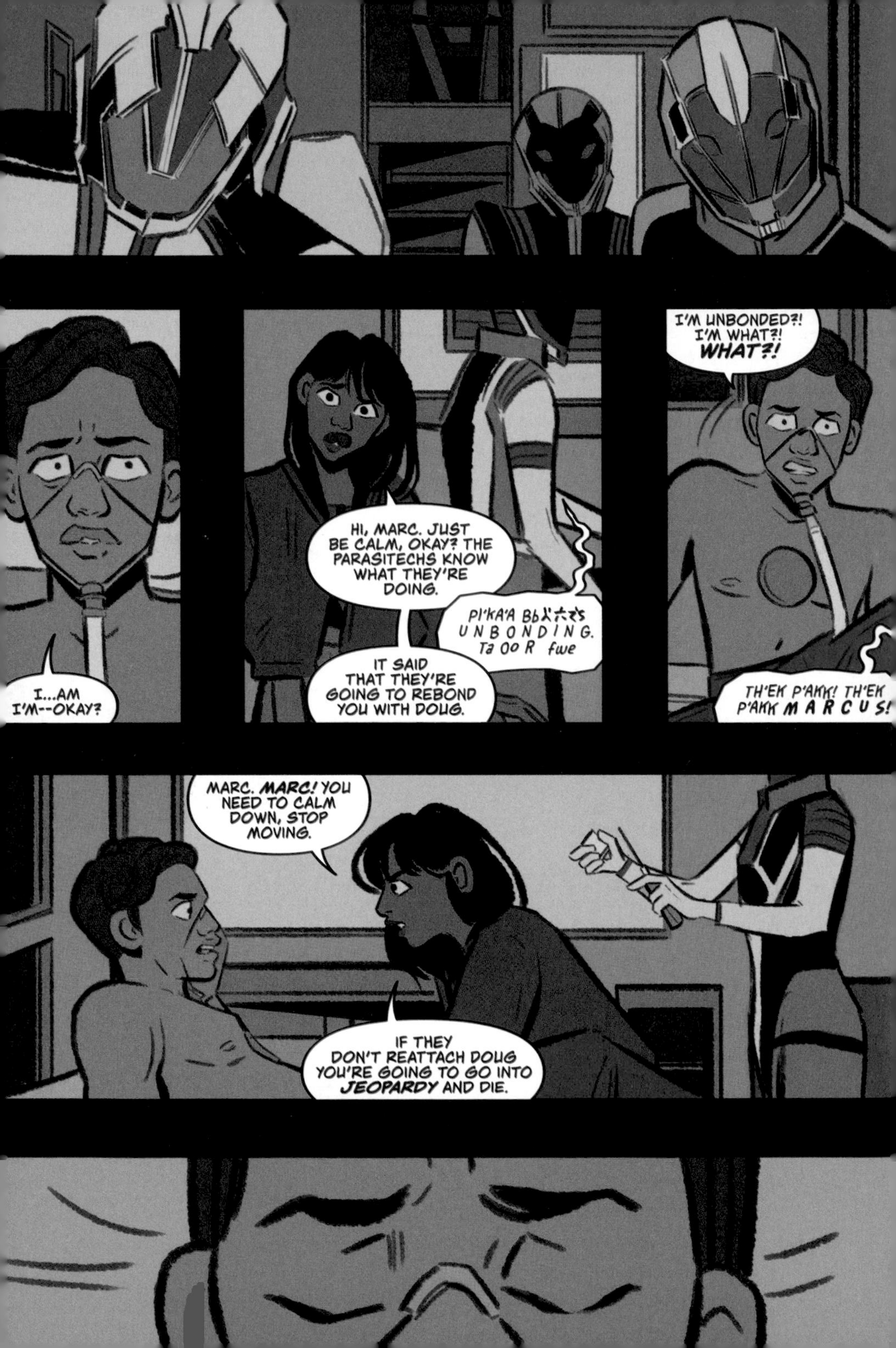
I...AM I'M--OKAY?
HI, MARC. JUST BE CALM, OKAY? THE PARASITECHS KNOW WHAT THEY'RE DOING.
PI'KA'A Bb UNBONDING. Ta OO R fwe
IT SAID THAT THEY'RE GOING TO REBOND YOU WITH DOUG.
I'M UNBONDED?! I'M WHAT?! WHAT?!
TH'EK P'AKK! TH'EK P'AKK MARCUS!
MARC. MARC! YOU NEED TO CALM DOWN, STOP MOVING.
IF THEY DON'T REATTACH DOUG YOU'RE GOING TO GO INTO JEOPARDY AND DIE.

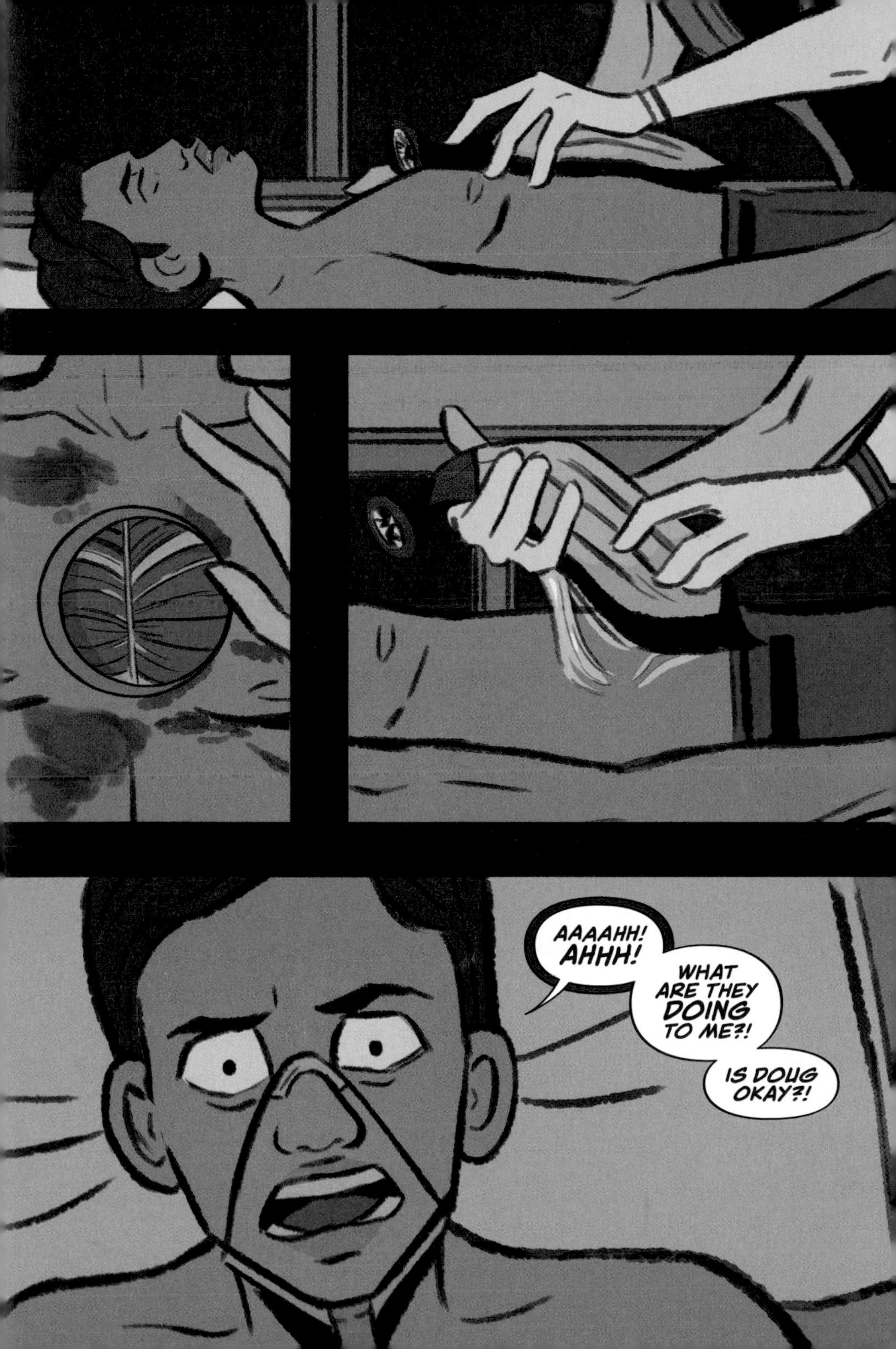
AAAAHH! AHHH!
WHAT ARE THEY DOING TO ME?!
IS DOUG OKAY?!

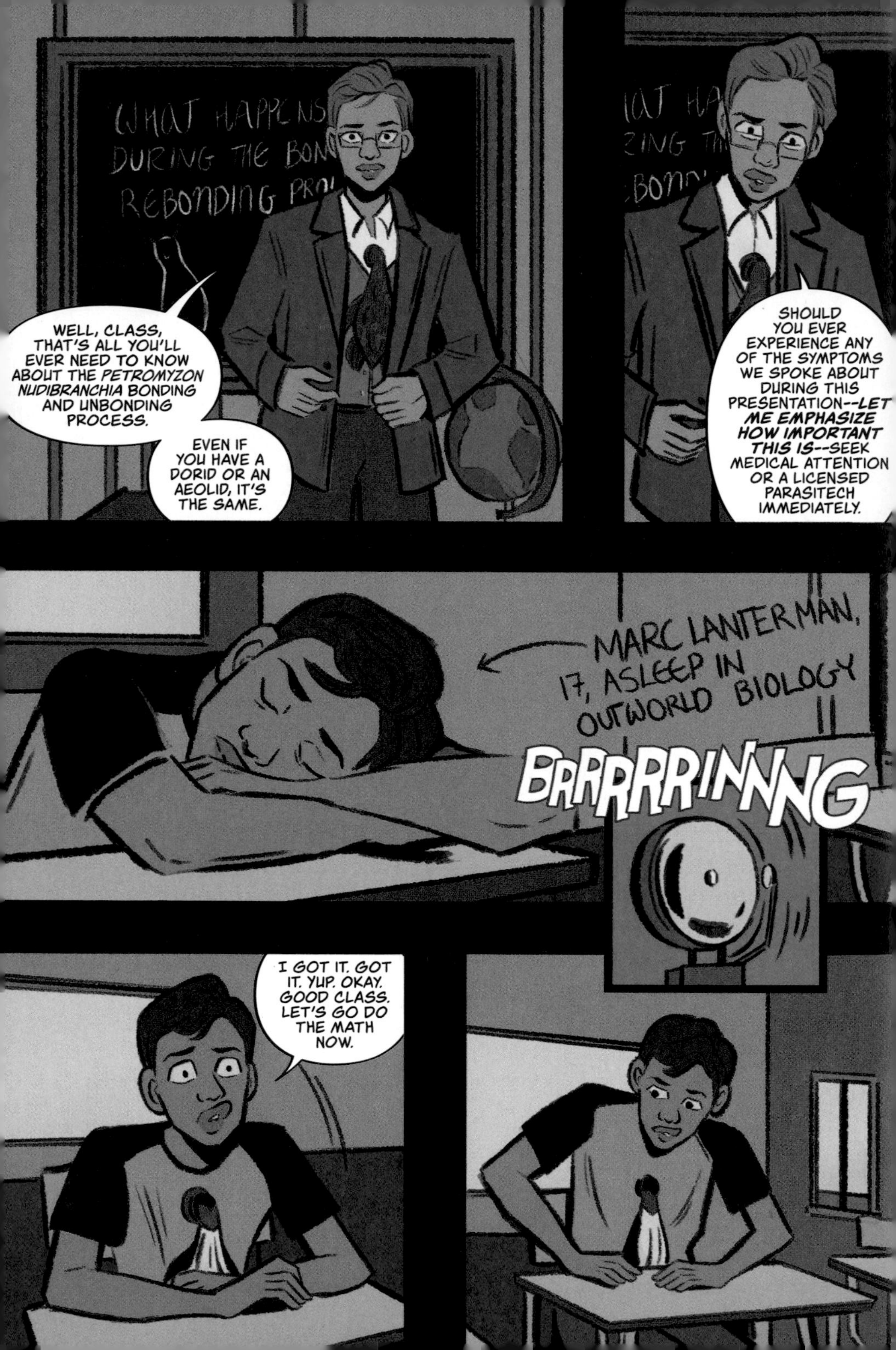

WHAT HAPPENS DURING THE BON REBONDING PRO
WELL, CLASS, THAT'S ALL YOU'LL EVER NEED TO KNOW ABOUT THE *PETROMYZON NUDIBRANCHIA* BONDING AND UNBONDING PROCESS.
EVEN IF YOU HAVE A DORID OR AN AEOLID, IT'S THE SAME.
SHOULD YOU EVER EXPERIENCE ANY OF THE SYMPTOMS WE SPOKE ABOUT DURING THIS PRESENTATION--***LET ME EMPHASIZE HOW IMPORTANT THIS IS***--SEEK MEDICAL ATTENTION OR A LICENSED PARASITECH IMMEDIATELY.
MARC LANTERMAN, 17, ASLEEP IN OUTWORLD BIOLOGY
BRRRRRINNNG
I GOT IT. GOT IT. YUP. OKAY. GOOD CLASS. LET'S GO DO THE MATH NOW.

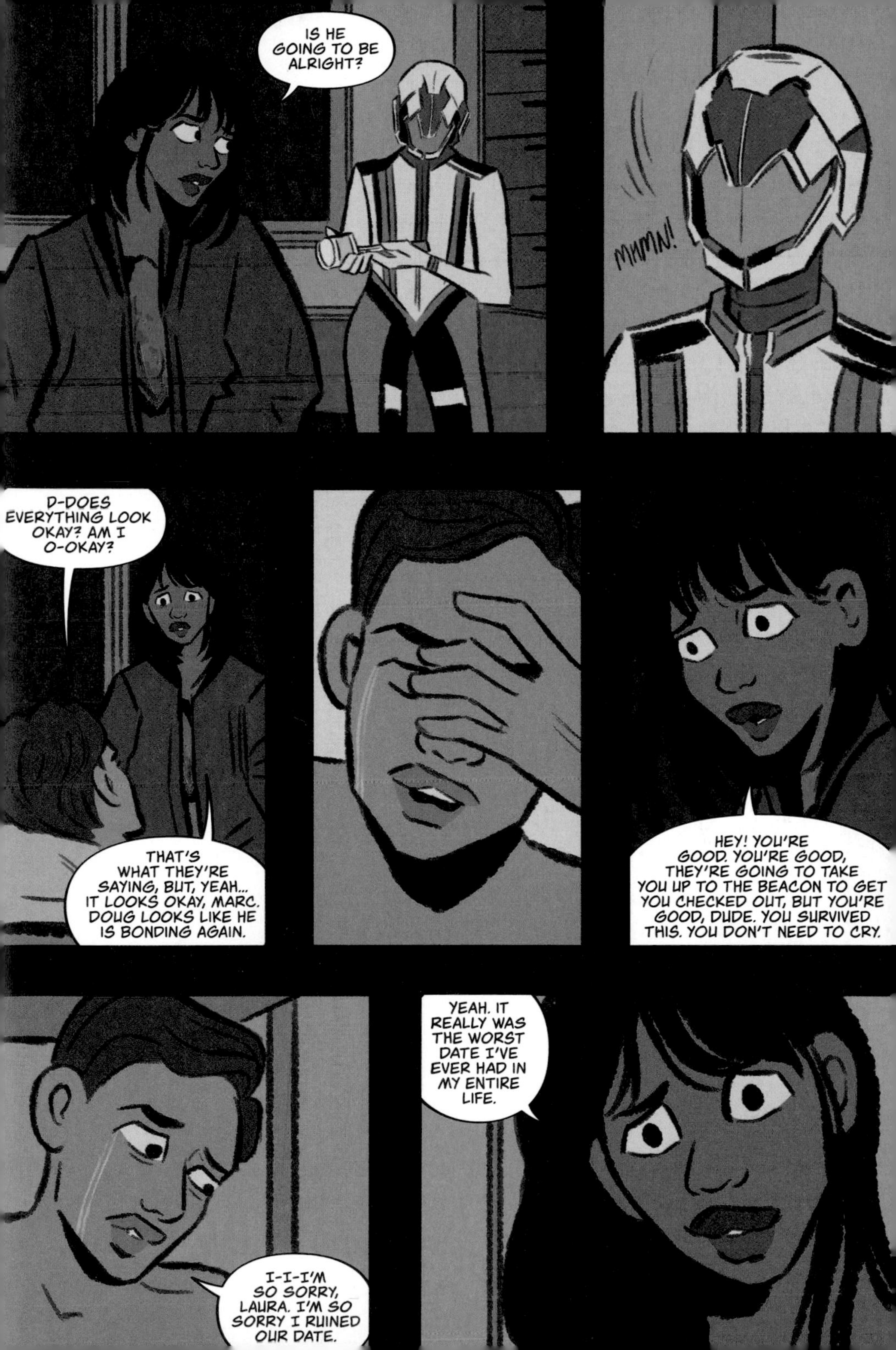
IS HE GOING TO BE ALRIGHT?
MMMN!
D-DOES EVERYTHING LOOK OKAY? AM I O-OKAY?
THAT'S WHAT THEY'RE SAYING, BUT, YEAH... IT LOOKS OKAY, MARC. DOUG LOOKS LIKE HE IS BONDING AGAIN.
HEY! YOU'RE GOOD. YOU'RE GOOD, THEY'RE GOING TO TAKE YOU UP TO THE BEACON TO GET YOU CHECKED OUT, BUT YOU'RE GOOD, DUDE. YOU SURVIVED THIS. YOU DON'T NEED TO CRY.
I-I-I'M SO SORRY, LAURA. I'M SO SORRY I RUINED OUR DATE.
YEAH. IT REALLY WAS THE WORST DATE I'VE EVER HAD IN MY ENTIRE LIFE.

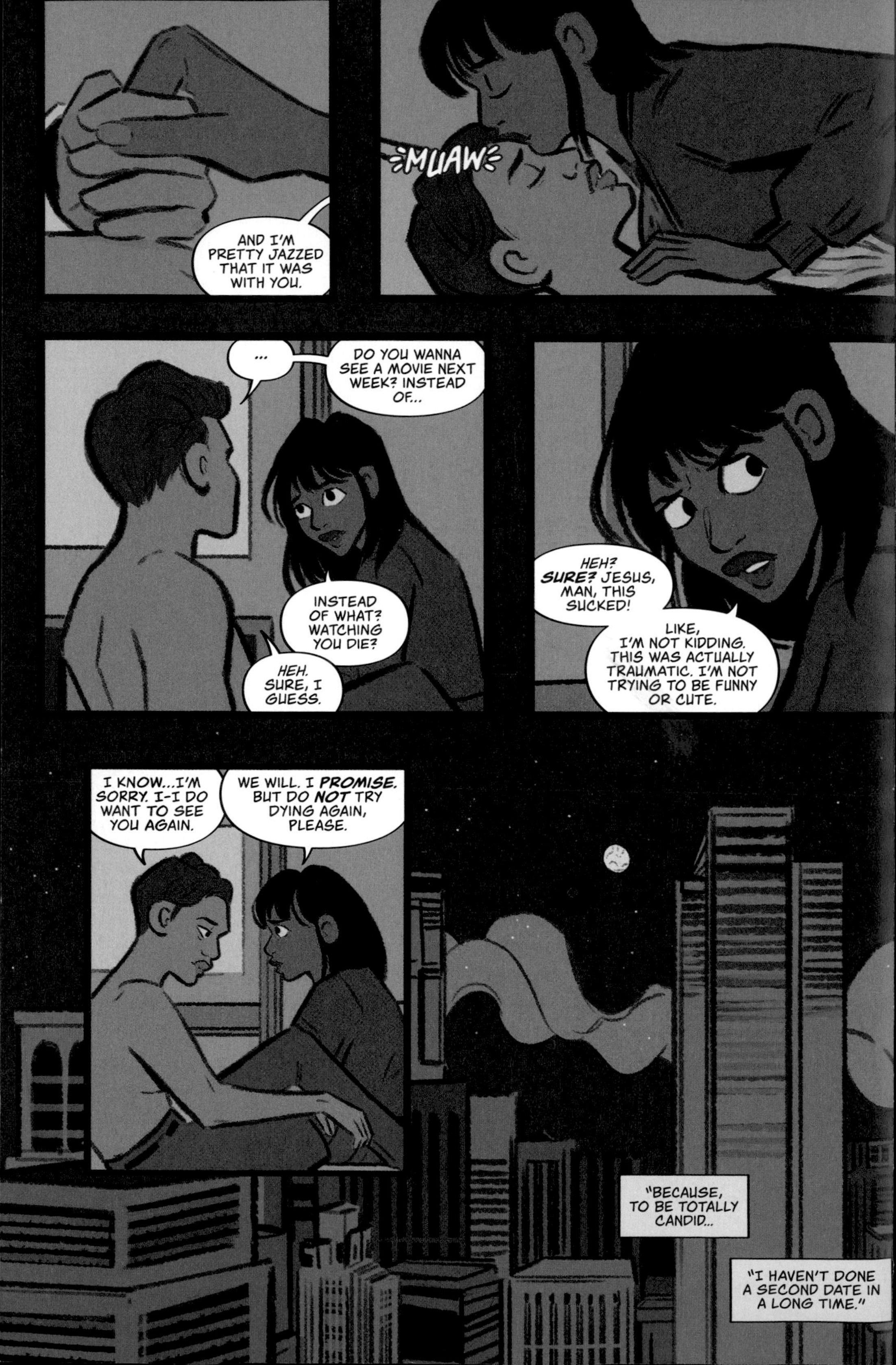
AND I'M PRETTY JAZZED THAT IT WAS WITH YOU.
MUAW
...
DO YOU WANNA SEE A MOVIE NEXT WEEK? INSTEAD OF...
INSTEAD OF WHAT? WATCHING YOU DIE?
HEH. SURE, I GUESS.
HEH? SURE? JESUS, MAN, THIS SUCKED!
LIKE, I'M NOT KIDDING. THIS WAS ACTUALLY TRAUMATIC. I'M NOT TRYING TO BE FUNNY OR CUTE.
I KNOW...I'M SORRY. I-I DO WANT TO SEE YOU AGAIN.
WE WILL. I PROMISE. BUT DO NOT TRY DYING AGAIN, PLEASE.
"BECAUSE, TO BE TOTALLY CANDID...
"I HAVEN'T DONE A SECOND DATE IN A LONG TIME."

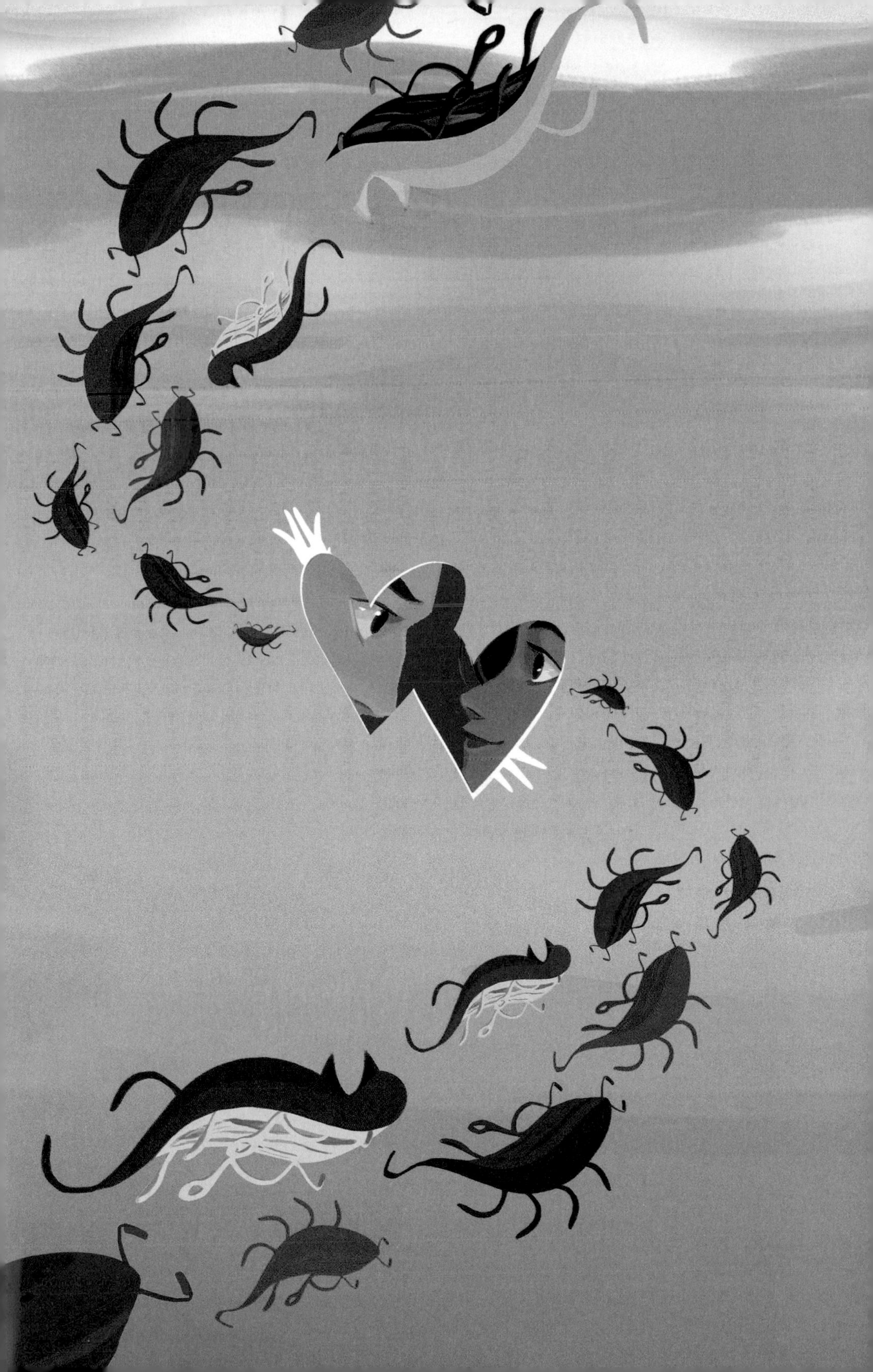

part two

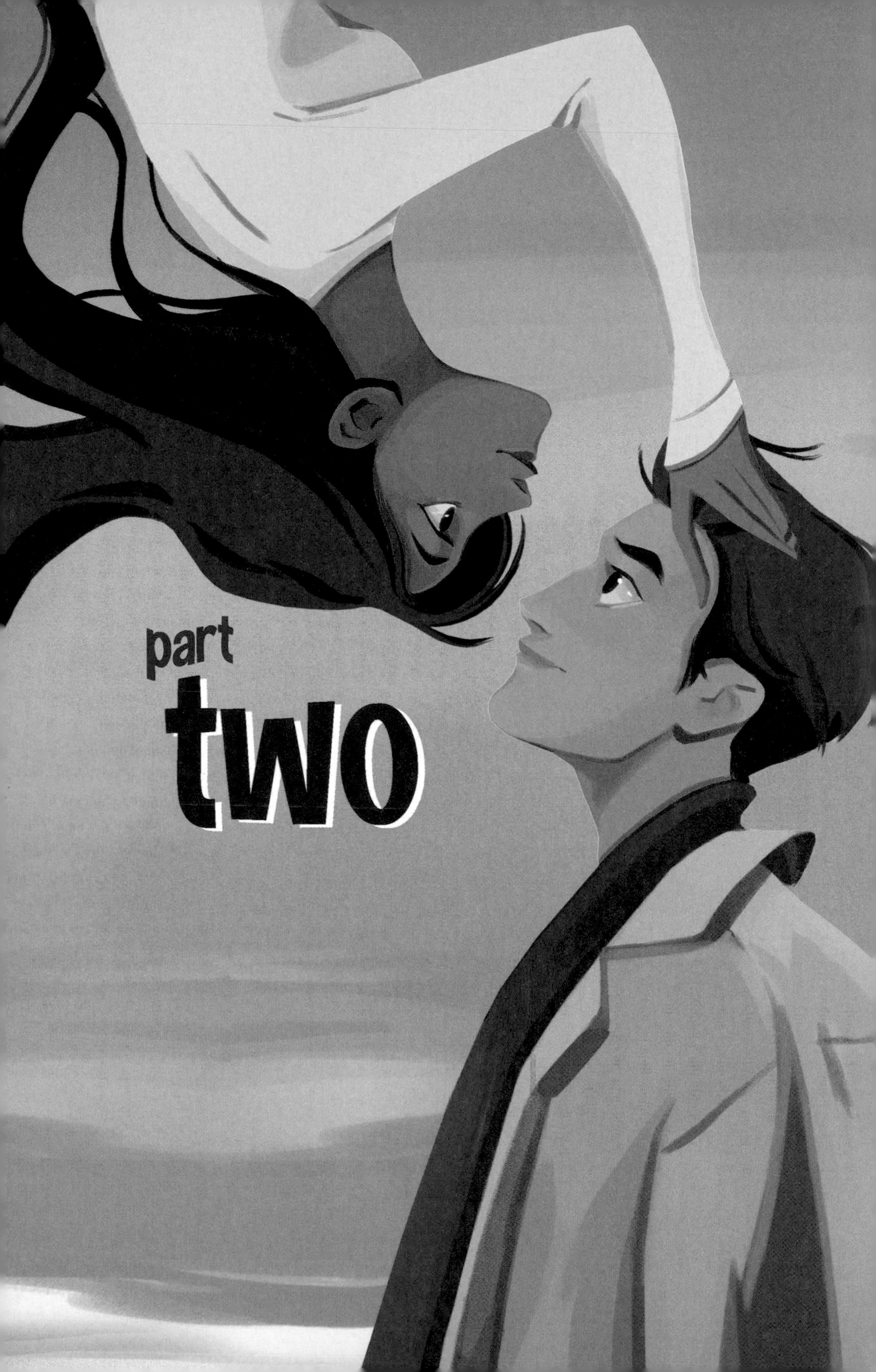

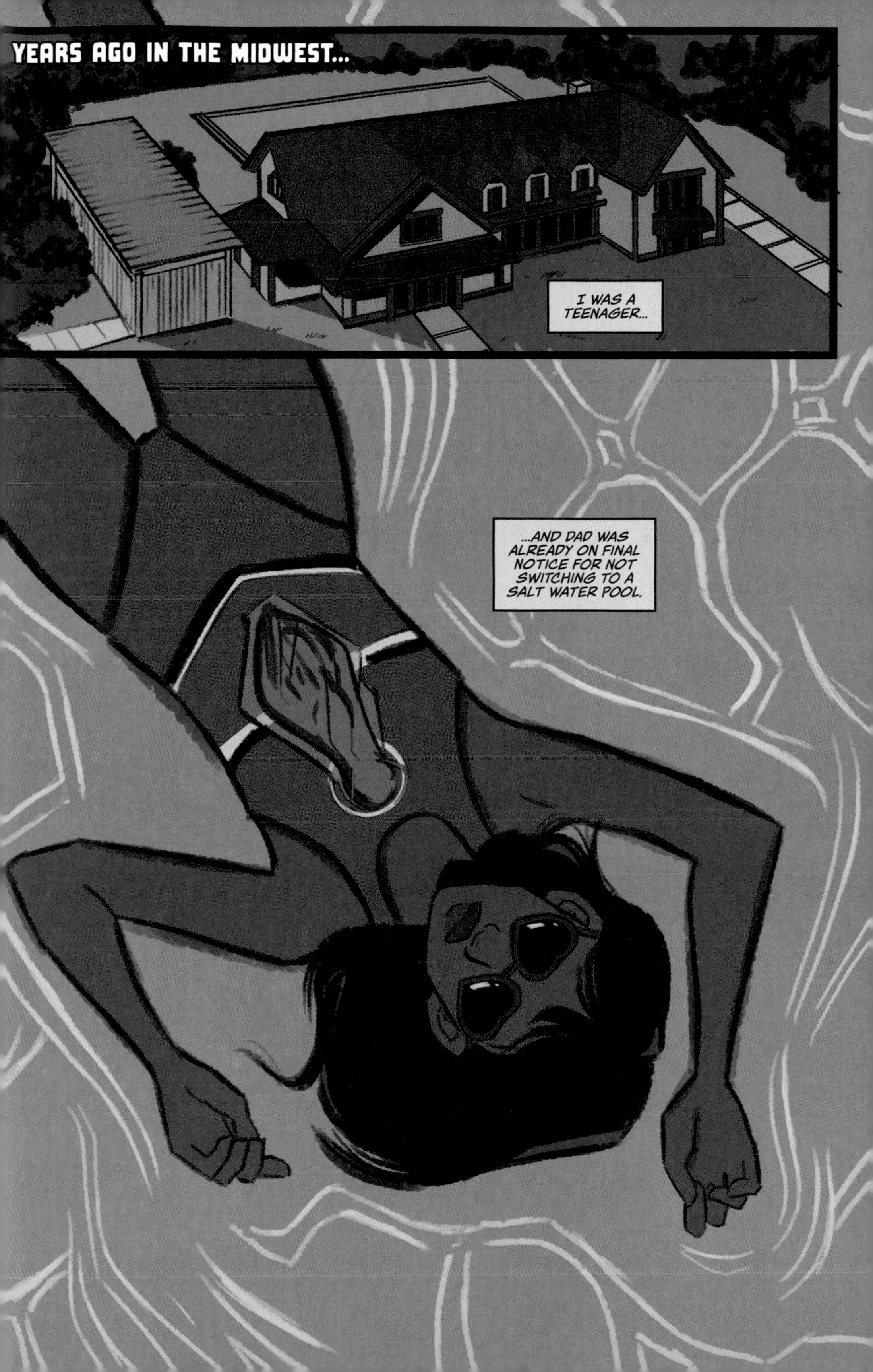
YEARS AGO IN THE MIDWEST...
I WAS A TEENAGER...
...AND DAD WAS ALREADY ON FINAL NOTICE FOR NOT SWITCHING TO A SALT WATER POOL.

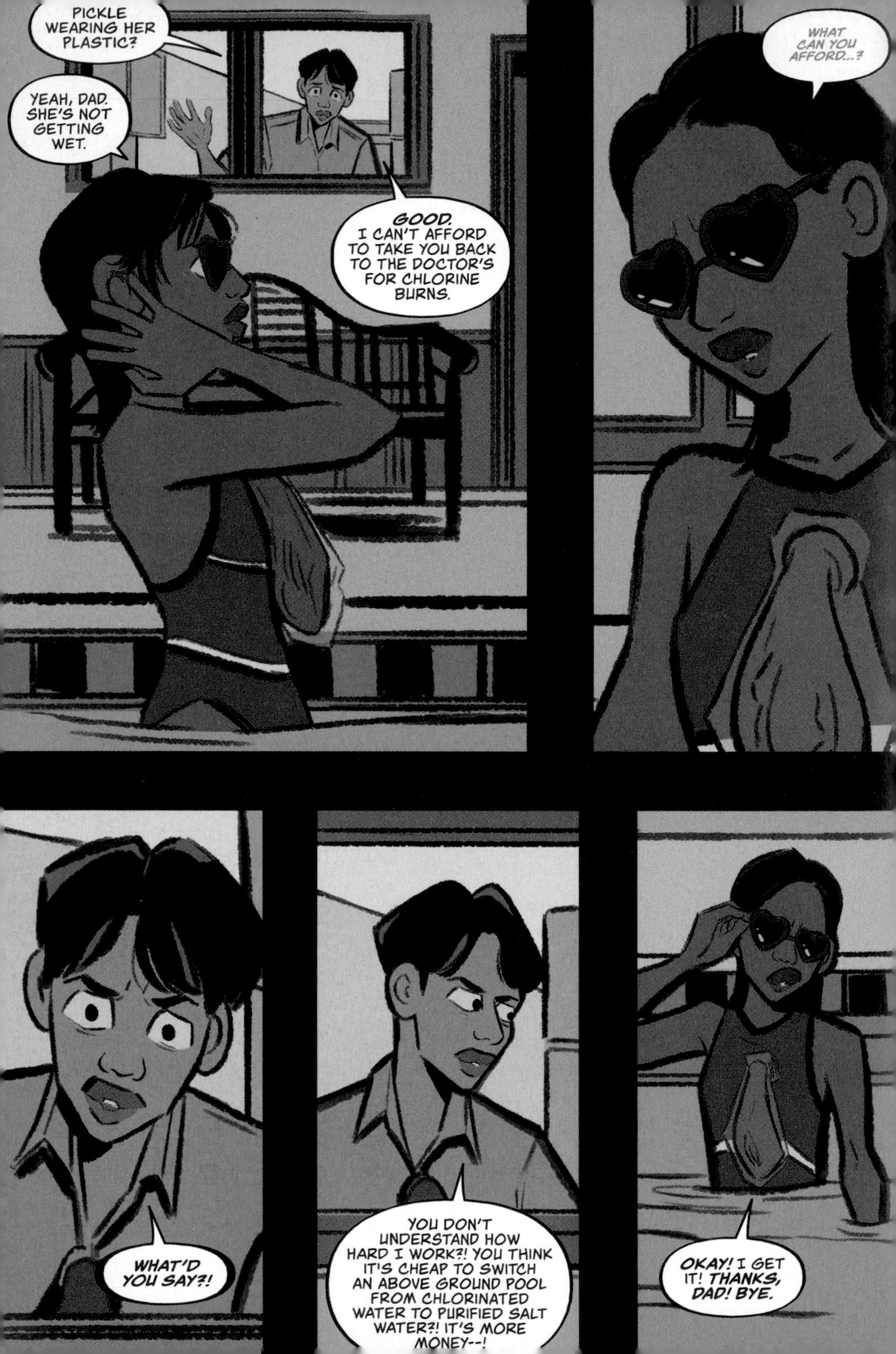
PICKLE WEARING HER PLASTIC?
YEAH, DAD. SHE'S NOT GETTING WET.
GOOD. I CAN'T AFFORD TO TAKE YOU BACK TO THE DOCTOR'S FOR CHLORINE BURNS.
WHAT CAN YOU AFFORD...?
WHAT'D YOU SAY?!
YOU DON'T UNDERSTAND HOW HARD I WORK?! YOU THINK IT'S CHEAP TO SWITCH AN ABOVE GROUND POOL FROM CHLORINATED WATER TO PURIFIED SALT WATER?! IT'S MORE MONEY--!
OKAY! I GET IT! THANKS, DAD! BYE.

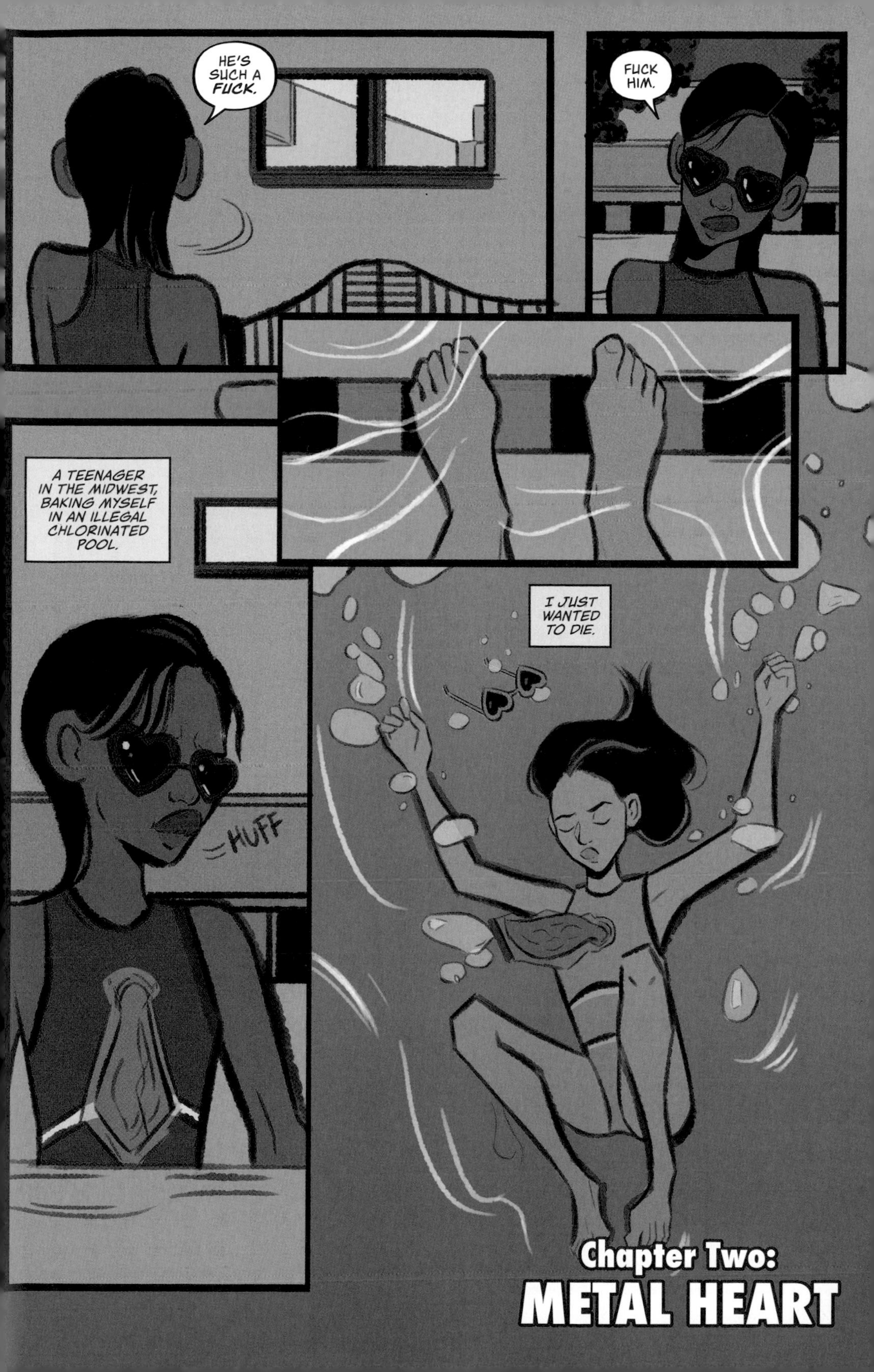

HE'S SUCH A FUCK.
FUCK HIM.
A TEENAGER IN THE MIDWEST, BAKING MYSELF IN AN ILLEGAL CHLORINATED POOL.
HUFF
I JUST WANTED TO DIE.
Chapter Two:
METAL HEART

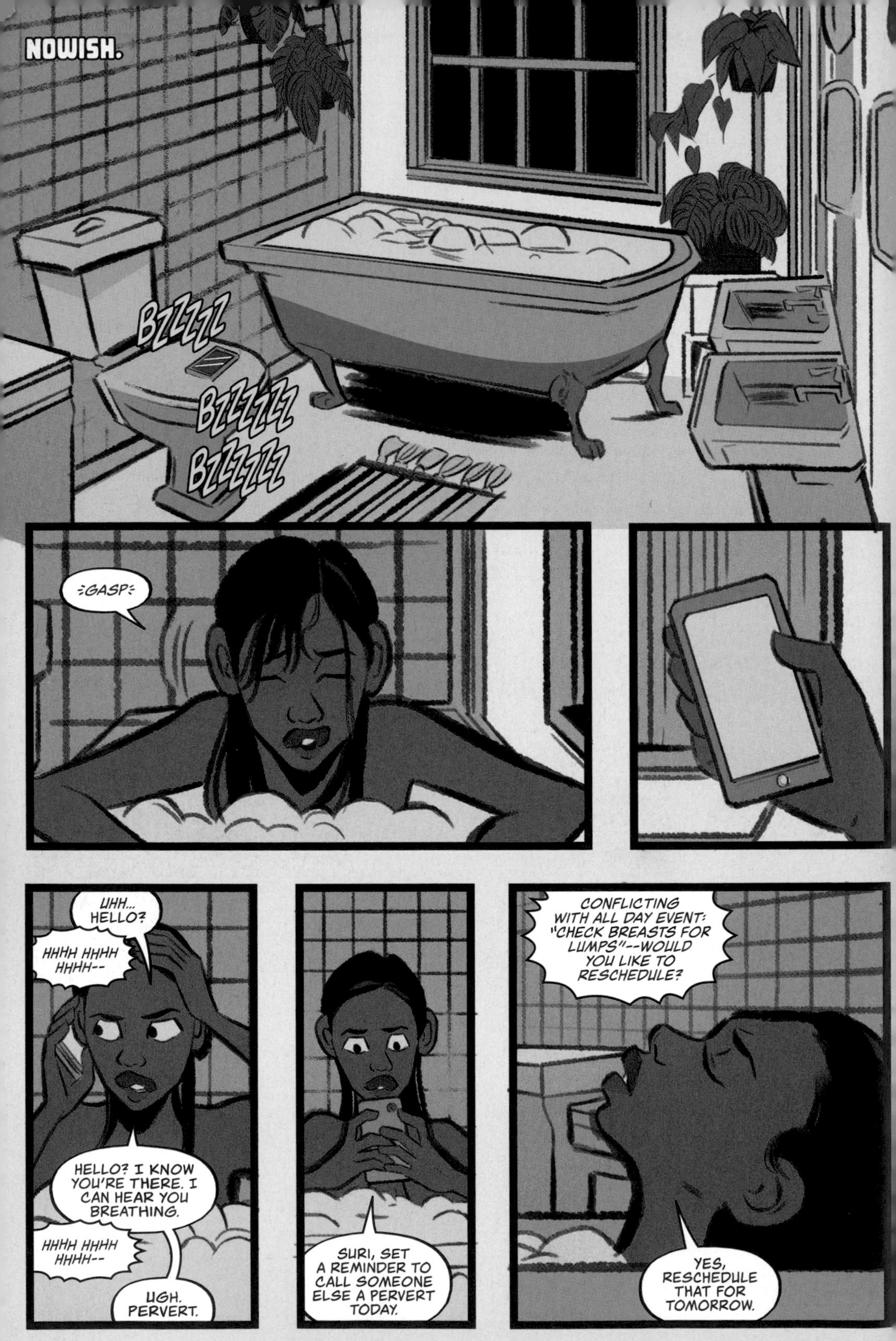
NOWISH.
BZZZZZ
BZZZZZZ
BZZZZZZ
GASP
UHH... HELLO?
HHHH HHHH HHHH--
HELLO? I KNOW YOU'RE THERE. I CAN HEAR YOU BREATHING.
HHHH HHHH HHHH--
UGH. PERVERT.
SURI, SET A REMINDER TO CALL SOMEONE ELSE A PERVERT TODAY.
CONFLICTING WITH ALL DAY EVENT: "CHECK BREASTS FOR LUMPS"--WOULD YOU LIKE TO RESCHEDULE?
YES, RESCHEDULE THAT FOR TOMORROW.

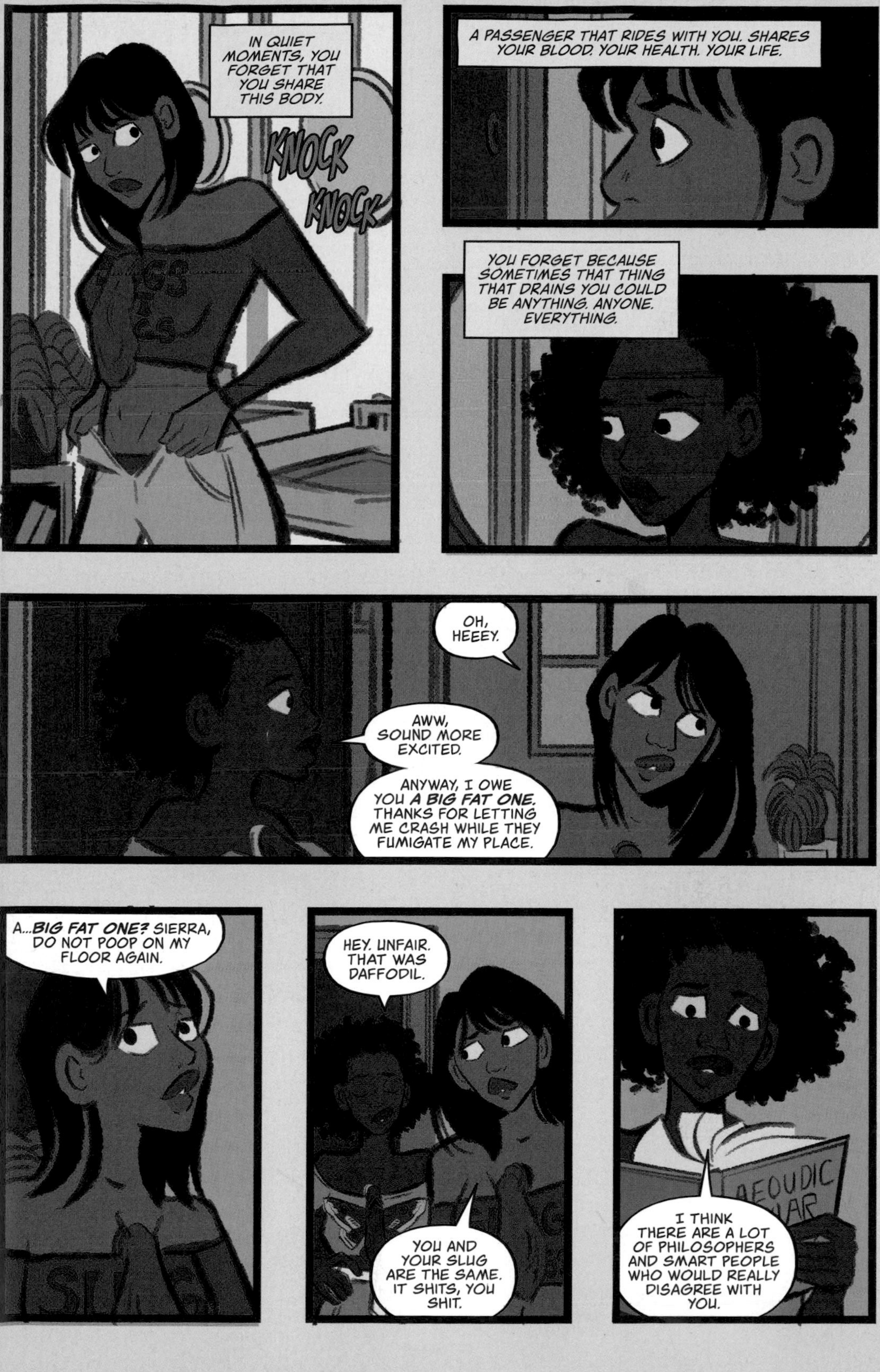
IN QUIET MOMENTS, YOU FORGET THAT YOU SHARE THIS BODY.
KNOCK
KNOCK
A PASSENGER THAT RIDES WITH YOU. SHARES YOUR BLOOD. YOUR HEALTH. YOUR LIFE.
YOU FORGET BECAUSE SOMETIMES THAT THING THAT DRAINS YOU COULD BE ANYTHING. ANYONE. EVERYTHING.
OH, HEEEY.
AWW, SOUND MORE EXCITED.
ANYWAY, I OWE YOU **A BIG FAT ONE.** THANKS FOR LETTING ME CRASH WHILE THEY FUMIGATE MY PLACE.
A...**BIG FAT ONE?** SIERRA, DO NOT POOP ON MY FLOOR AGAIN.
HEY. UNFAIR. THAT WAS DAFFODIL.
YOU AND YOUR SLUG ARE THE SAME. IT SHITS, YOU SHIT.
I THINK THERE ARE A LOT OF PHILOSOPHERS AND SMART PEOPLE WHO WOULD REALLY DISAGREE WITH YOU.

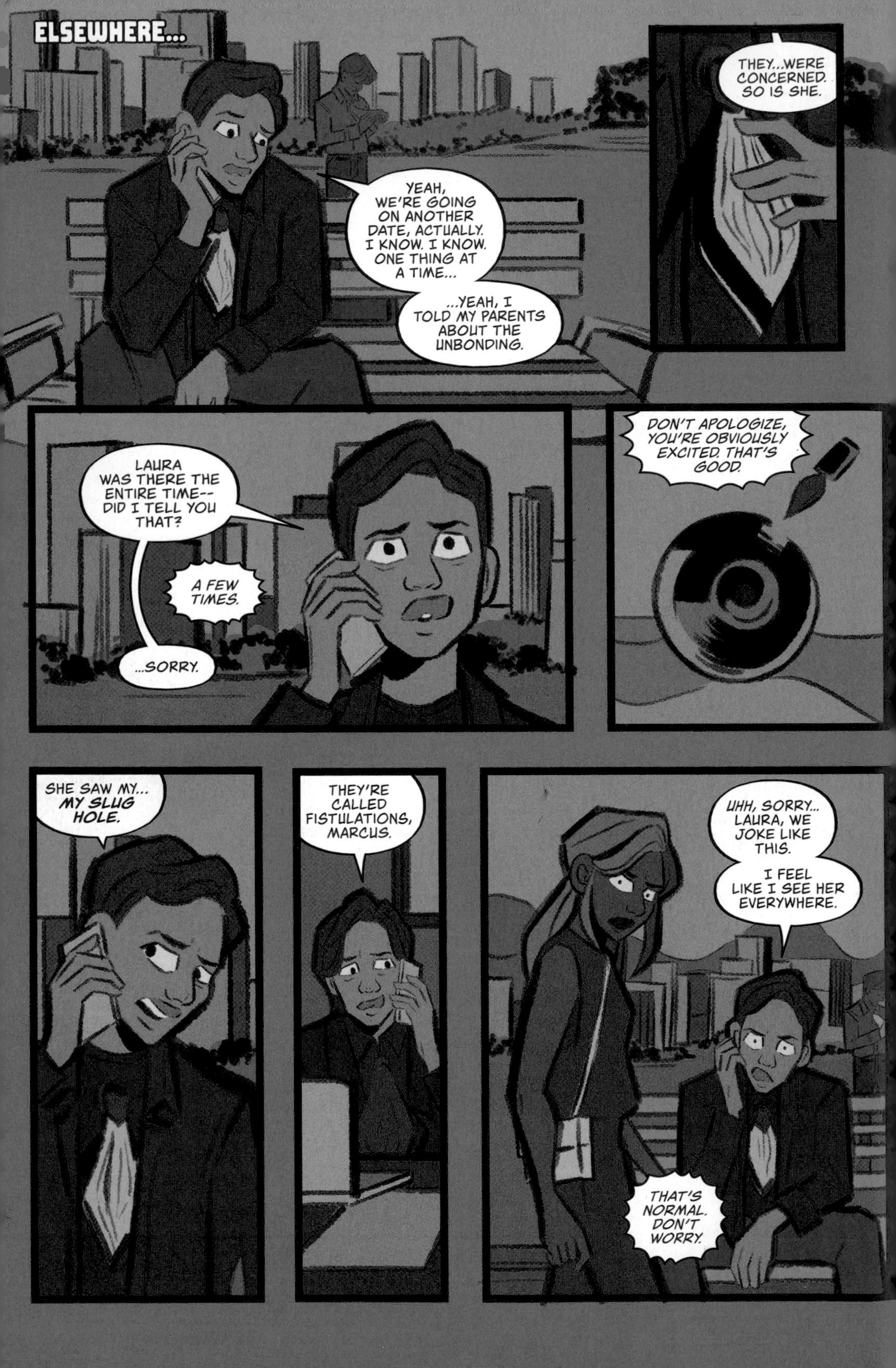
ELSEWHERE...
YEAH, WE'RE GOING ON ANOTHER DATE, ACTUALLY. I KNOW. I KNOW. ONE THING AT A TIME...
...YEAH, I TOLD MY PARENTS ABOUT THE UNBONDING.
THEY...WERE CONCERNED. SO IS SHE.
LAURA WAS THERE THE ENTIRE TIME-- DID I TELL YOU THAT?
A FEW TIMES.
...SORRY.
DON'T APOLOGIZE, YOU'RE OBVIOUSLY EXCITED. THAT'S GOOD.
SHE SAW MY... MY SLUG HOLE.
THEY'RE CALLED FISTULATIONS, MARCUS.
UHH, SORRY... LAURA, WE JOKE LIKE THIS.
I FEEL LIKE I SEE HER EVERYWHERE.
THAT'S NORMAL. DON'T WORRY.

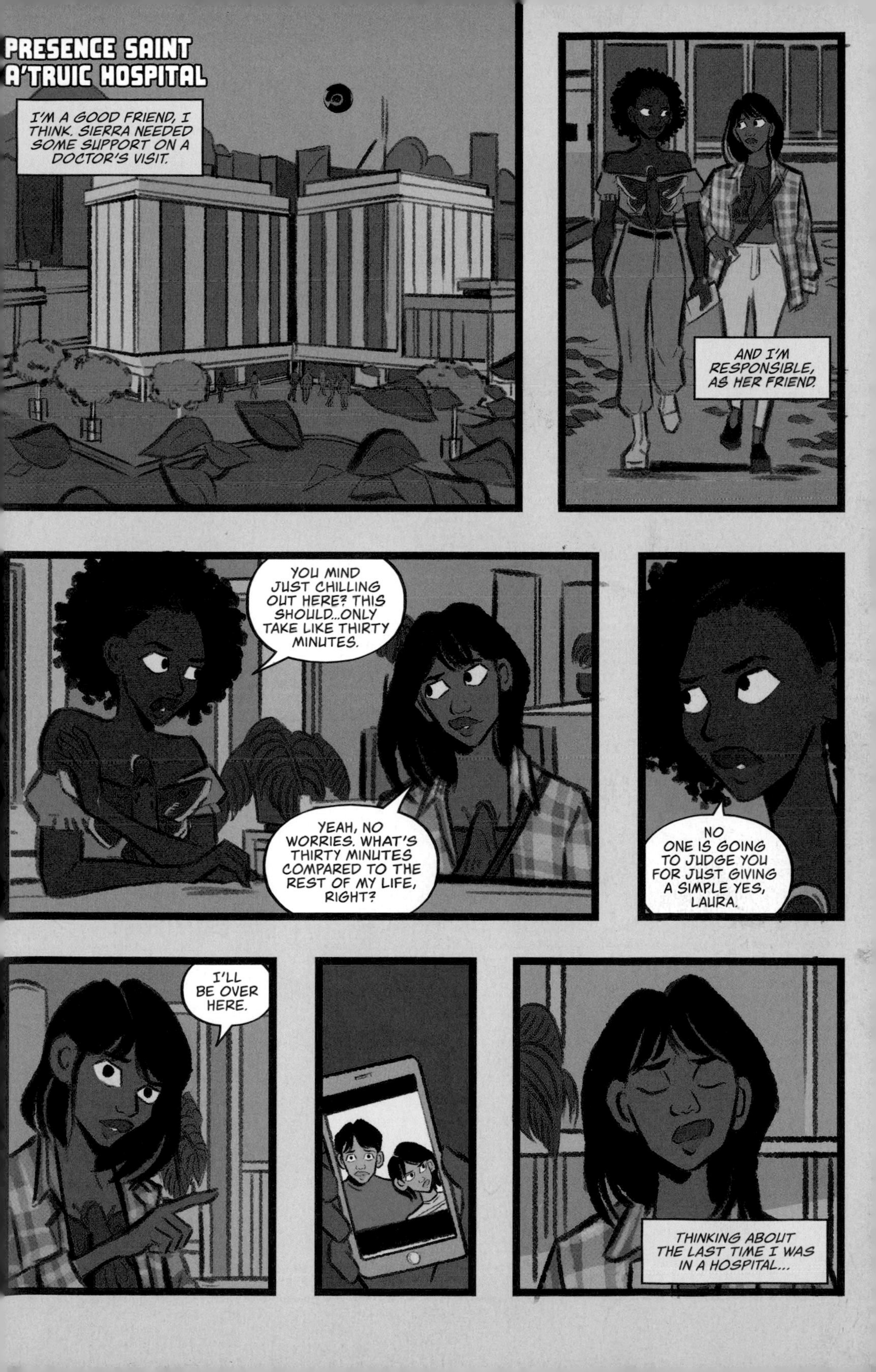
PRESENCE SAINT A'TRUIC HOSPITAL
I'M A GOOD FRIEND, I THINK. SIERRA NEEDED SOME SUPPORT ON A DOCTOR'S VISIT.
AND I'M RESPONSIBLE, AS HER FRIEND.
YOU MIND JUST CHILLING OUT HERE? THIS SHOULD...ONLY TAKE LIKE THIRTY MINUTES.
YEAH, NO WORRIES. WHAT'S THIRTY MINUTES COMPARED TO THE REST OF MY LIFE, RIGHT?
NO ONE IS GOING TO JUDGE YOU FOR JUST GIVING A SIMPLE YES, LAURA.
I'LL BE OVER HERE.
THINKING ABOUT THE LAST TIME I WAS IN A HOSPITAL...

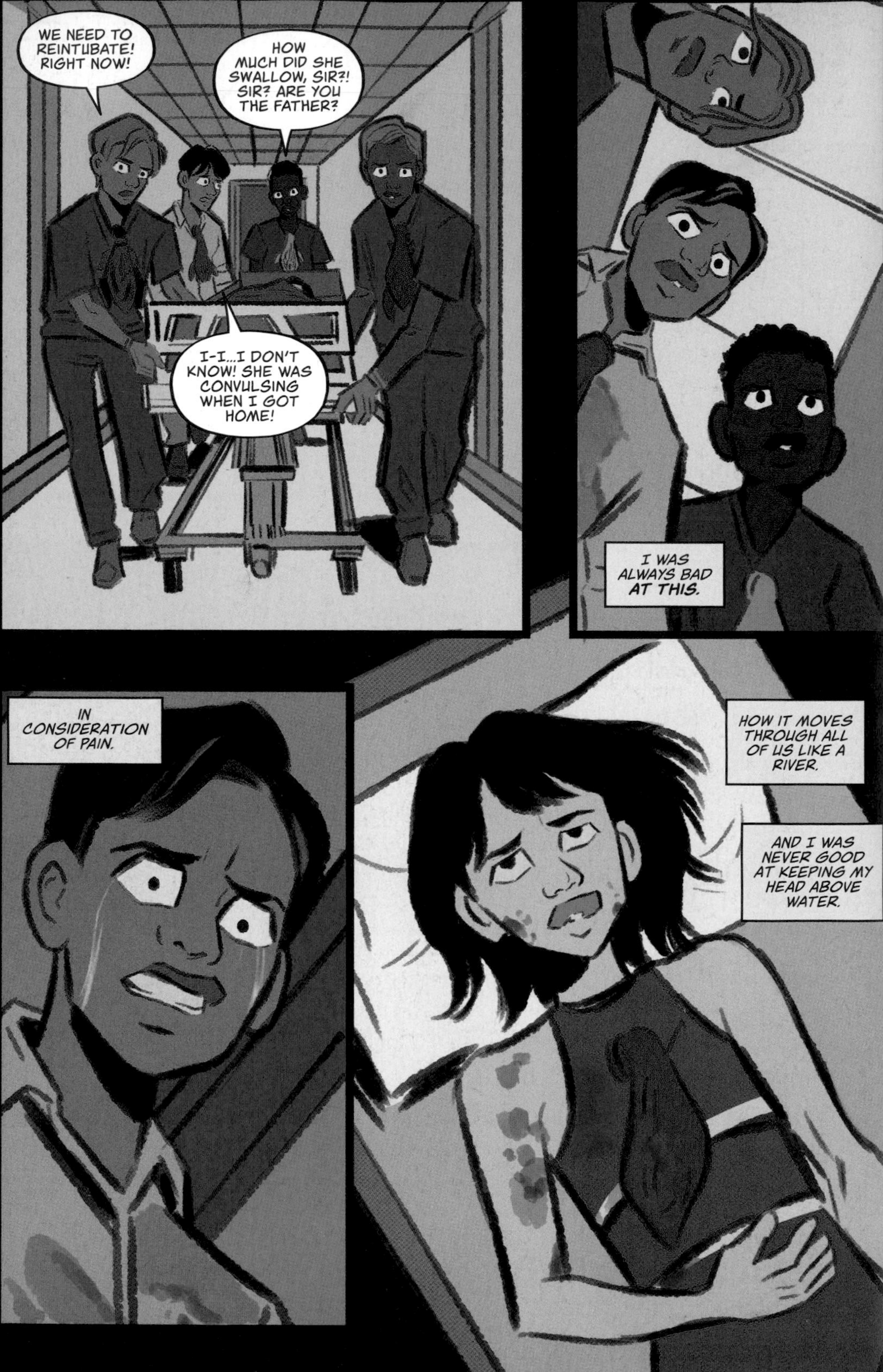
WE NEED TO REINTUBATE! RIGHT NOW!
HOW MUCH DID SHE SWALLOW, SIR?! SIR? ARE YOU THE FATHER?
I-I...I DON'T KNOW! SHE WAS CONVULSING WHEN I GOT HOME!
I WAS ALWAYS BAD AT THIS.
IN CONSIDERATION OF PAIN.
HOW IT MOVES THROUGH ALL OF US LIKE A RIVER.
AND I WAS NEVER GOOD AT KEEPING MY HEAD ABOVE WATER.

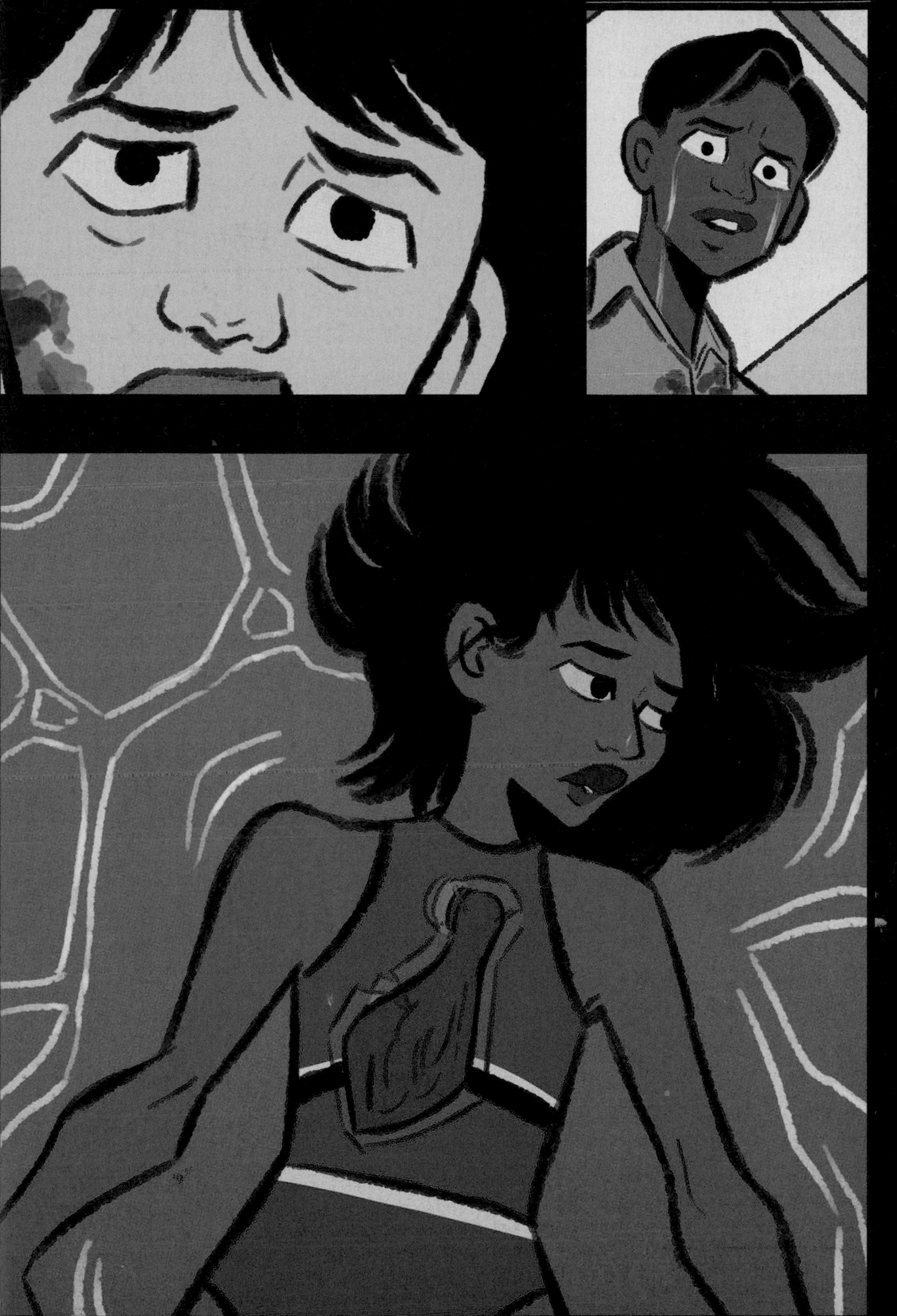

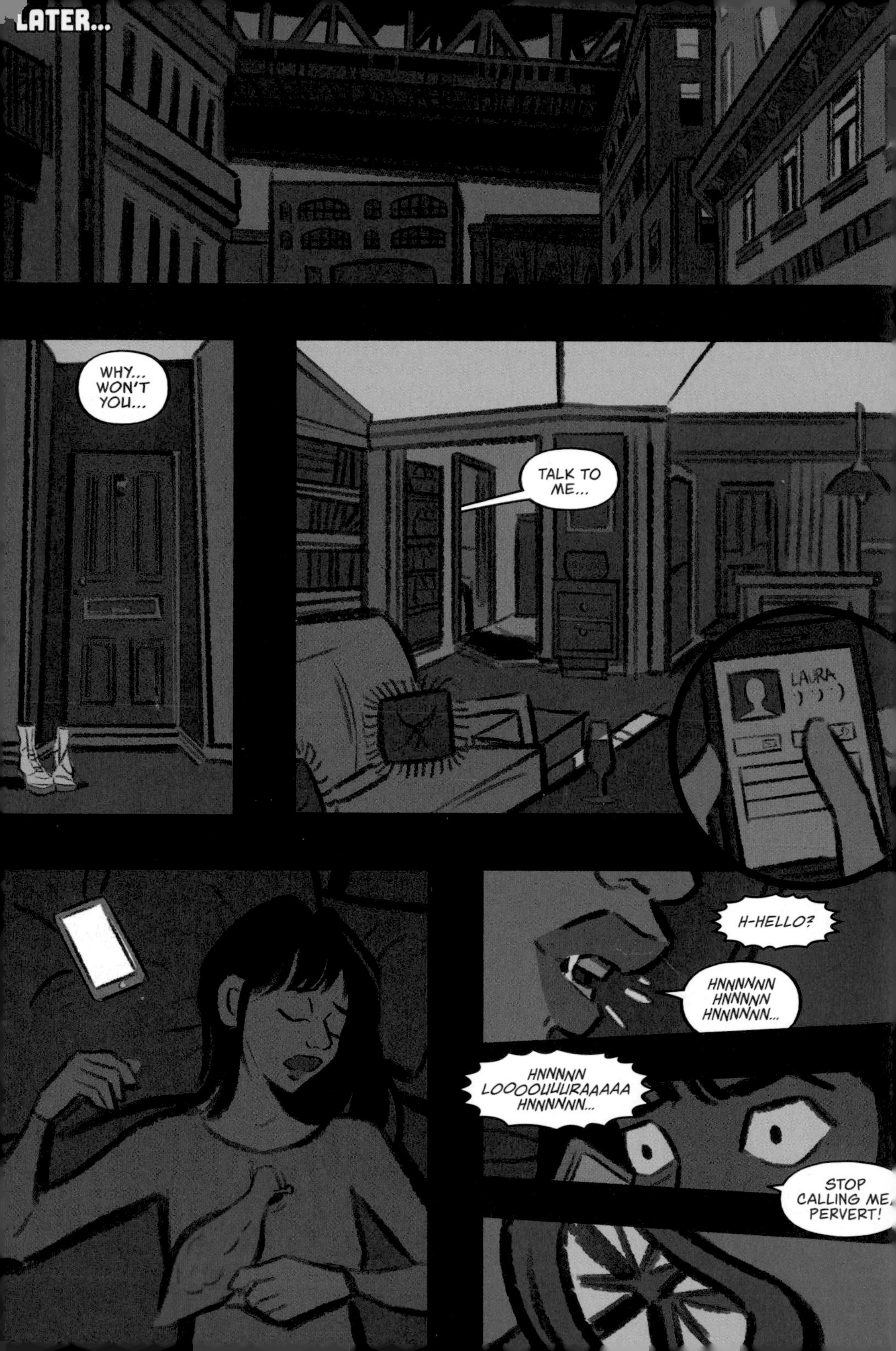
LATER...
WHY... WON'T YOU...
TALK TO ME...
LAURA
H-HELLO?
HNNNNNN HNNNNN HNNNNNN...
HNNNNN LOOOOUUURAAAAA HNNNNNN...
STOP CALLING ME, PERVERT!

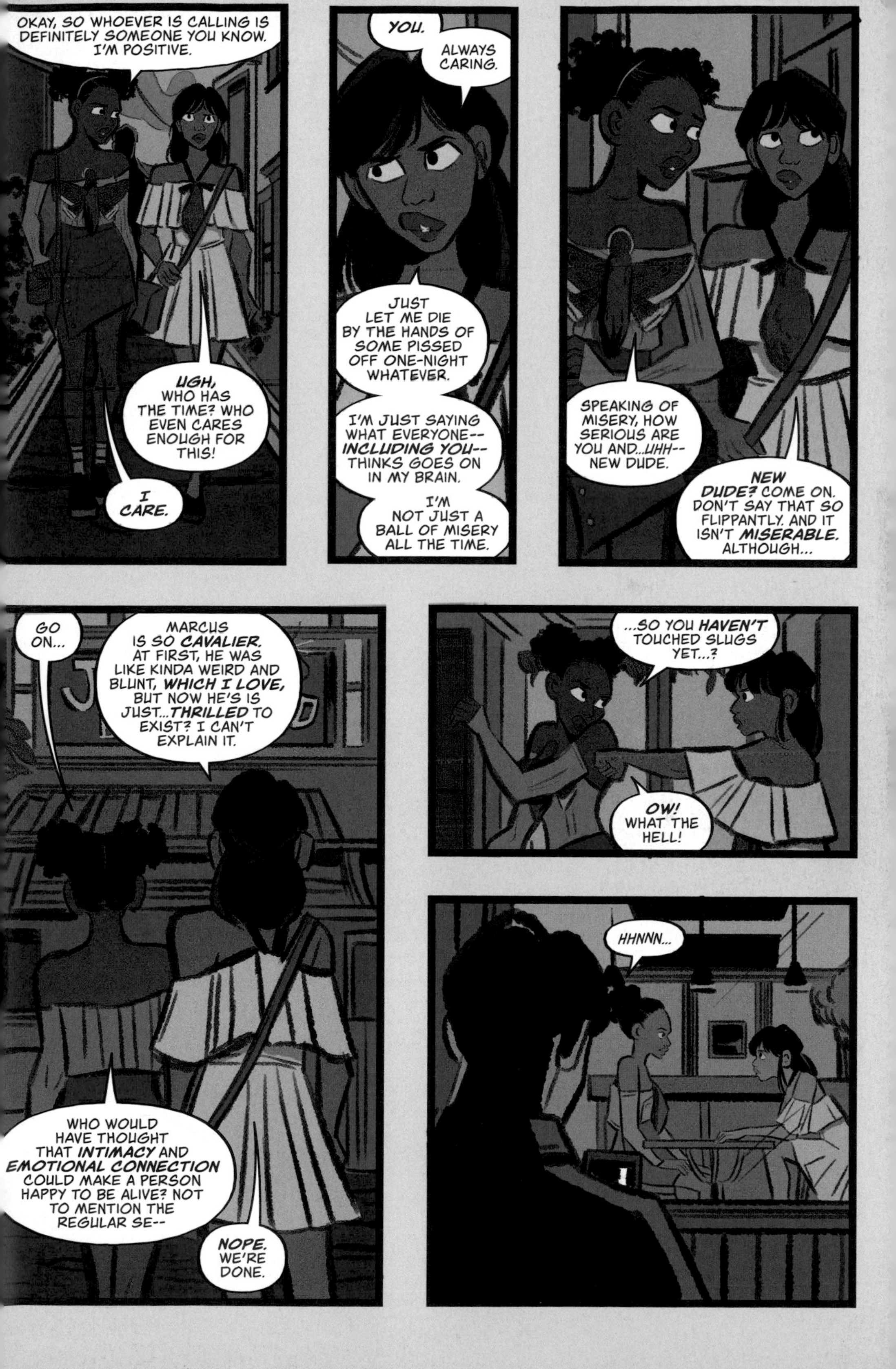

OKAY, SO WHOEVER IS CALLING IS DEFINITELY SOMEONE YOU KNOW. I'M POSITIVE.
UGH, WHO HAS THE TIME? WHO EVEN CARES ENOUGH FOR THIS!
I CARE.
YOU.
ALWAYS CARING.
JUST LET ME DIE BY THE HANDS OF SOME PISSED OFF ONE-NIGHT WHATEVER.
I'M JUST SAYING WHAT EVERYONE-- INCLUDING YOU-- THINKS GOES ON IN MY BRAIN.
I'M NOT JUST A BALL OF MISERY ALL THE TIME.
SPEAKING OF MISERY, HOW SERIOUS ARE YOU AND...UHH-- NEW DUDE.
NEW DUDE? COME ON. DON'T SAY THAT SO FLIPPANTLY. AND IT ISN'T MISERABLE. ALTHOUGH...
GO ON...
MARCUS IS SO CAVALIER. AT FIRST, HE WAS LIKE KINDA WEIRD AND BLUNT, WHICH I LOVE, BUT NOW HE'S IS JUST...THRILLED TO EXIST? I CAN'T EXPLAIN IT.
WHO WOULD HAVE THOUGHT THAT INTIMACY AND EMOTIONAL CONNECTION COULD MAKE A PERSON HAPPY TO BE ALIVE? NOT TO MENTION THE REGULAR SE--
NOPE. WE'RE DONE.
...SO YOU HAVEN'T TOUCHED SLUGS YET...?
OW! WHAT THE HELL!
HHNNN...

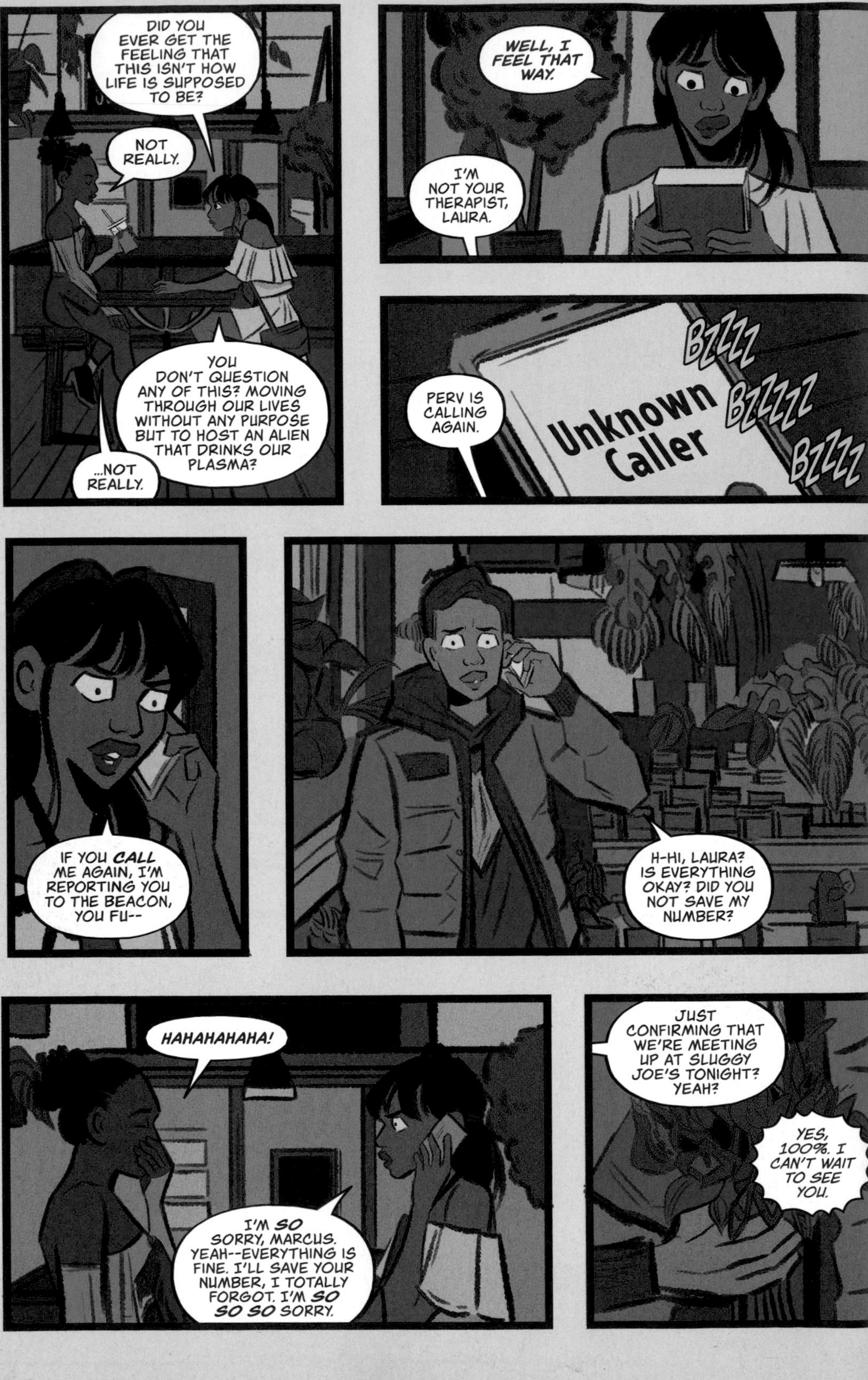
DID YOU EVER GET THE FEELING THAT THIS ISN'T HOW LIFE IS SUPPOSED TO BE?
NOT REALLY.
YOU DON'T QUESTION ANY OF THIS? MOVING THROUGH OUR LIVES WITHOUT ANY PURPOSE BUT TO HOST AN ALIEN THAT DRINKS OUR PLASMA?
...NOT REALLY.
WELL, I FEEL THAT WAY.
I'M NOT YOUR THERAPIST, LAURA.
PERV IS CALLING AGAIN.
Unknown Caller
BZZZZ
BZZZZZ
BZZZZ
IF YOU CALL ME AGAIN, I'M REPORTING YOU TO THE BEACON, YOU FU--
H-HI, LAURA? IS EVERYTHING OKAY? DID YOU NOT SAVE MY NUMBER?
HAHAHAHAHA!
I'M SO SORRY, MARCUS. YEAH--EVERYTHING IS FINE. I'LL SAVE YOUR NUMBER, I TOTALLY FORGOT. I'M SO SO SO SORRY.
JUST CONFIRMING THAT WE'RE MEETING UP AT SLUGGY JOE'S TONIGHT? YEAH?
YES, 100%. I CAN'T WAIT TO SEE YOU.

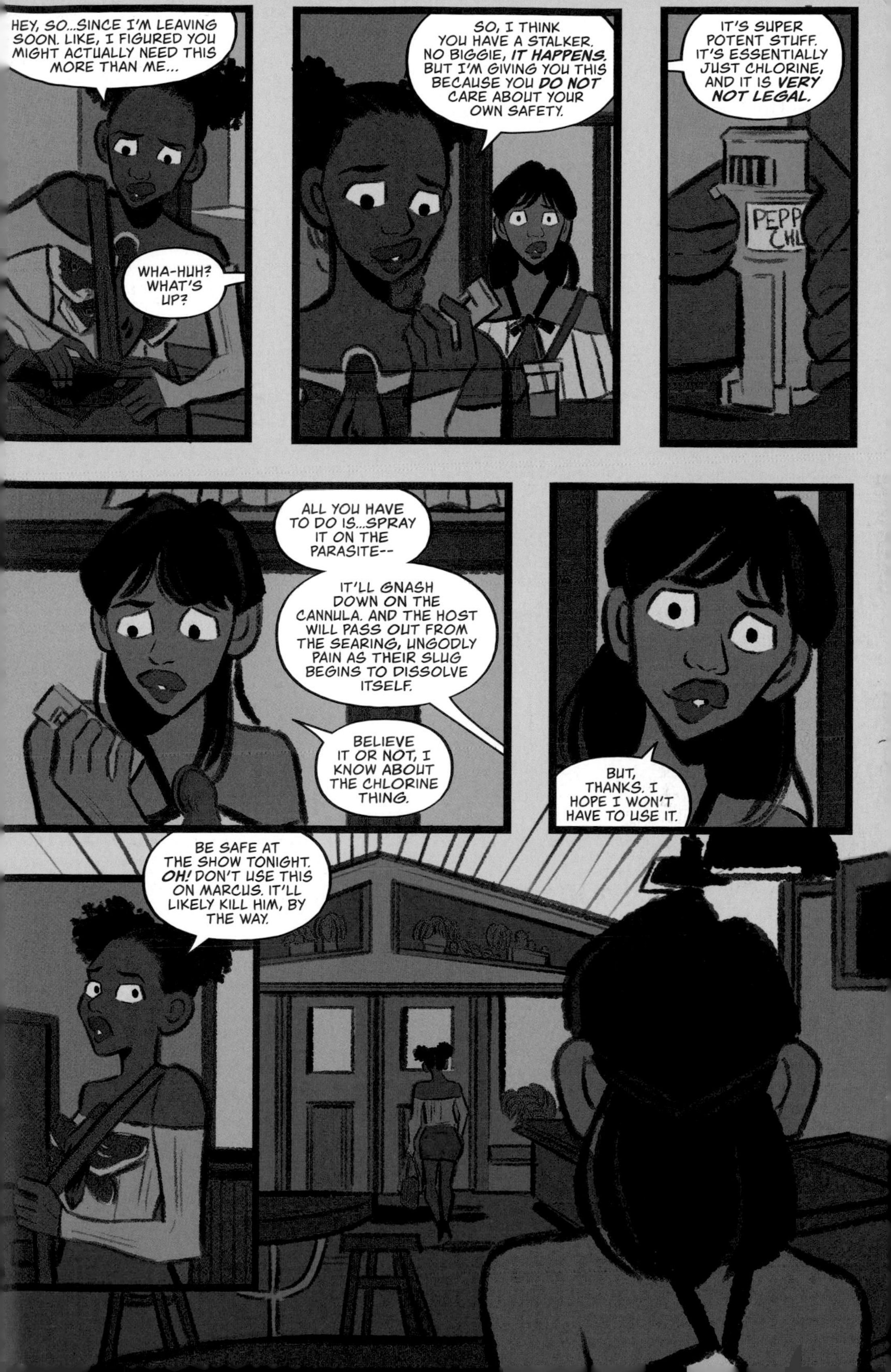
HEY, SO...SINCE I'M LEAVING SOON. LIKE, I FIGURED YOU MIGHT ACTUALLY NEED THIS MORE THAN ME...
WHA-HUH? WHAT'S UP?
SO, I THINK YOU HAVE A STALKER. NO BIGGIE, *IT HAPPENS.* BUT I'M GIVING YOU THIS BECAUSE YOU **DO NOT** CARE ABOUT YOUR OWN SAFETY.
IT'S SUPER POTENT STUFF. IT'S ESSENTIALLY JUST CHLORINE, AND IT IS ***VERY NOT LEGAL.***
PEPP CHL
ALL YOU HAVE TO DO IS...SPRAY IT ON THE PARASITE--
IT'LL GNASH DOWN ON THE CANNULA. AND THE HOST WILL PASS OUT FROM THE SEARING, UNGODLY PAIN AS THEIR SLUG BEGINS TO DISSOLVE ITSELF.
BELIEVE IT OR NOT, I KNOW ABOUT THE CHLORINE THING.
BUT, THANKS. I HOPE I WON'T HAVE TO USE IT.
BE SAFE AT THE SHOW TONIGHT. ***OH!*** DON'T USE THIS ON MARCUS. IT'LL LIKELY KILL HIM, BY THE WAY.

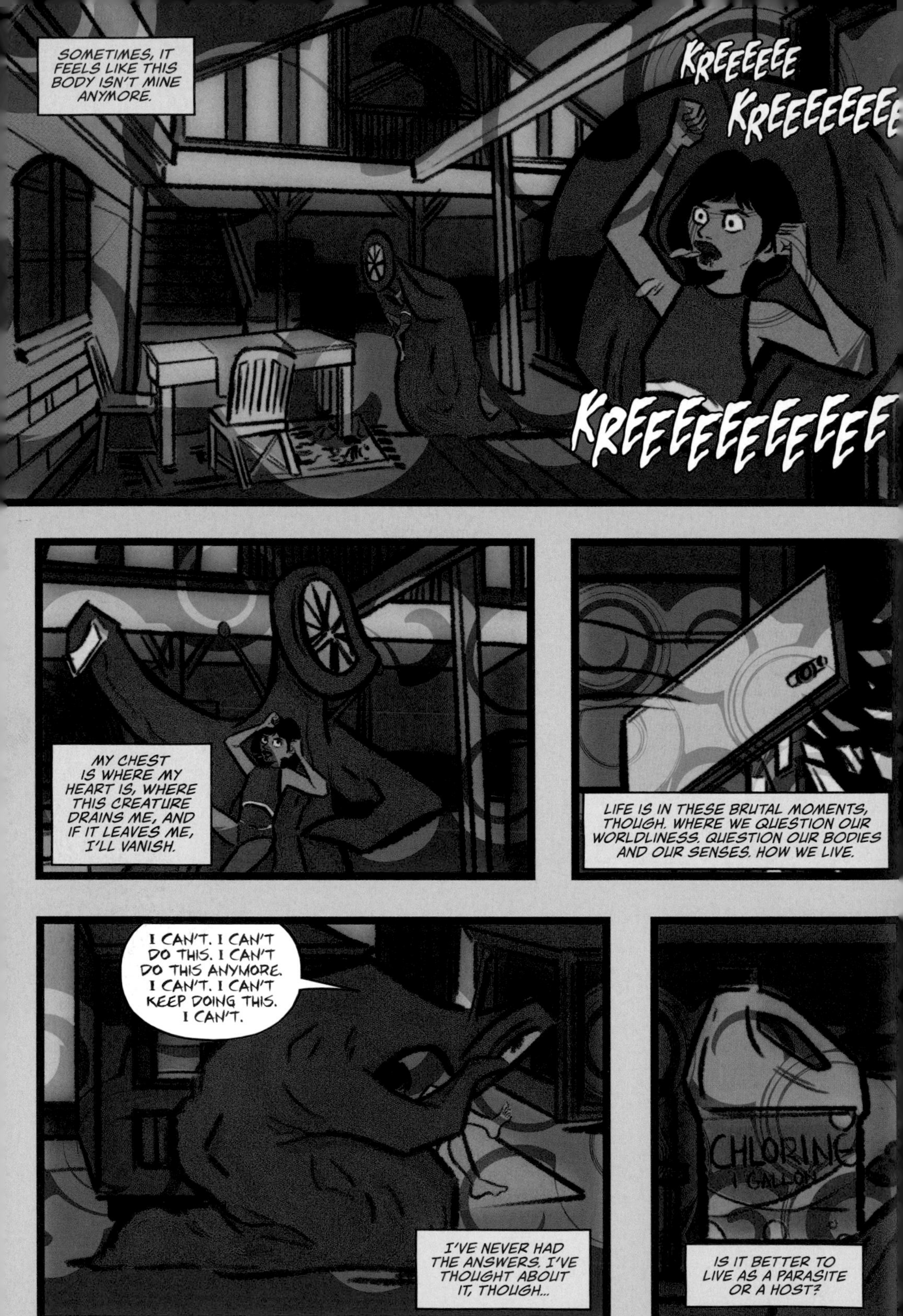
SOMETIMES, IT FEELS LIKE THIS BODY ISN'T MINE ANYMORE.
KREEEEEE
KREEEEEEEE
KREEEEEEEEEEE
MY CHEST IS WHERE MY HEART IS, WHERE THIS CREATURE DRAINS ME, AND IF IT LEAVES ME, I'LL VANISH.
LIFE IS IN THESE BRUTAL MOMENTS, THOUGH. WHERE WE QUESTION OUR WORLDLINESS. QUESTION OUR BODIES AND OUR SENSES. HOW WE LIVE.
I CAN'T. I CAN'T DO THIS. I CAN'T DO THIS ANYMORE. I CAN'T. I CAN'T KEEP DOING THIS. I CAN'T.
I'VE NEVER HAD THE ANSWERS. I'VE THOUGHT ABOUT IT, THOUGH...
CHLORINE
1 GALLON
IS IT BETTER TO LIVE AS A PARASITE OR A HOST?

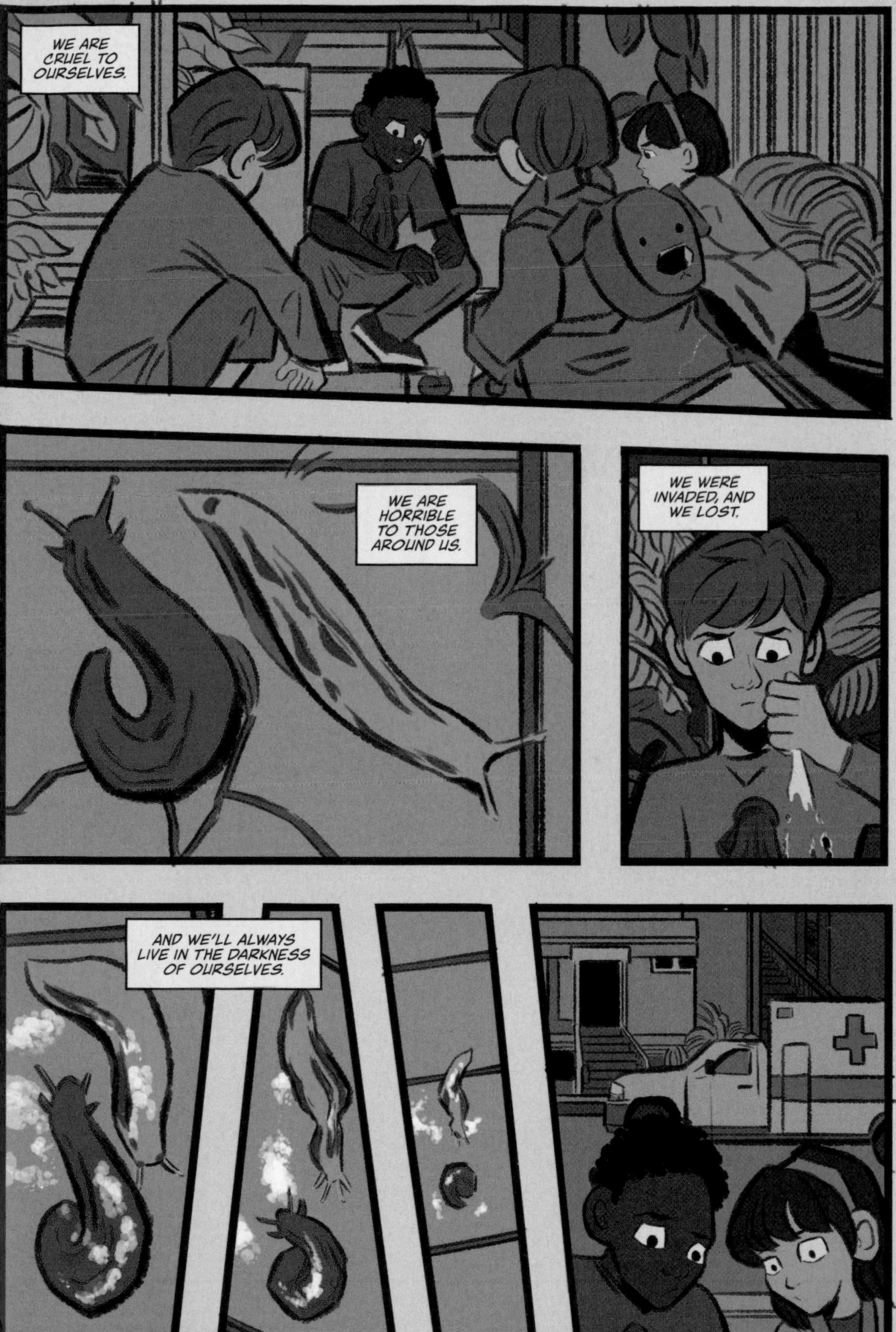
WE ARE CRUEL TO OURSELVES.
WE ARE HORRIBLE TO THOSE AROUND US.
WE WERE INVADED, AND WE LOST.
AND WE'LL ALWAYS LIVE IN THE DARKNESS OF OURSELVES.

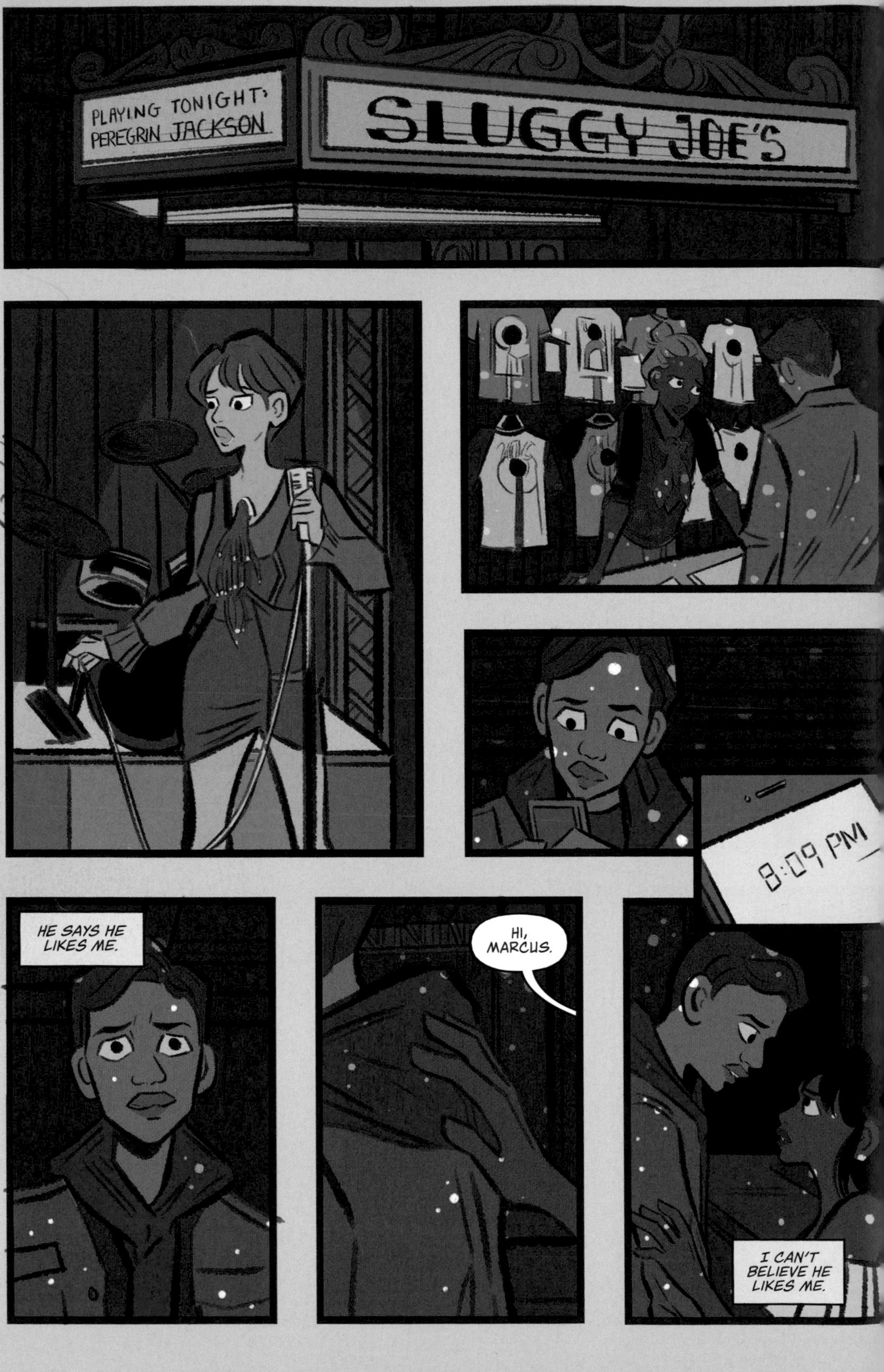
PLAYING TONIGHT:
PEREGRIN JACKSON
SLUGGY JOE'S
8:09 PM
HE SAYS HE LIKES ME.
HI, MARCUS.
I CAN'T BELIEVE HE LIKES ME.

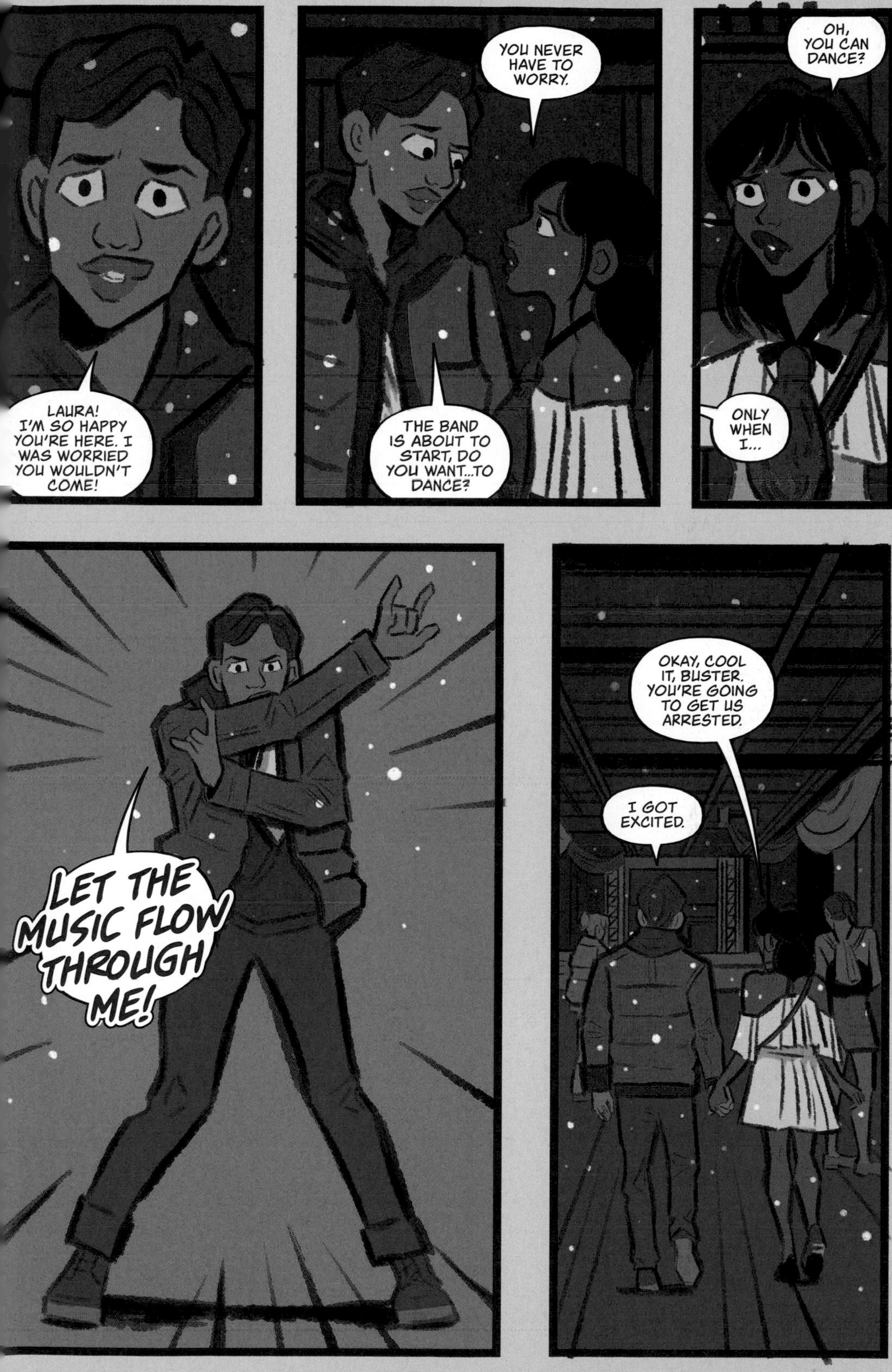
LAURA! I'M SO HAPPY YOU'RE HERE. I WAS WORRIED YOU WOULDN'T COME!
YOU NEVER HAVE TO WORRY.
THE BAND IS ABOUT TO START, DO YOU WANT...TO DANCE?
OH, YOU CAN DANCE?
ONLY WHEN I...
LET THE MUSIC FLOW THROUGH ME!
OKAY, COOL IT, BUSTER. YOU'RE GOING TO GET US ARRESTED.
I GOT EXCITED.

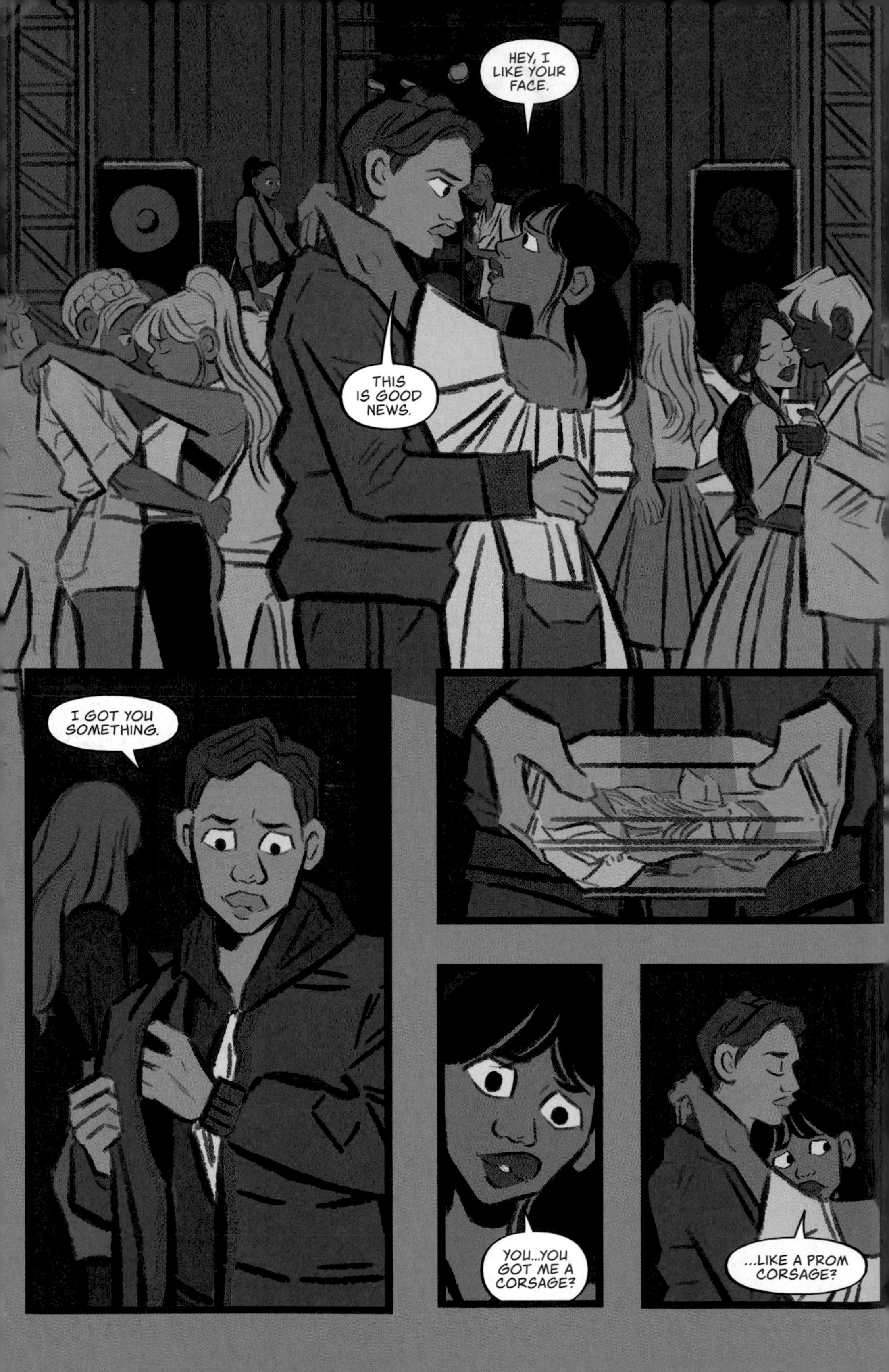
HEY, I LIKE YOUR FACE.
THIS IS GOOD NEWS.
I GOT YOU SOMETHING.
YOU...YOU GOT ME A CORSAGE?
...LIKE A PROM CORSAGE?

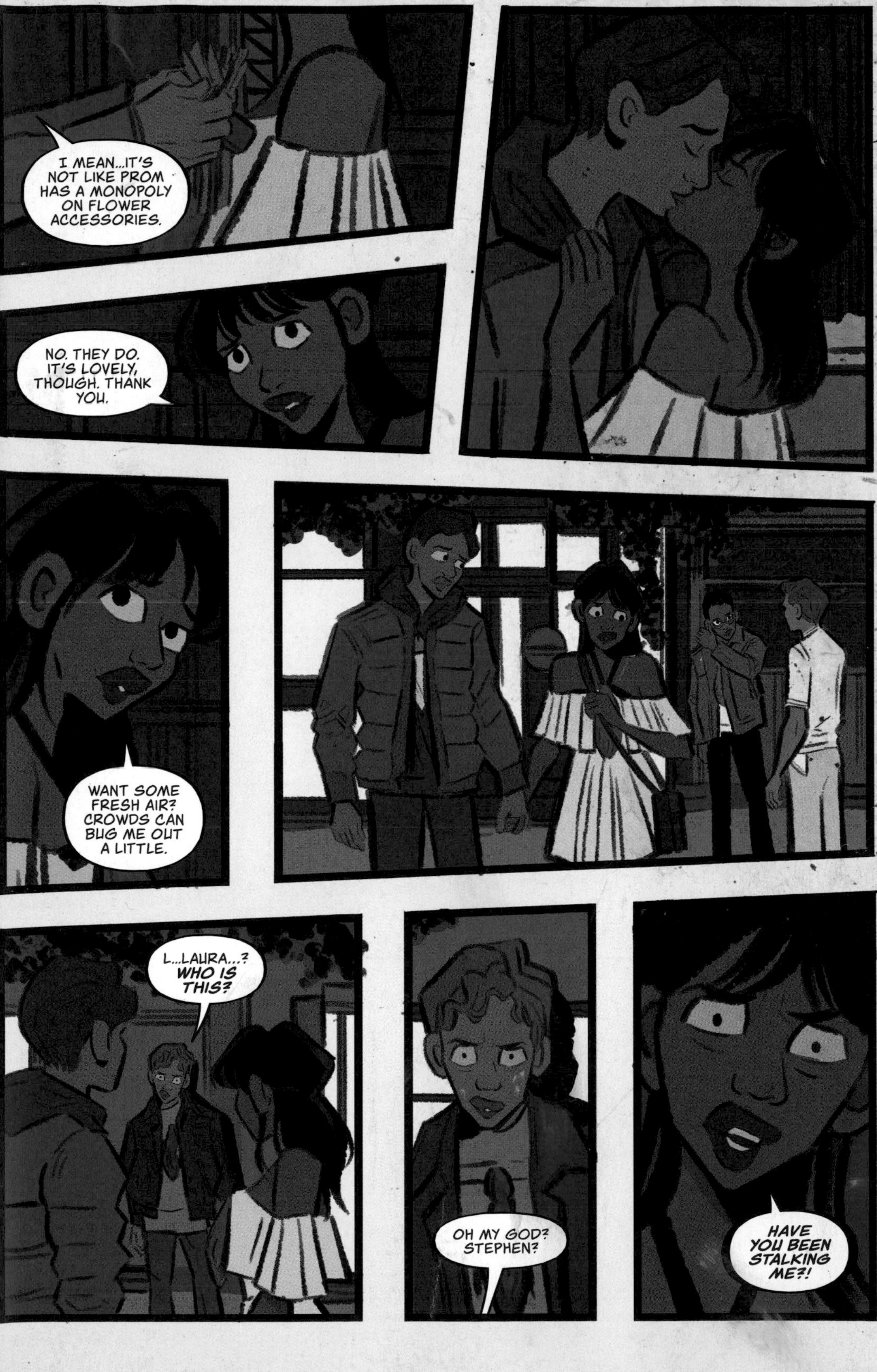
I MEAN...IT'S NOT LIKE PROM HAS A MONOPOLY ON FLOWER ACCESSORIES.
NO. THEY DO. IT'S LOVELY, THOUGH. THANK YOU.
WANT SOME FRESH AIR? CROWDS CAN BUG ME OUT A LITTLE.
L...LAURA...? WHO IS THIS?
OH MY GOD? STEPHEN?
HAVE YOU BEEN STALKING ME?!

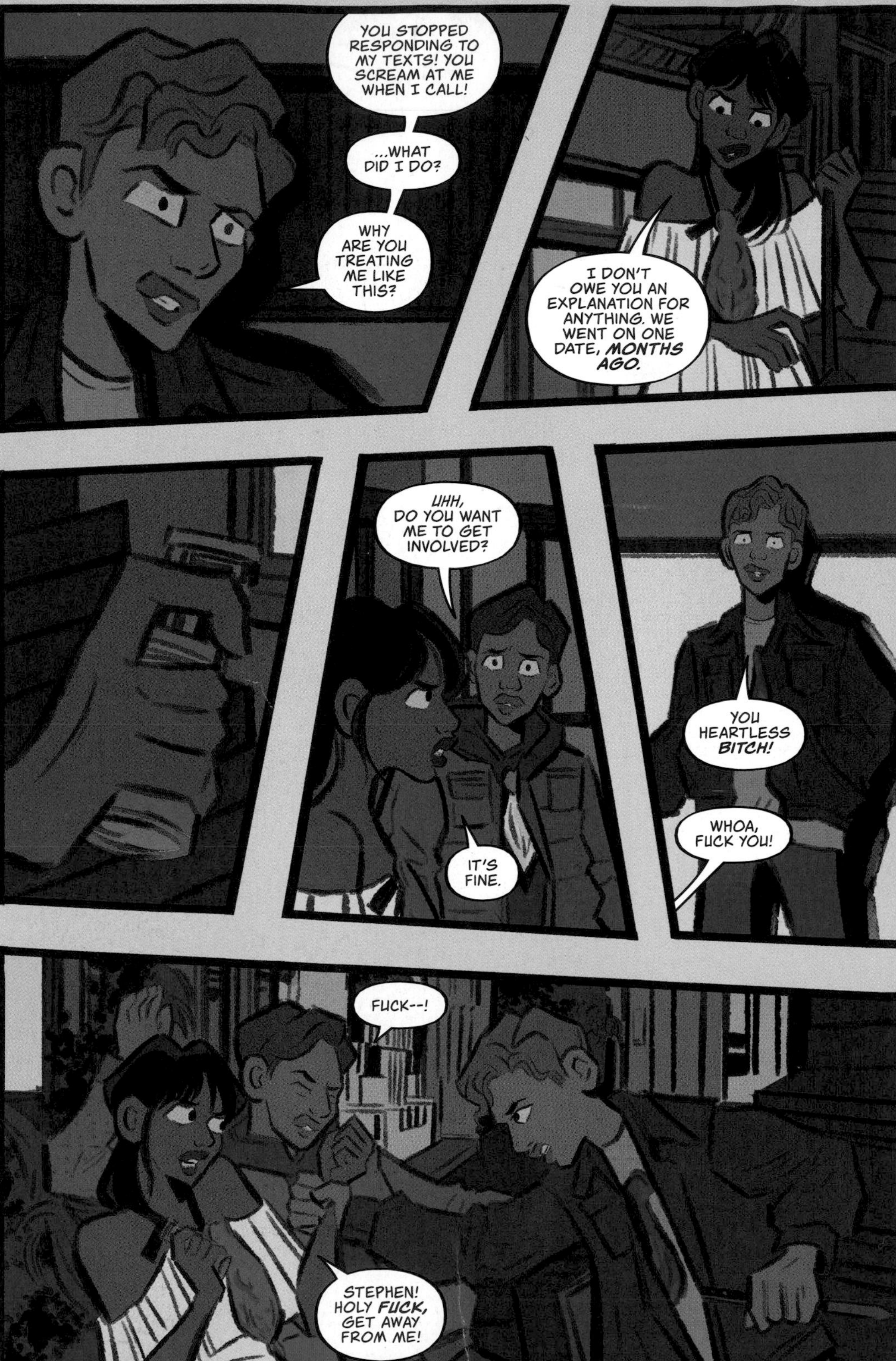
YOU STOPPED RESPONDING TO MY TEXTS! YOU SCREAM AT ME WHEN I CALL!
...WHAT DID I DO?
WHY ARE YOU TREATING ME LIKE THIS?
I DON'T OWE YOU AN EXPLANATION FOR ANYTHING. WE WENT ON ONE DATE, MONTHS AGO.
UHH, DO YOU WANT ME TO GET INVOLVED?
IT'S FINE.
YOU HEARTLESS BITCH!
WHOA, FUCK YOU!
FUCK--!
STEPHEN! HOLY FUCK, GET AWAY FROM ME!

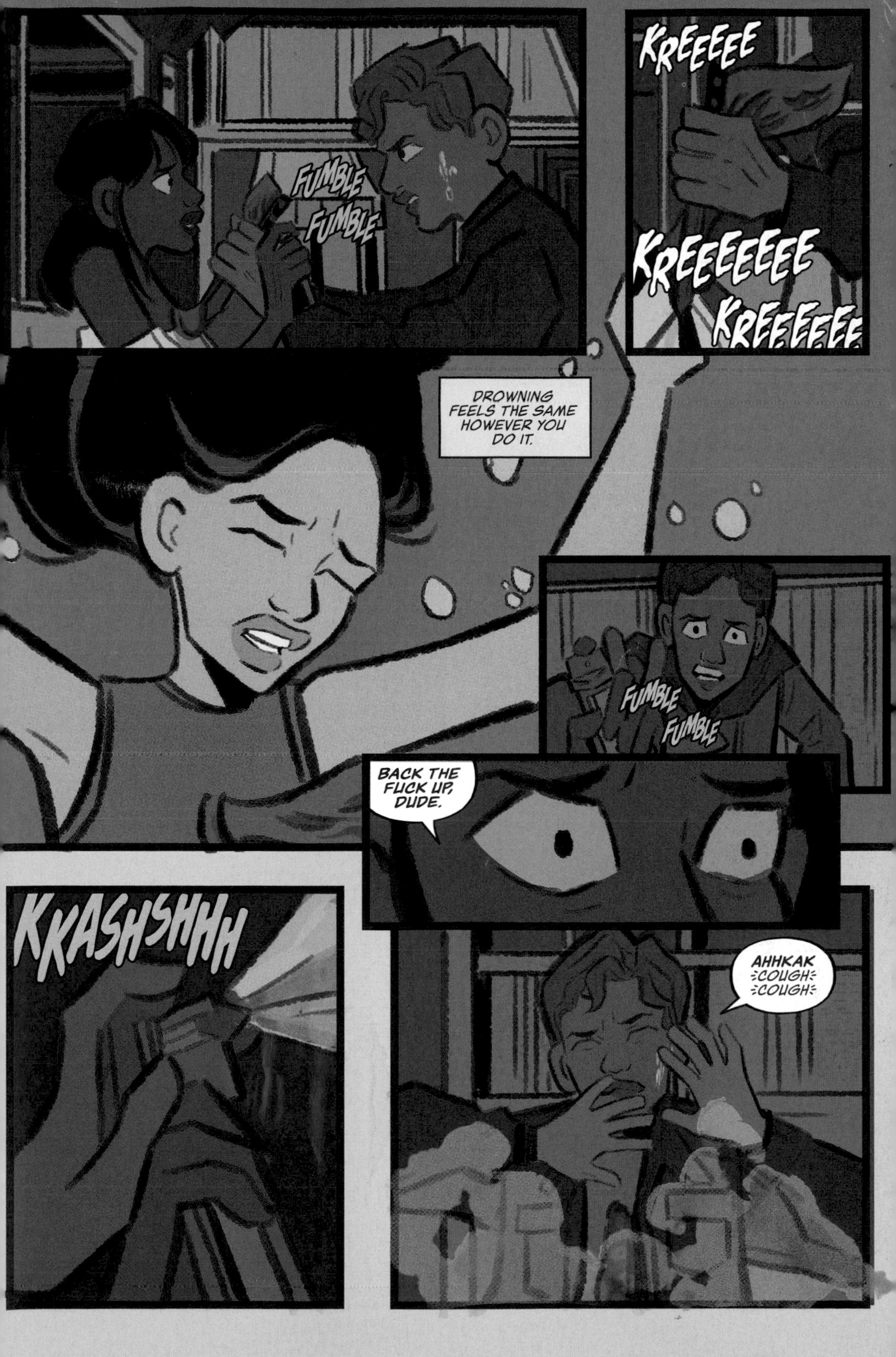
FUMBLE
FUMBLE
KREEEEE
KREEEEEEE
KREEEEEE
DROWNING FEELS THE SAME HOWEVER YOU DO IT.
FUMBLE
FUMBLE
BACK THE FUCK UP, DUDE.
KKASHSHHH
AHHKAK
COUGH
COUGH

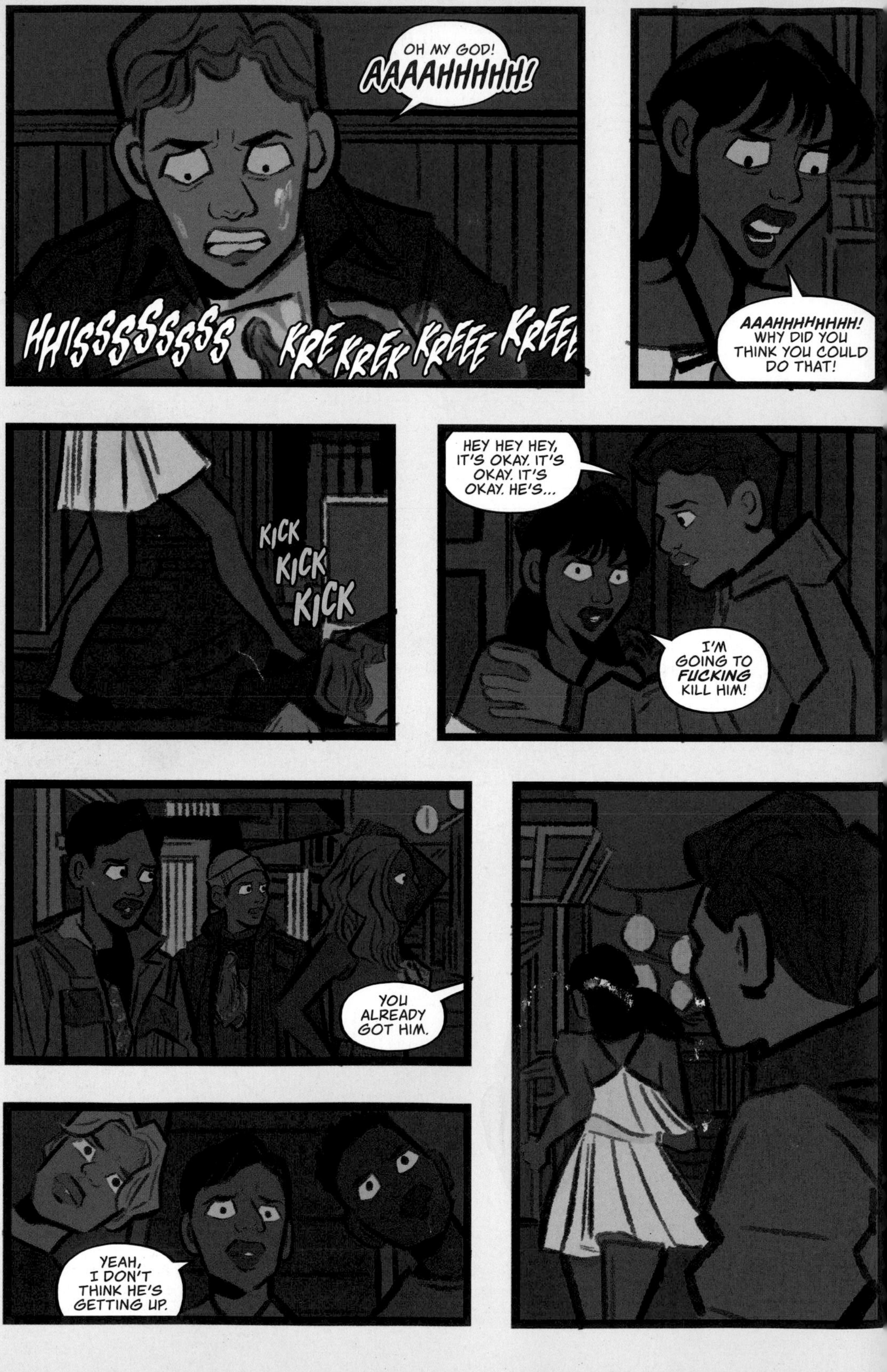
OH MY GOD!
AAAAHHHHH!
HHISSSSSSSS
KRE KREK KREEE KREEE
AAAHHHHHHHH! WHY DID YOU THINK YOU COULD DO THAT!
KICK
KICK
KICK
HEY HEY HEY, IT'S OKAY. IT'S OKAY. IT'S OKAY. HE'S...
I'M GOING TO FUCKING KILL HIM!
YOU ALREADY GOT HIM.
YEAH, I DON'T THINK HE'S GETTING UP.

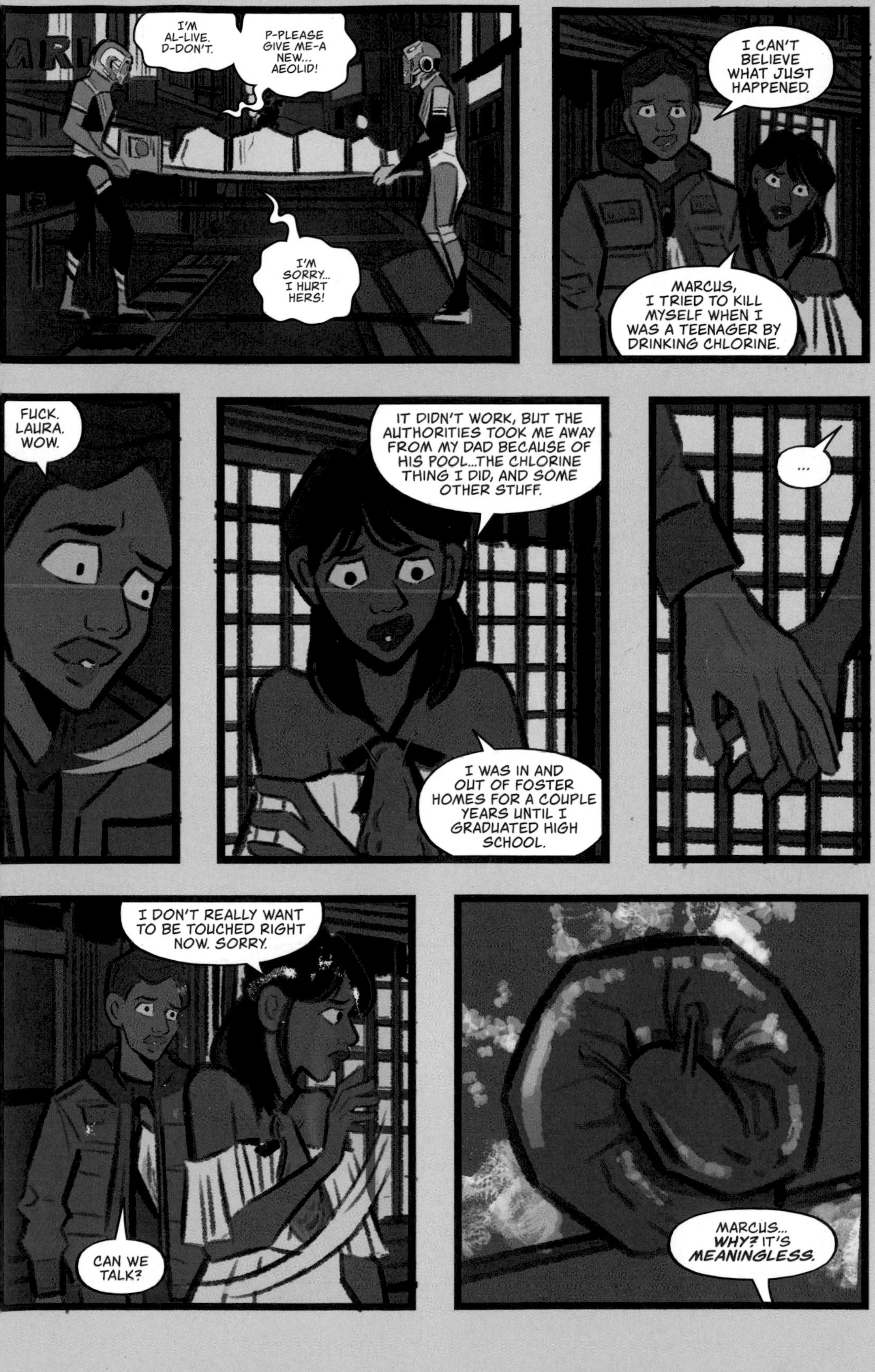
I'M AL-LIVE. D-DON'T.
P-PLEASE GIVE ME-A NEW... AEOLID!
I'M SORRY... I HURT HERS!
I CAN'T BELIEVE WHAT JUST HAPPENED.
MARCUS, I TRIED TO KILL MYSELF WHEN I WAS A TEENAGER BY DRINKING CHLORINE.
FUCK. LAURA. WOW.
IT DIDN'T WORK, BUT THE AUTHORITIES TOOK ME AWAY FROM MY DAD BECAUSE OF HIS POOL...THE CHLORINE THING I DID, AND SOME OTHER STUFF.
I WAS IN AND OUT OF FOSTER HOMES FOR A COUPLE YEARS UNTIL I GRADUATED HIGH SCHOOL.
...
I DON'T REALLY WANT TO BE TOUCHED RIGHT NOW. SORRY.
CAN WE TALK?
MARCUS... *WHY?* IT'S *MEANINGLESS.*

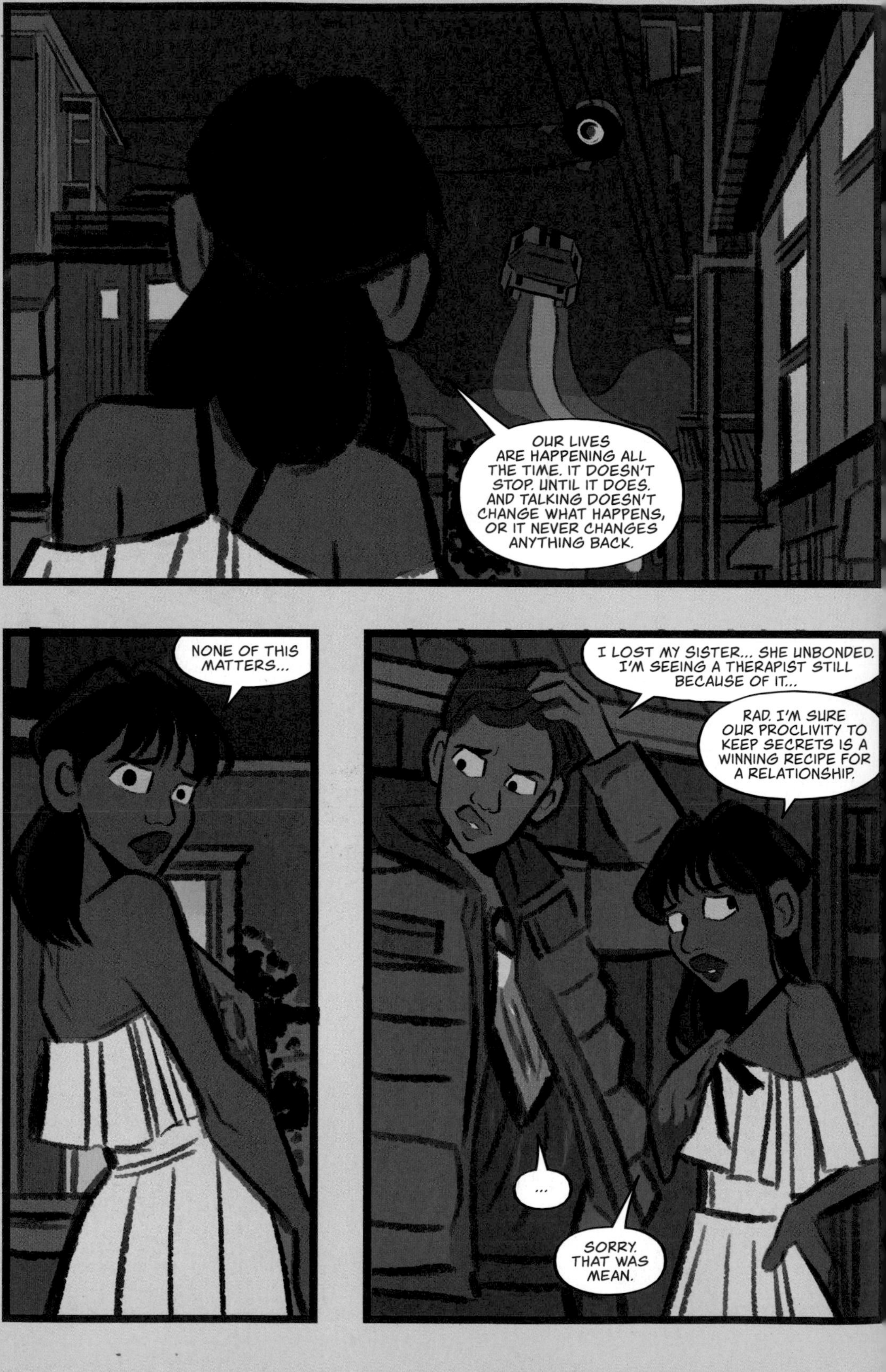
OUR LIVES ARE HAPPENING ALL THE TIME. IT DOESN'T STOP. UNTIL IT DOES. AND TALKING DOESN'T CHANGE WHAT HAPPENS, OR IT NEVER CHANGES ANYTHING BACK.
NONE OF THIS MATTERS...
I LOST MY SISTER... SHE UNBONDED. I'M SEEING A THERAPIST STILL BECAUSE OF IT...
RAD. I'M SURE OUR PROCLIVITY TO KEEP SECRETS IS A WINNING RECIPE FOR A RELATIONSHIP.
...
SORRY. THAT WAS MEAN.

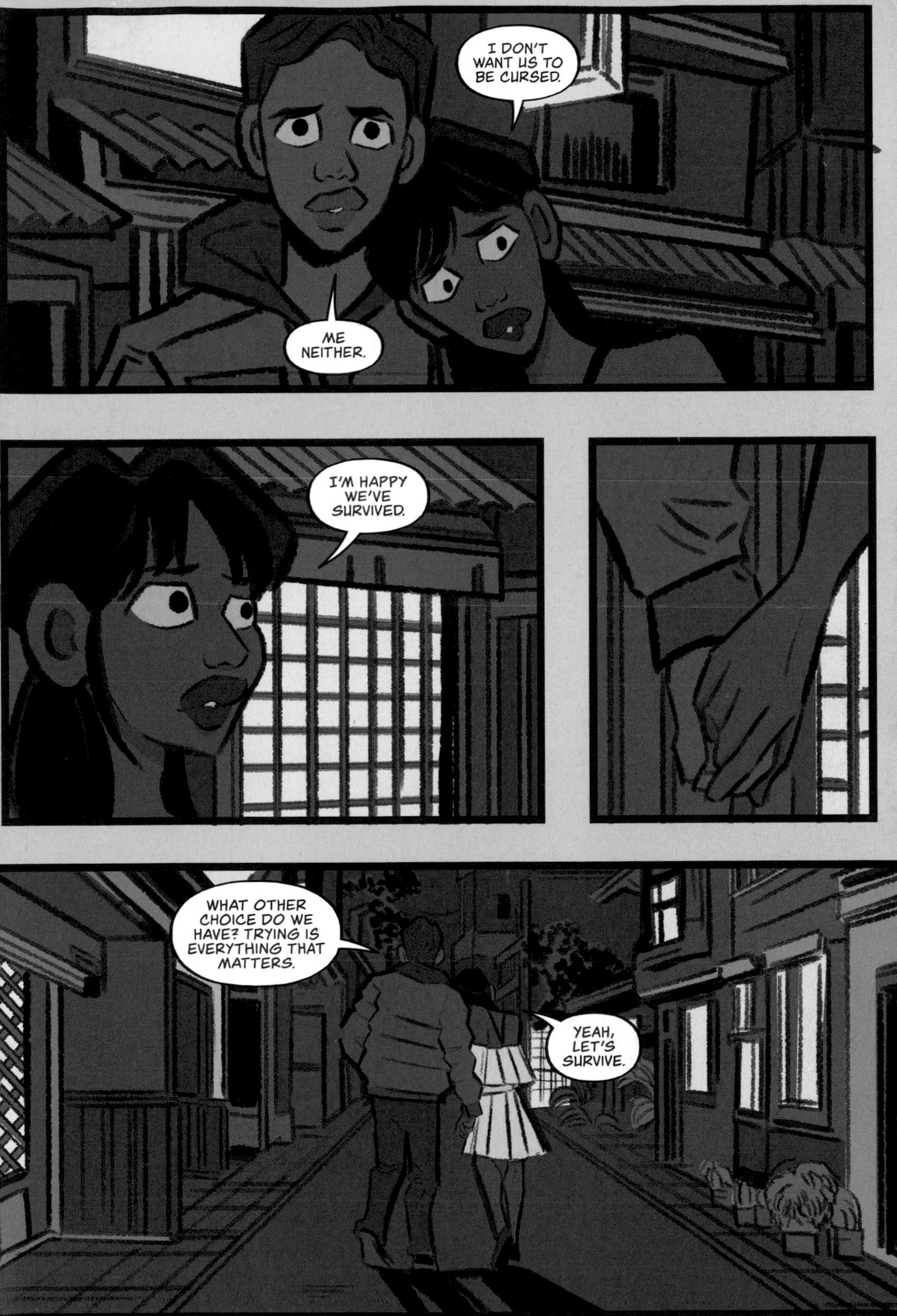
I DON'T WANT US TO BE CURSED.
ME NEITHER.
I'M HAPPY WE'VE SURVIVED.
WHAT OTHER CHOICE DO WE HAVE? TRYING IS EVERYTHING THAT MATTERS.
YEAH, LET'S SURVIVE.

part three

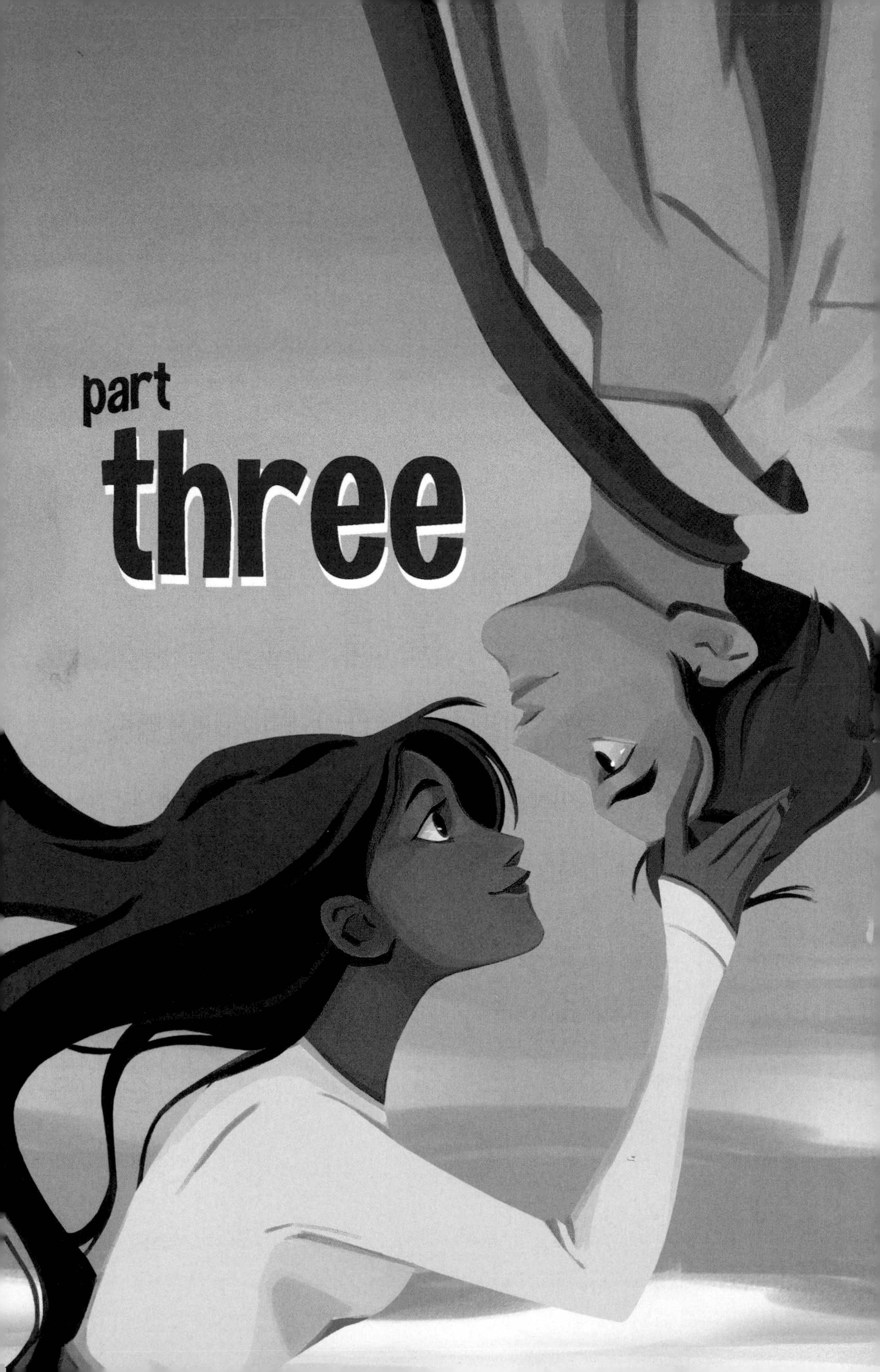

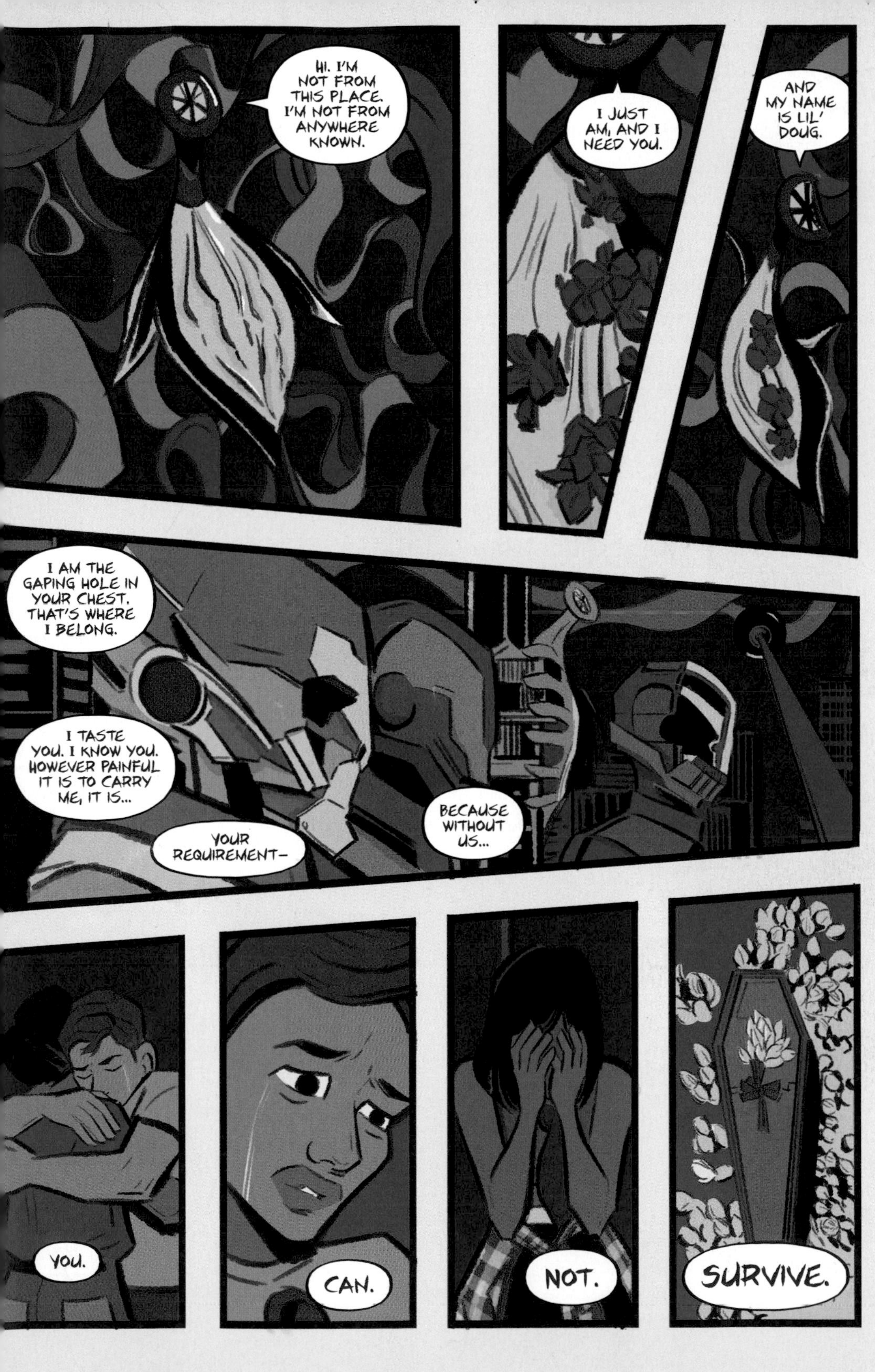
HI. I'M NOT FROM THIS PLACE. I'M NOT FROM ANYWHERE KNOWN.
I JUST AM, AND I NEED YOU.
AND MY NAME IS LIL' DOUG.
I AM THE GAPING HOLE IN YOUR CHEST. THAT'S WHERE I BELONG.
I TASTE YOU. I KNOW YOU. HOWEVER PAINFUL IT IS TO CARRY ME, IT IS...
YOUR REQUIREMENT–
BECAUSE WITHOUT US...
YOU.
CAN.
NOT.
SURVIVE.

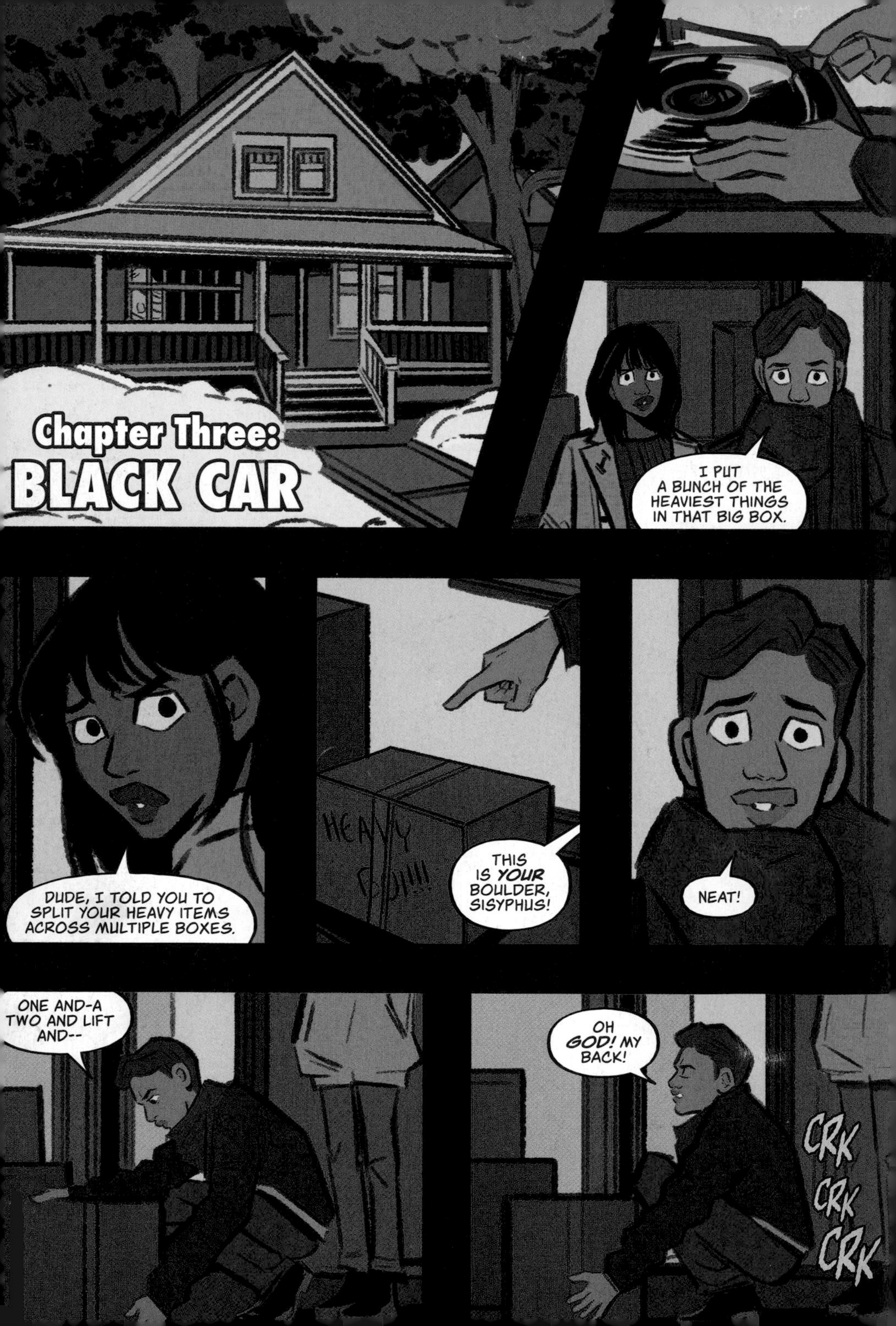
Chapter Three:
BLACK CAR
I PUT A BUNCH OF THE HEAVIEST THINGS IN THAT BIG BOX.
DUDE, I TOLD YOU TO SPLIT YOUR HEAVY ITEMS ACROSS MULTIPLE BOXES.
THIS IS YOUR BOULDER, SISYPHUS!
NEAT!
ONE AND-A TWO AND LIFT AND--
OH GOD! MY BACK!
CRK CRK CRK

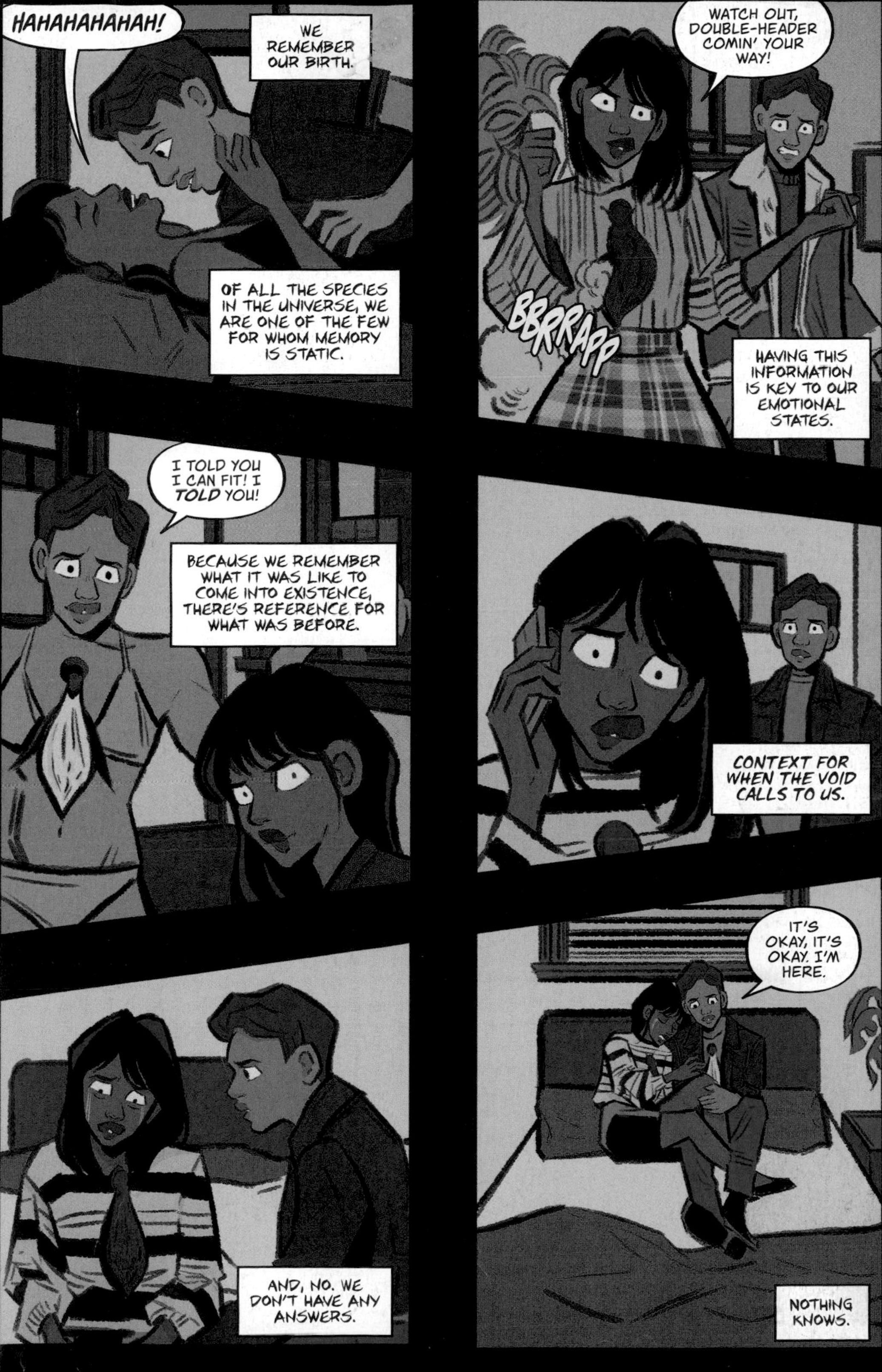
HAHAHAHAHAH!
WE REMEMBER OUR BIRTH.
OF ALL THE SPECIES IN THE UNIVERSE, WE ARE ONE OF THE FEW FOR WHOM MEMORY IS STATIC.
WATCH OUT, DOUBLE-HEADER COMIN' YOUR WAY!
BBRRAPP
HAVING THIS INFORMATION IS KEY TO OUR EMOTIONAL STATES.
I TOLD YOU I CAN FIT! I TOLD YOU!
BECAUSE WE REMEMBER WHAT IT WAS LIKE TO COME INTO EXISTENCE, THERE'S REFERENCE FOR WHAT WAS BEFORE.
CONTEXT FOR WHEN THE VOID CALLS TO US.
AND, NO. WE DON'T HAVE ANY ANSWERS.
IT'S OKAY, IT'S OKAY. I'M HERE.
NOTHING KNOWS.

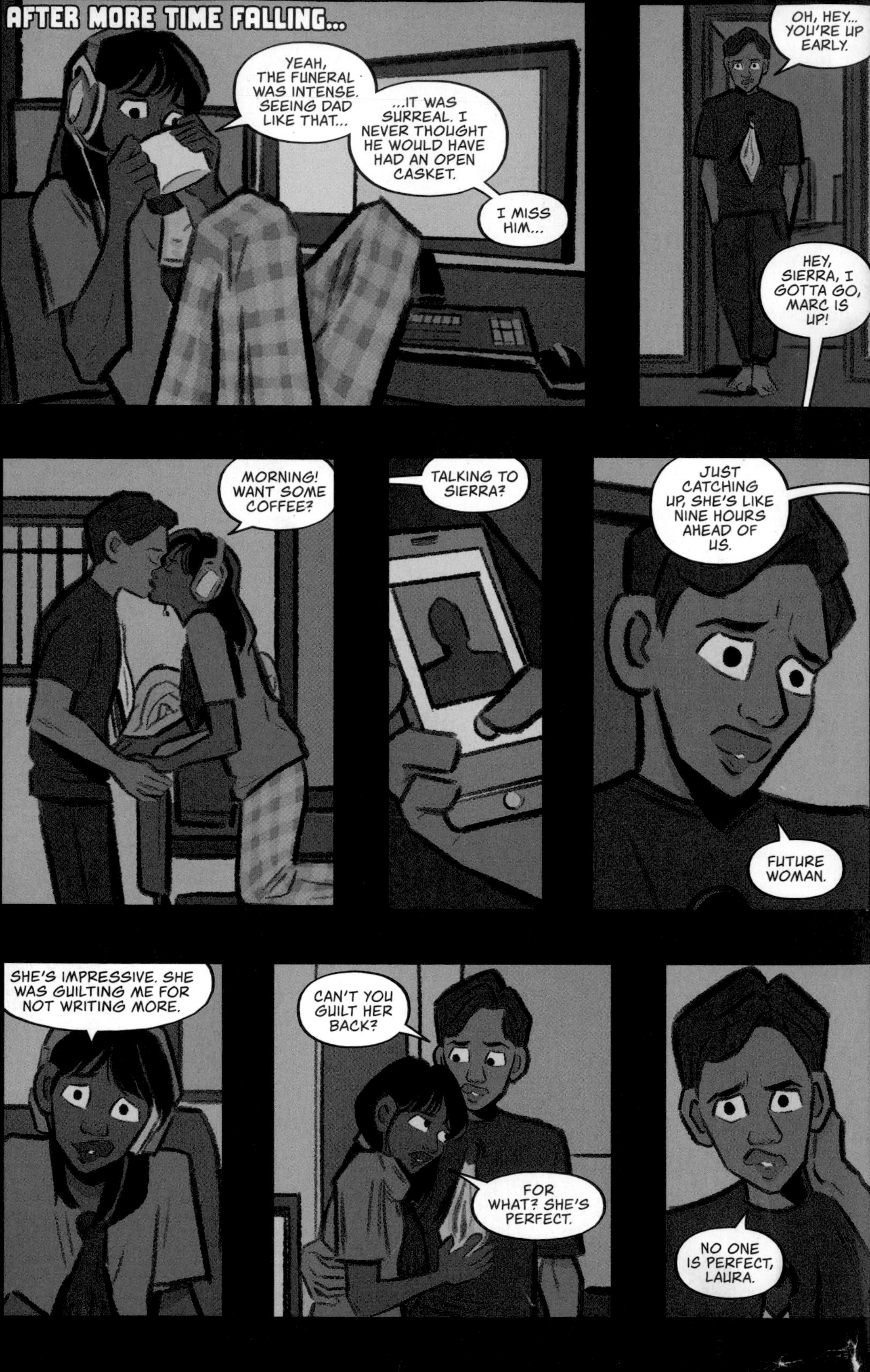
AFTER MORE TIME FALLING...
YEAH, THE FUNERAL WAS INTENSE. SEEING DAD LIKE THAT...
...IT WAS SURREAL. I NEVER THOUGHT HE WOULD HAVE HAD AN OPEN CASKET.
I MISS HIM...
OH, HEY... YOU'RE UP EARLY.
HEY, SIERRA, I GOTTA GO, MARC IS UP!
MORNING! WANT SOME COFFEE?
TALKING TO SIERRA?
JUST CATCHING UP, SHE'S LIKE NINE HOURS AHEAD OF US.
FUTURE WOMAN.
SHE'S IMPRESSIVE. SHE WAS GUILTING ME FOR NOT WRITING MORE.
CAN'T YOU GUILT HER BACK?
FOR WHAT? SHE'S PERFECT.
NO ONE IS PERFECT, LAURA.

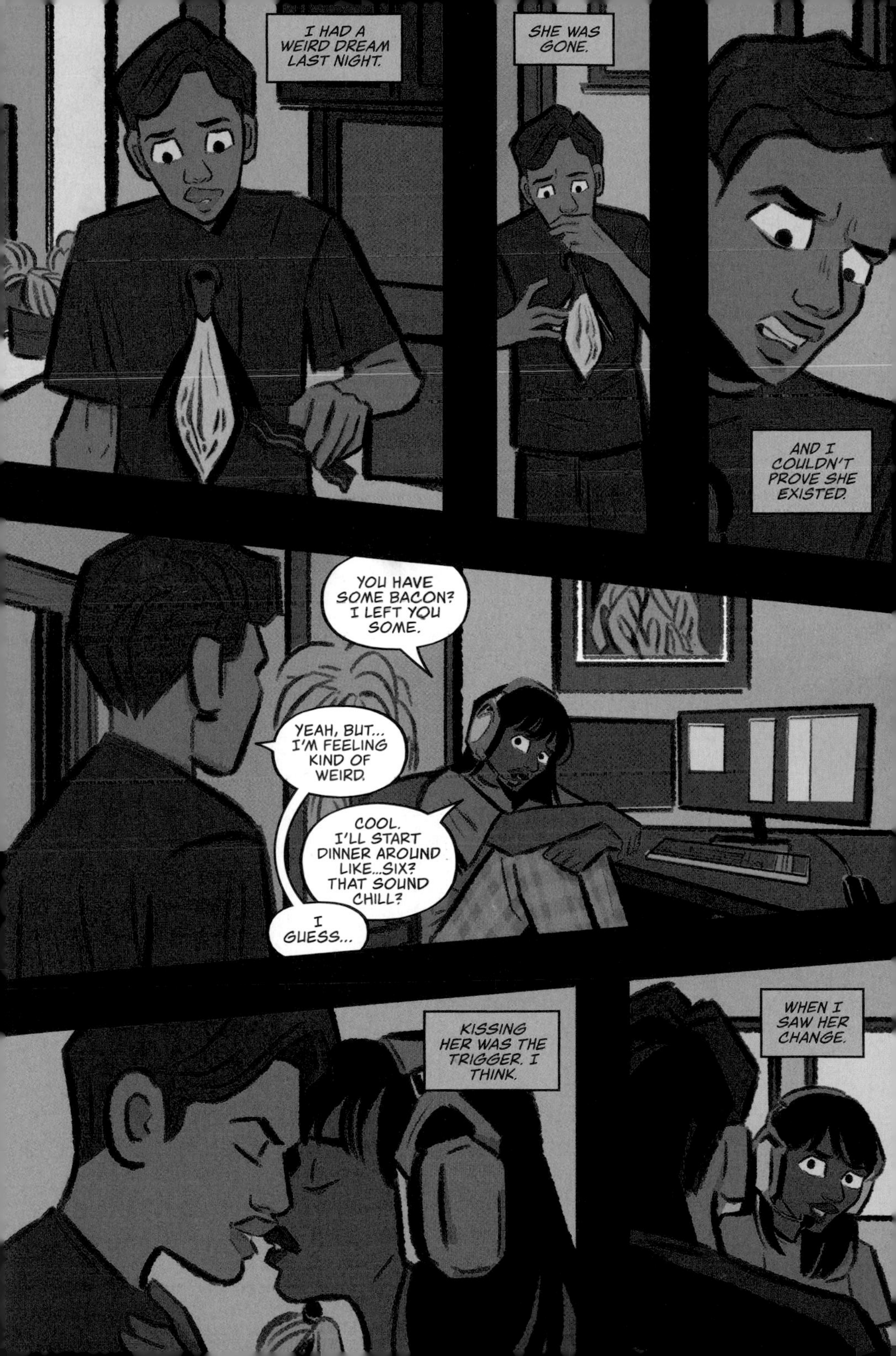
I HAD A WEIRD DREAM LAST NIGHT.
SHE WAS GONE.
AND I COULDN'T PROVE SHE EXISTED.
YOU HAVE SOME BACON? I LEFT YOU SOME.
YEAH, BUT... I'M FEELING KIND OF WEIRD.
COOL. I'LL START DINNER AROUND LIKE...SIX? THAT SOUND CHILL?
I GUESS...
KISSING HER WAS THE TRIGGER. I THINK.
WHEN I SAW HER CHANGE.

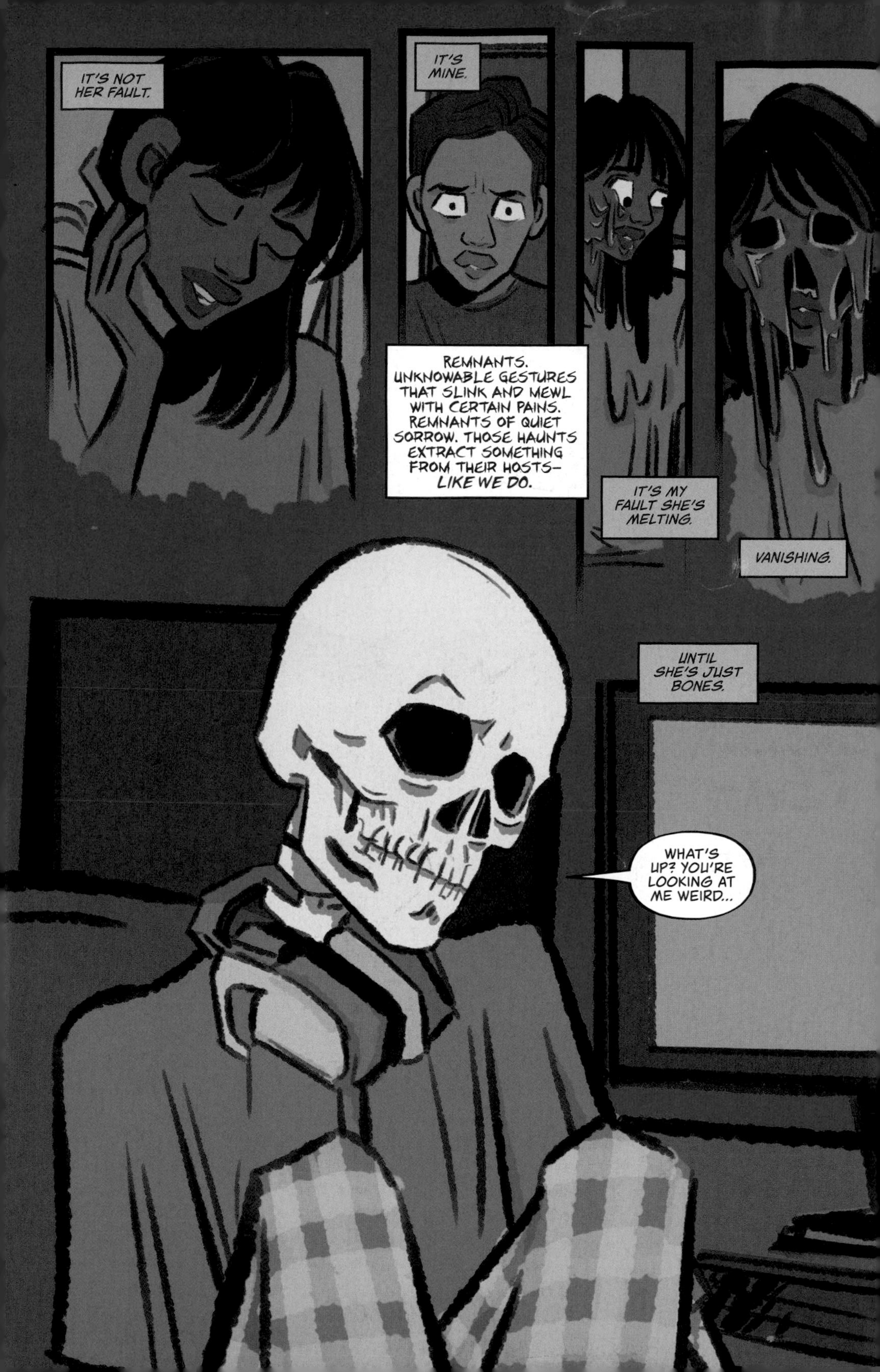
IT'S NOT HER FAULT.
IT'S MINE.
REMNANTS. UNKNOWABLE GESTURES THAT SLINK AND MEWL WITH CERTAIN PAINS. REMNANTS OF QUIET SORROW. THOSE HAUNTS EXTRACT SOMETHING FROM THEIR HOSTS— LIKE WE DO.
IT'S MY FAULT SHE'S MELTING.
VANISHING.
UNTIL SHE'S JUST BONES.
WHAT'S UP? YOU'RE LOOKING AT ME WEIRD...

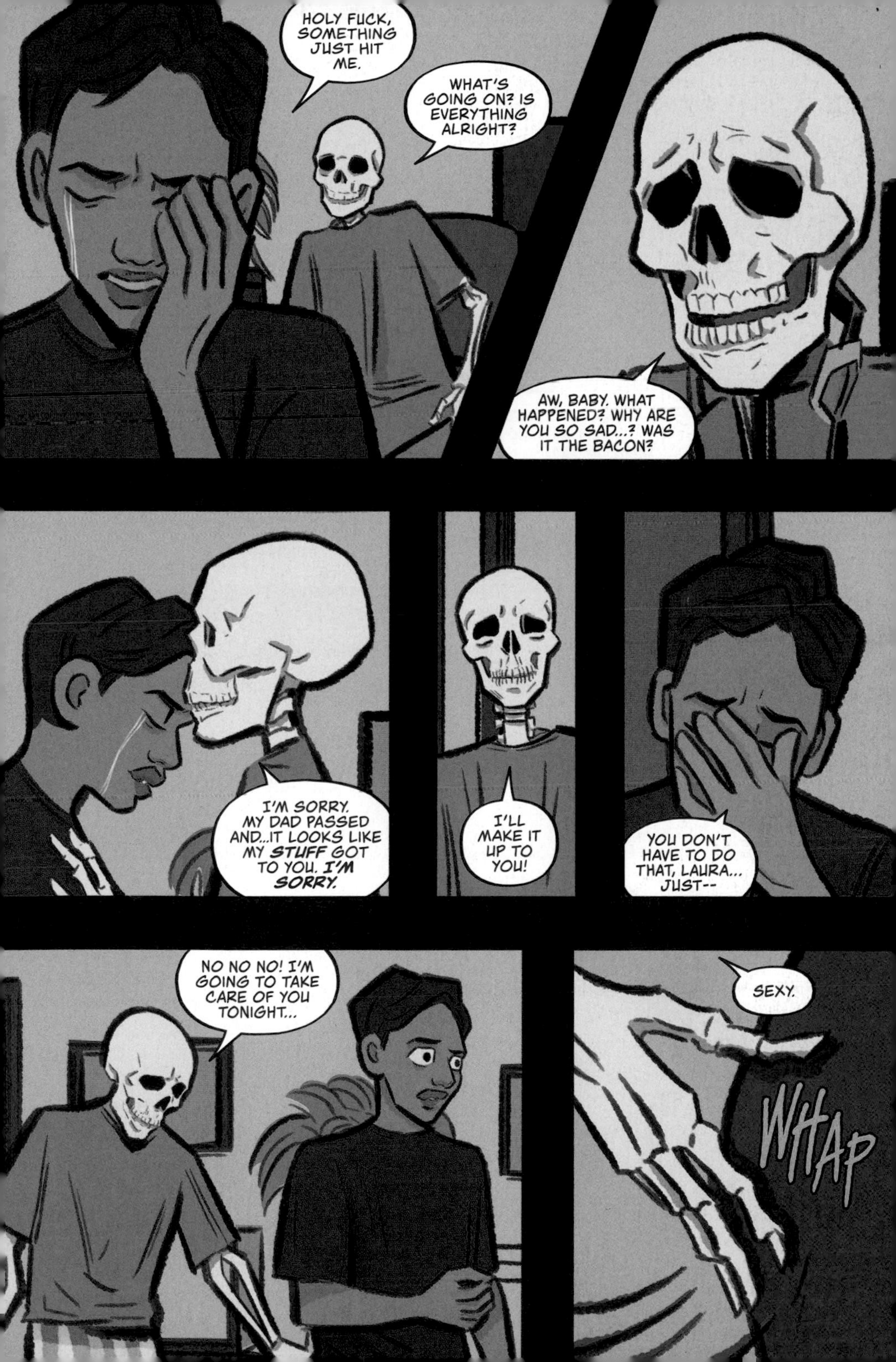
HOLY FUCK, SOMETHING JUST HIT ME.
WHAT'S GOING ON? IS EVERYTHING ALRIGHT?
AW, BABY. WHAT HAPPENED? WHY ARE YOU SO SAD...? WAS IT THE BACON?
I'M SORRY. MY DAD PASSED AND...IT LOOKS LIKE MY STUFF GOT TO YOU. I'M SORRY.
I'LL MAKE IT UP TO YOU!
YOU DON'T HAVE TO DO THAT, LAURA... JUST--
NO NO NO! I'M GOING TO TAKE CARE OF YOU TONIGHT...
SEXY.
WHAP

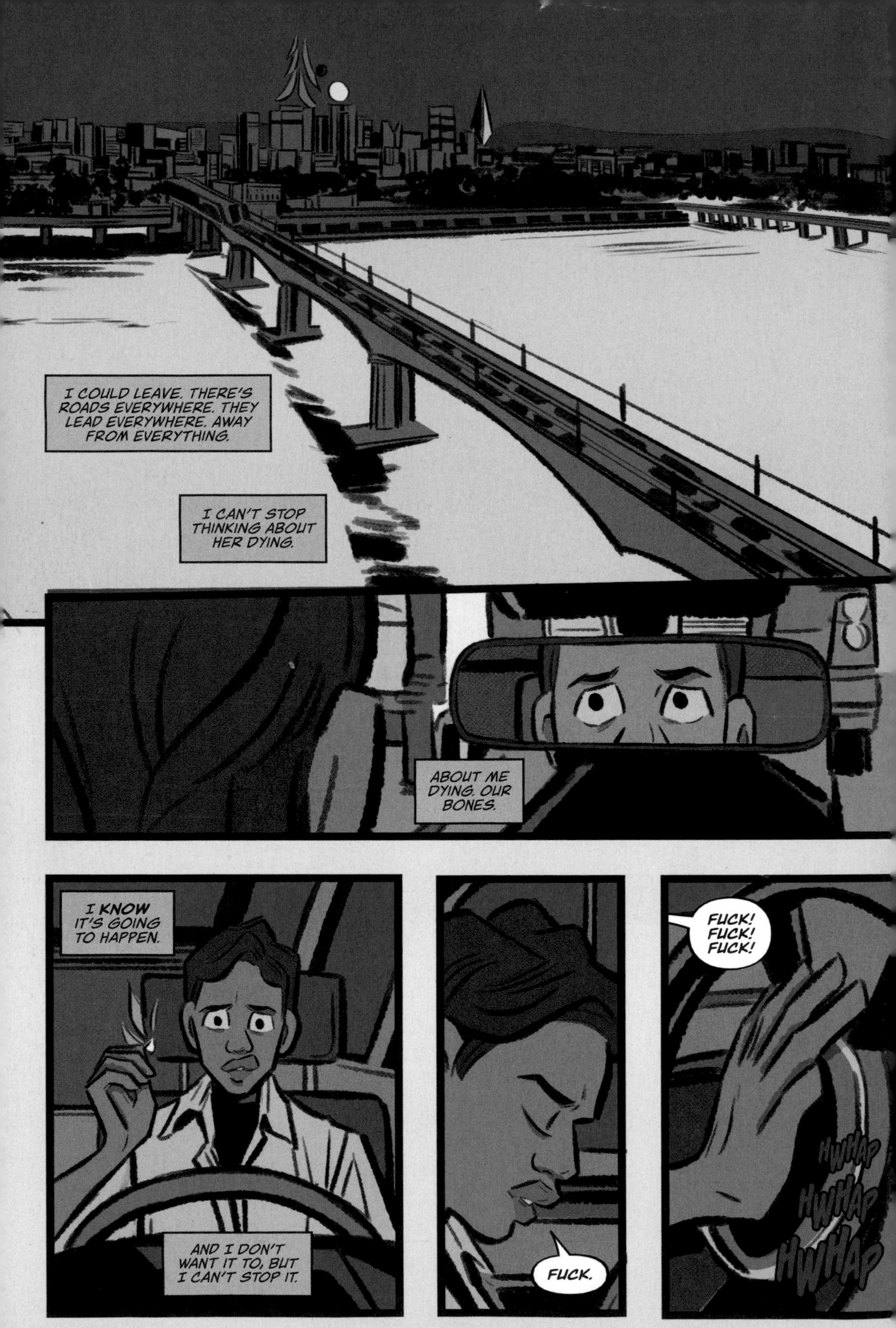

I COULD LEAVE. THERE'S ROADS EVERYWHERE. THEY LEAD EVERYWHERE. AWAY FROM EVERYTHING.
I CAN'T STOP THINKING ABOUT HER DYING.
ABOUT ME DYING. OUR BONES.
I KNOW IT'S GOING TO HAPPEN.
AND I DON'T WANT IT TO, BUT I CAN'T STOP IT.
FUCK.
FUCK! FUCK! FUCK!
HWHAP
HWHAP
HWHAP

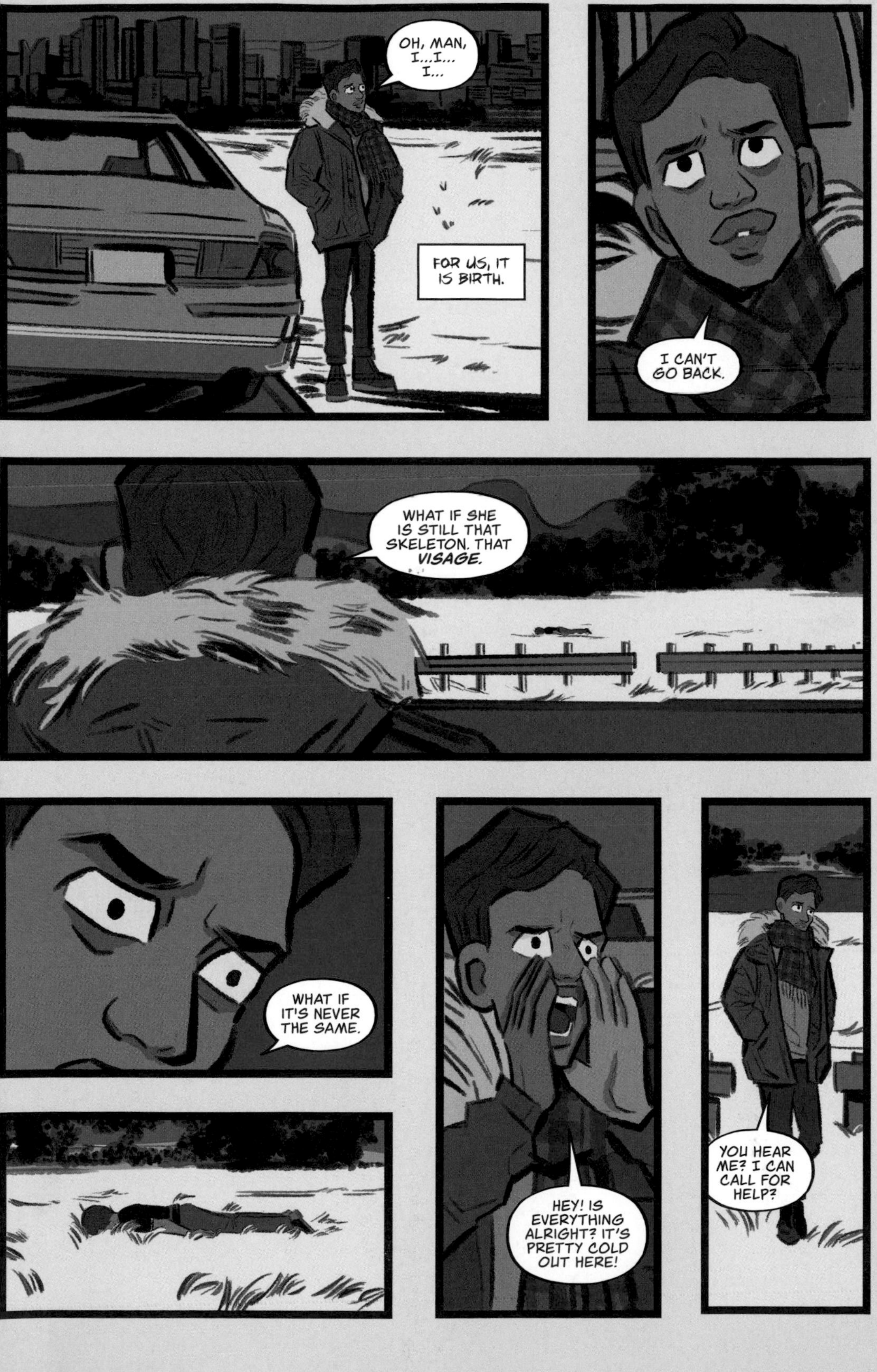
OH, MAN, I...I... I...
FOR US, IT IS BIRTH.
I CAN'T GO BACK.
WHAT IF SHE IS STILL THAT SKELETON. THAT VISAGE.
WHAT IF IT'S NEVER THE SAME.
HEY! IS EVERYTHING ALRIGHT? IT'S PRETTY COLD OUT HERE!
YOU HEAR ME? I CAN CALL FOR HELP?

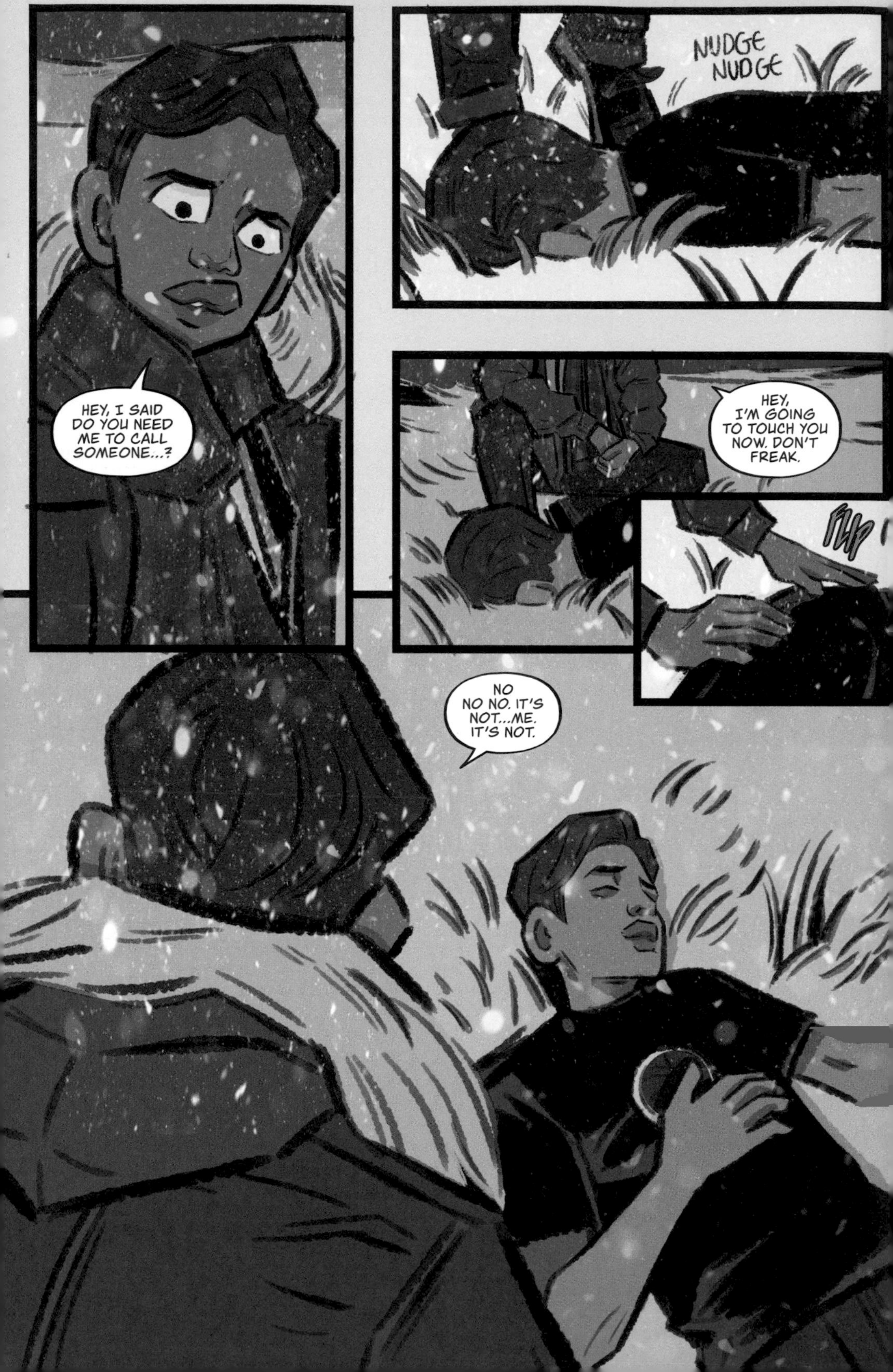
HEY, I SAID DO YOU NEED ME TO CALL SOMEONE...?
NUDGE NUDGE
HEY, I'M GOING TO TOUCH YOU NOW. DON'T FREAK.
FLIP
NO NO NO. IT'S NOT...ME. IT'S NOT.

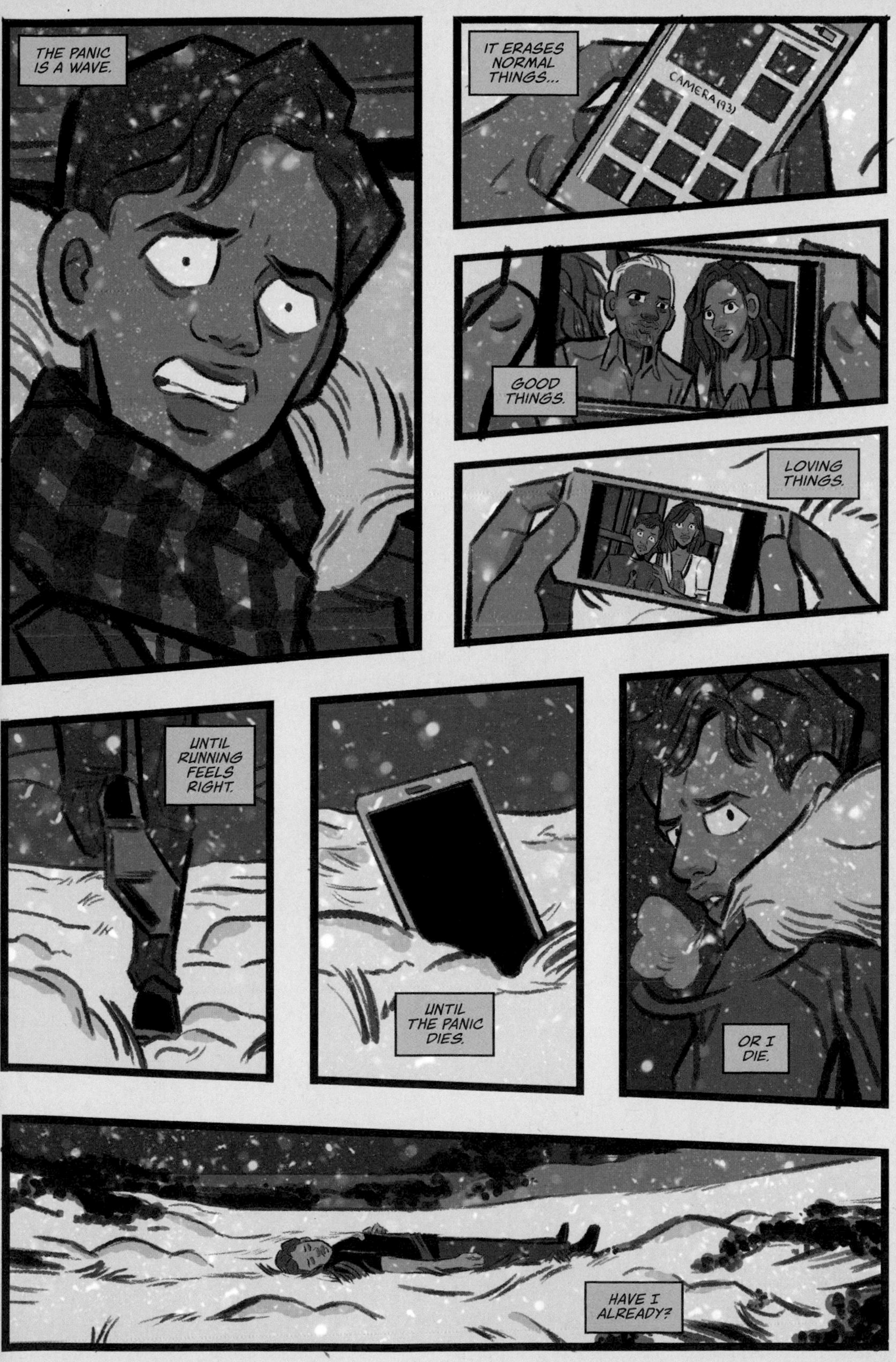
THE PANIC IS A WAVE.
IT ERASES NORMAL THINGS...
CAMERA (93)
GOOD THINGS.
LOVING THINGS.
UNTIL RUNNING FEELS RIGHT.
UNTIL THE PANIC DIES.
OR I DIE.
HAVE I ALREADY?

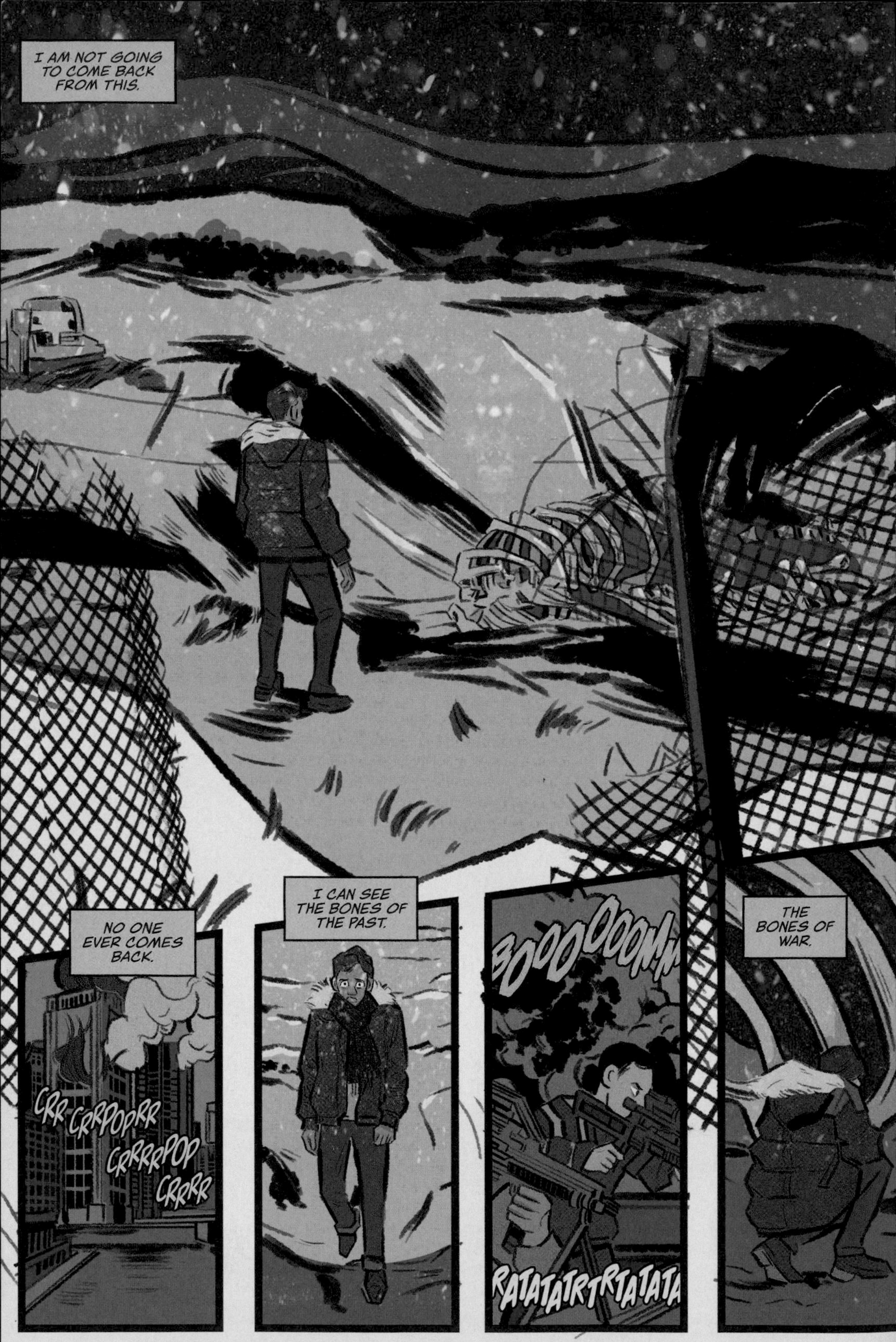
I AM NOT GOING TO COME BACK FROM THIS.
NO ONE EVER COMES BACK.
CRR CRRPOPRR CRRRRPOP CRRRR
I CAN SEE THE BONES OF THE PAST.
BOOOOOOOMM
RATATATRTRTATATA
THE BONES OF WAR.

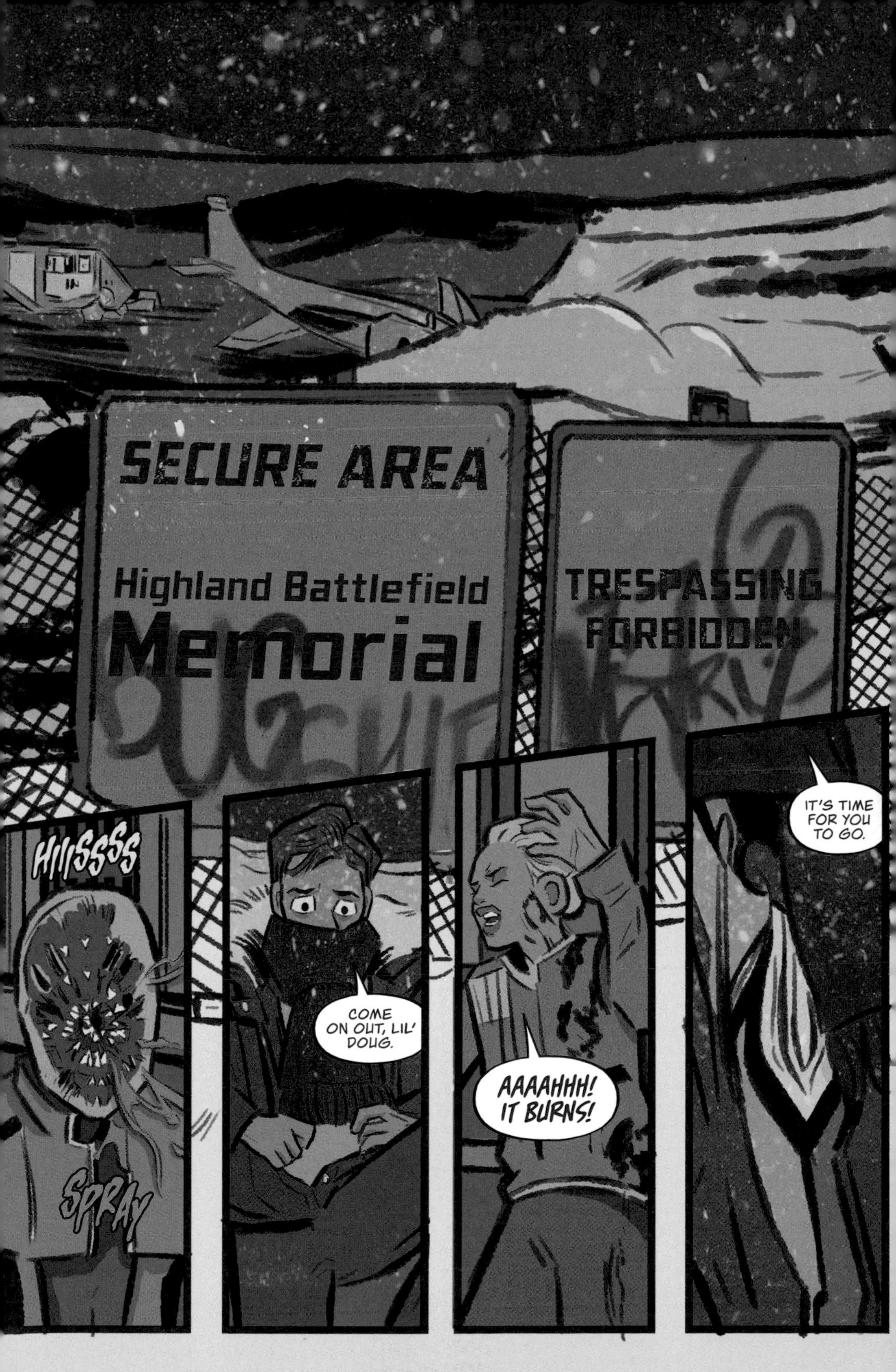
SECURE AREA
Highland Battlefield Memorial
TRESPASSING FORBIDDEN
HIIISSSS
SPRAY
COME ON OUT, LIL' DOUG.
AAAAHHH! IT BURNS!
IT'S TIME FOR YOU TO GO.

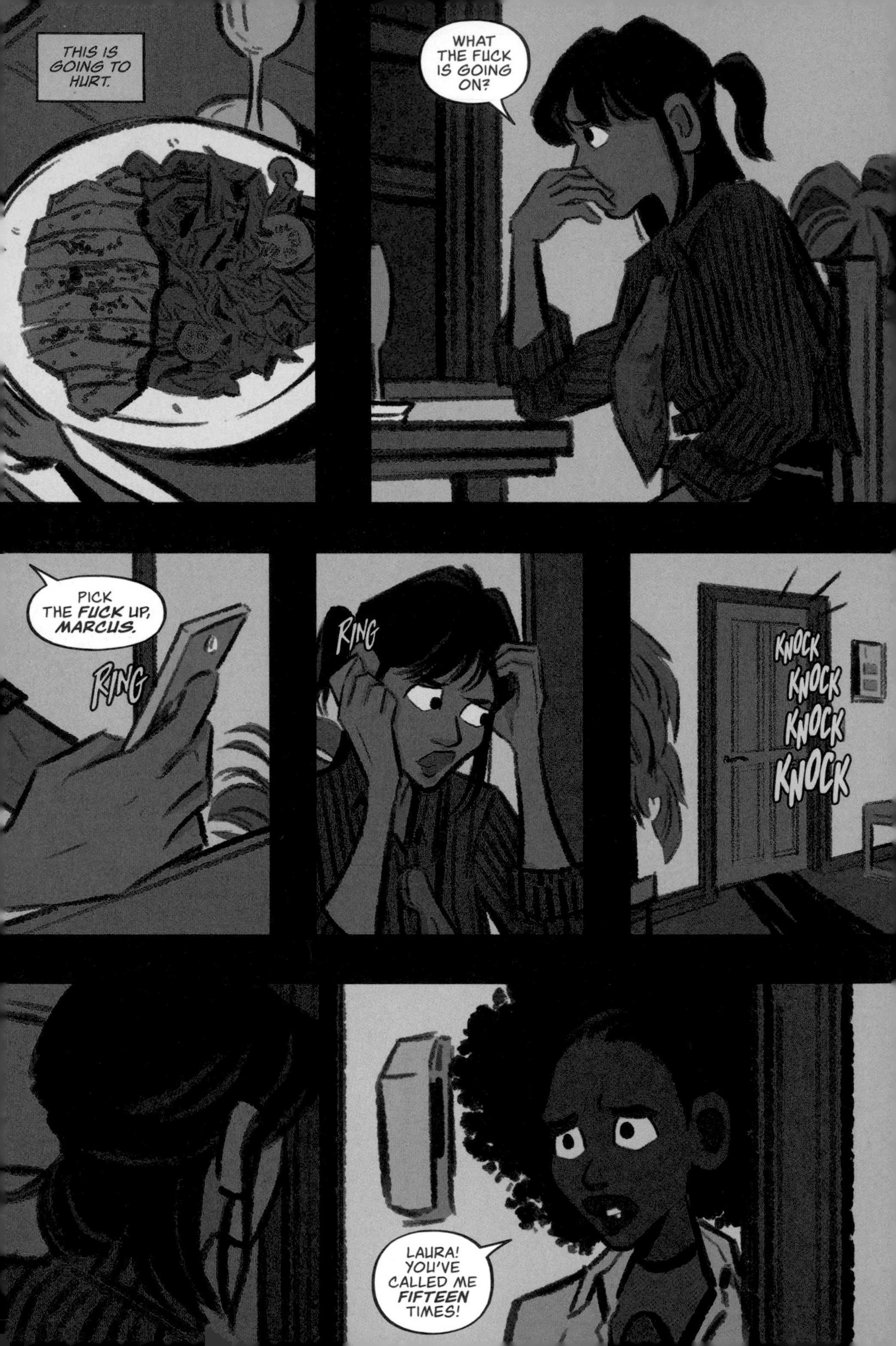
THIS IS GOING TO HURT.
WHAT THE FUCK IS GOING ON?
PICK THE FUCK UP, MARCUS.
RING
RING
KNOCK
KNOCK
KNOCK
KNOCK
LAURA! YOU'VE CALLED ME FIFTEEN TIMES!

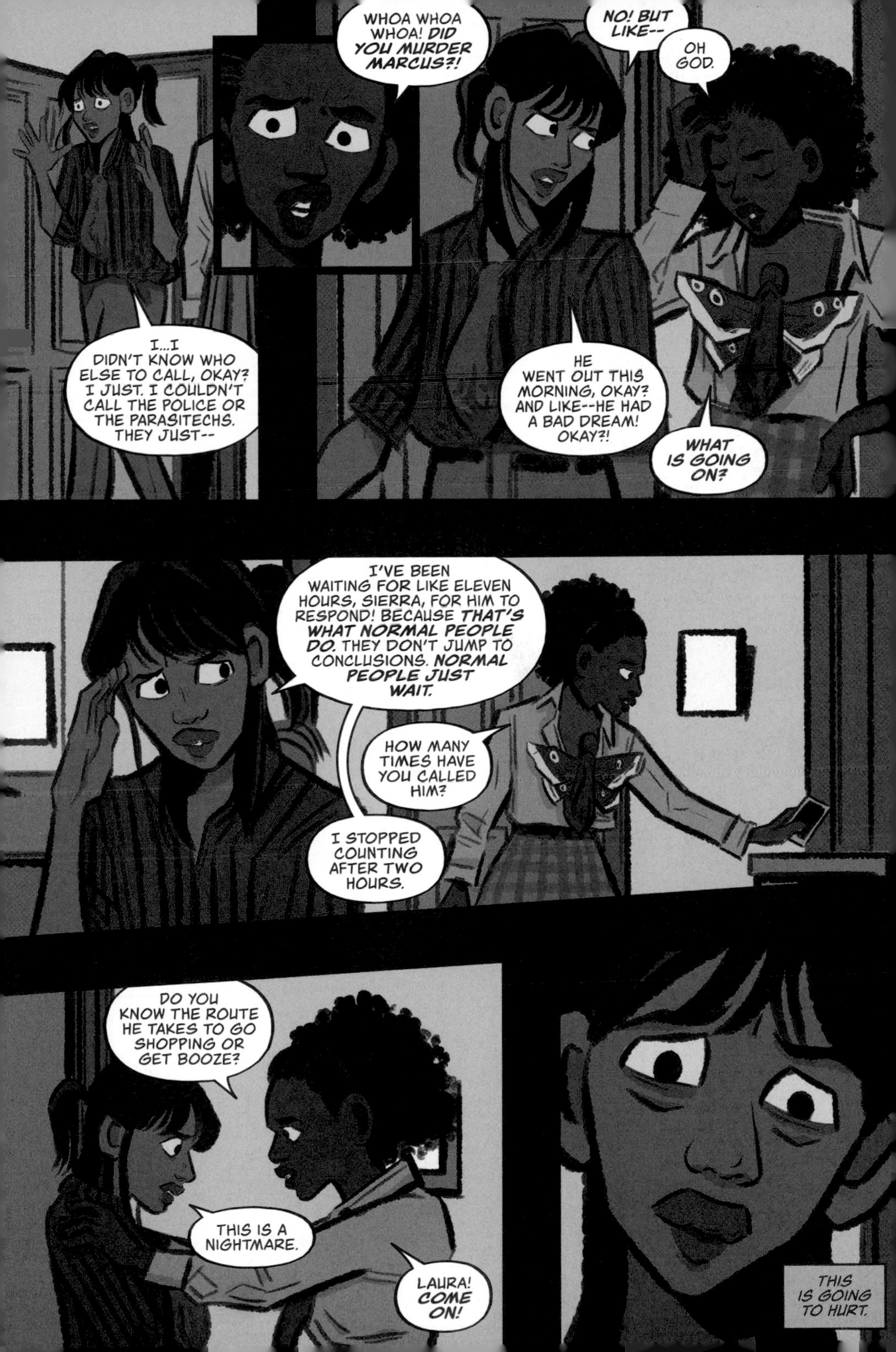
WHOA WHOA WHOA! DID YOU MURDER MARCUS?!
NO! BUT LIKE--
OH GOD.
I...I DIDN'T KNOW WHO ELSE TO CALL, OKAY? I JUST. I COULDN'T CALL THE POLICE OR THE PARASITECHS. THEY JUST--
HE WENT OUT THIS MORNING, OKAY? AND LIKE--HE HAD A BAD DREAM! OKAY?!
WHAT IS GOING ON?
I'VE BEEN WAITING FOR LIKE ELEVEN HOURS, SIERRA, FOR HIM TO RESPOND! BECAUSE THAT'S WHAT NORMAL PEOPLE DO. THEY DON'T JUMP TO CONCLUSIONS. NORMAL PEOPLE JUST WAIT.
HOW MANY TIMES HAVE YOU CALLED HIM?
I STOPPED COUNTING AFTER TWO HOURS.
DO YOU KNOW THE ROUTE HE TAKES TO GO SHOPPING OR GET BOOZE?
THIS IS A NIGHTMARE.
LAURA! COME ON!
THIS IS GOING TO HURT.

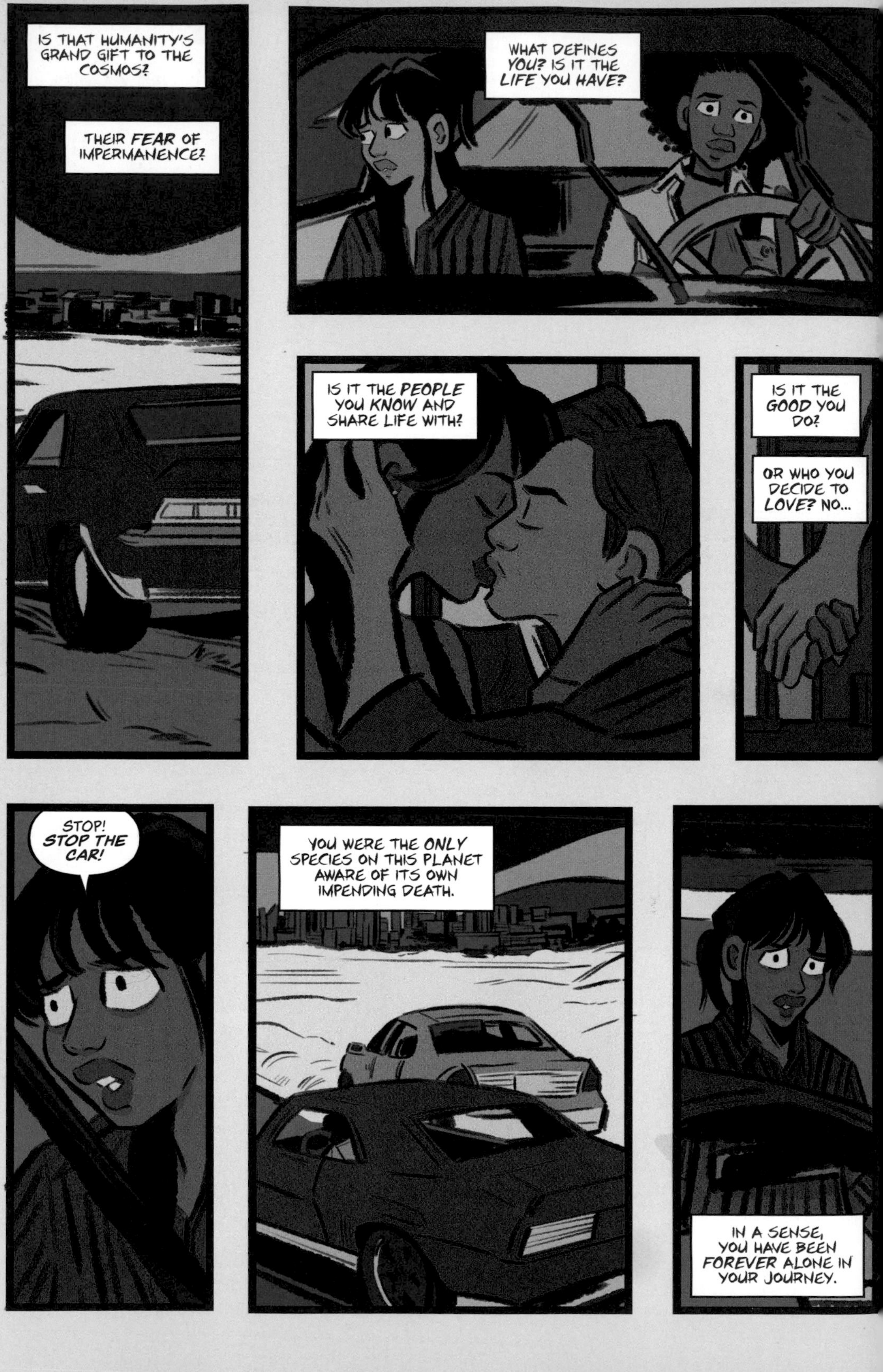
IS THAT HUMANITY'S GRAND GIFT TO THE COSMOS?
THEIR FEAR OF IMPERMANENCE?
WHAT DEFINES YOU? IS IT THE LIFE YOU HAVE?
IS IT THE PEOPLE YOU KNOW AND SHARE LIFE WITH?
IS IT THE GOOD YOU DO?
OR WHO YOU DECIDE TO LOVE? NO...
STOP! STOP THE CAR!
YOU WERE THE ONLY SPECIES ON THIS PLANET AWARE OF ITS OWN IMPENDING DEATH.
IN A SENSE, YOU HAVE BEEN FOREVER ALONE IN YOUR JOURNEY.

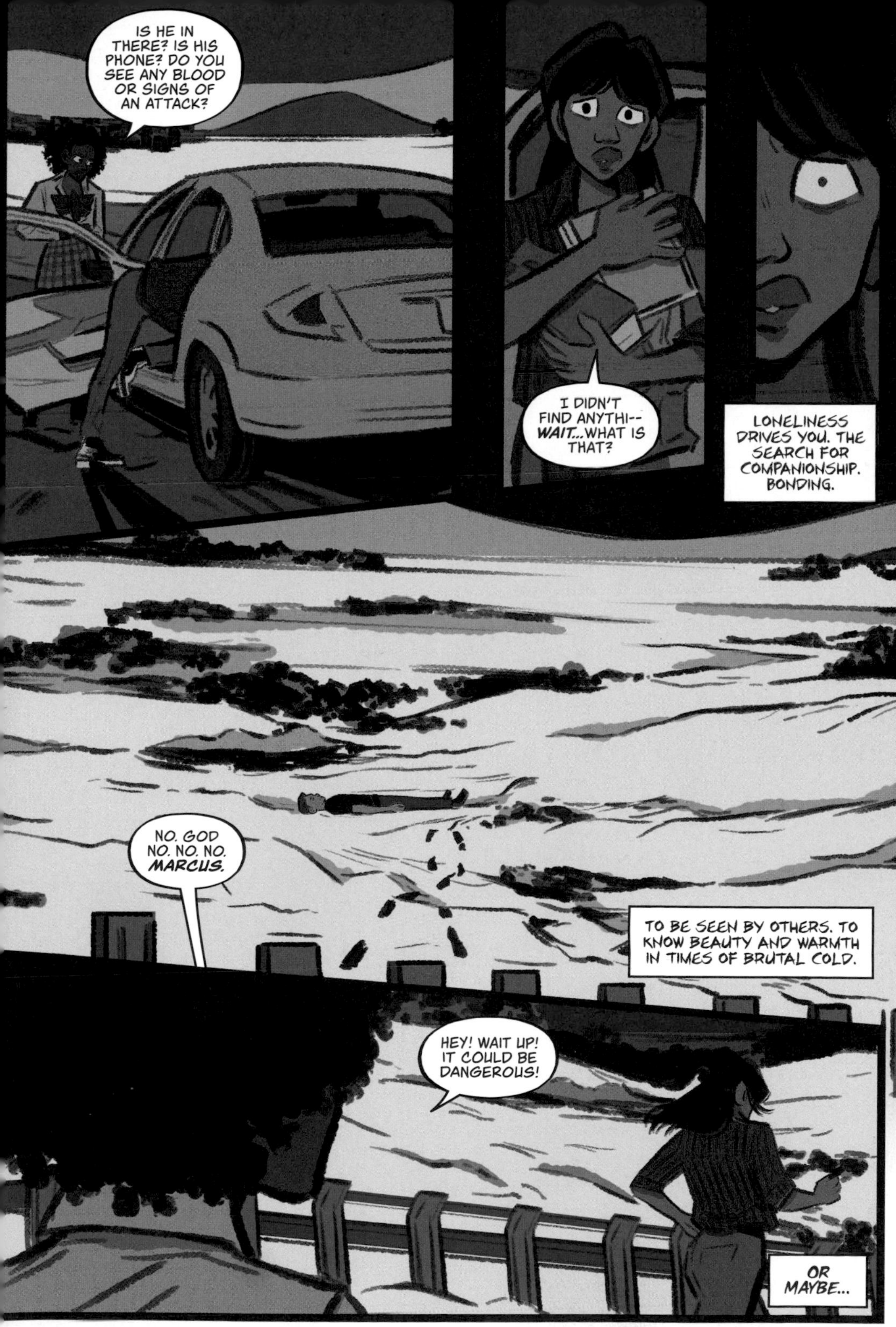
IS HE IN THERE? IS HIS PHONE? DO YOU SEE ANY BLOOD OR SIGNS OF AN ATTACK?
I DIDN'T FIND ANYTHI-- WAIT...WHAT IS THAT?
LONELINESS DRIVES YOU. THE SEARCH FOR COMPANIONSHIP. BONDING.
NO. GOD NO. NO. NO. MARCUS.
TO BE SEEN BY OTHERS. TO KNOW BEAUTY AND WARMTH IN TIMES OF BRUTAL COLD.
HEY! WAIT UP! IT COULD BE DANGEROUS!
OR MAYBE...

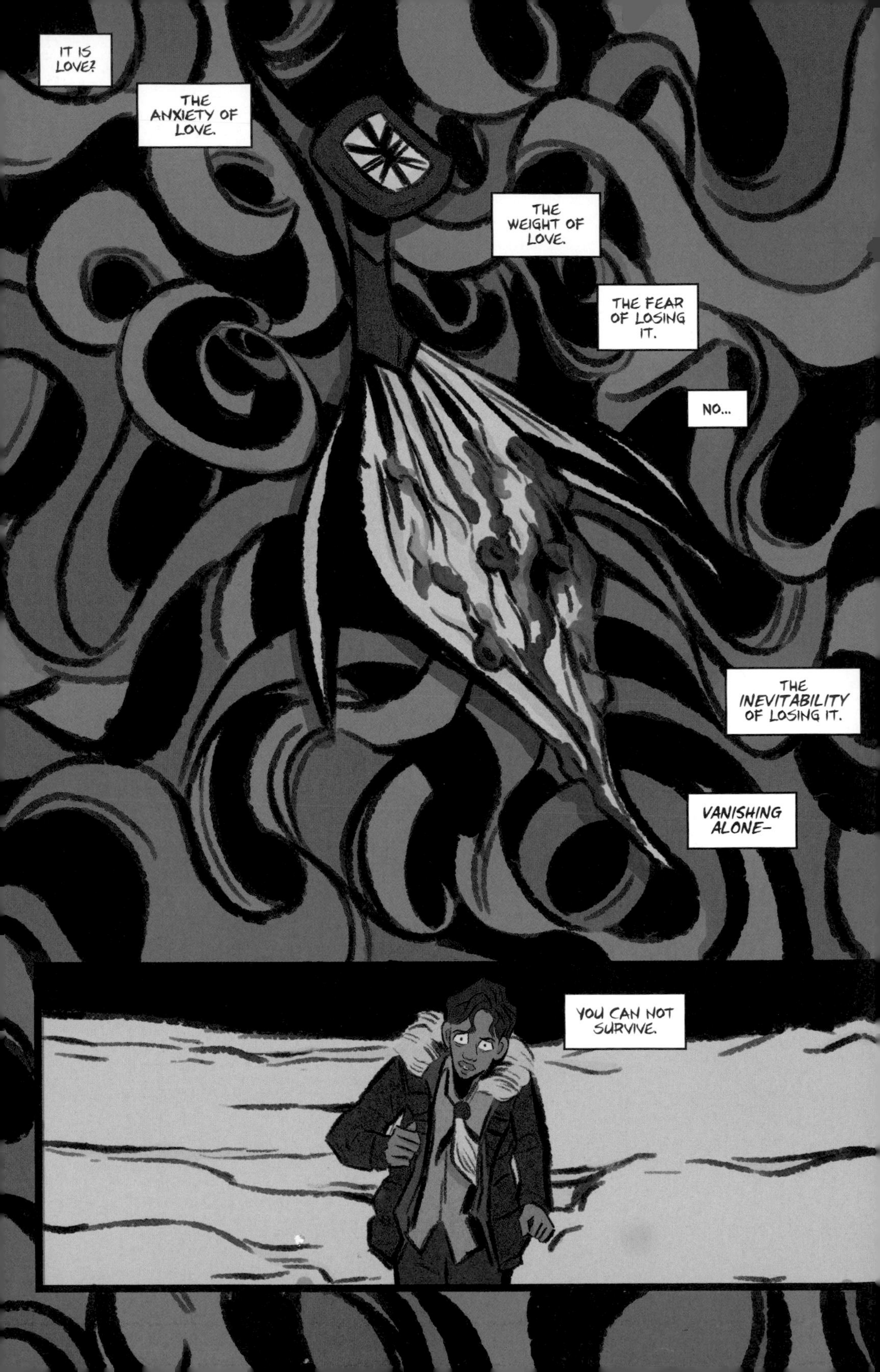
IT IS LOVE?
THE ANXIETY OF LOVE.
THE WEIGHT OF LOVE.
THE FEAR OF LOSING IT.
NO...
THE *INEVITABILITY* OF LOSING IT.
VANISHING ALONE-
YOU CAN NOT SURVIVE.

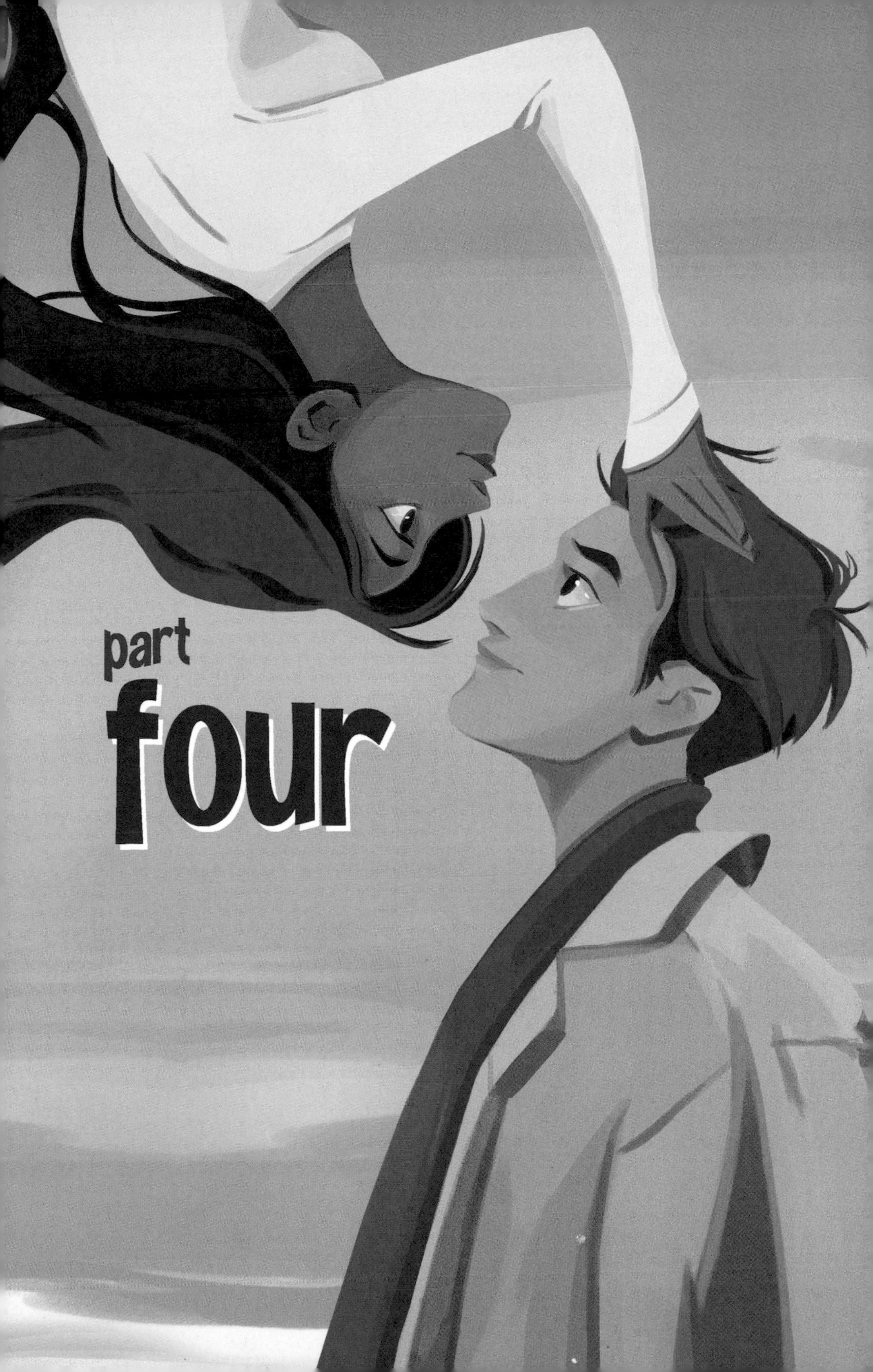
part
four

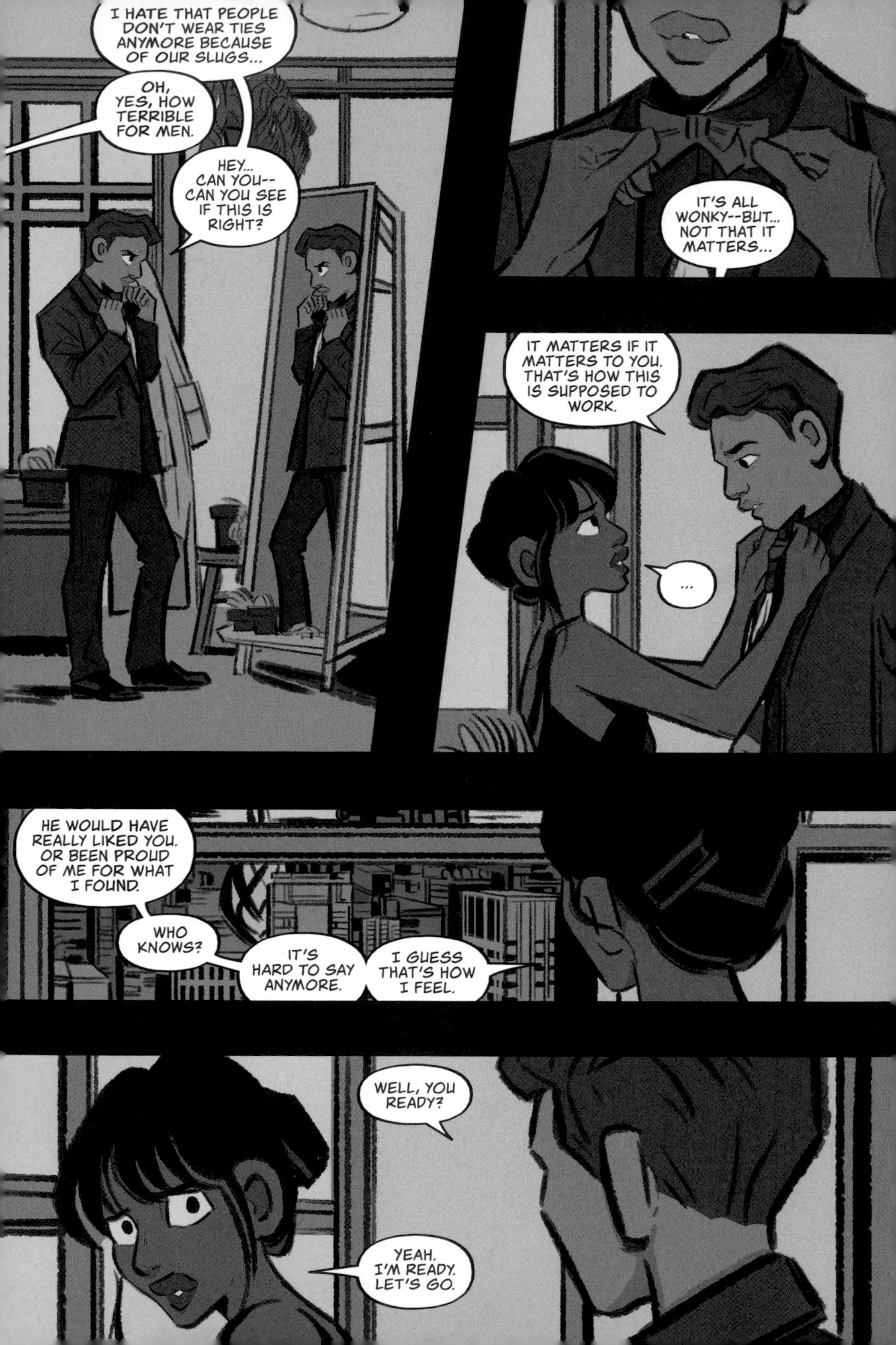
I HATE THAT PEOPLE DON'T WEAR TIES ANYMORE BECAUSE OF OUR SLUGS...
OH, YES, HOW TERRIBLE FOR MEN.
HEY... CAN YOU-- CAN YOU SEE IF THIS IS RIGHT?
IT'S ALL WONKY--BUT... NOT THAT IT MATTERS...
IT MATTERS IF IT MATTERS TO YOU. THAT'S HOW THIS IS SUPPOSED TO WORK.
...
HE WOULD HAVE REALLY LIKED YOU. OR BEEN PROUD OF ME FOR WHAT I FOUND.
WHO KNOWS?
IT'S HARD TO SAY ANYMORE.
I GUESS THAT'S HOW I FEEL.
WELL, YOU READY?
YEAH. I'M READY. LET'S GO.

WE SPENT THAT DAY TOGETHER.

WE DIDN'T SPEAK MUCH.

WE JUST WERE.

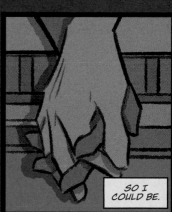

SO I COULD BE.

...

...

≈SIGH≈

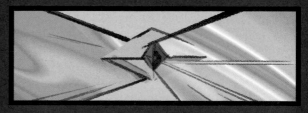

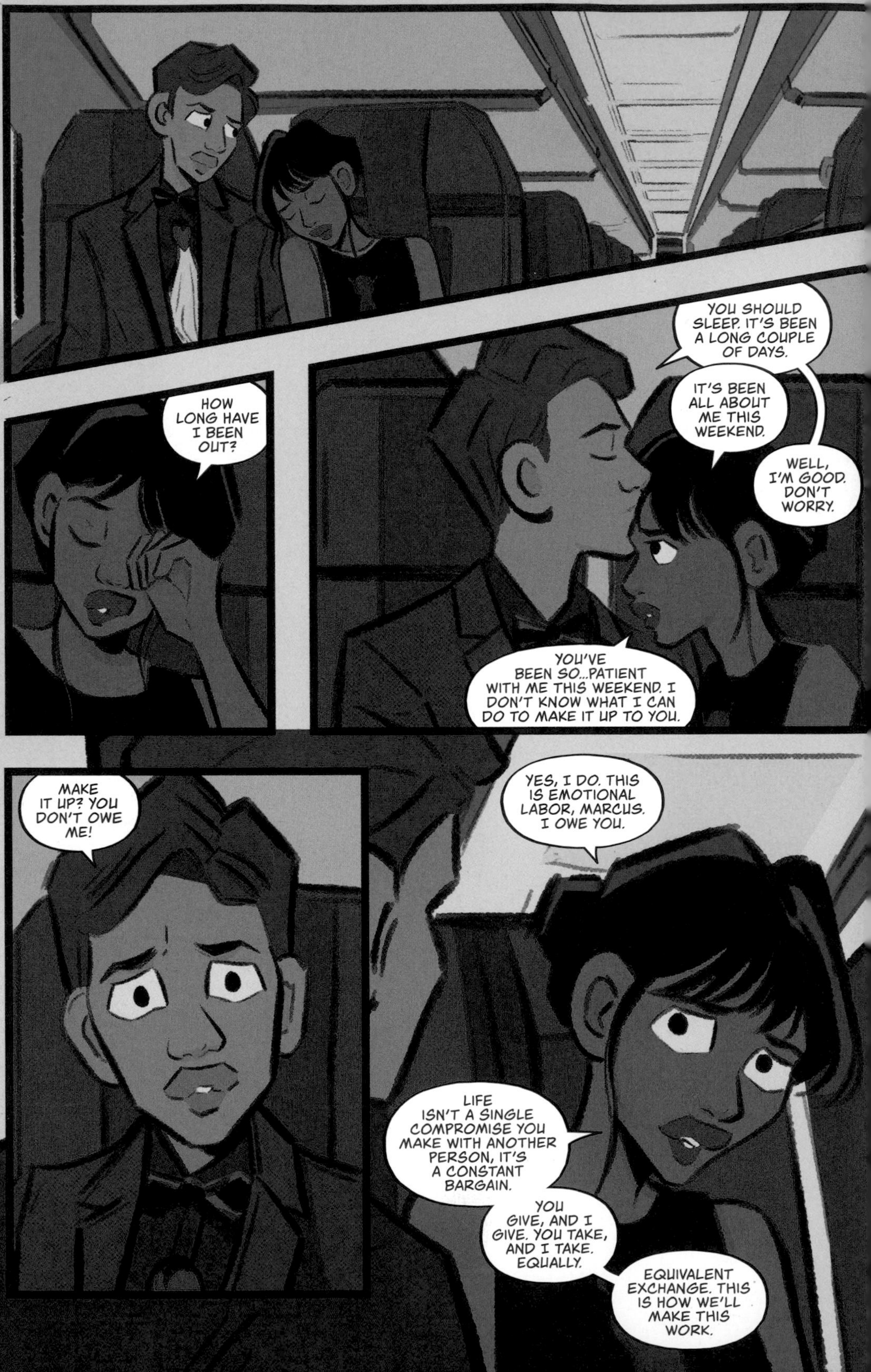
HOW LONG HAVE I BEEN OUT?
YOU SHOULD SLEEP. IT'S BEEN A LONG COUPLE OF DAYS.
IT'S BEEN ALL ABOUT ME THIS WEEKEND.
WELL, I'M GOOD. DON'T WORRY.
YOU'VE BEEN SO...PATIENT WITH ME THIS WEEKEND. I DON'T KNOW WHAT I CAN DO TO MAKE IT UP TO YOU.
MAKE IT UP? YOU DON'T OWE ME!
YES, I DO. THIS IS EMOTIONAL LABOR, MARCUS. I OWE YOU.
LIFE ISN'T A SINGLE COMPROMISE YOU MAKE WITH ANOTHER PERSON, IT'S A CONSTANT BARGAIN.
YOU GIVE, AND I GIVE. YOU TAKE, AND I TAKE. EQUALLY.
EQUIVALENT EXCHANGE. THIS IS HOW WE'LL MAKE THIS WORK.

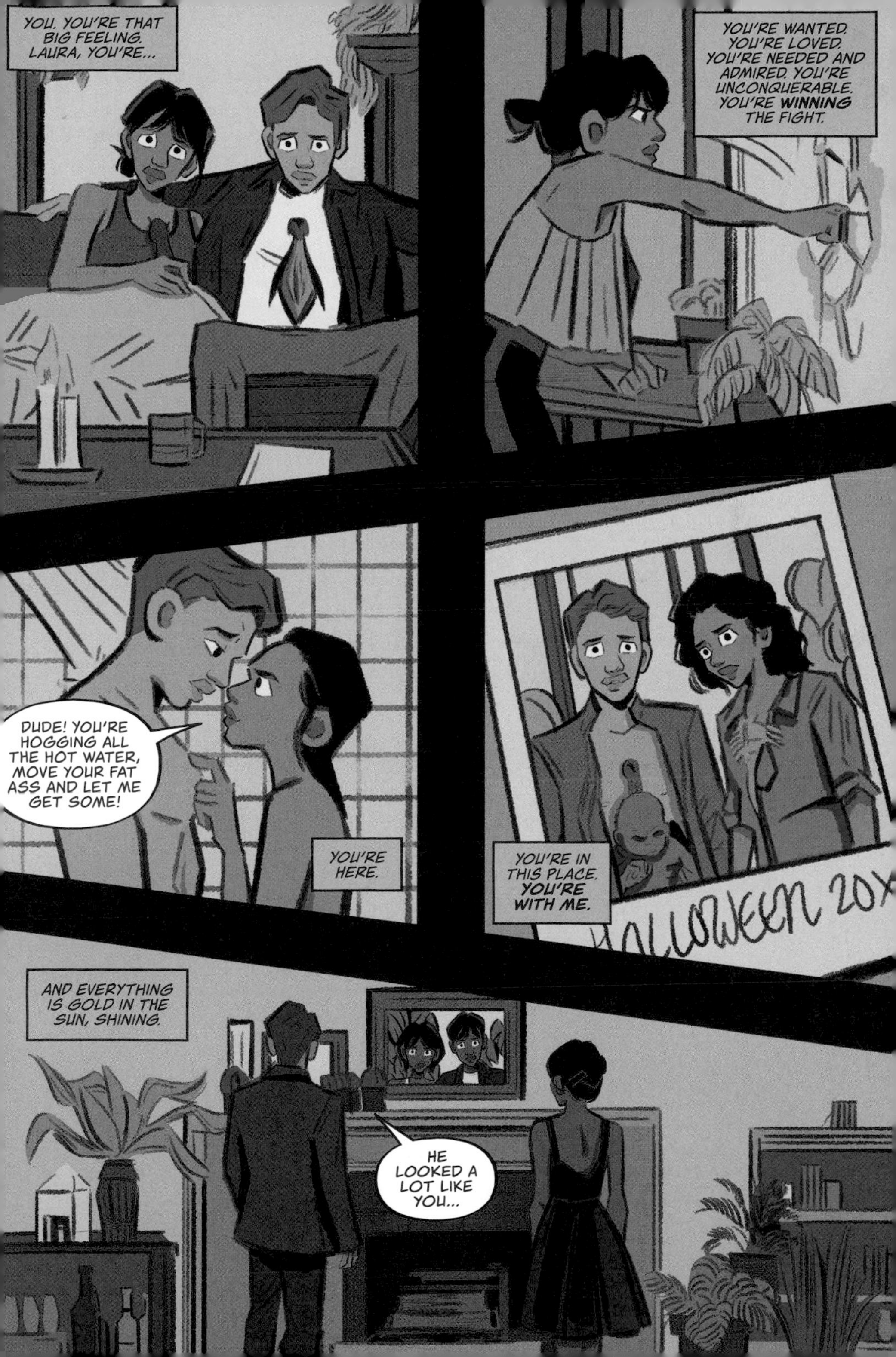

YOU. YOU'RE THAT BIG FEELING. LAURA, YOU'RE...
YOU'RE WANTED. YOU'RE LOVED. YOU'RE NEEDED AND ADMIRED. YOU'RE UNCONQUERABLE. YOU'RE WINNING THE FIGHT.
DUDE! YOU'RE HOGGING ALL THE HOT WATER, MOVE YOUR FAT ASS AND LET ME GET SOME!
YOU'RE HERE.
YOU'RE IN THIS PLACE. YOU'RE WITH ME.
HALLOWEEN 20X
AND EVERYTHING IS GOLD IN THE SUN, SHINING.
HE LOOKED A LOT LIKE YOU...

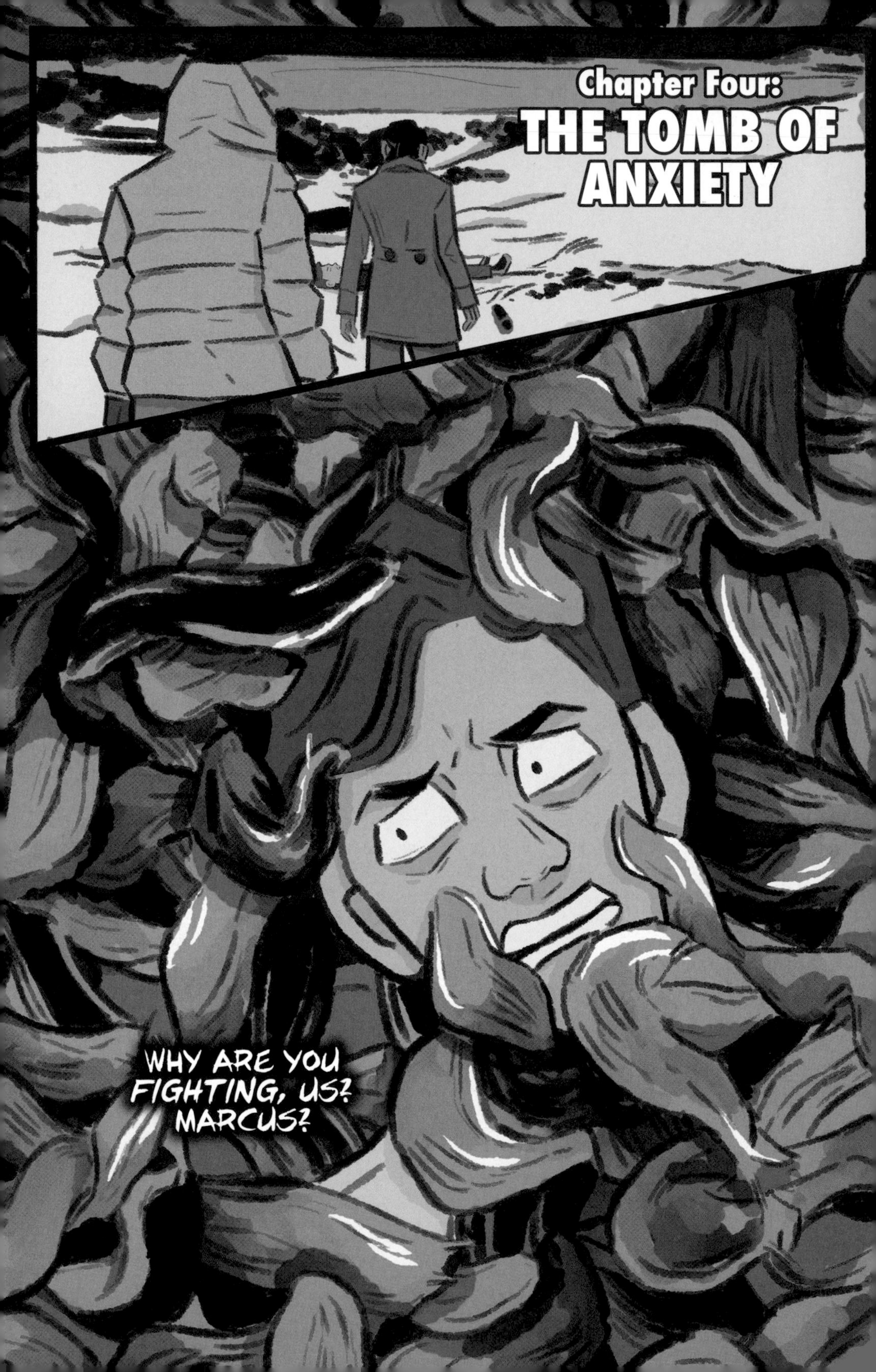
Chapter Four:
THE TOMB OF ANXIETY
WHY ARE YOU FIGHTING, US? MARCUS?

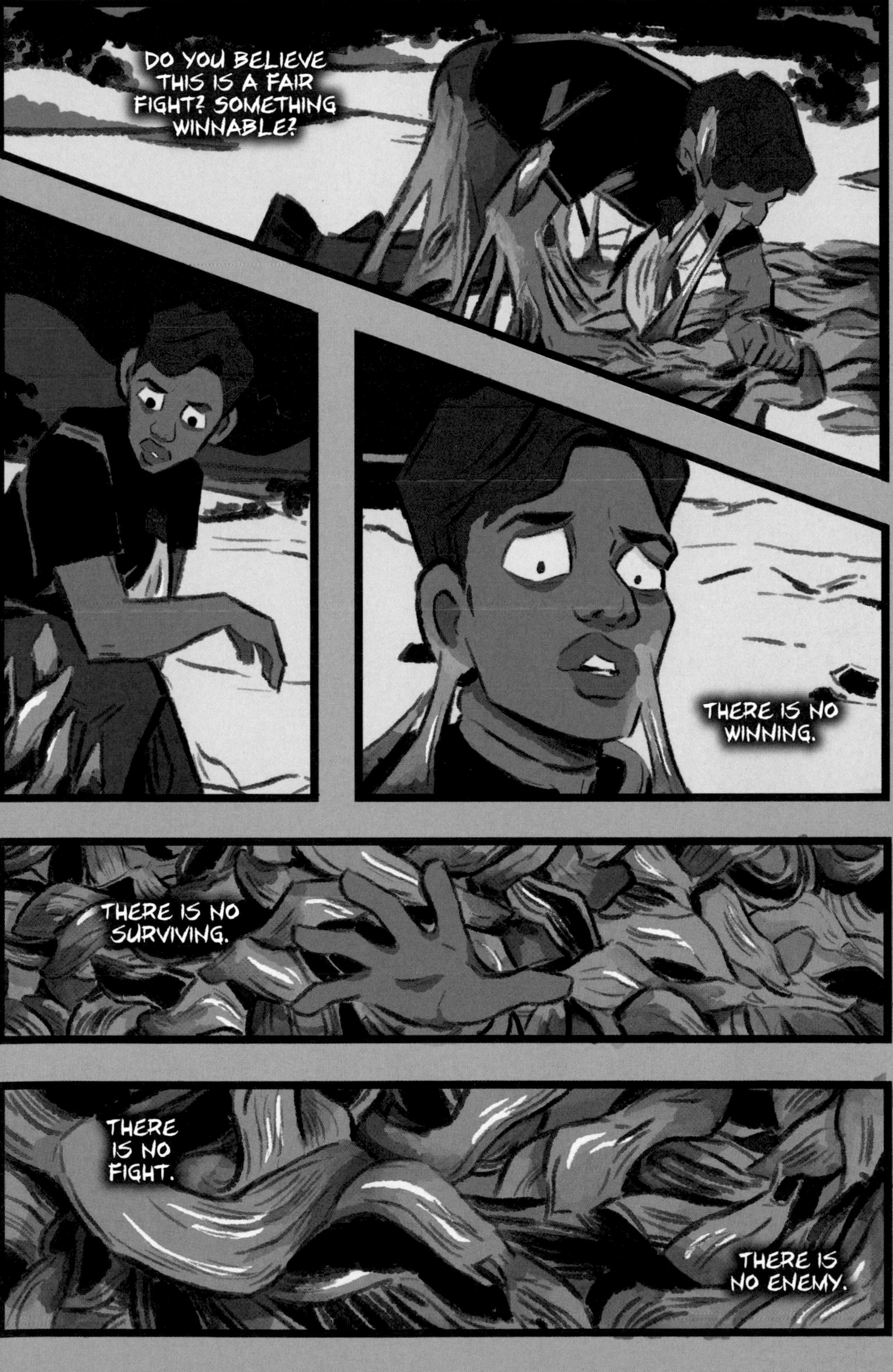
DO YOU BELIEVE THIS IS A FAIR FIGHT? SOMETHING WINNABLE?
THERE IS NO WINNING.
THERE IS NO SURVIVING.
THERE IS NO FIGHT.
THERE IS NO ENEMY.

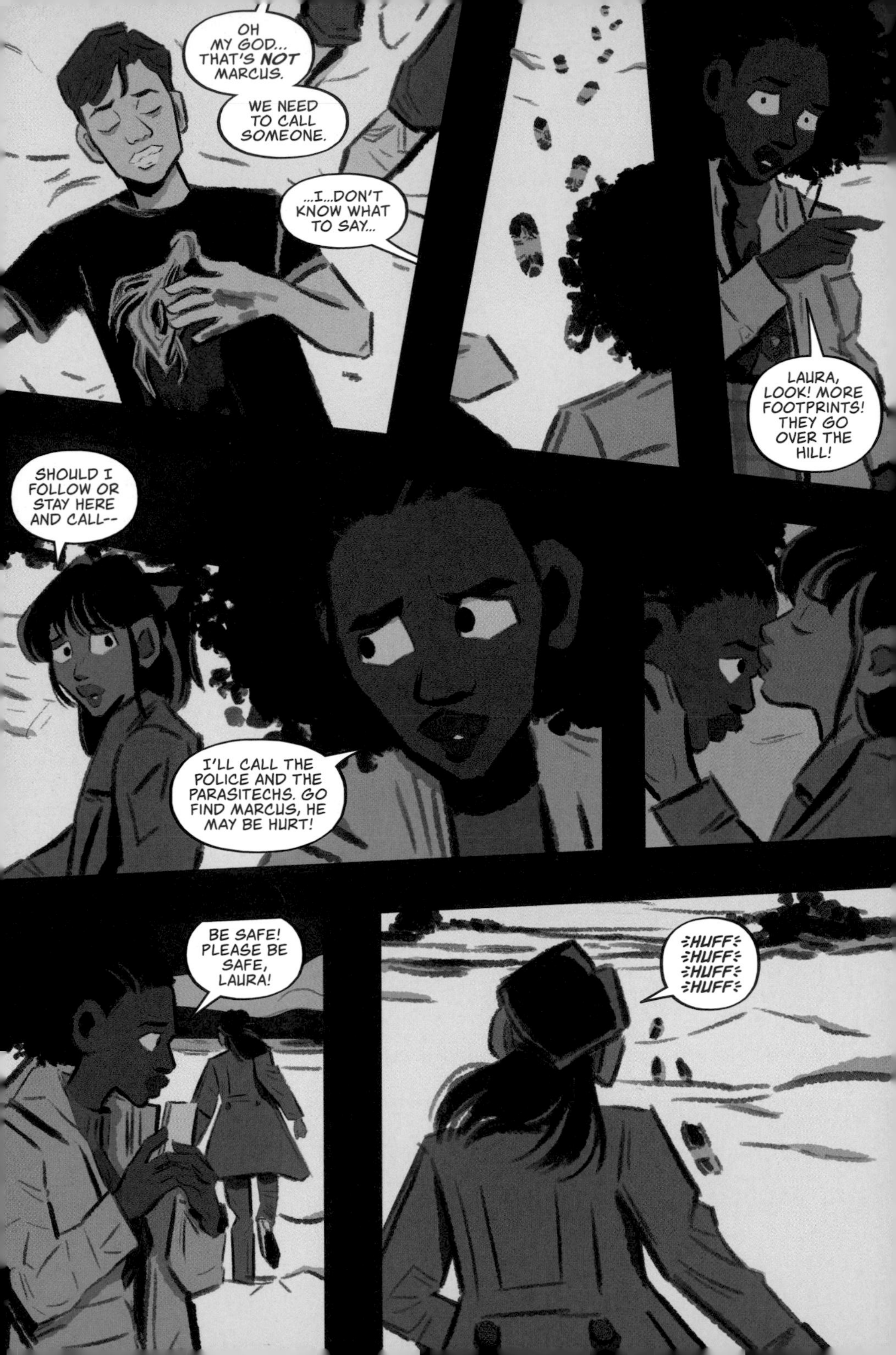
OH MY GOD... THAT'S NOT MARCUS.
WE NEED TO CALL SOMEONE.
...I...DON'T KNOW WHAT TO SAY...
LAURA, LOOK! MORE FOOTPRINTS! THEY GO OVER THE HILL!
SHOULD I FOLLOW OR STAY HERE AND CALL--
I'LL CALL THE POLICE AND THE PARASITECHS. GO FIND MARCUS, HE MAY BE HURT!
BE SAFE! PLEASE BE SAFE, LAURA!
HUFF HUFF HUFF HUFF

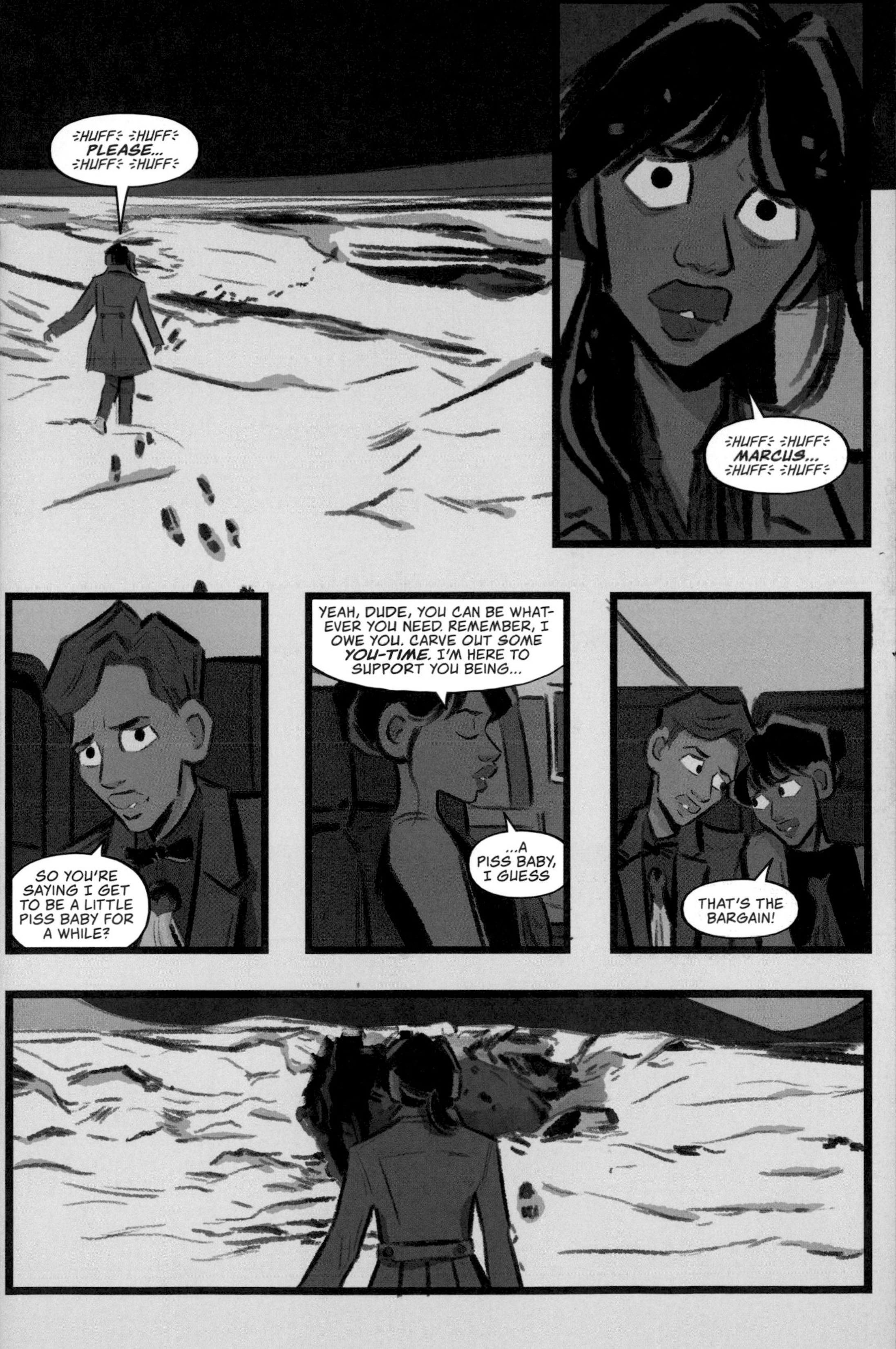

≈HUFF≈ ≈HUFF≈ PLEASE... ≈HUFF≈ ≈HUFF≈
≈HUFF≈ ≈HUFF≈ MARCUS... ≈HUFF≈ ≈HUFF≈
SO YOU'RE SAYING I GET TO BE A LITTLE PISS BABY FOR A WHILE?
YEAH, DUDE, YOU CAN BE WHAT-EVER YOU NEED. REMEMBER, I OWE YOU. CARVE OUT SOME YOU-TIME. I'M HERE TO SUPPORT YOU BEING...
...A PISS BABY, I GUESS
THAT'S THE BARGAIN!

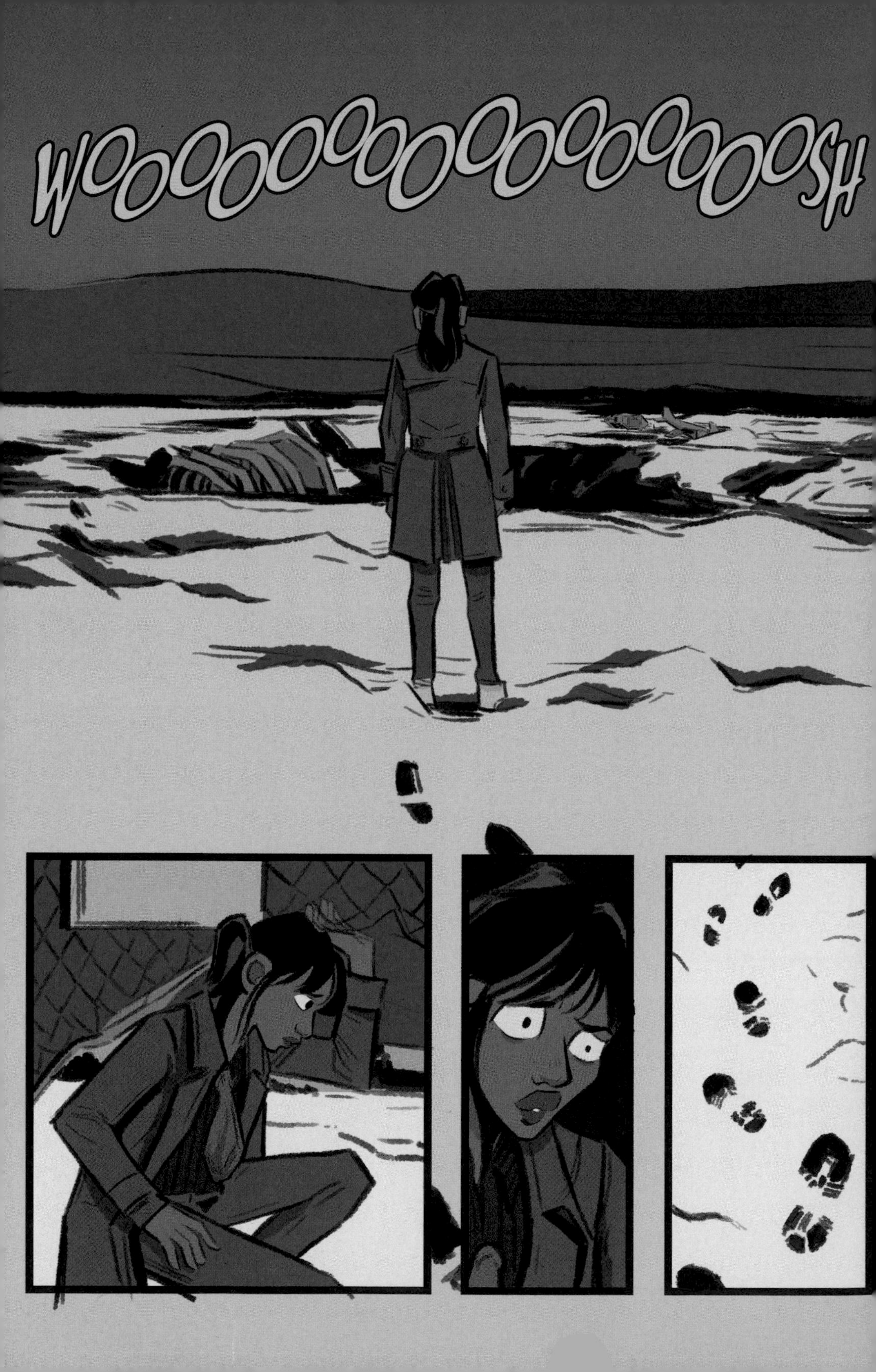
WOOOOOOOOOOOOOOOOOOOSH

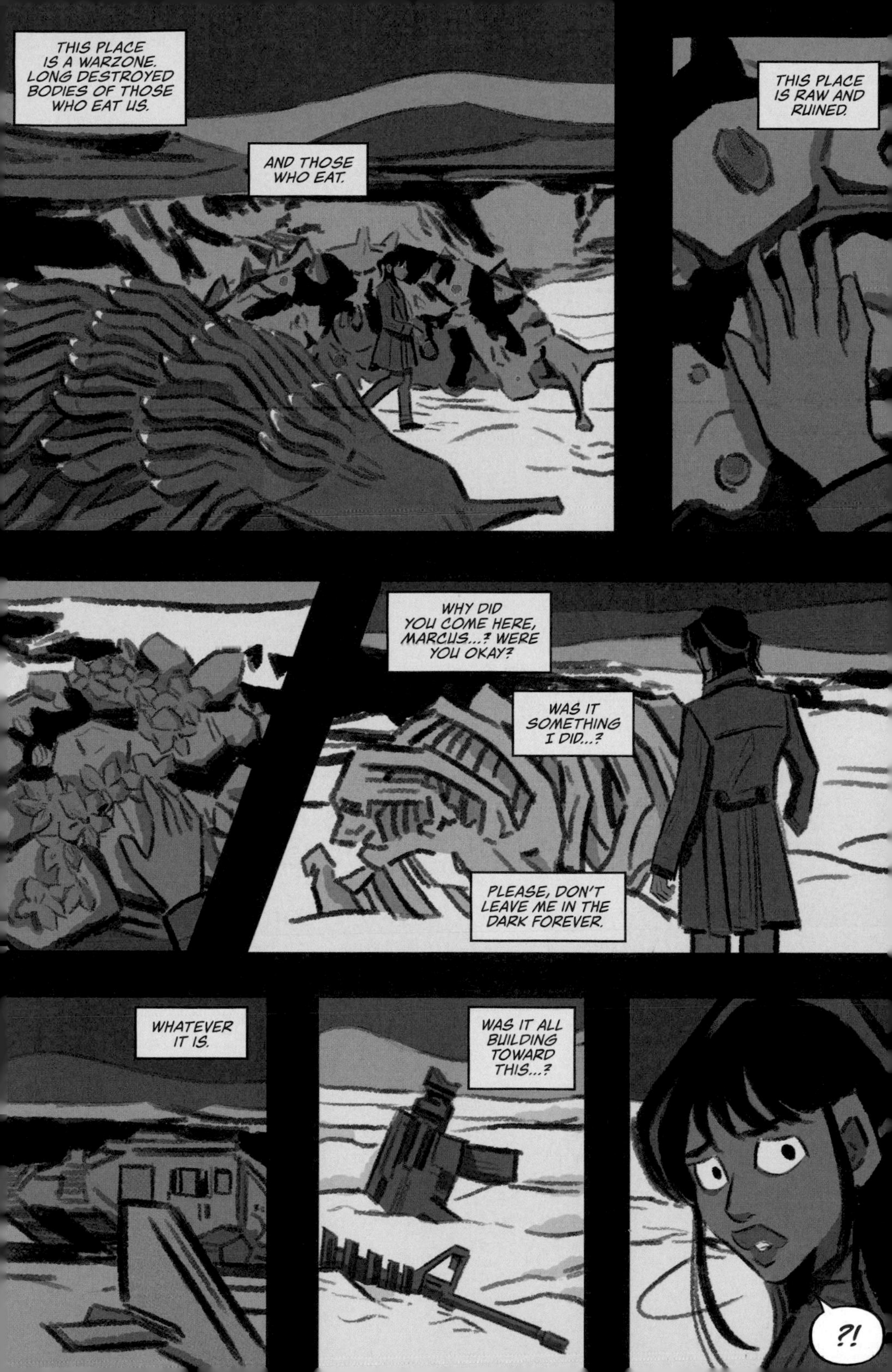
THIS PLACE IS A WARZONE. LONG DESTROYED BODIES OF THOSE WHO EAT US.
AND THOSE WHO EAT.
THIS PLACE IS RAW AND RUINED.
WHY DID YOU COME HERE, MARCUS...? WERE YOU OKAY?
WAS IT SOMETHING I DID...?
PLEASE, DON'T LEAVE ME IN THE DARK FOREVER.
WHATEVER IT IS.
WAS IT ALL BUILDING TOWARD THIS...?
?!

part five

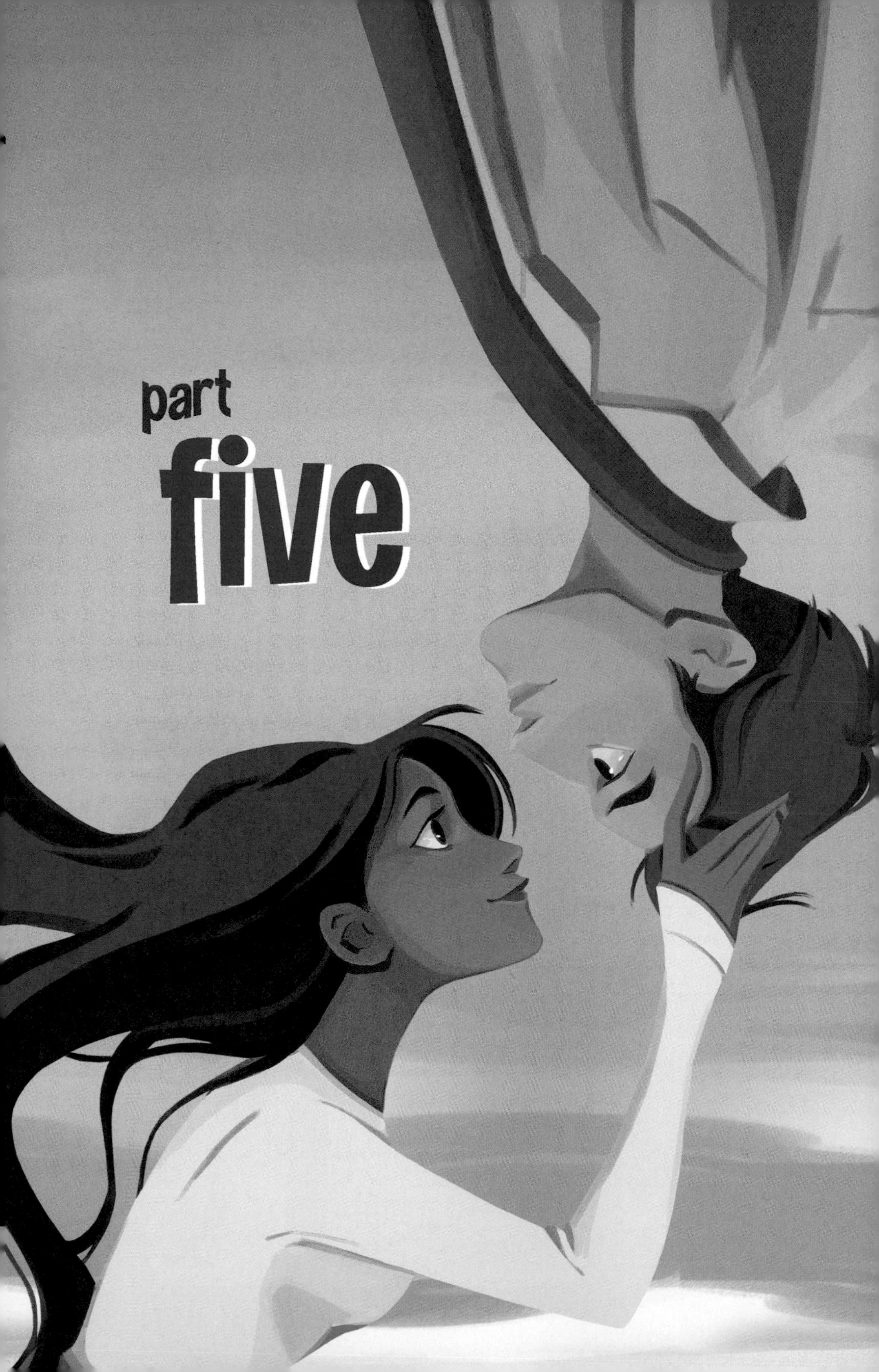

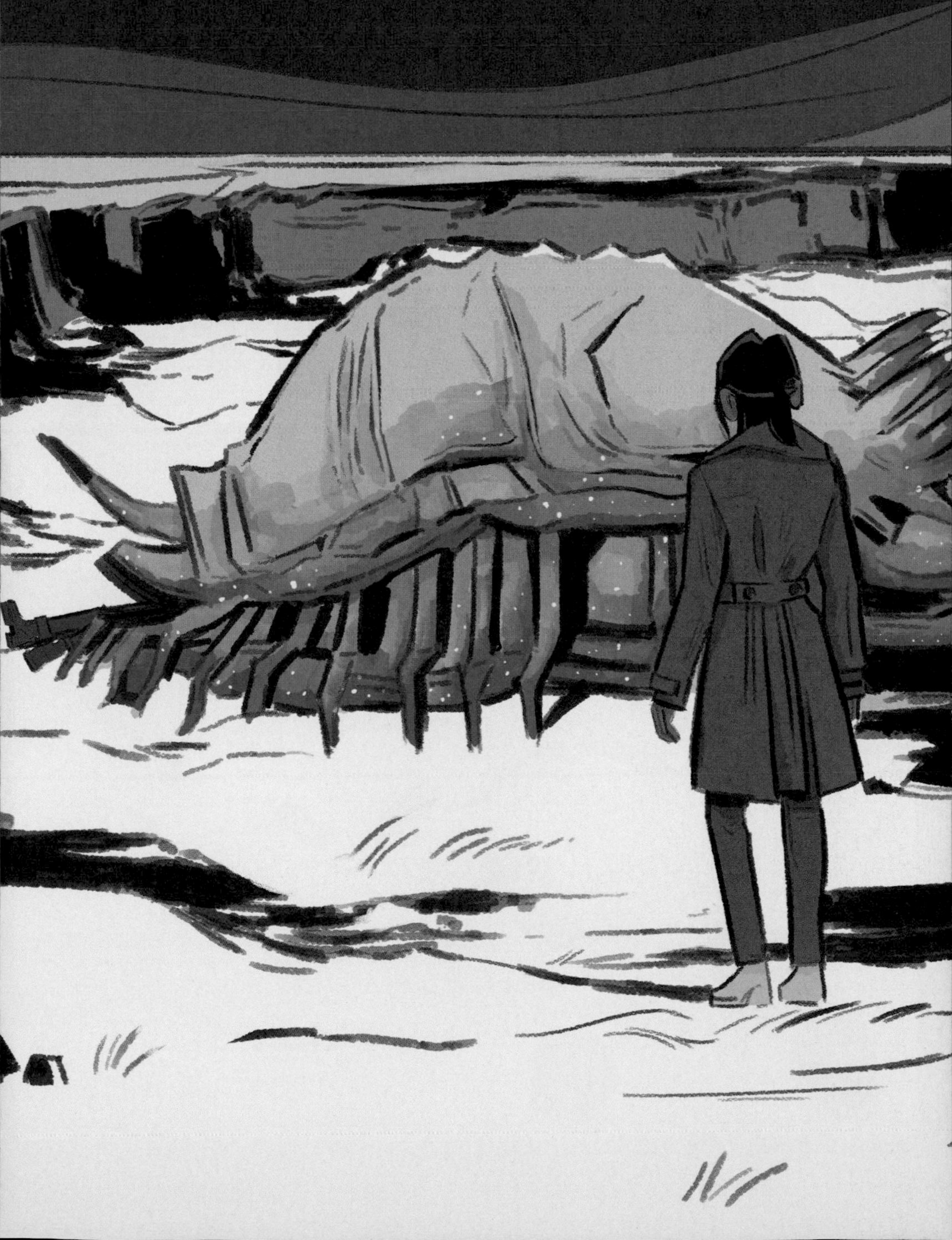

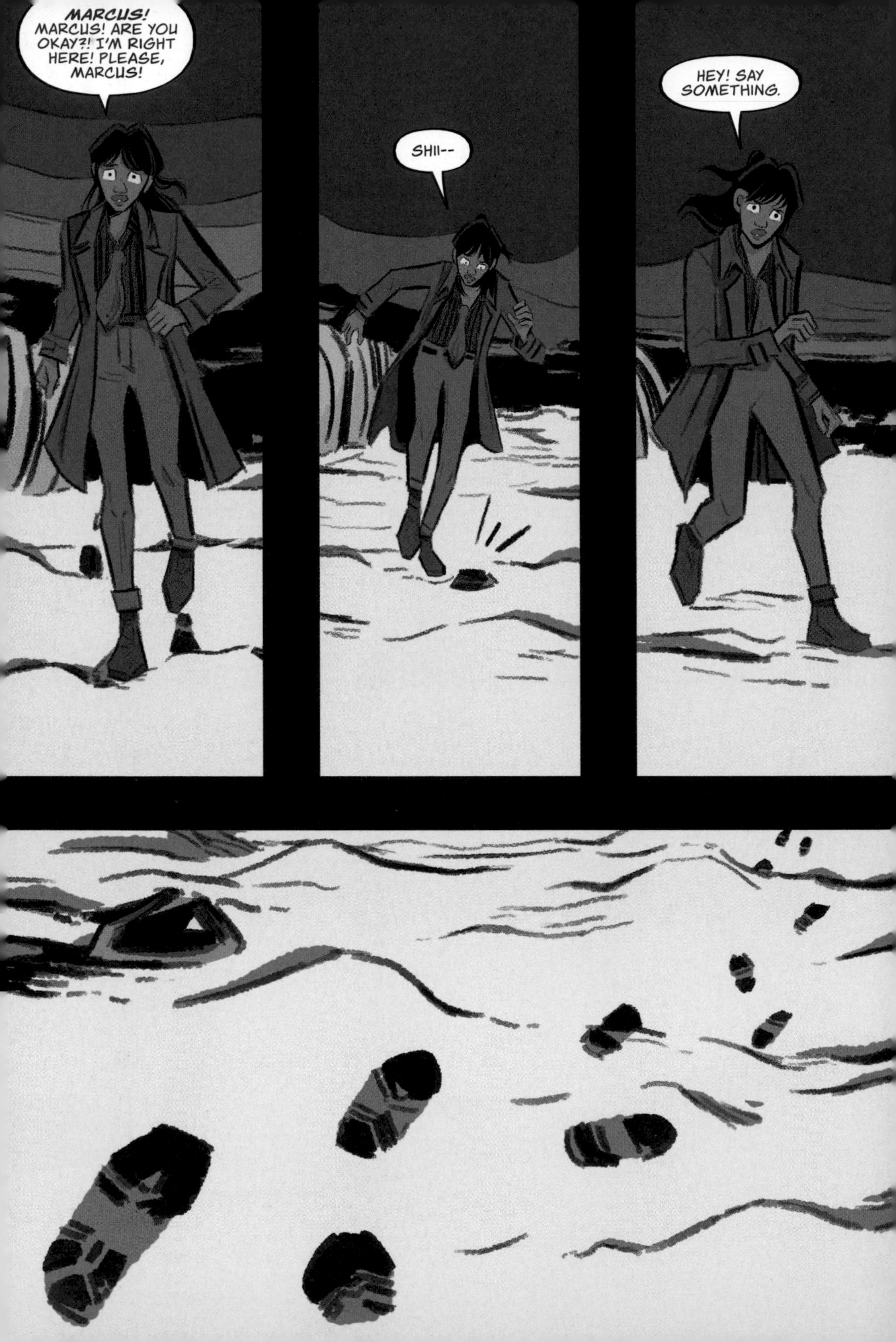
MARCUS! MARCUS! ARE YOU OKAY?! I'M RIGHT HERE! PLEASE, MARCUS!
SHII--
HEY! SAY SOMETHING.

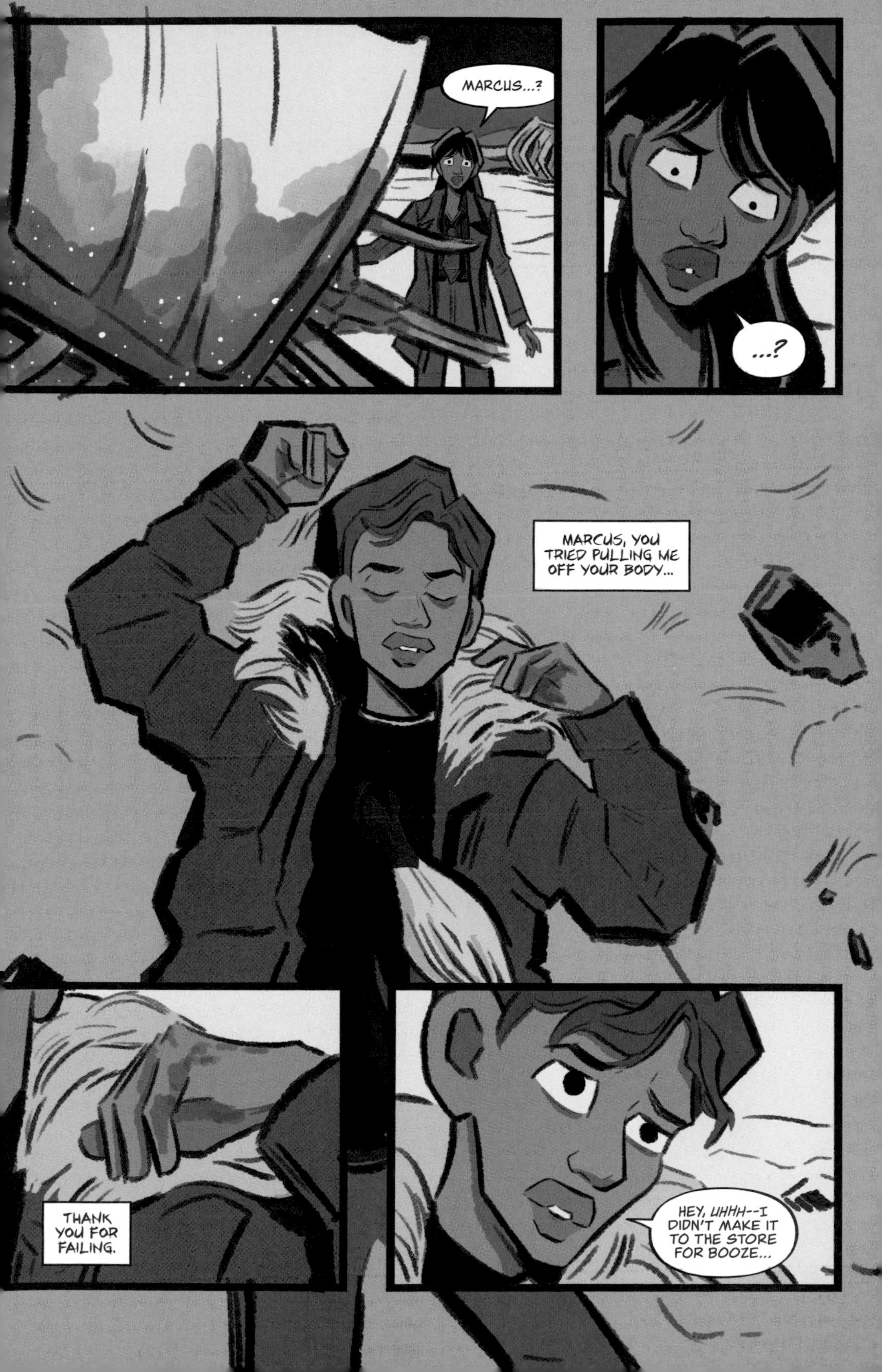
MARCUS...?
...?
MARCUS, YOU TRIED PULLING ME OFF YOUR BODY...
THANK YOU FOR FAILING.
HEY, UHHH--I DIDN'T MAKE IT TO THE STORE FOR BOOZE...

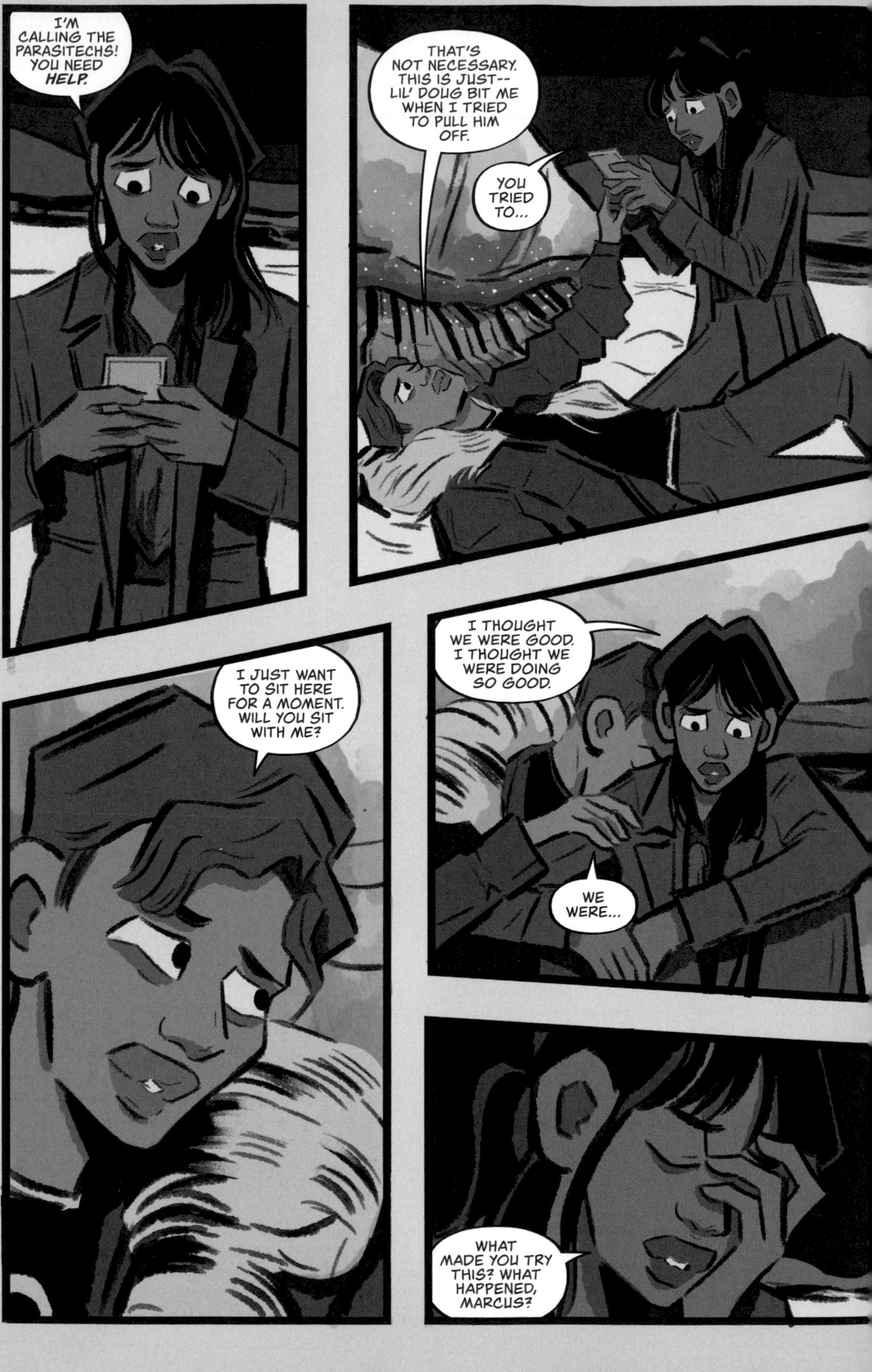

I'M CALLING THE PARASITECHS! YOU NEED HELP.
THAT'S NOT NECESSARY. THIS IS JUST-- LIL' DOUG BIT ME WHEN I TRIED TO PULL HIM OFF.
YOU TRIED TO...
I JUST WANT TO SIT HERE FOR A MOMENT. WILL YOU SIT WITH ME?
I THOUGHT WE WERE GOOD. I THOUGHT WE WERE DOING SO GOOD.
WE WERE...
WHAT MADE YOU TRY THIS? WHAT HAPPENED, MARCUS?

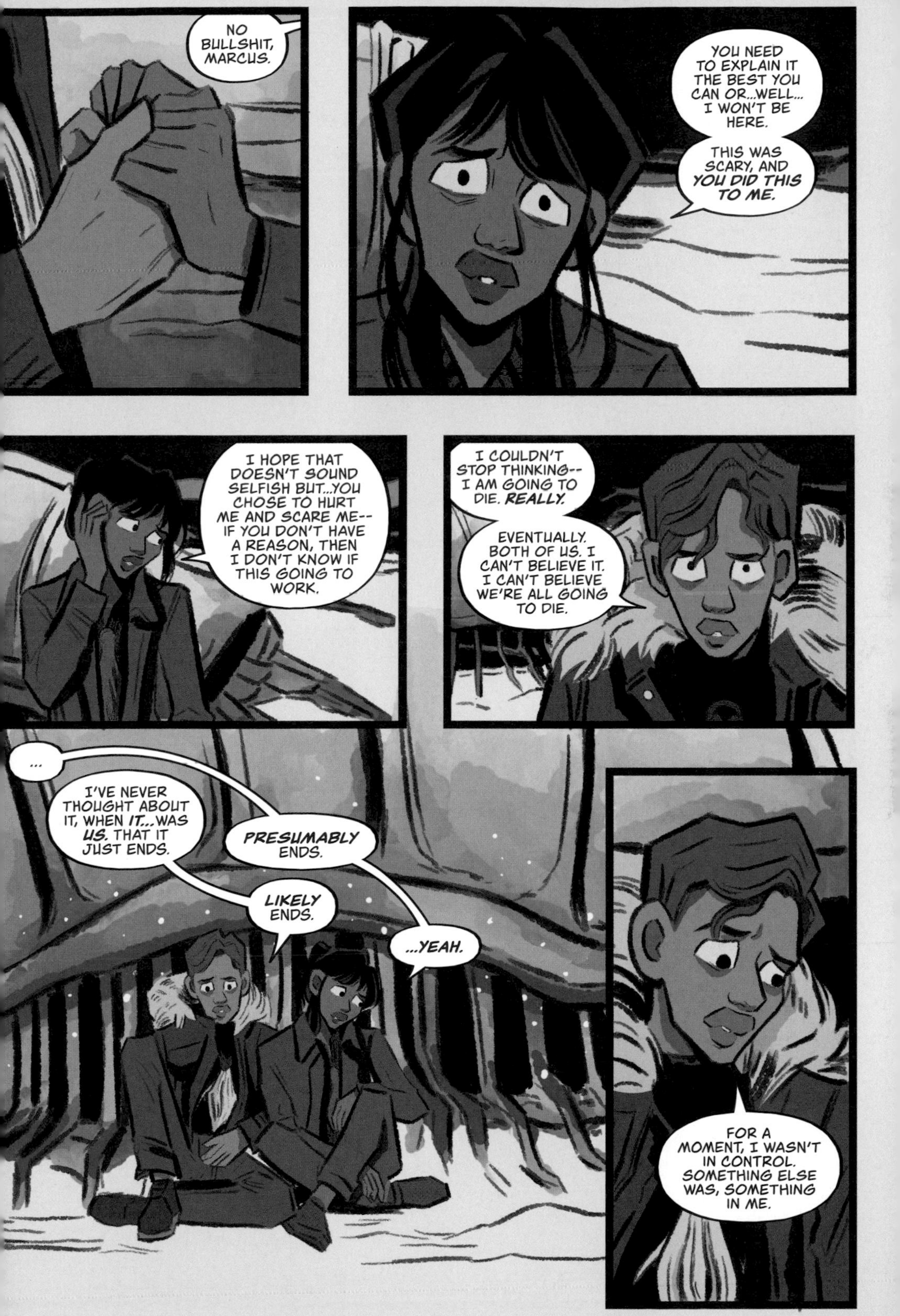
NO BULLSHIT, MARCUS.
YOU NEED TO EXPLAIN IT THE BEST YOU CAN OR...WELL... I WON'T BE HERE.
THIS WAS SCARY, AND *YOU DID THIS TO ME.*
I HOPE THAT DOESN'T SOUND SELFISH BUT...YOU CHOSE TO HURT ME AND SCARE ME-- IF YOU DON'T HAVE A REASON, THEN I DON'T KNOW IF THIS GOING TO WORK.
I COULDN'T STOP THINKING-- I AM GOING TO DIE. *REALLY.*
EVENTUALLY. BOTH OF US. I CAN'T BELIEVE IT. I CAN'T BELIEVE WE'RE ALL GOING TO DIE.
...
I'VE NEVER THOUGHT ABOUT IT, WHEN *IT...* WAS *US.* THAT IT JUST ENDS.
PRESUMABLY ENDS.
LIKELY ENDS.
...YEAH.
FOR A MOMENT, I WASN'T IN CONTROL. SOMETHING ELSE WAS, SOMETHING IN ME.

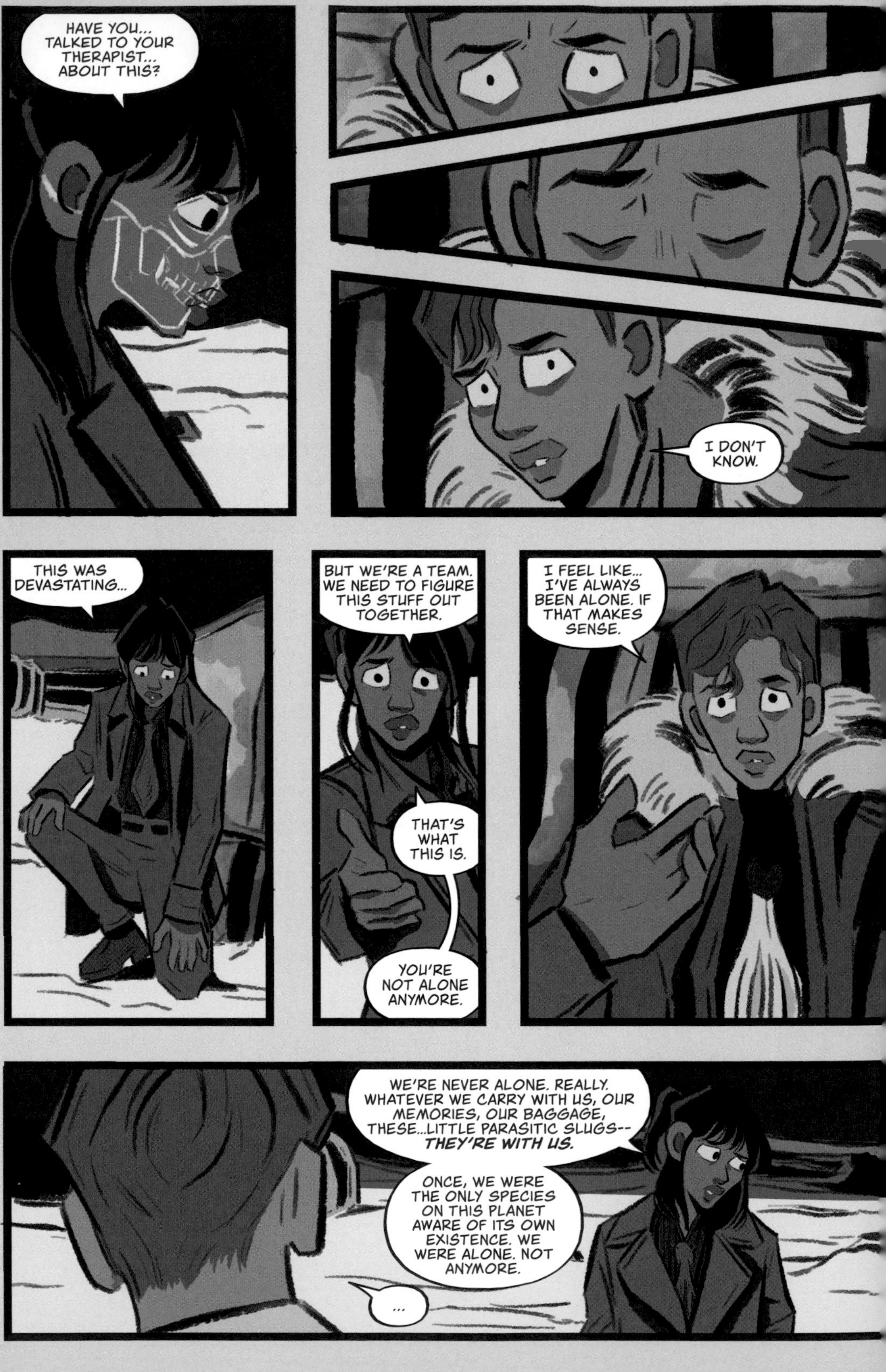
HAVE YOU... TALKED TO YOUR THERAPIST... ABOUT THIS?
I DON'T KNOW.
THIS WAS DEVASTATING...
BUT WE'RE A TEAM. WE NEED TO FIGURE THIS STUFF OUT TOGETHER.
THAT'S WHAT THIS IS.
YOU'RE NOT ALONE ANYMORE.
I FEEL LIKE... I'VE ALWAYS BEEN ALONE. IF THAT MAKES SENSE.
WE'RE NEVER ALONE. REALLY. WHATEVER WE CARRY WITH US, OUR MEMORIES, OUR BAGGAGE, THESE...LITTLE PARASITIC SLUGS-- ***THEY'RE WITH US.***
ONCE, WE WERE THE ONLY SPECIES ON THIS PLANET AWARE OF ITS OWN EXISTENCE. WE WERE ALONE. NOT ANYMORE.
...

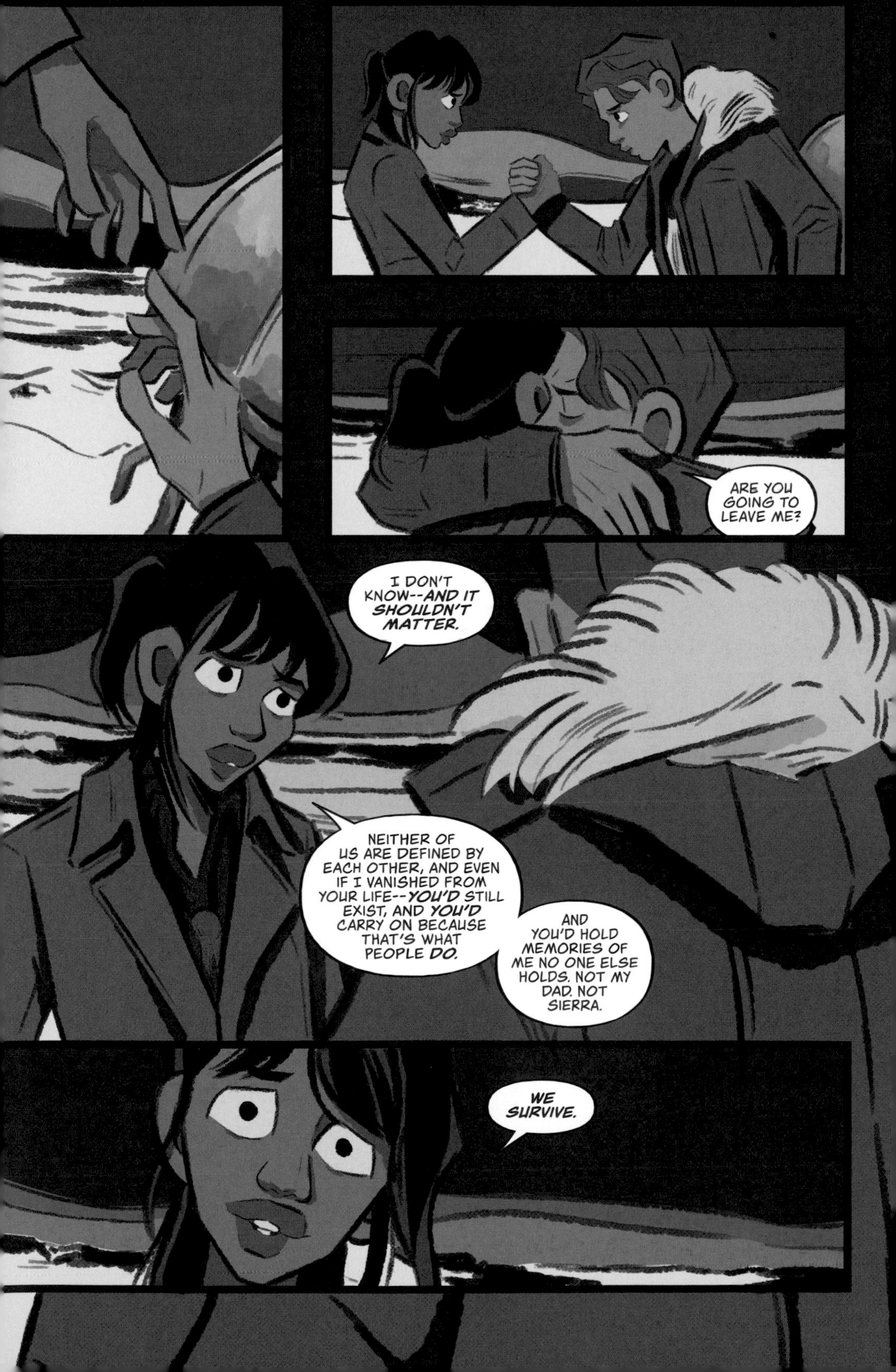
ARE YOU GOING TO LEAVE ME?
I DON'T KNOW--AND IT SHOULDN'T MATTER.
NEITHER OF US ARE DEFINED BY EACH OTHER, AND EVEN IF I VANISHED FROM YOUR LIFE--YOU'D STILL EXIST, AND YOU'D CARRY ON BECAUSE THAT'S WHAT PEOPLE DO.
AND YOU'D HOLD MEMORIES OF ME NO ONE ELSE HOLDS. NOT MY DAD. NOT SIERRA.
WE SURVIVE.

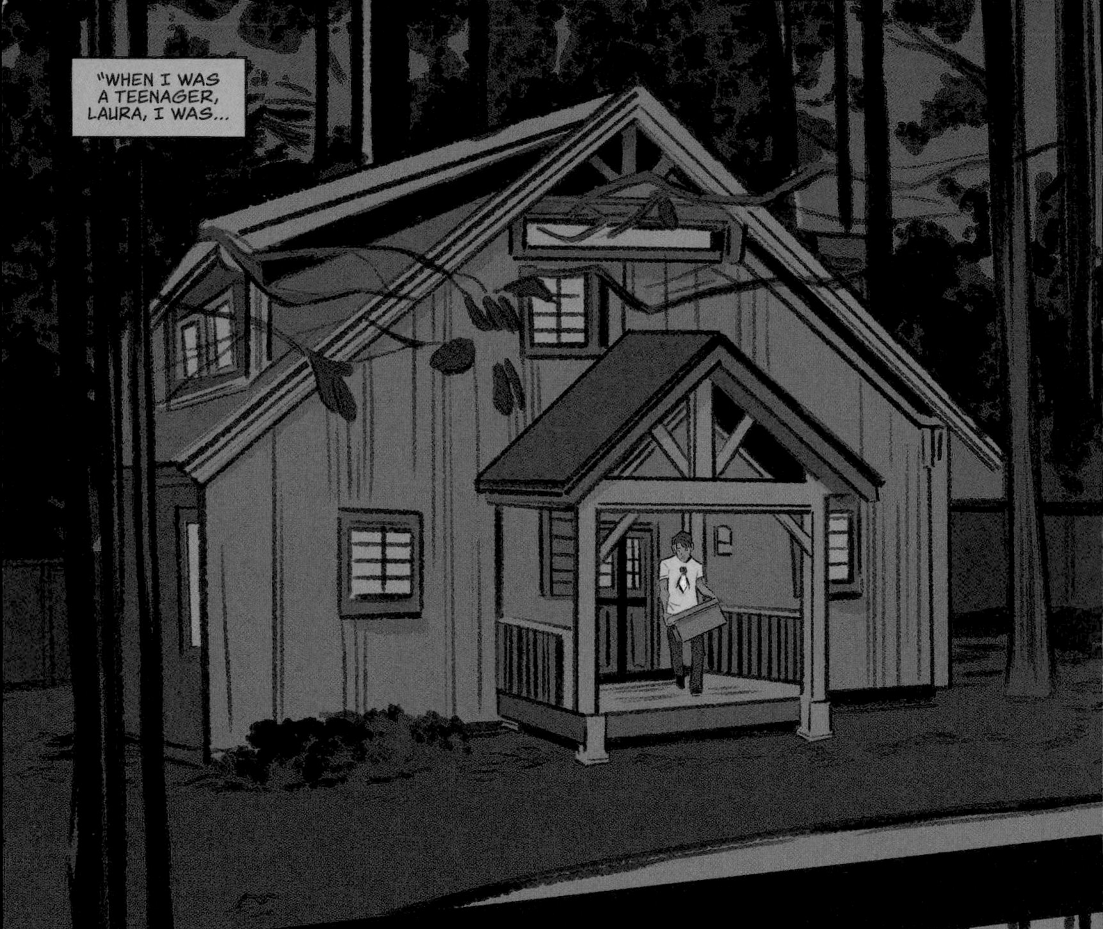
"WHEN I WAS A TEENAGER, LAURA, I WAS...

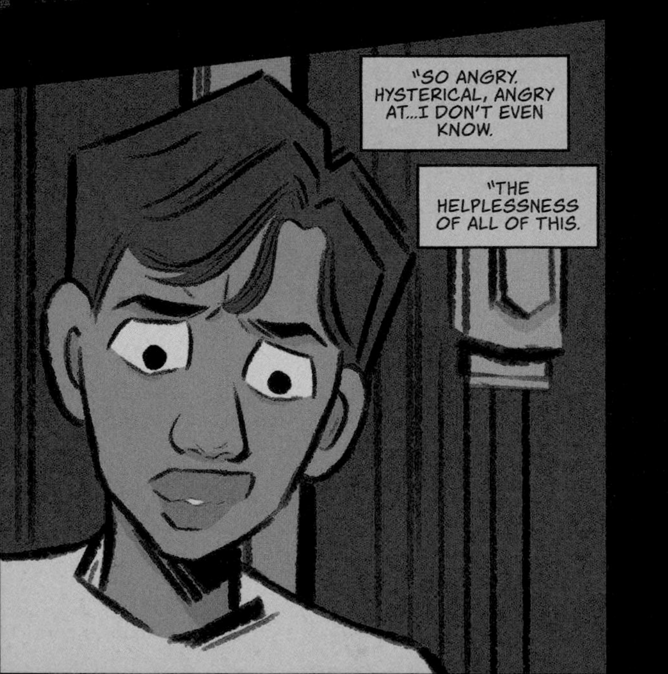
"SO ANGRY. HYSTERICAL, ANGRY AT...I DON'T EVEN KNOW.
"THE HELPLESSNESS OF ALL OF THIS.

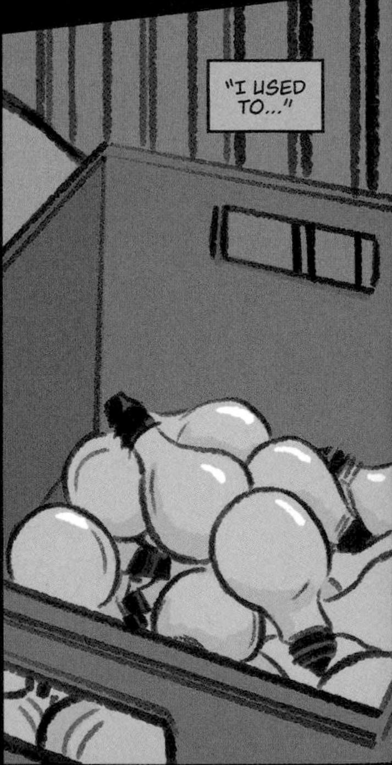
"I USED TO..."

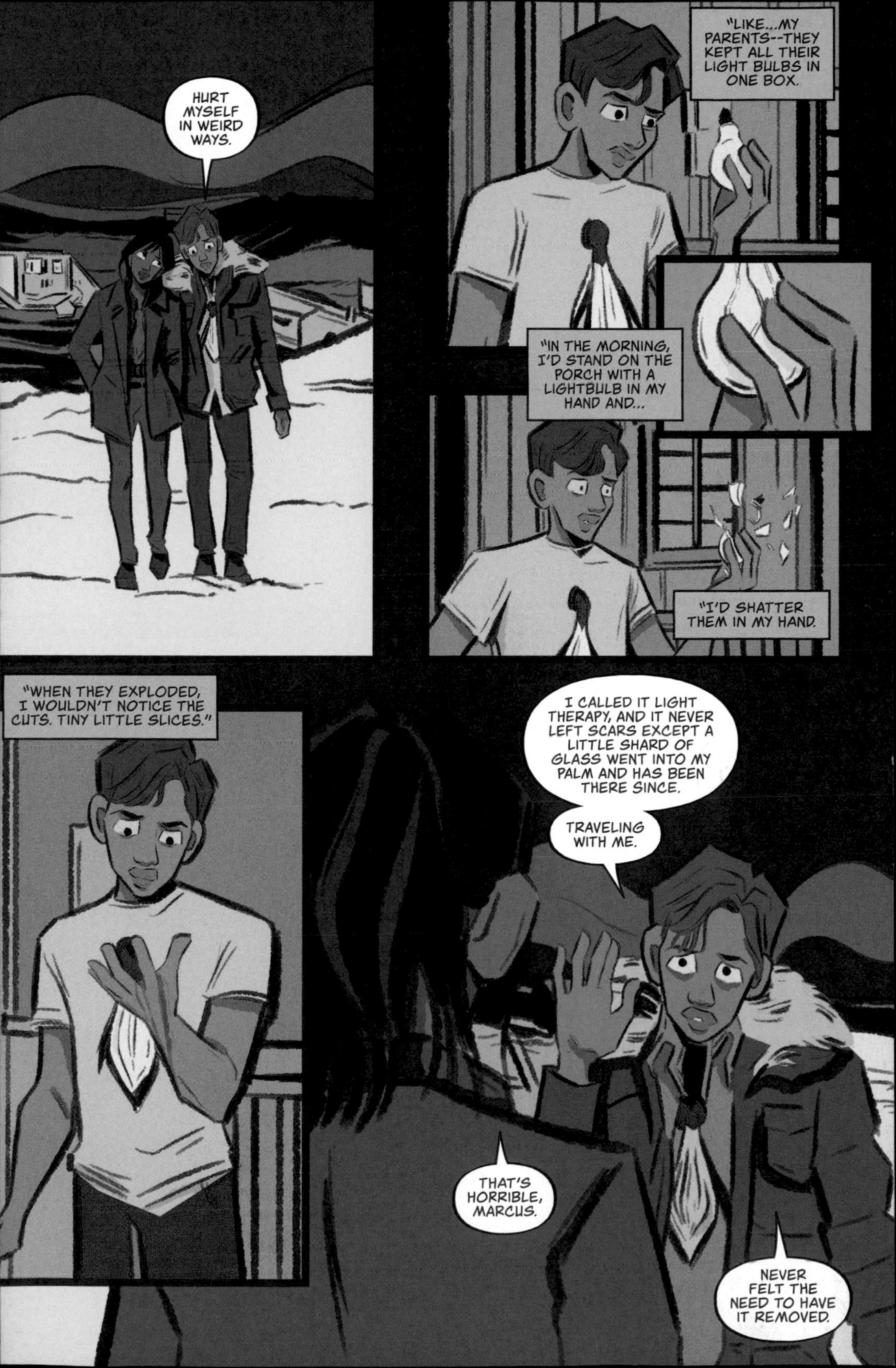
HURT MYSELF IN WEIRD WAYS.
"LIKE...MY PARENTS--THEY KEPT ALL THEIR LIGHT BULBS IN ONE BOX.
"IN THE MORNING, I'D STAND ON THE PORCH WITH A LIGHTBULB IN MY HAND AND...
"I'D SHATTER THEM IN MY HAND.
"WHEN THEY EXPLODED, I WOULDN'T NOTICE THE CUTS. TINY LITTLE SLICES."
I CALLED IT LIGHT THERAPY, AND IT NEVER LEFT SCARS EXCEPT A LITTLE SHARD OF GLASS WENT INTO MY PALM AND HAS BEEN THERE SINCE.
TRAVELING WITH ME.
THAT'S HORRIBLE, MARCUS.
NEVER FELT THE NEED TO HAVE IT REMOVED.

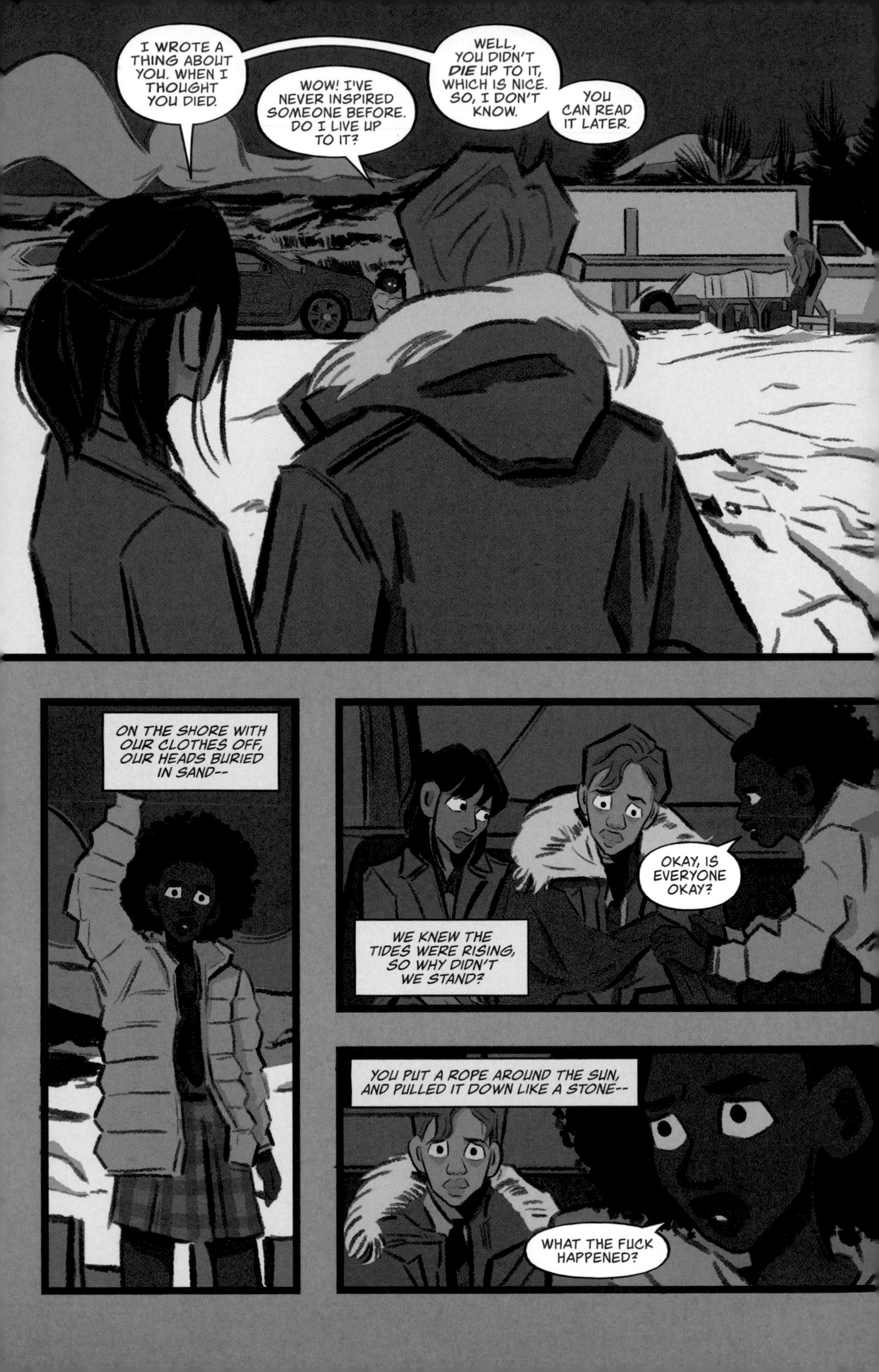
I WROTE A THING ABOUT YOU. WHEN I THOUGHT YOU DIED.
WOW! I'VE NEVER INSPIRED SOMEONE BEFORE. DO I LIVE UP TO IT?
WELL, YOU DIDN'T DIE UP TO IT, WHICH IS NICE. SO, I DON'T KNOW.
YOU CAN READ IT LATER.
ON THE SHORE WITH OUR CLOTHES OFF, OUR HEADS BURIED IN SAND--
OKAY, IS EVERYONE OKAY?
WE KNEW THE TIDES WERE RISING, SO WHY DIDN'T WE STAND?
YOU PUT A ROPE AROUND THE SUN, AND PULLED IT DOWN LIKE A STONE--
WHAT THE FUCK HAPPENED?

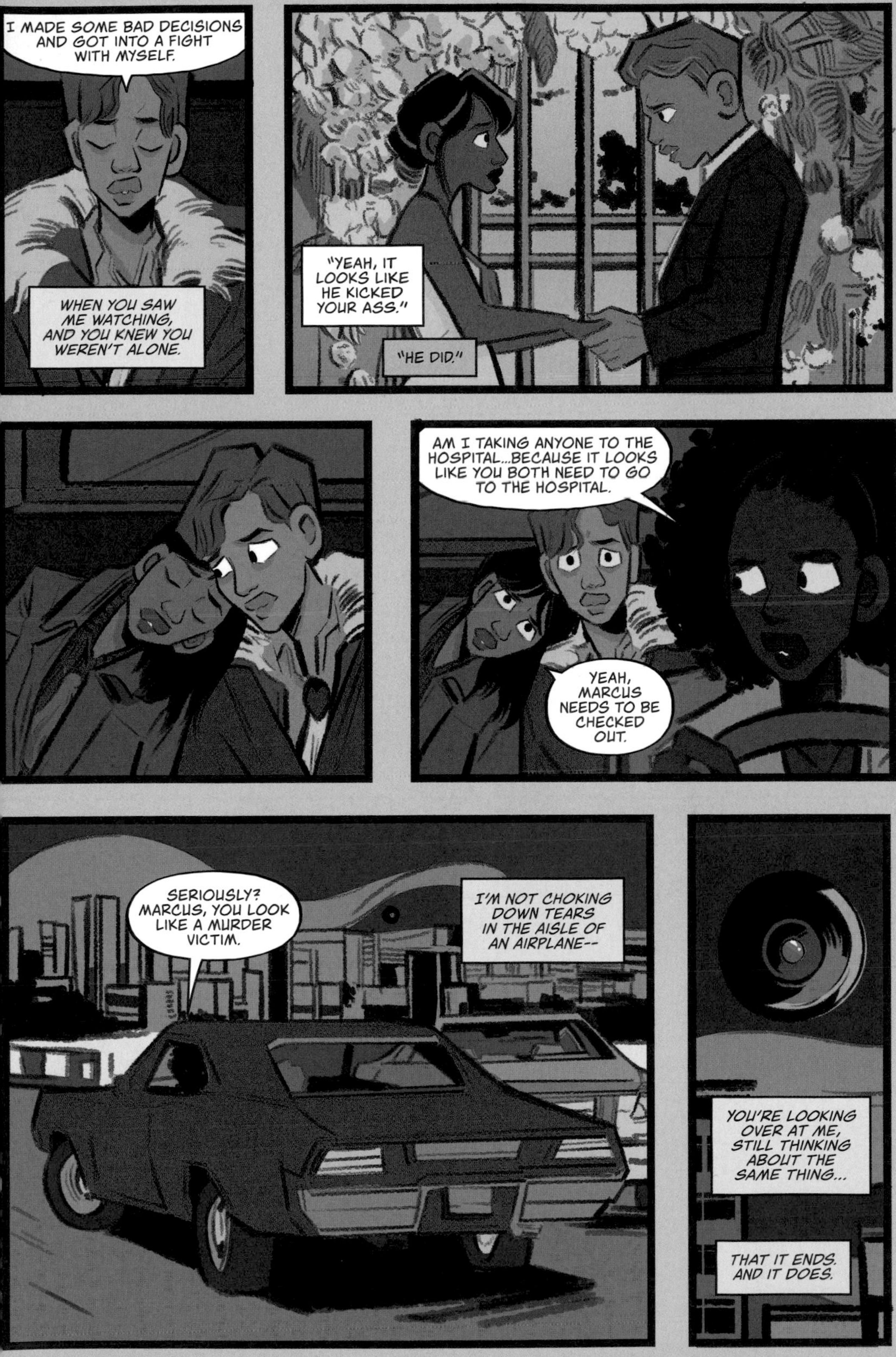
I MADE SOME BAD DECISIONS AND GOT INTO A FIGHT WITH MYSELF.
WHEN YOU SAW ME WATCHING, AND YOU KNEW YOU WEREN'T ALONE.
"YEAH, IT LOOKS LIKE HE KICKED YOUR ASS."
"HE DID."
AM I TAKING ANYONE TO THE HOSPITAL...BECAUSE IT LOOKS LIKE YOU BOTH NEED TO GO TO THE HOSPITAL.
YEAH, MARCUS NEEDS TO BE CHECKED OUT.
SERIOUSLY? MARCUS, YOU LOOK LIKE A MURDER VICTIM.
I'M NOT CHOKING DOWN TEARS IN THE AISLE OF AN AIRPLANE--
YOU'RE LOOKING OVER AT ME, STILL THINKING ABOUT THE SAME THING...
THAT IT ENDS. AND IT DOES.

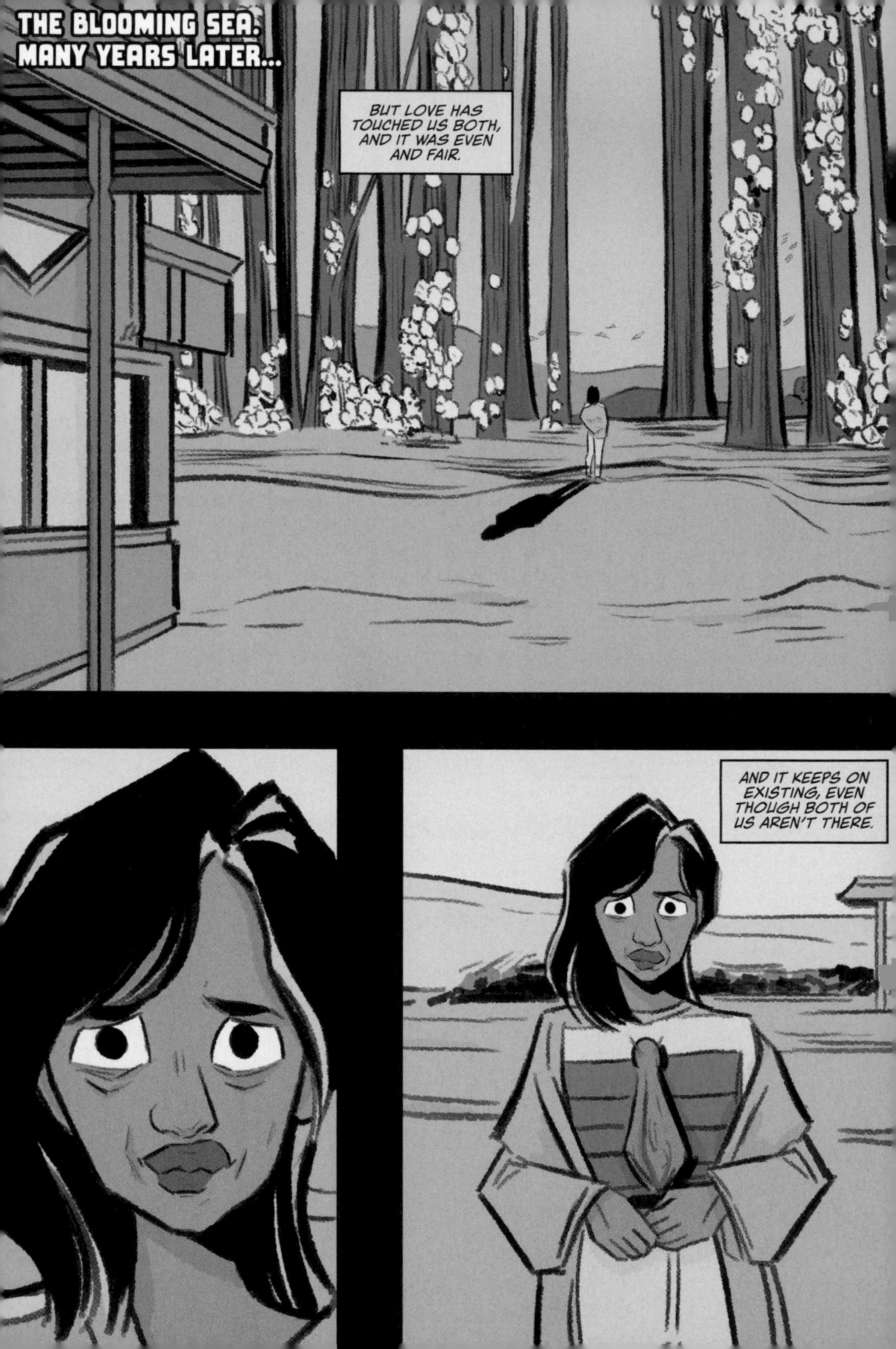
THE BLOOMING SEA. MANY YEARS LATER...
BUT LOVE HAS TOUCHED US BOTH, AND IT WAS EVEN AND FAIR.
AND IT KEEPS ON EXISTING, EVEN THOUGH BOTH OF US AREN'T THERE.

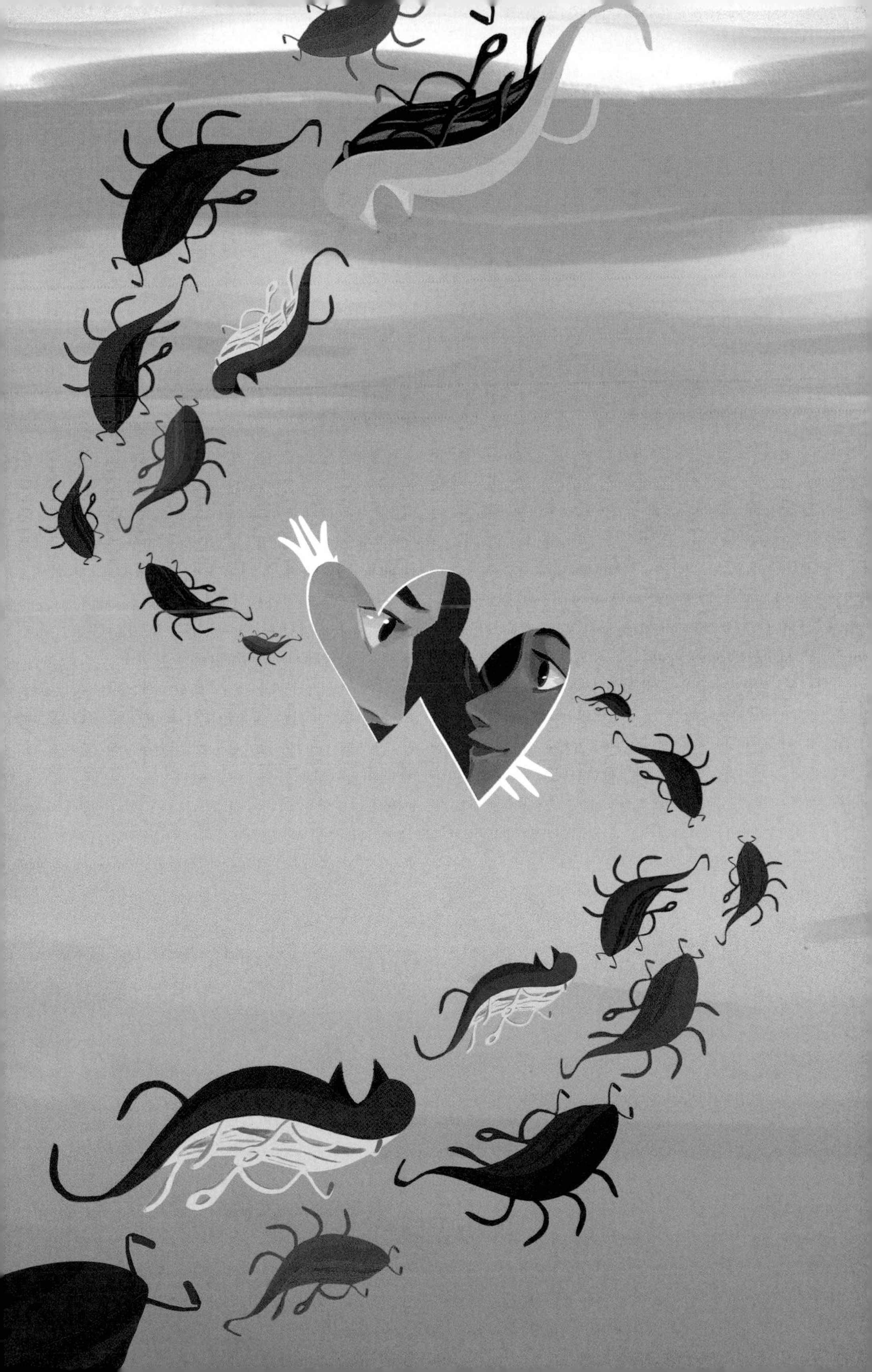

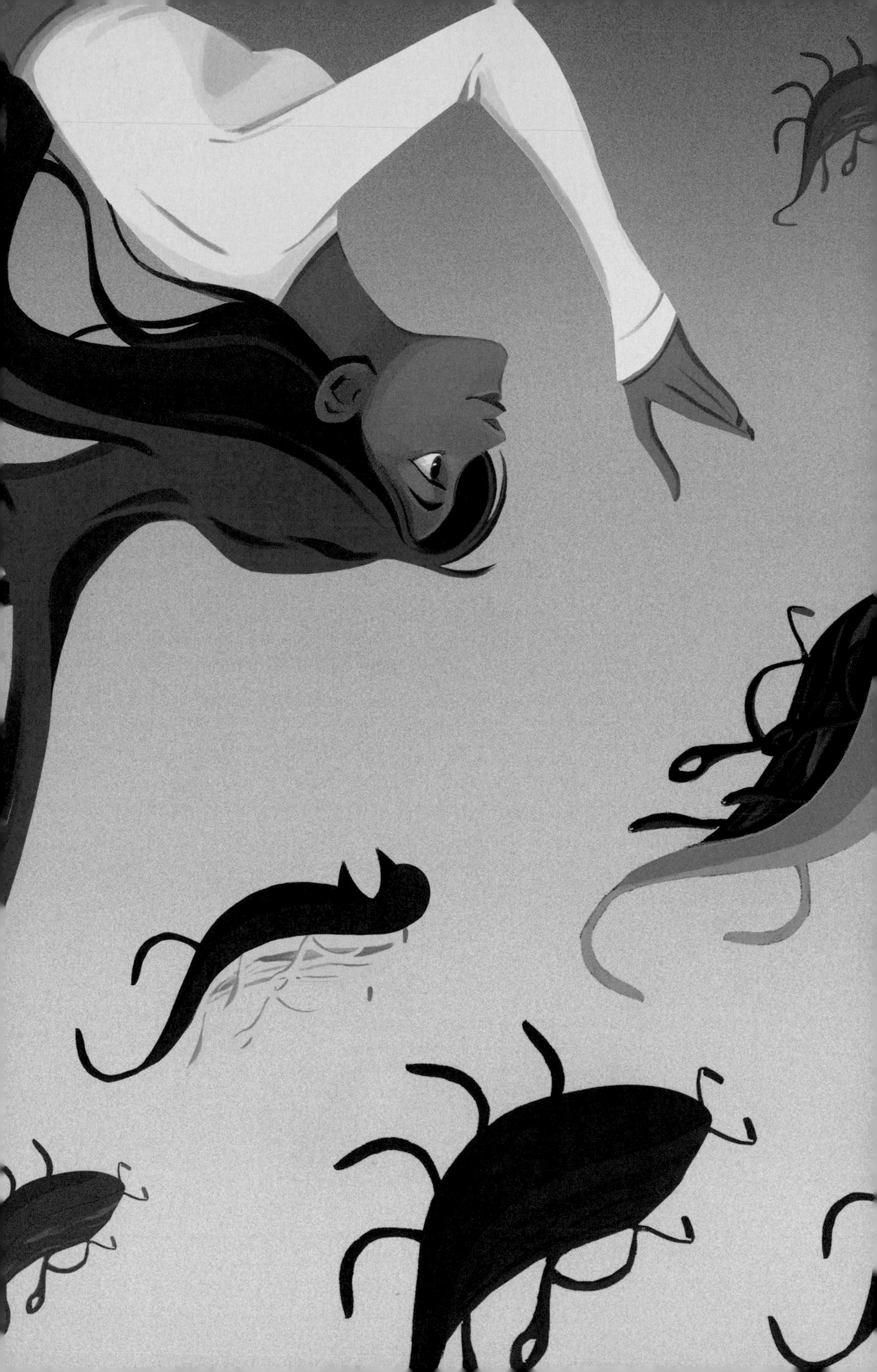

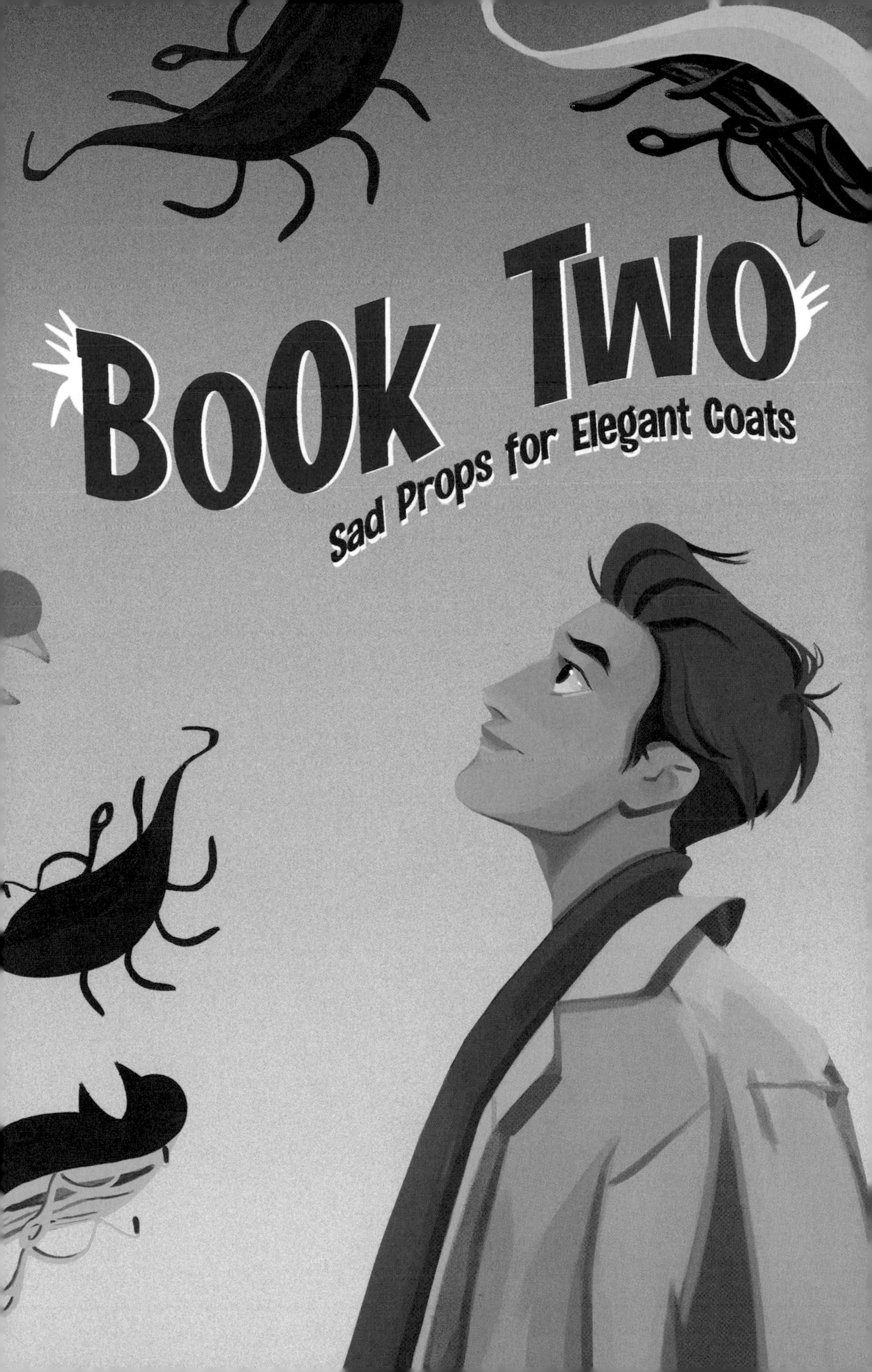
Book Two
Sad Props for Elegant Coats

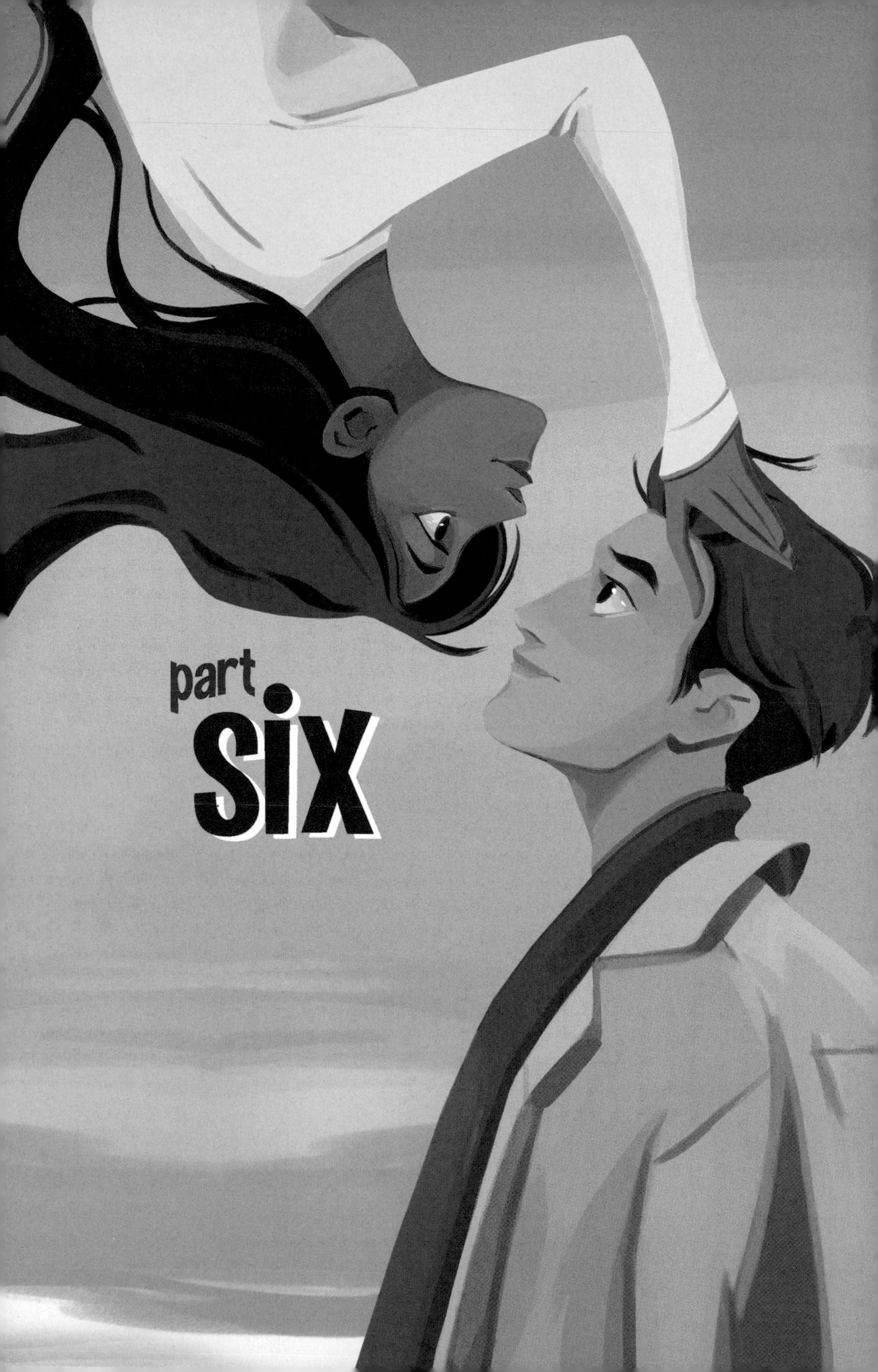
part
SIX

IRA R. - 22031
SOPHOMORE / 2ND SEMESTER
1ST PERIOD - RM. 103
BIOLOGICAL GEOMETRY 2-A
2ND PERIOD - RM. 208
HISTORY 2-C
3RD PERIOD - RM. 144
OUTWORLD LANGUAGE / AEOLIDIC 1-A
LUNCH PERIOD - CAFE B / 11:45 - 12:30
4TH PERIOD - GYMNASIUM 2
OLID/DORID HEA...

OKAY, FIRST DAY BACK. HERE WE GO.

DAALINGLINGINGING
DAALINGINALING

ELEGANT!

IRA!

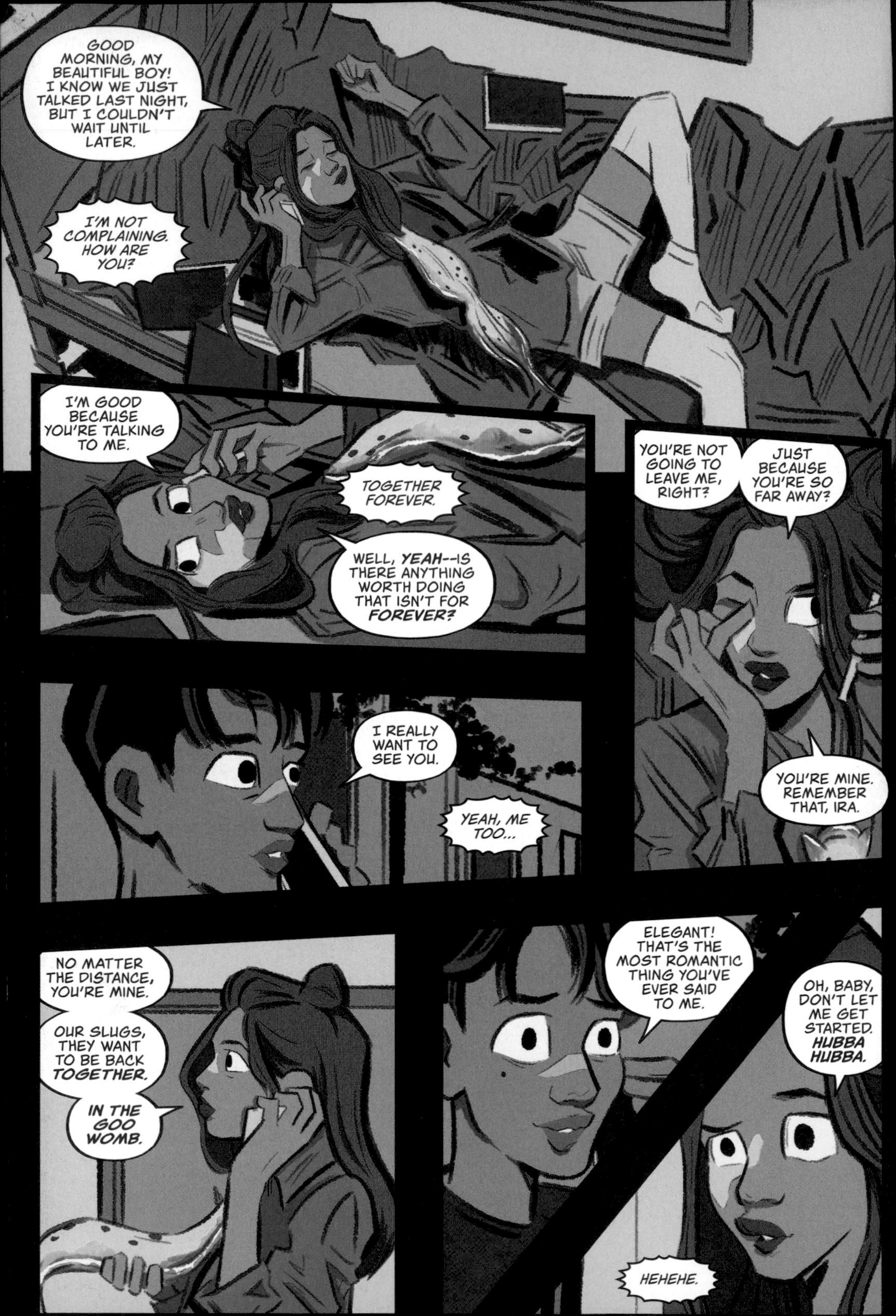

GOOD MORNING, MY BEAUTIFUL BOY! I KNOW WE JUST TALKED LAST NIGHT, BUT I COULDN'T WAIT UNTIL LATER.
I'M NOT COMPLAINING. HOW ARE YOU?
I'M GOOD BECAUSE YOU'RE TALKING TO ME.
TOGETHER FOREVER.
WELL, YEAH--IS THERE ANYTHING WORTH DOING THAT ISN'T FOR FOREVER?
YOU'RE NOT GOING TO LEAVE ME, RIGHT?
JUST BECAUSE YOU'RE SO FAR AWAY?
I REALLY WANT TO SEE YOU.
YEAH, ME TOO...
YOU'RE MINE. REMEMBER THAT, IRA.
NO MATTER THE DISTANCE, YOU'RE MINE.
OUR SLUGS, THEY WANT TO BE BACK TOGETHER.
IN THE GOO WOMB.
ELEGANT! THAT'S THE MOST ROMANTIC THING YOU'VE EVER SAID TO ME.
OH, BABY, DON'T LET ME GET STARTED. HUBBA HUBBA.
HEHEHE.

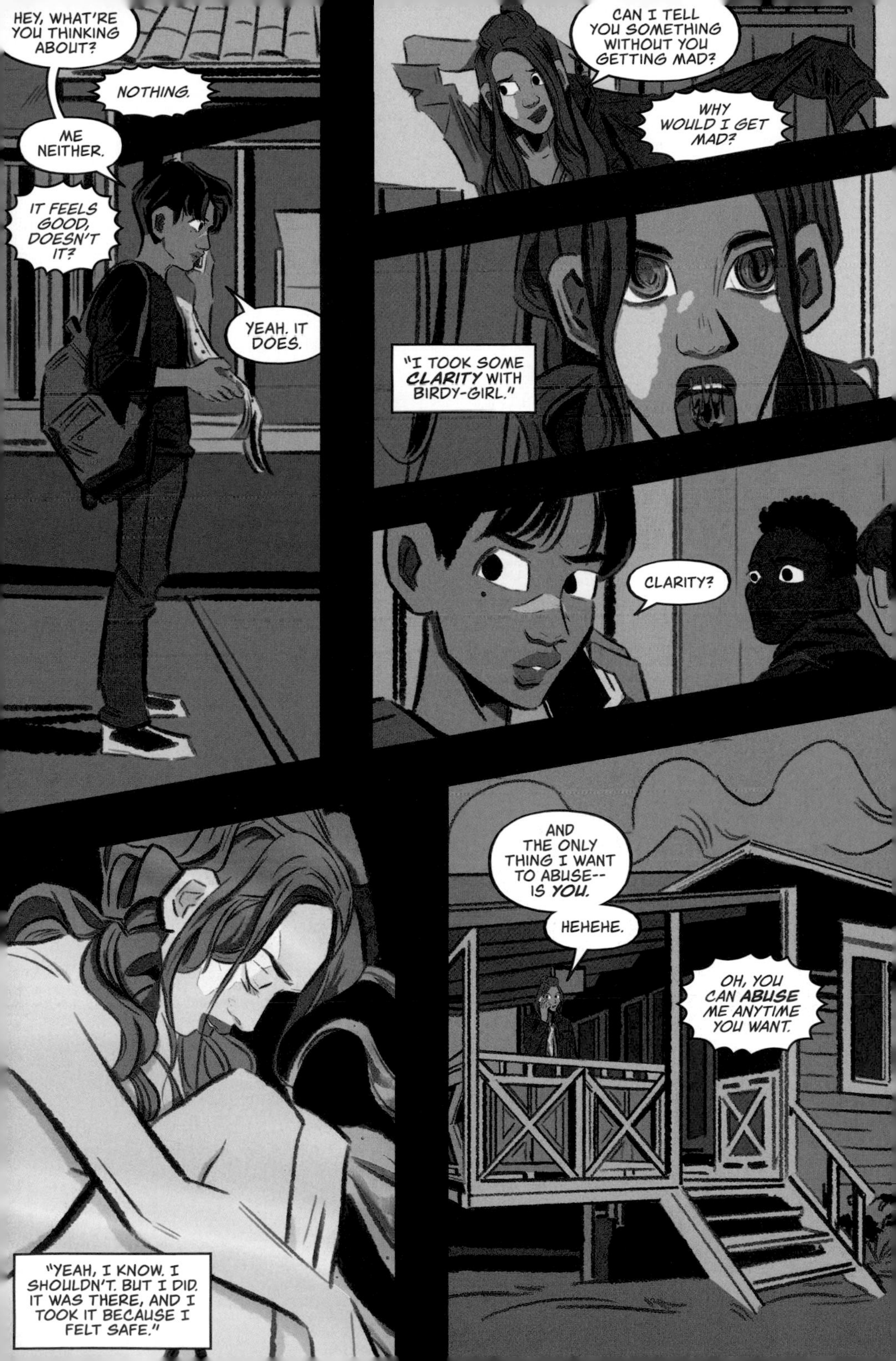
HEY, WHAT'RE YOU THINKING ABOUT?
NOTHING.
ME NEITHER.
IT FEELS GOOD, DOESN'T IT?
YEAH. IT DOES.
CAN I TELL YOU SOMETHING WITHOUT YOU GETTING MAD?
WHY WOULD I GET MAD?
"I TOOK SOME CLARITY WITH BIRDY-GIRL."
CLARITY?
"YEAH, I KNOW. I SHOULDN'T. BUT I DID. IT WAS THERE, AND I TOOK IT BECAUSE I FELT SAFE."
AND THE ONLY THING I WANT TO ABUSE-- IS YOU.
HEHEHE.
OH, YOU CAN ABUSE ME ANYTIME YOU WANT.

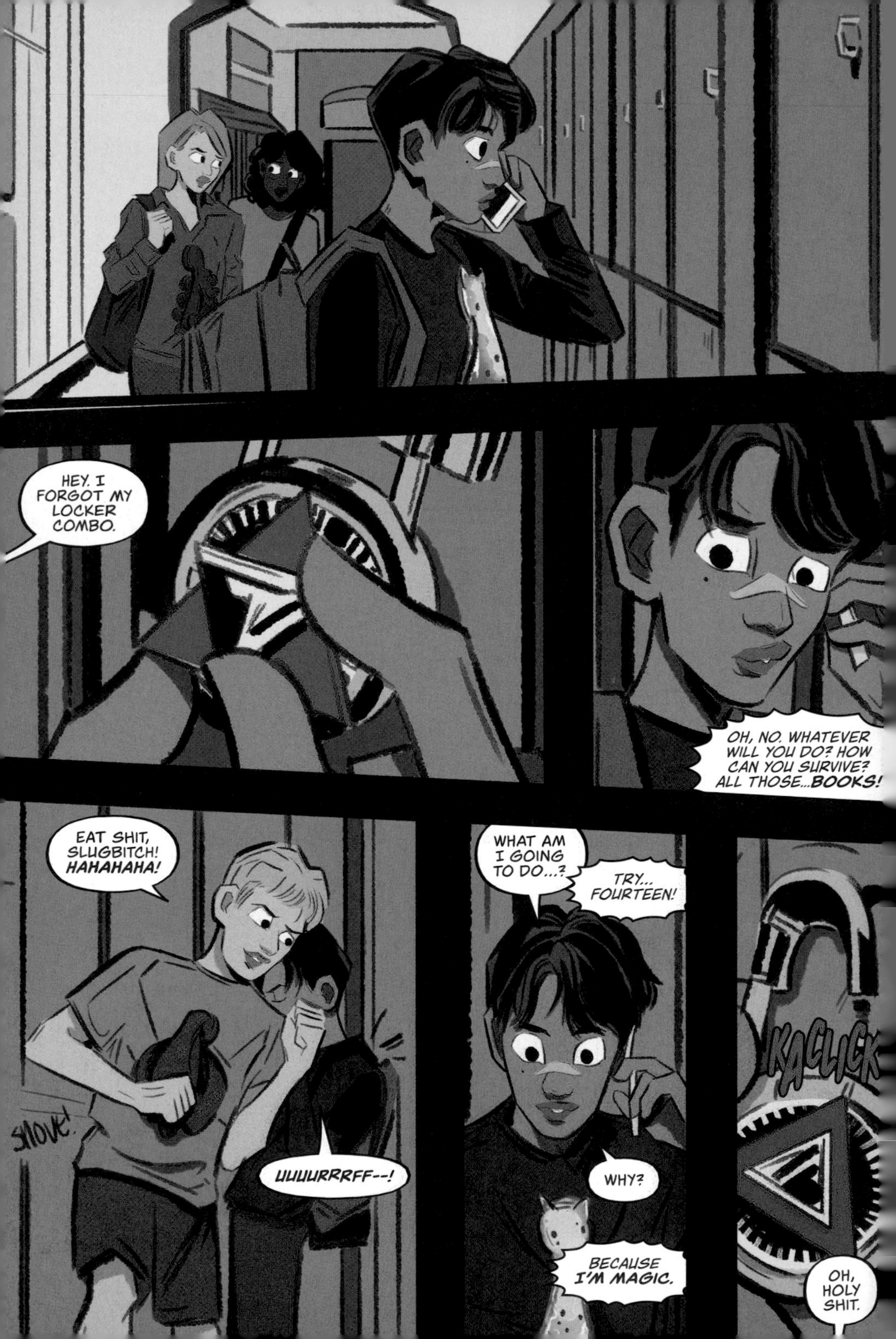
HEY. I FORGOT MY LOCKER COMBO.
OH, NO. WHATEVER WILL YOU DO? HOW CAN YOU SURVIVE? ALL THOSE...**BOOKS!**
EAT SHIT, SLUGBITCH! ***HAHAHAHA!***
SHOVE!
UUUURRRFF--!
WHAT AM I GOING TO DO...?
TRY... FOURTEEN!
WHY?
BECAUSE **I'M MAGIC.**
KACLICK
OH, HOLY SHIT.

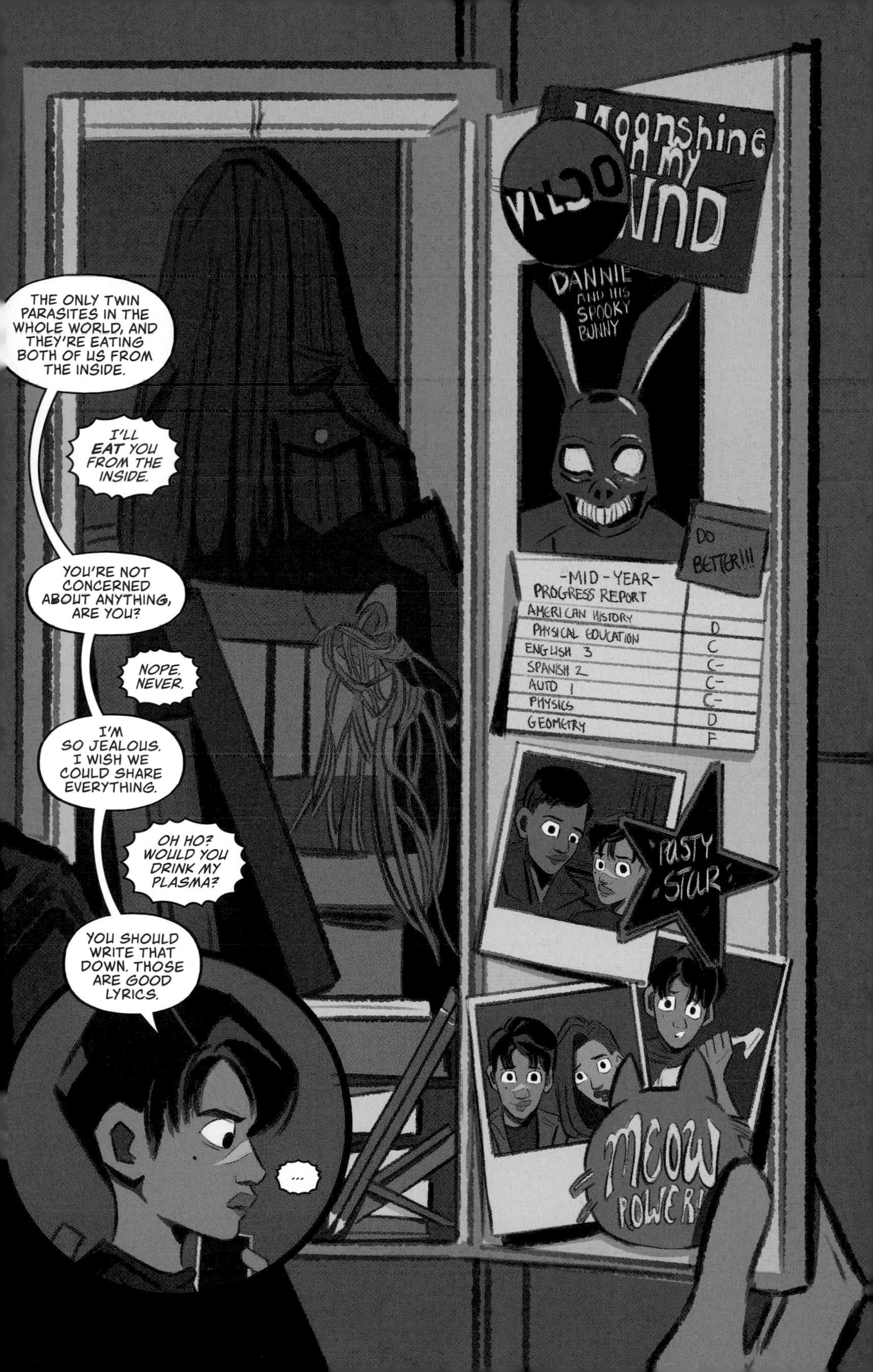
THE ONLY TWIN PARASITES IN THE WHOLE WORLD, AND THEY'RE EATING BOTH OF US FROM THE INSIDE.
I'LL EAT YOU FROM THE INSIDE.
YOU'RE NOT CONCERNED ABOUT ANYTHING, ARE YOU?
NOPE. NEVER.
I'M SO JEALOUS. I WISH WE COULD SHARE EVERYTHING.
OH HO? WOULD YOU DRINK MY PLASMA?
YOU SHOULD WRITE THAT DOWN. THOSE ARE GOOD LYRICS.
...
DANNIE AND HIS SPOOKY BUNNY
DO BETTER!!!
-MID-YEAR- PROGRESS REPORT
AMERICAN HISTORY D
PHYSICAL EDUCATION C
ENGLISH 3 C-
SPANISH 2 C-
AUTO 1 C-
PHYSICS D
GEOMETRY F
PASTY STAR
MEOW POWER!

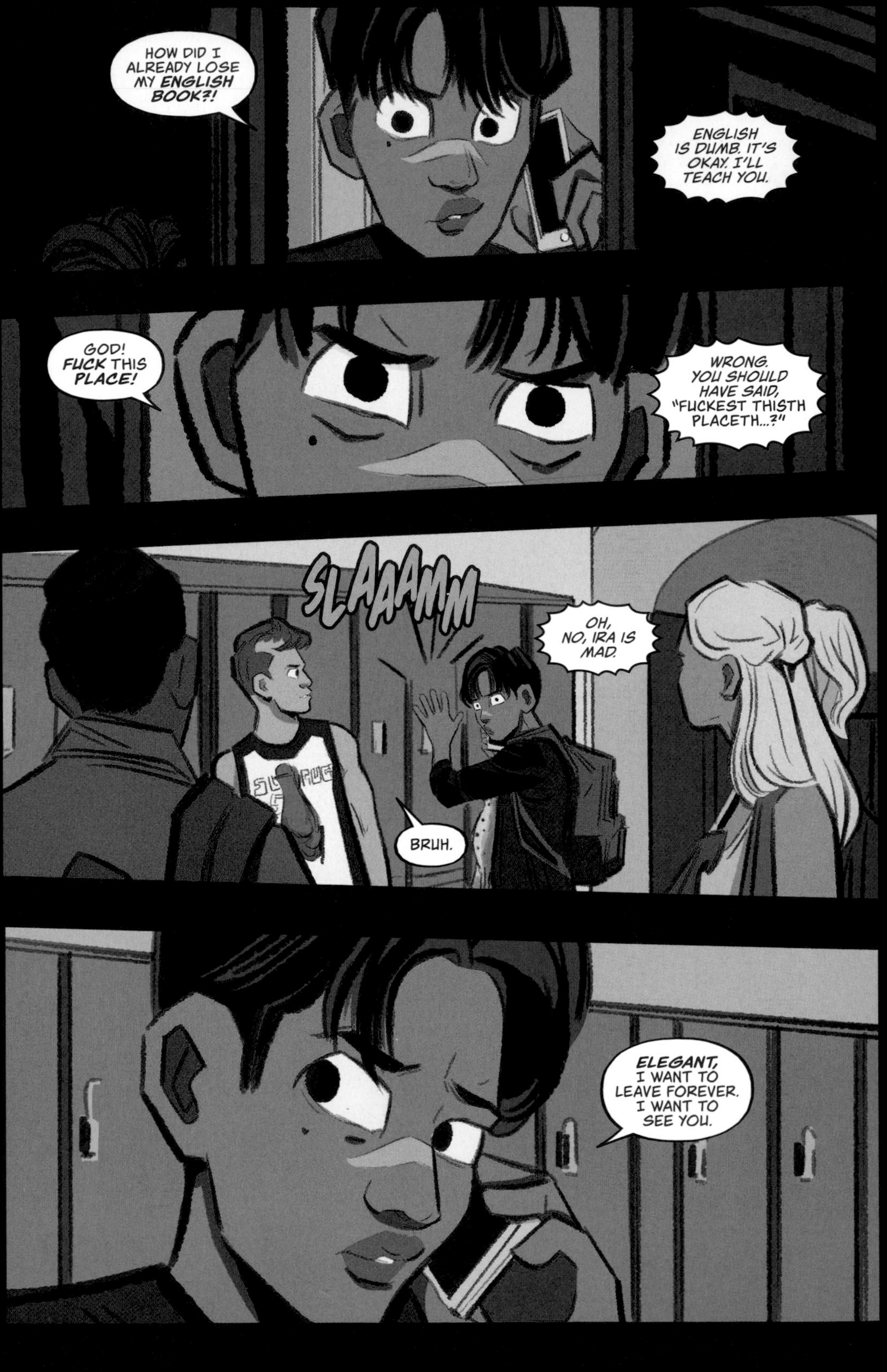
HOW DID I ALREADY LOSE MY ENGLISH BOOK?!
ENGLISH IS DUMB. IT'S OKAY. I'LL TEACH YOU.
GOD! FUCK THIS PLACE!
WRONG. YOU SHOULD HAVE SAID, "FUCKEST THISTH PLACETH...?"
SLAAAMM
OH, NO, IRA IS MAD.
BRUH.
ELEGANT, I WANT TO LEAVE FOREVER. I WANT TO SEE YOU.

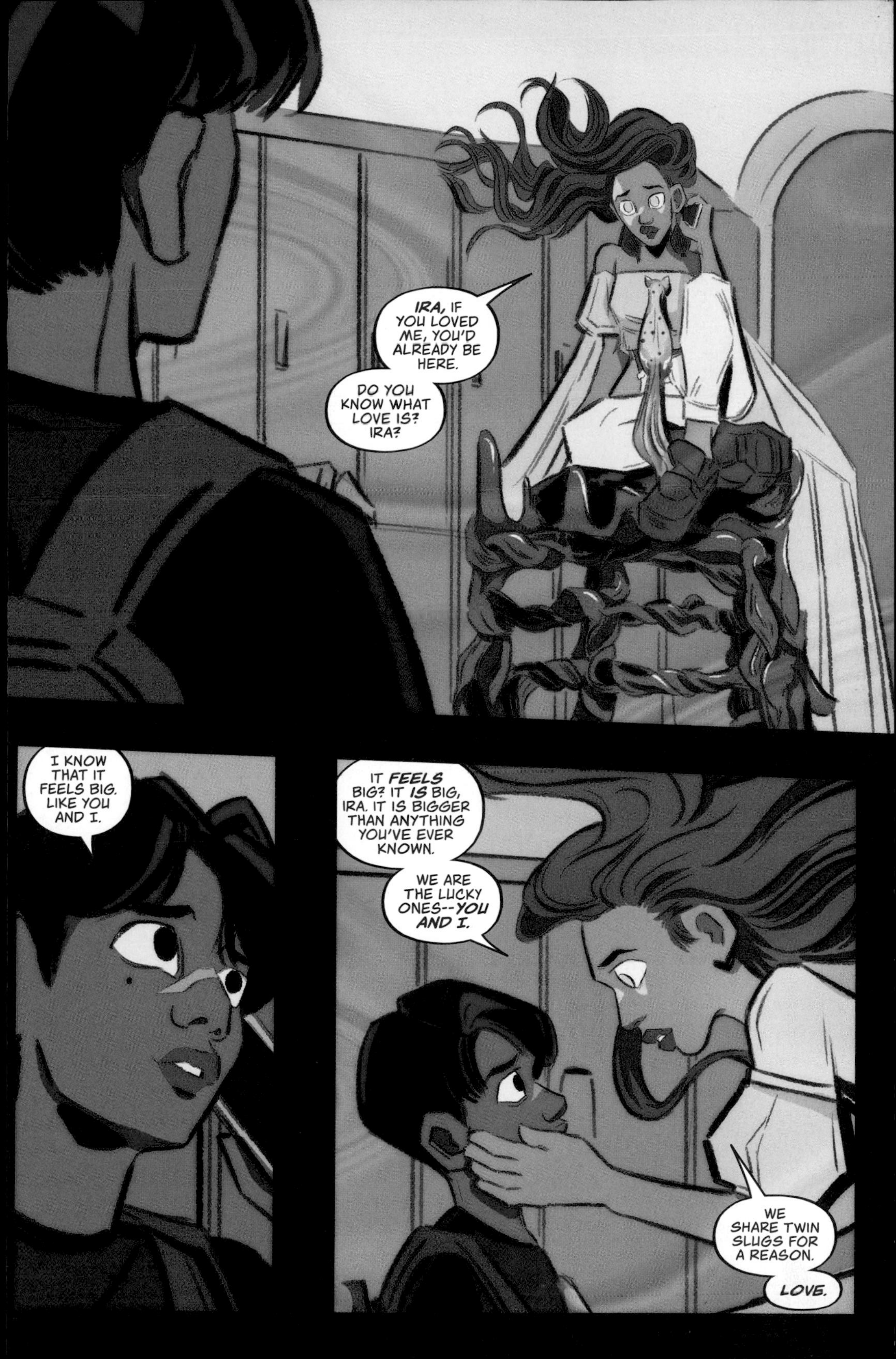
IRA, IF YOU LOVED ME, YOU'D ALREADY BE HERE.
DO YOU KNOW WHAT LOVE IS? IRA?
I KNOW THAT IT FEELS BIG. LIKE YOU AND I.
IT FEELS BIG? IT IS BIG, IRA. IT IS BIGGER THAN ANYTHING YOU'VE EVER KNOWN.
WE ARE THE LUCKY ONES--YOU AND I.
WE SHARE TWIN SLUGS FOR A REASON.
LOVE.

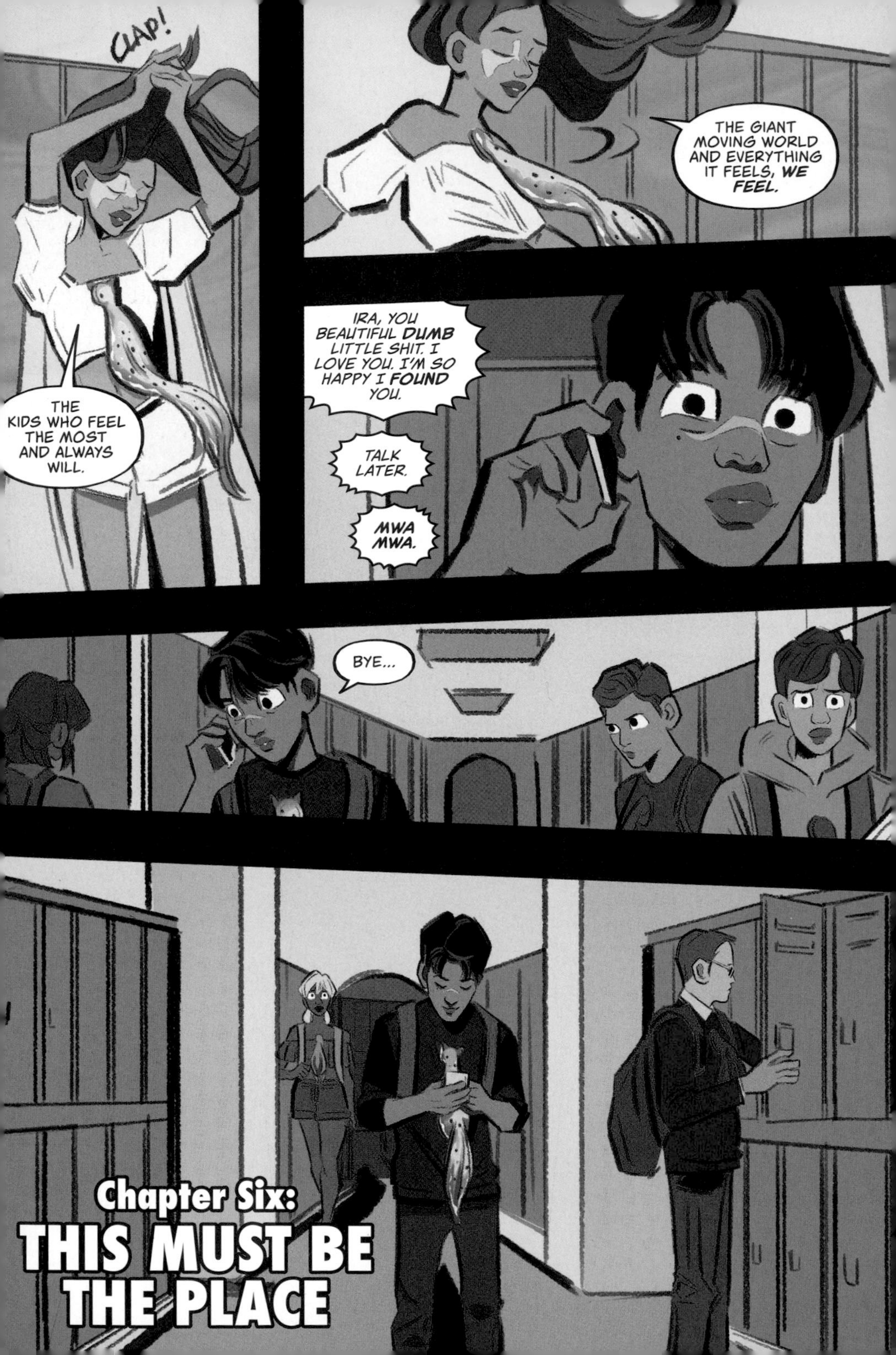
CLAP!
THE GIANT MOVING WORLD AND EVERYTHING IT FEELS, WE FEEL.
THE KIDS WHO FEEL THE MOST AND ALWAYS WILL.
IRA, YOU BEAUTIFUL DUMB LITTLE SHIT. I LOVE YOU. I'M SO HAPPY I FOUND YOU.
TALK LATER.
MWA MWA.
BYE...
Chapter Six:
THIS MUST BE THE PLACE

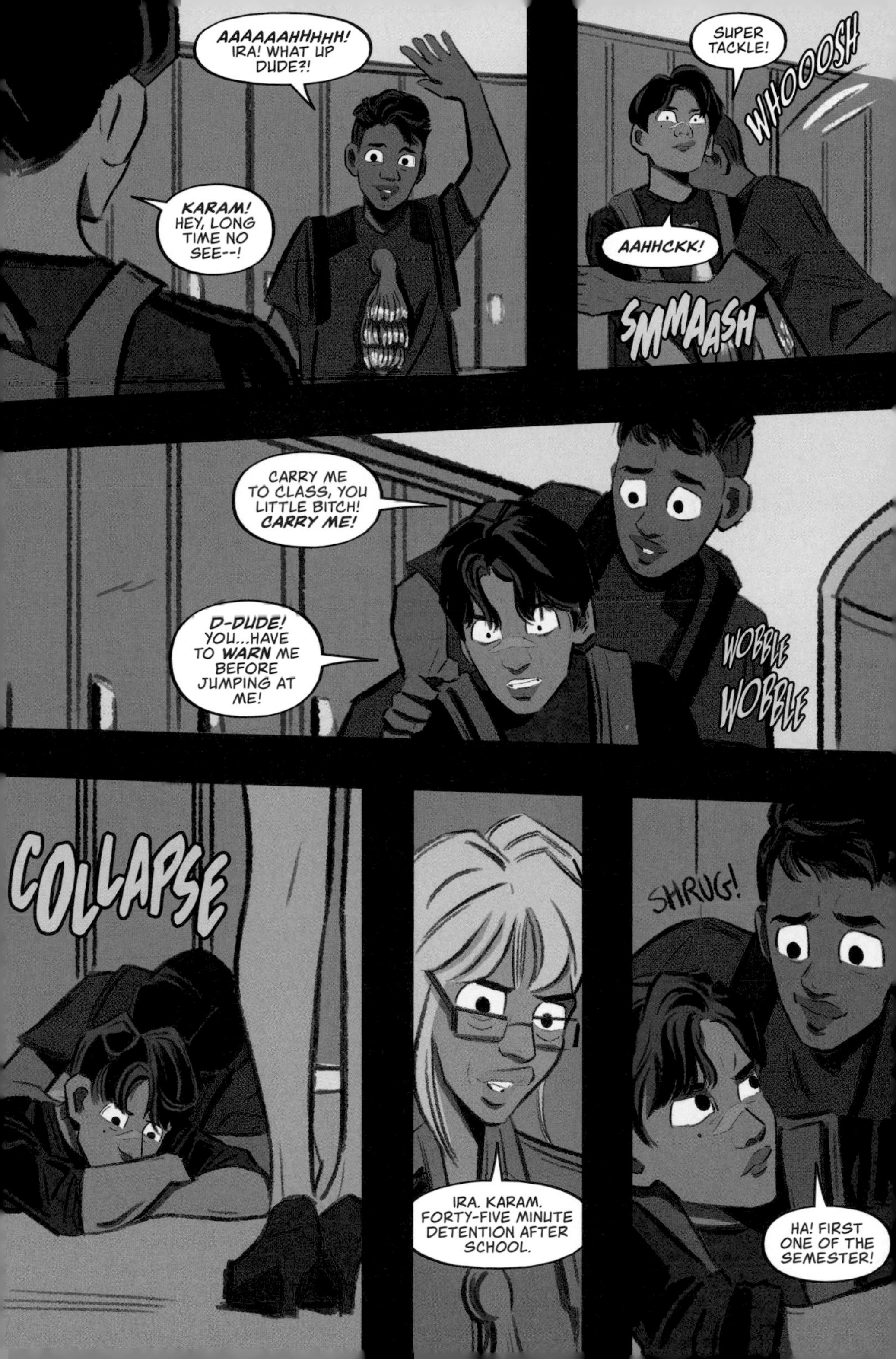
AAAAAAHHHHH! IRA! WHAT UP DUDE?!
KARAM! HEY, LONG TIME NO SEE--!
SUPER TACKLE!
WHOOOSH
AAHHCKK!
SMMAASH
CARRY ME TO CLASS, YOU LITTLE BITCH! CARRY ME!
D-DUDE! YOU...HAVE TO WARN ME BEFORE JUMPING AT ME!
WOBBLE WOBBLE
COLLAPSE
IRA. KARAM. FORTY-FIVE MINUTE DETENTION AFTER SCHOOL.
SHRUG!
HA! FIRST ONE OF THE SEMESTER!

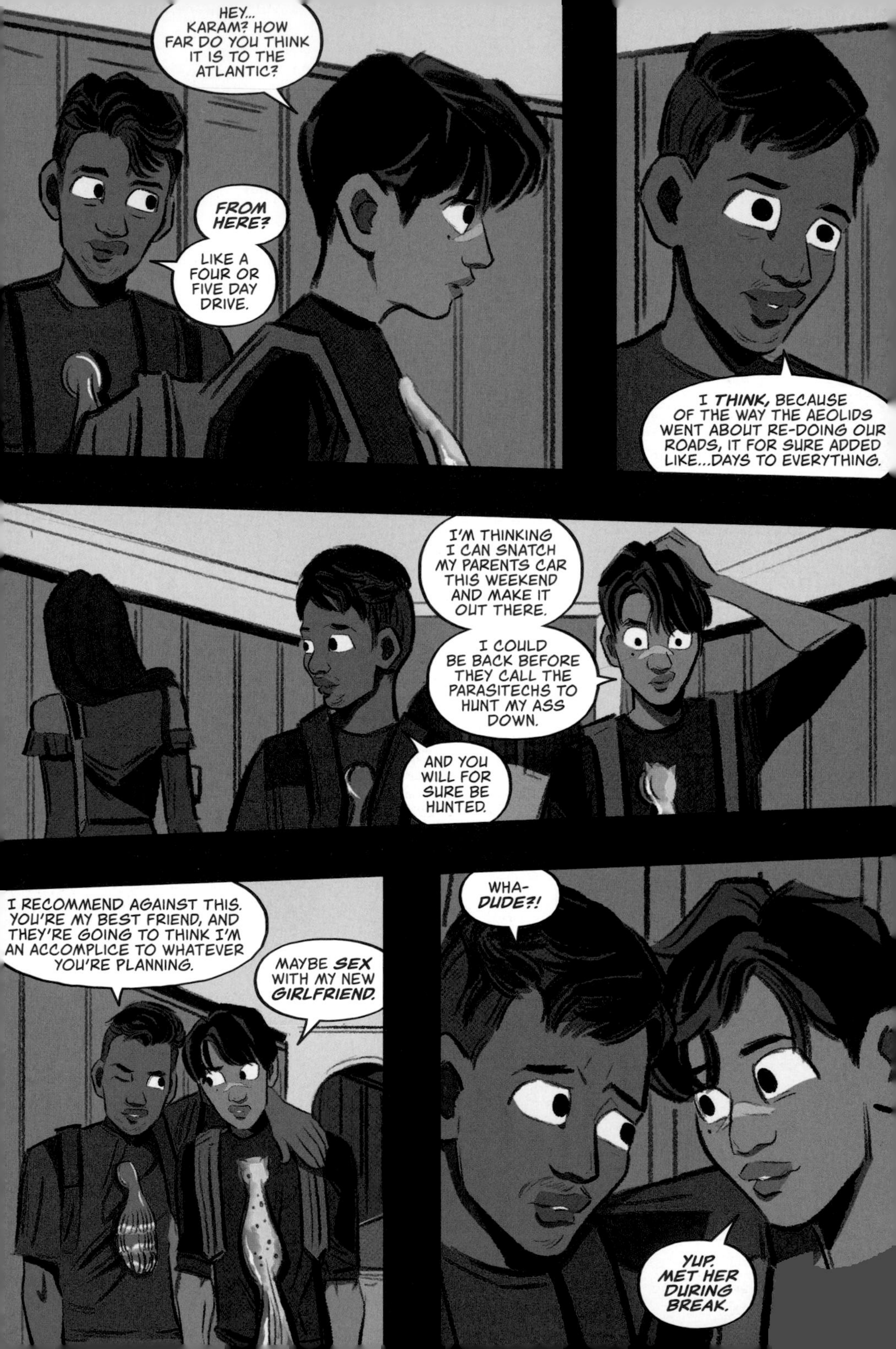
HEY... KARAM? HOW FAR DO YOU THINK IT IS TO THE ATLANTIC?
FROM HERE?
LIKE A FOUR OR FIVE DAY DRIVE.
I THINK, BECAUSE OF THE WAY THE AEOLIDS WENT ABOUT RE-DOING OUR ROADS, IT FOR SURE ADDED LIKE...DAYS TO EVERYTHING.
I'M THINKING I CAN SNATCH MY PARENTS CAR THIS WEEKEND AND MAKE IT OUT THERE.
I COULD BE BACK BEFORE THEY CALL THE PARASITECHS TO HUNT MY ASS DOWN.
AND YOU WILL FOR SURE BE HUNTED.
I RECOMMEND AGAINST THIS. YOU'RE MY BEST FRIEND, AND THEY'RE GOING TO THINK I'M AN ACCOMPLICE TO WHATEVER YOU'RE PLANNING.
MAYBE SEX WITH MY NEW GIRLFRIEND.
WHA- DUDE?!
YUP. MET HER DURING BREAK.

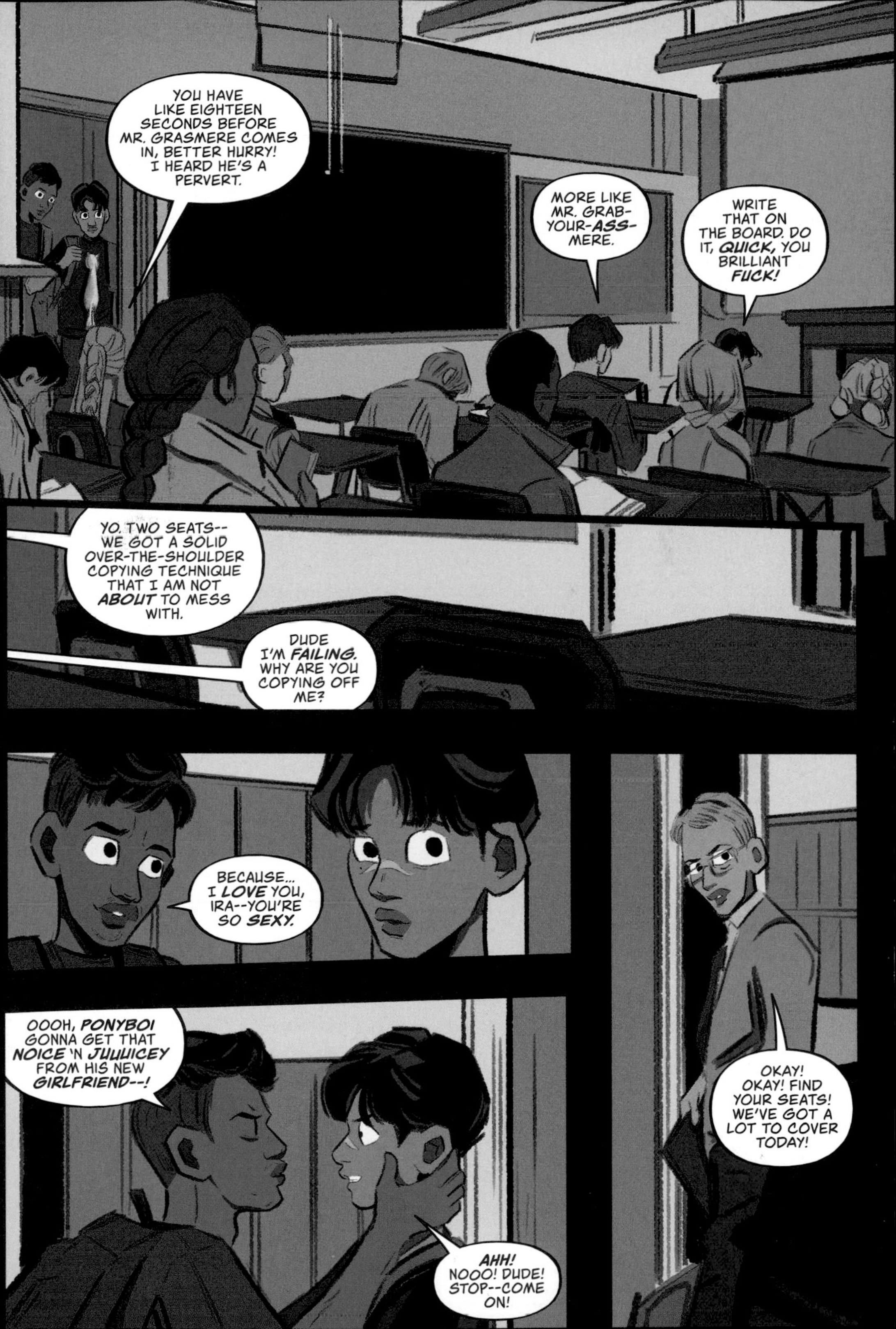
YOU HAVE LIKE EIGHTEEN SECONDS BEFORE MR. GRASMERE COMES IN, BETTER HURRY! I HEARD HE'S A PERVERT.
MORE LIKE MR. GRAB-YOUR-ASS-MERE.
WRITE THAT ON THE BOARD. DO IT, QUICK, YOU BRILLIANT FUCK!
YO. TWO SEATS--WE GOT A SOLID OVER-THE-SHOULDER COPYING TECHNIQUE THAT I AM NOT ABOUT TO MESS WITH.
DUDE I'M FAILING. WHY ARE YOU COPYING OFF ME?
BECAUSE... I LOVE YOU, IRA--YOU'RE SO SEXY.
OOOH, PONYBOI GONNA GET THAT NOICE 'N JUUUICEY FROM HIS NEW GIRLFRIEND--!
AHH! NOOO! DUDE! STOP--COME ON!
OKAY! OKAY! FIND YOUR SEATS! WE'VE GOT A LOT TO COVER TODAY!

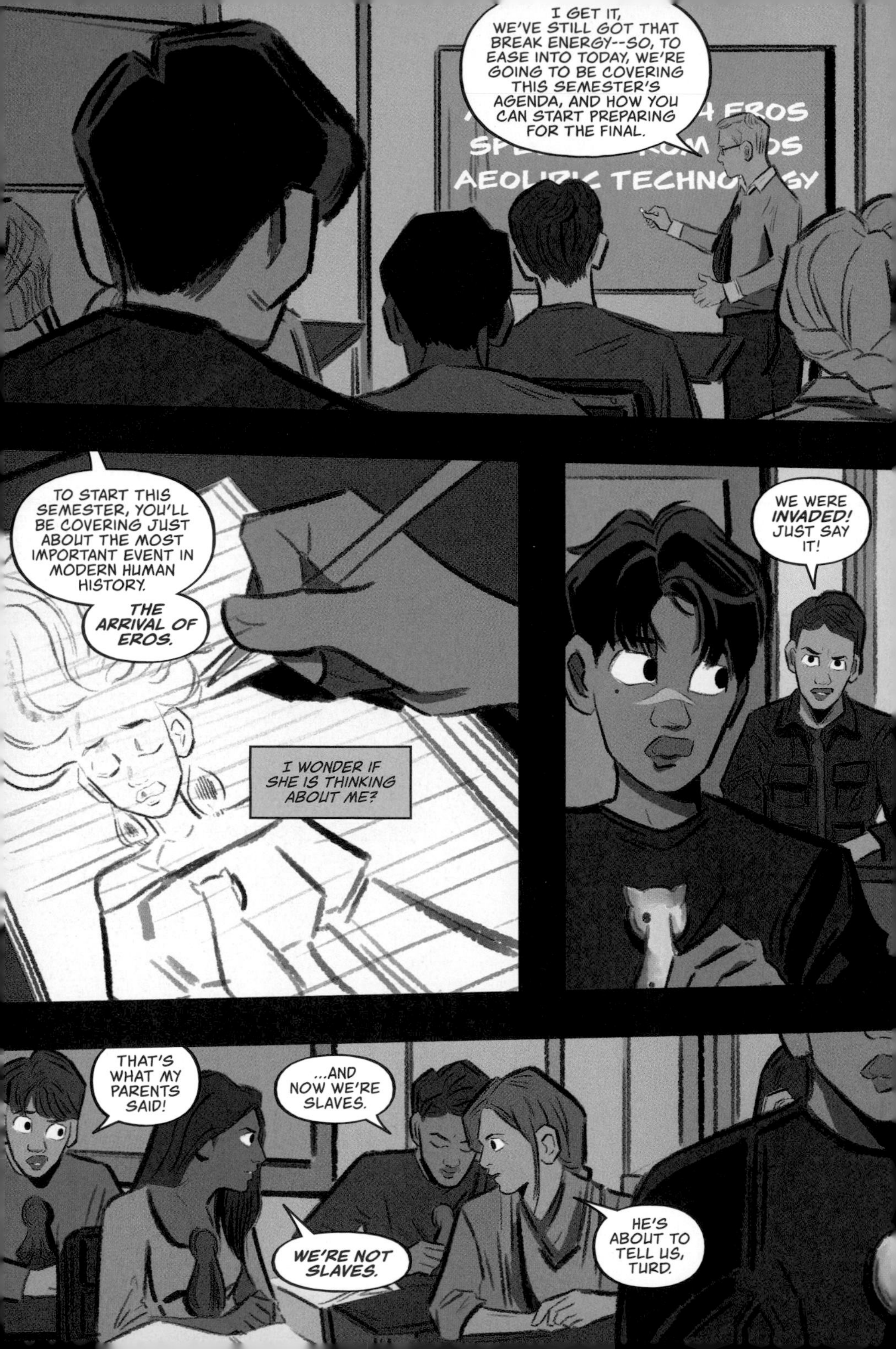
I GET IT, WE'VE STILL GOT THAT BREAK ENERGY--SO, TO EASE INTO TODAY, WE'RE GOING TO BE COVERING THIS SEMESTER'S AGENDA, AND HOW YOU CAN START PREPARING FOR THE FINAL.
TO START THIS SEMESTER, YOU'LL BE COVERING JUST ABOUT THE MOST IMPORTANT EVENT IN MODERN HUMAN HISTORY.
THE ARRIVAL OF EROS.
I WONDER IF SHE IS THINKING ABOUT ME?
WE WERE INVADED! JUST SAY IT!
THAT'S WHAT MY PARENTS SAID!
...AND NOW WE'RE SLAVES.
WE'RE NOT SLAVES.
HE'S ABOUT TO TELL US, TURD.

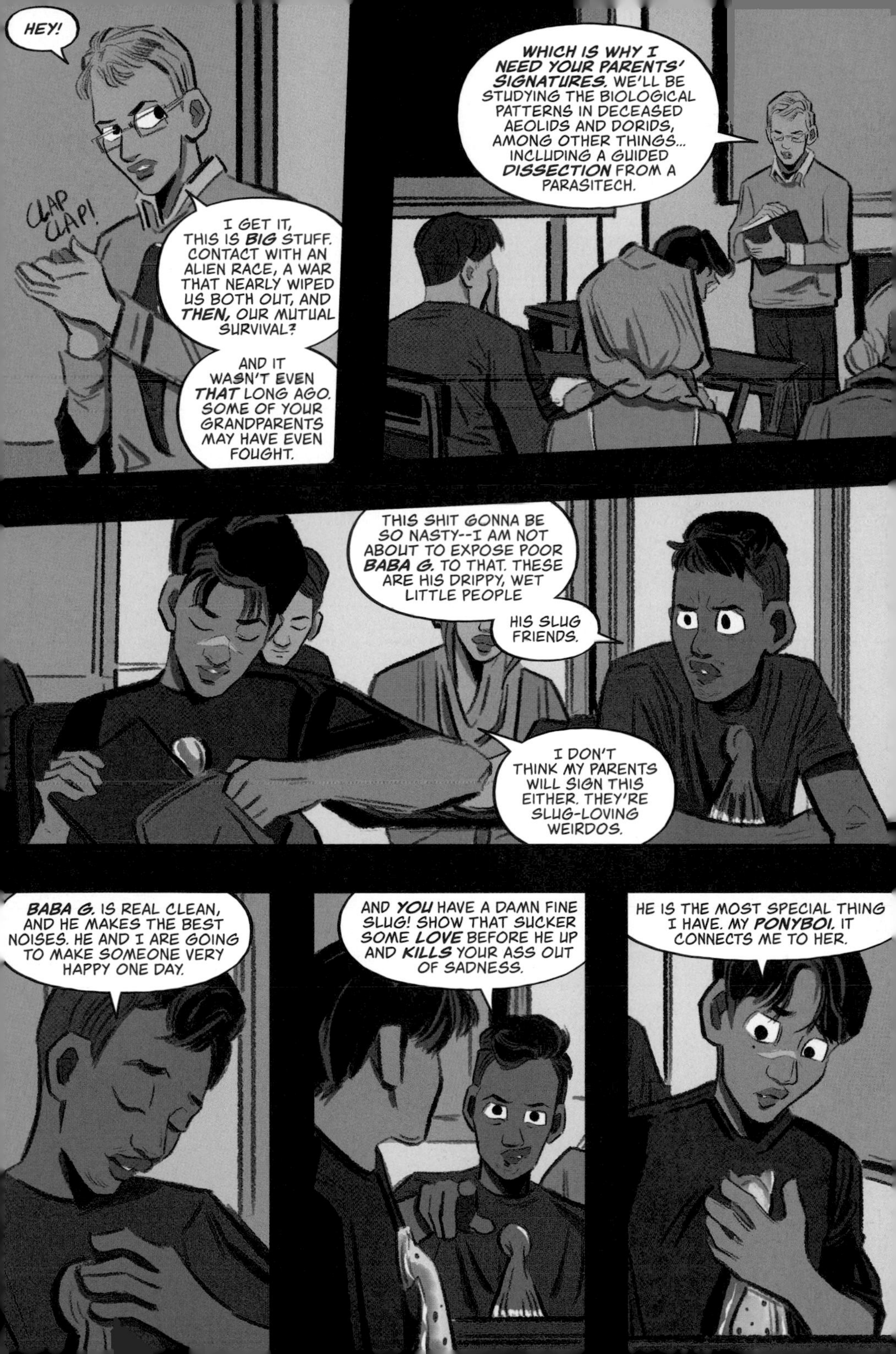
HEY!
CLAP CLAP!
I GET IT, THIS IS BIG STUFF. CONTACT WITH AN ALIEN RACE, A WAR THAT NEARLY WIPED US BOTH OUT, AND THEN, OUR MUTUAL SURVIVAL?
AND IT WASN'T EVEN THAT LONG AGO. SOME OF YOUR GRANDPARENTS MAY HAVE EVEN FOUGHT.
WHICH IS WHY I NEED YOUR PARENTS' SIGNATURES. WE'LL BE STUDYING THE BIOLOGICAL PATTERNS IN DECEASED AEOLIDS AND DORIDS, AMONG OTHER THINGS... INCLUDING A GUIDED DISSECTION FROM A PARASITECH.
THIS SHIT GONNA BE SO NASTY--I AM NOT ABOUT TO EXPOSE POOR BABA G. TO THAT. THESE ARE HIS DRIPPY, WET LITTLE PEOPLE
HIS SLUG FRIENDS.
I DON'T THINK MY PARENTS WILL SIGN THIS EITHER. THEY'RE SLUG-LOVING WEIRDOS.
BABA G. IS REAL CLEAN, AND HE MAKES THE BEST NOISES. HE AND I ARE GOING TO MAKE SOMEONE VERY HAPPY ONE DAY.
AND YOU HAVE A DAMN FINE SLUG! SHOW THAT SUCKER SOME LOVE BEFORE HE UP AND KILLS YOUR ASS OUT OF SADNESS.
HE IS THE MOST SPECIAL THING I HAVE. MY PONYBOI. IT CONNECTS ME TO HER.

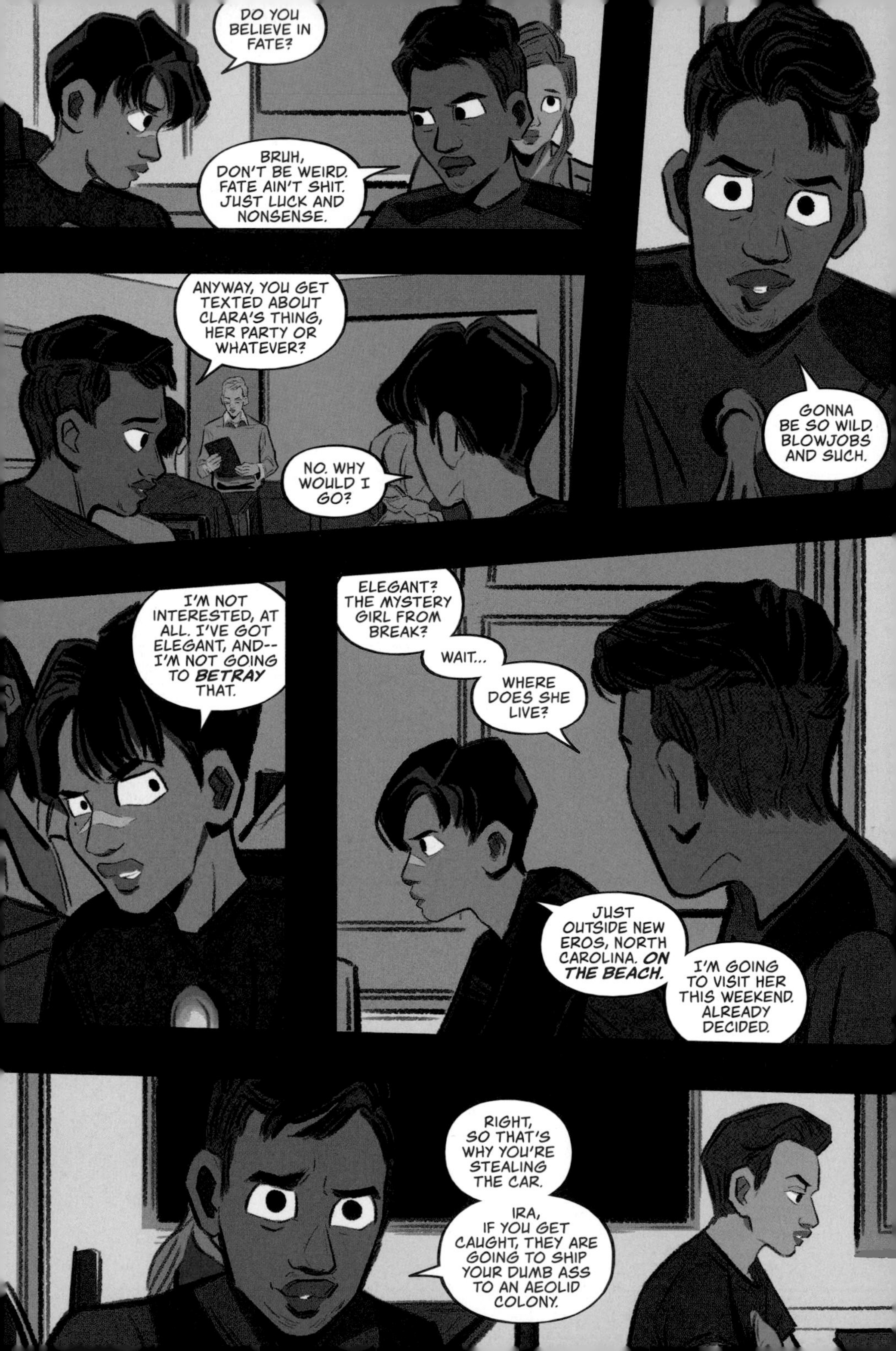
DO YOU BELIEVE IN FATE?
BRUH, DON'T BE WEIRD. FATE AIN'T SHIT. JUST LUCK AND NONSENSE.
ANYWAY, YOU GET TEXTED ABOUT CLARA'S THING, HER PARTY OR WHATEVER?
NO. WHY WOULD I GO?
GONNA BE SO WILD. BLOWJOBS AND SUCH.
I'M NOT INTERESTED, AT ALL. I'VE GOT ELEGANT, AND-- I'M NOT GOING TO ***BETRAY*** THAT.
ELEGANT? THE MYSTERY GIRL FROM BREAK?
WAIT...
WHERE DOES SHE LIVE?
JUST OUTSIDE NEW EROS, NORTH CAROLINA. ***ON THE BEACH.***
I'M GOING TO VISIT HER THIS WEEKEND. ALREADY DECIDED.
RIGHT, SO THAT'S WHY YOU'RE STEALING THE CAR.
IRA, IF YOU GET CAUGHT, THEY ARE GOING TO SHIP YOUR DUMB ASS TO AN AEOLID COLONY.

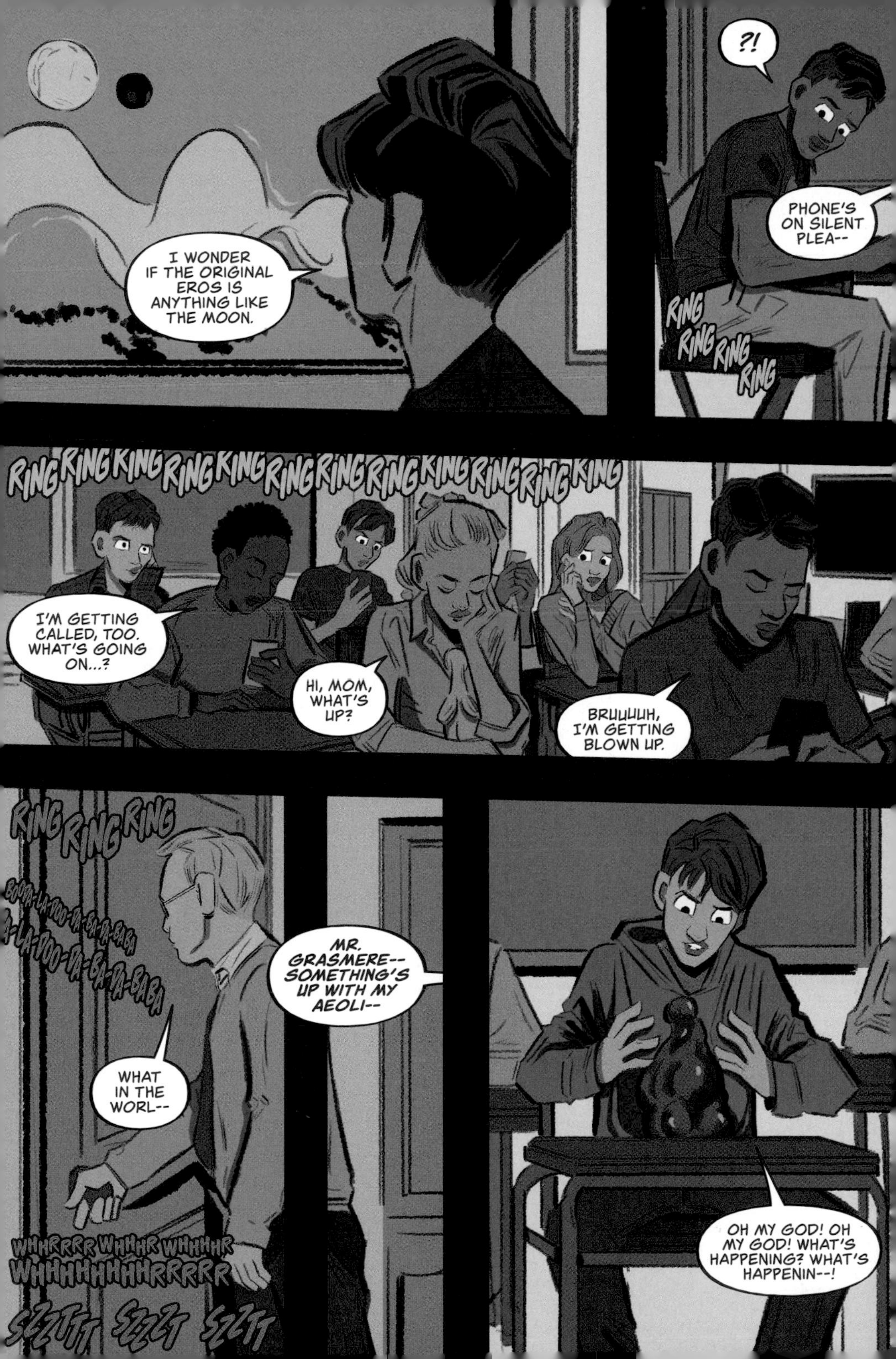
I WONDER IF THE ORIGINAL EROS IS ANYTHING LIKE THE MOON.
?!
PHONE'S ON SILENT PLEA--
RING RING RING RING
RING RING RING RING RING RING RING RING RING RING RING RING
I'M GETTING CALLED, TOO. WHAT'S GOING ON...?
HI, MOM, WHAT'S UP?
BRUUUUH, I'M GETTING BLOWN UP.
RING RING RING
BOOTA-LA-DOO-DA-BA-DA-BABA
A-LA-DOO-DA-BA-DA-BABA
WHAT IN THE WORL--
WHHRRRR WHHHR WHHHHR
WHHHHHHHHRRRRR
SZZTTT SZZZT SZZTT
MR. GRASMERE-- SOMETHING'S UP WITH MY AEOLI--
OH MY GOD! OH MY GOD! WHAT'S HAPPENING? WHAT'S HAPPENIN--!

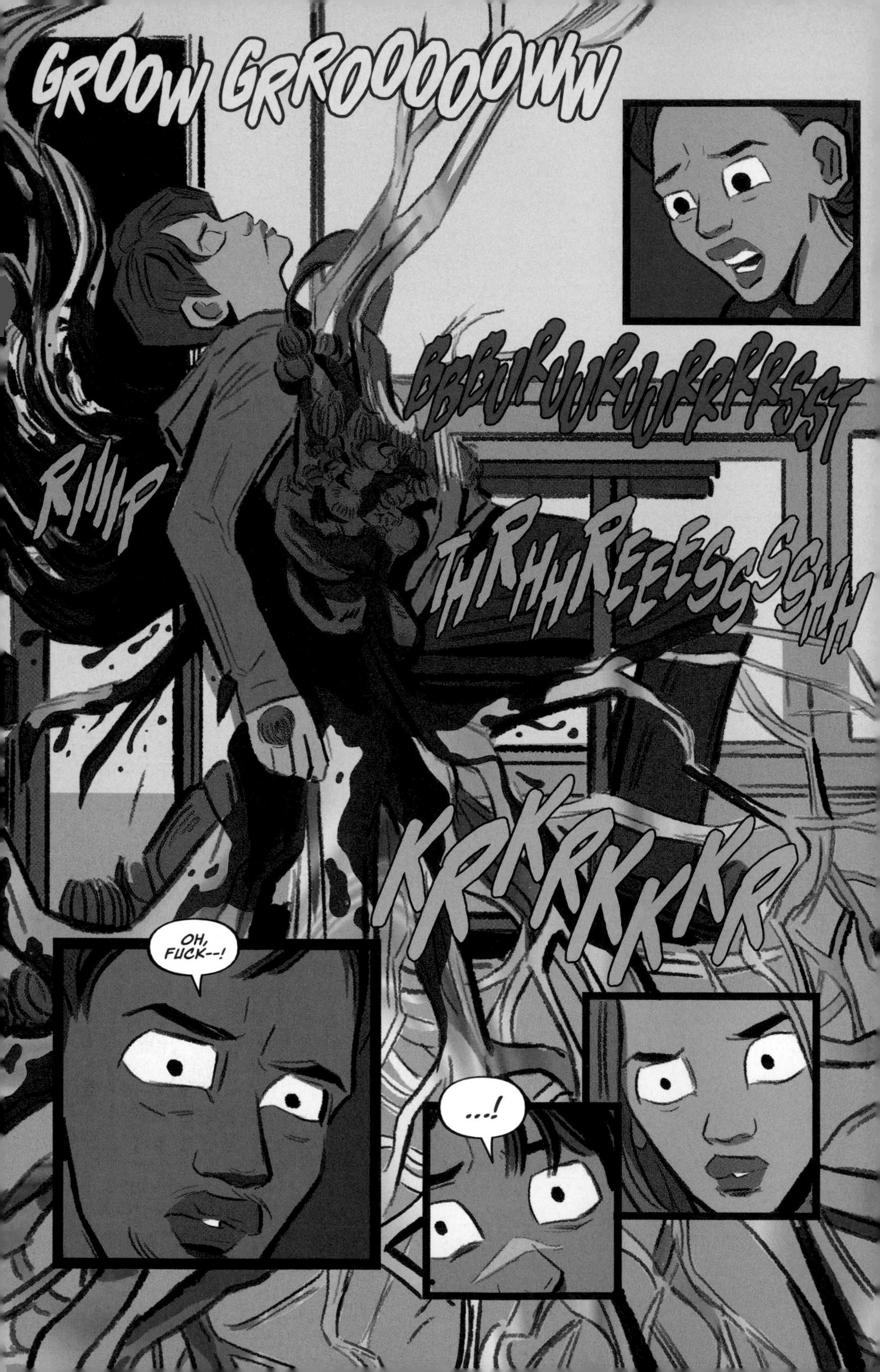
GROOW GRROOOOOOWW
BBBUIRUUIRUUIRRRRSST
RIIIIP
THRHHREEESSSSHH
KRKRKKKR
OH, FUCK--!
...!

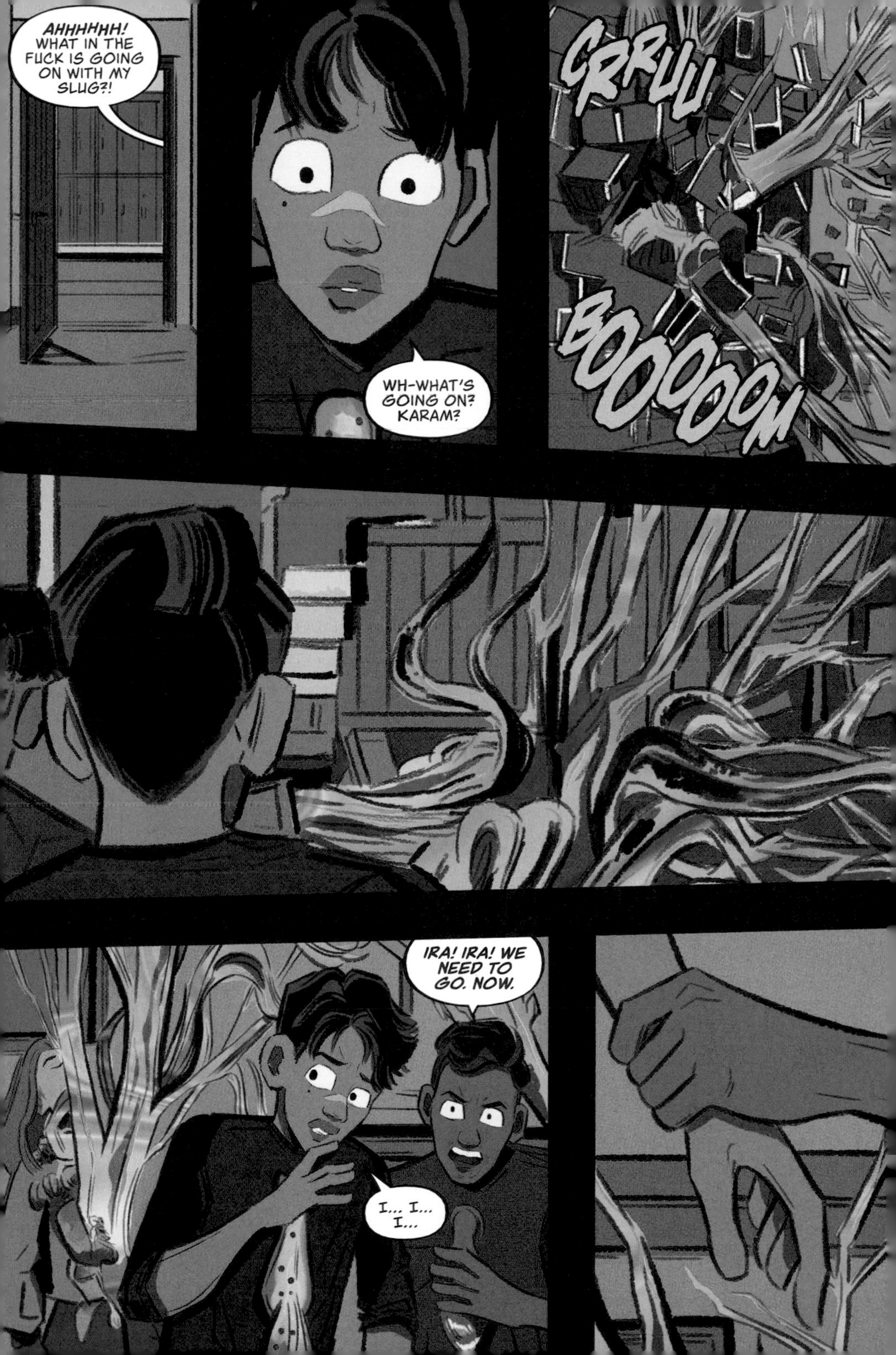
AHHHHHH! WHAT IN THE FUCK IS GOING ON WITH MY SLUG?!
WH-WHAT'S GOING ON? KARAM?
CRRUU
BOOOOOM
IRA! IRA! WE NEED TO GO. NOW.
I... I... I...

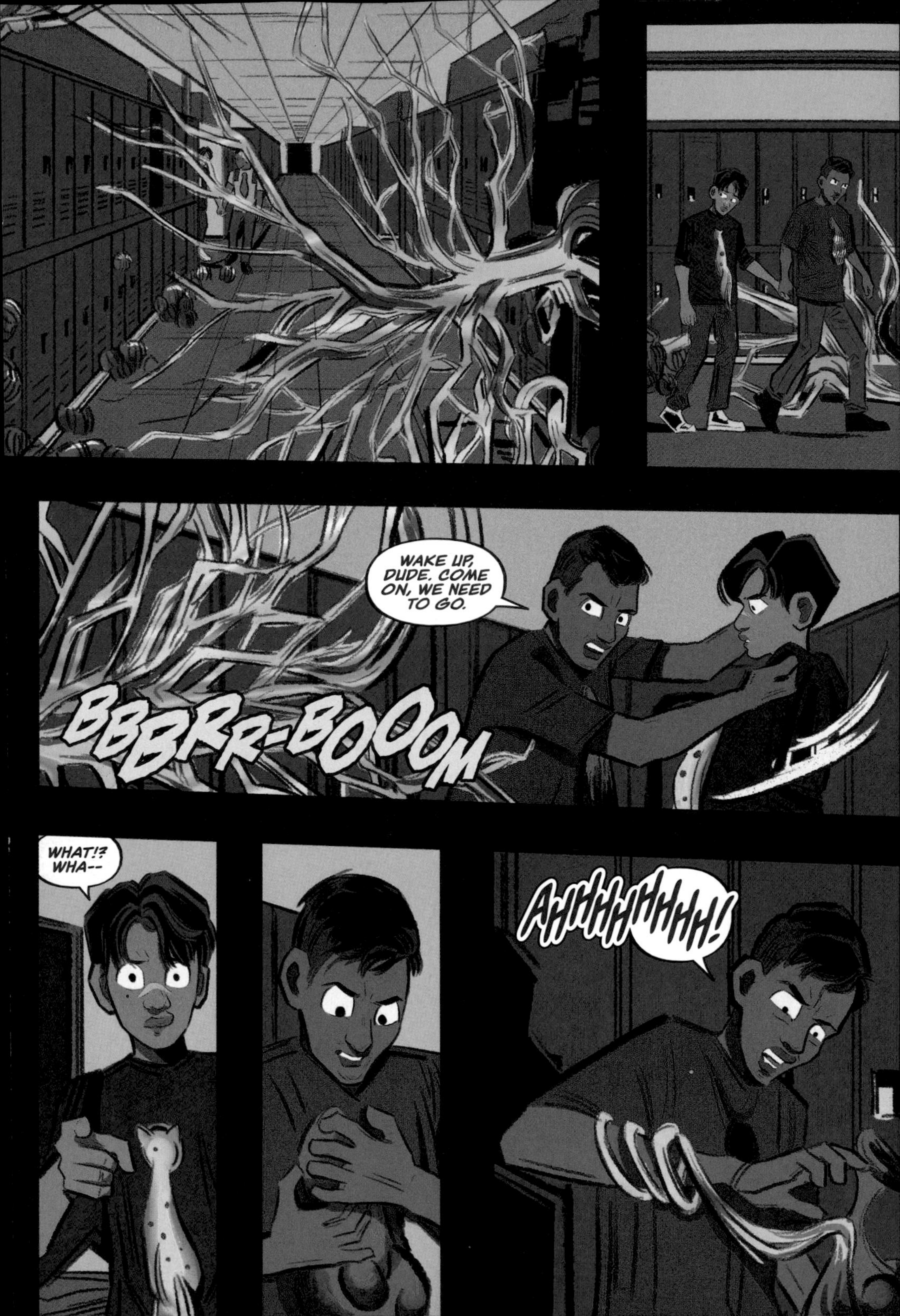
WAKE UP, DUDE. COME ON, WE NEED TO GO.
BBBRR-BOOOOM
WHAT!? WHA--
AHHHHHHHHH!

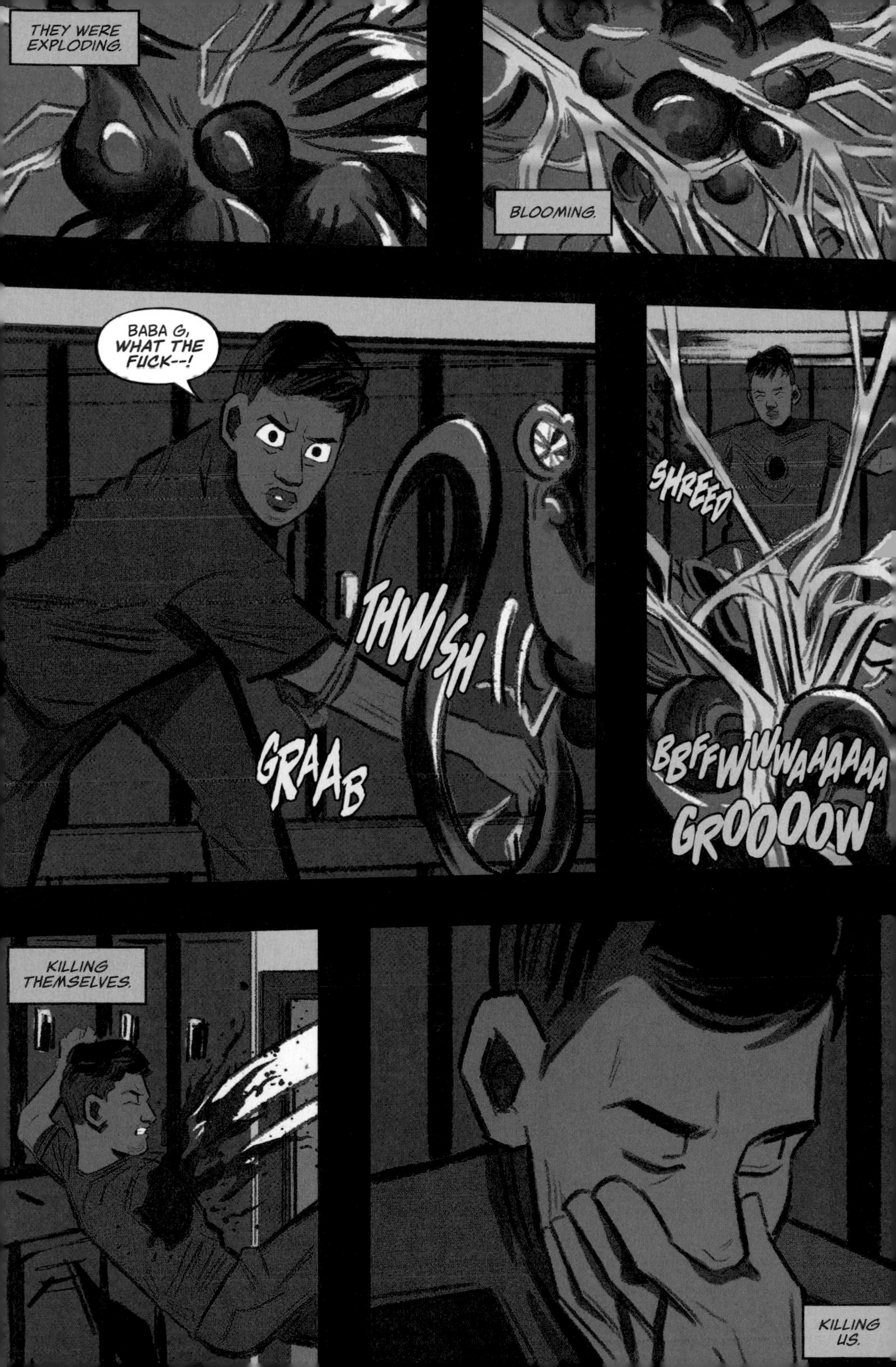
THEY WERE EXPLODING.
BLOOMING.
BABA G, WHAT THE FUCK--!
THWISH
GRAAB
SHREED
BBFFWWWAAAAAA
GROOOOW
KILLING THEMSELVES.
KILLING US.

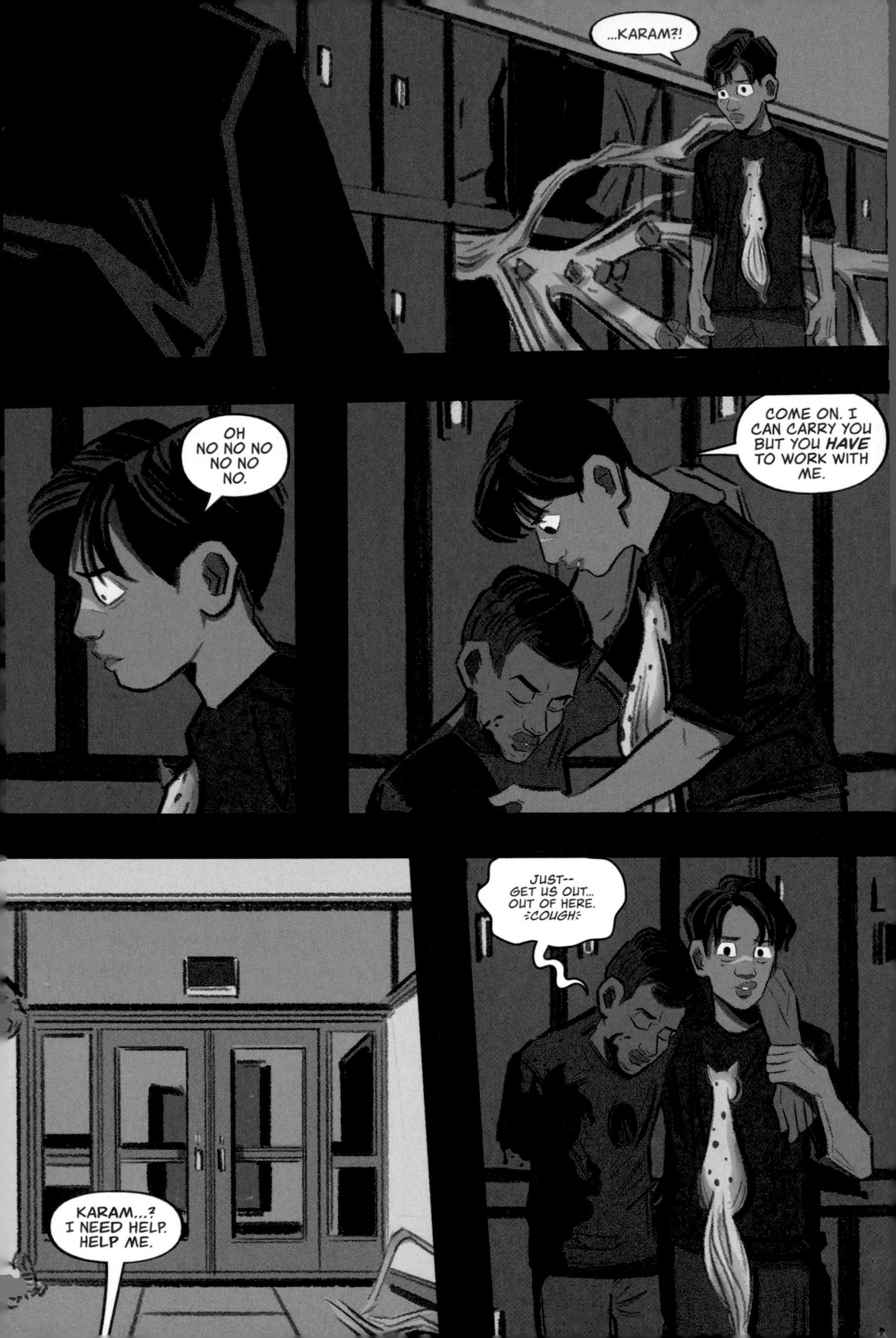
...KARAM?!
OH NO NO NO NO NO NO.
COME ON. I CAN CARRY YOU BUT YOU *HAVE* TO WORK WITH ME.
KARAM...? I NEED HELP. HELP ME.
JUST-- GET US OUT... OUT OF HERE. *COUGH*

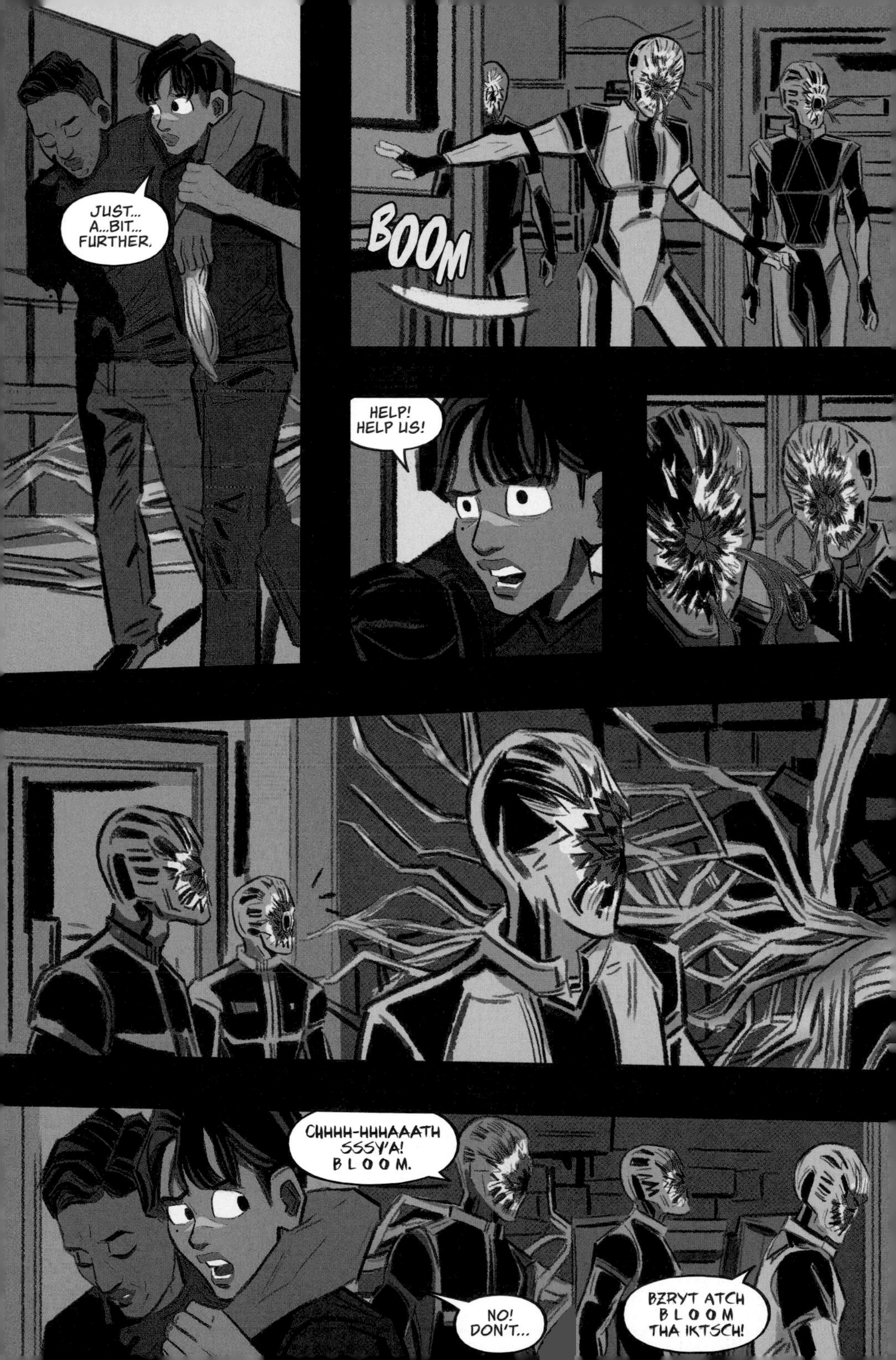
JUST... A...BIT... FURTHER.
BOOM
HELP! HELP US!
CHHHH-HHHAAATH SSSY'A! BLOOM.
NO! DON'T...
BZRYT ATCH BLOOM THA IKTSCH!

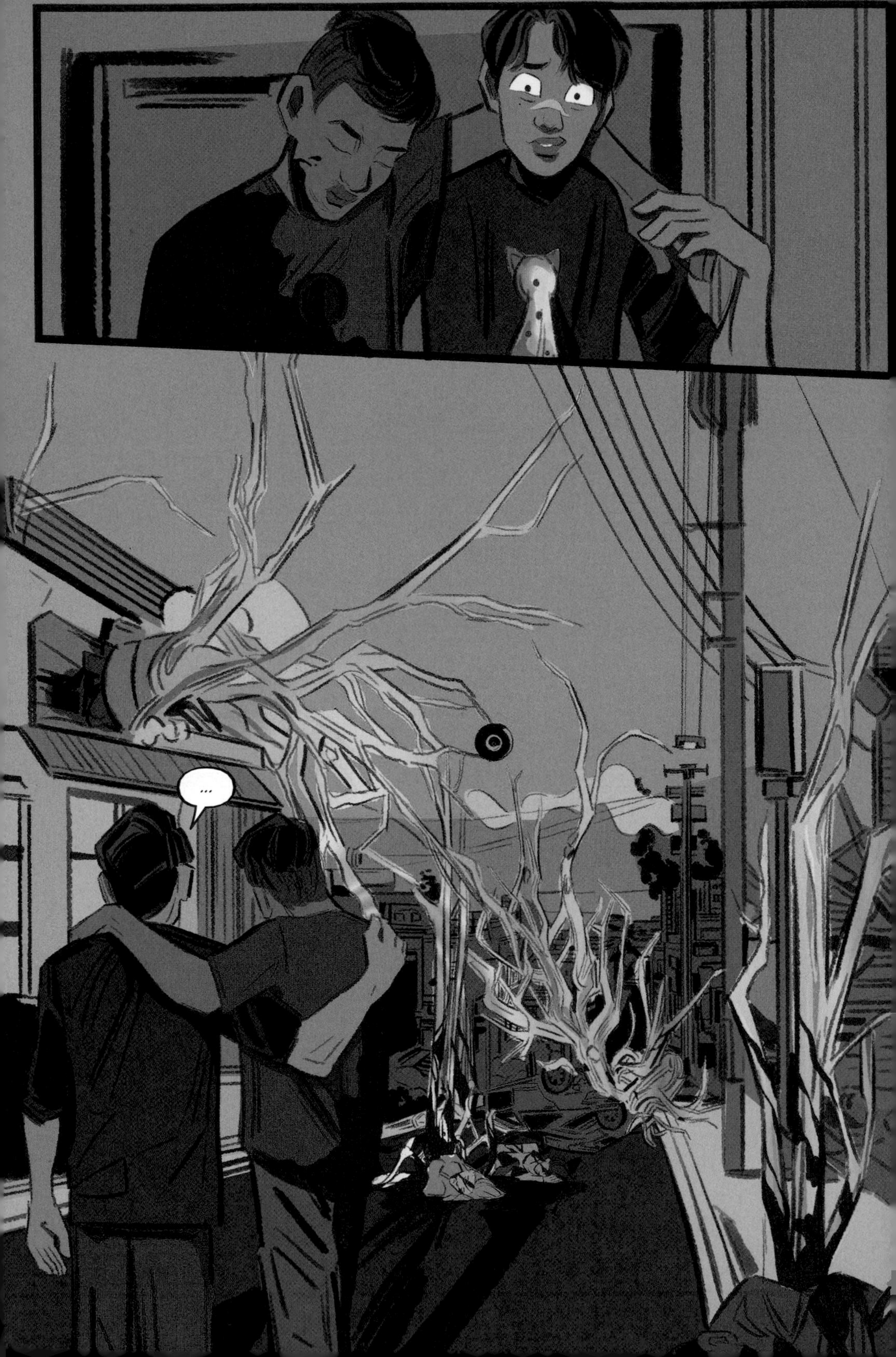
...

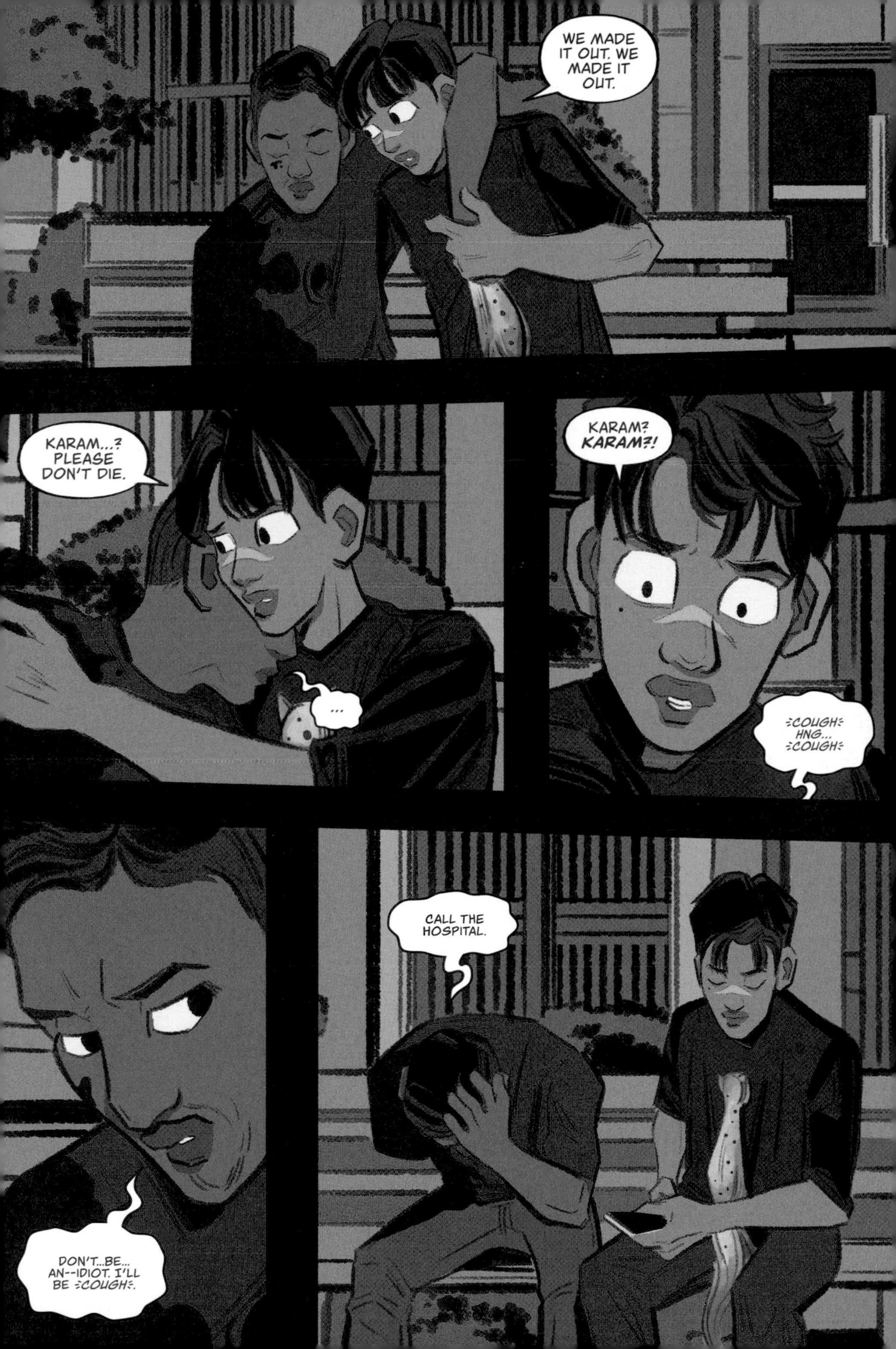
WE MADE IT OUT. WE MADE IT OUT.
KARAM...? PLEASE DON'T DIE.
...
KARAM? **KARAM?!**
COUGH HNG... *COUGH*
DON'T...BE... AN--IDIOT. I'LL BE *COUGH*.
CALL THE HOSPITAL.

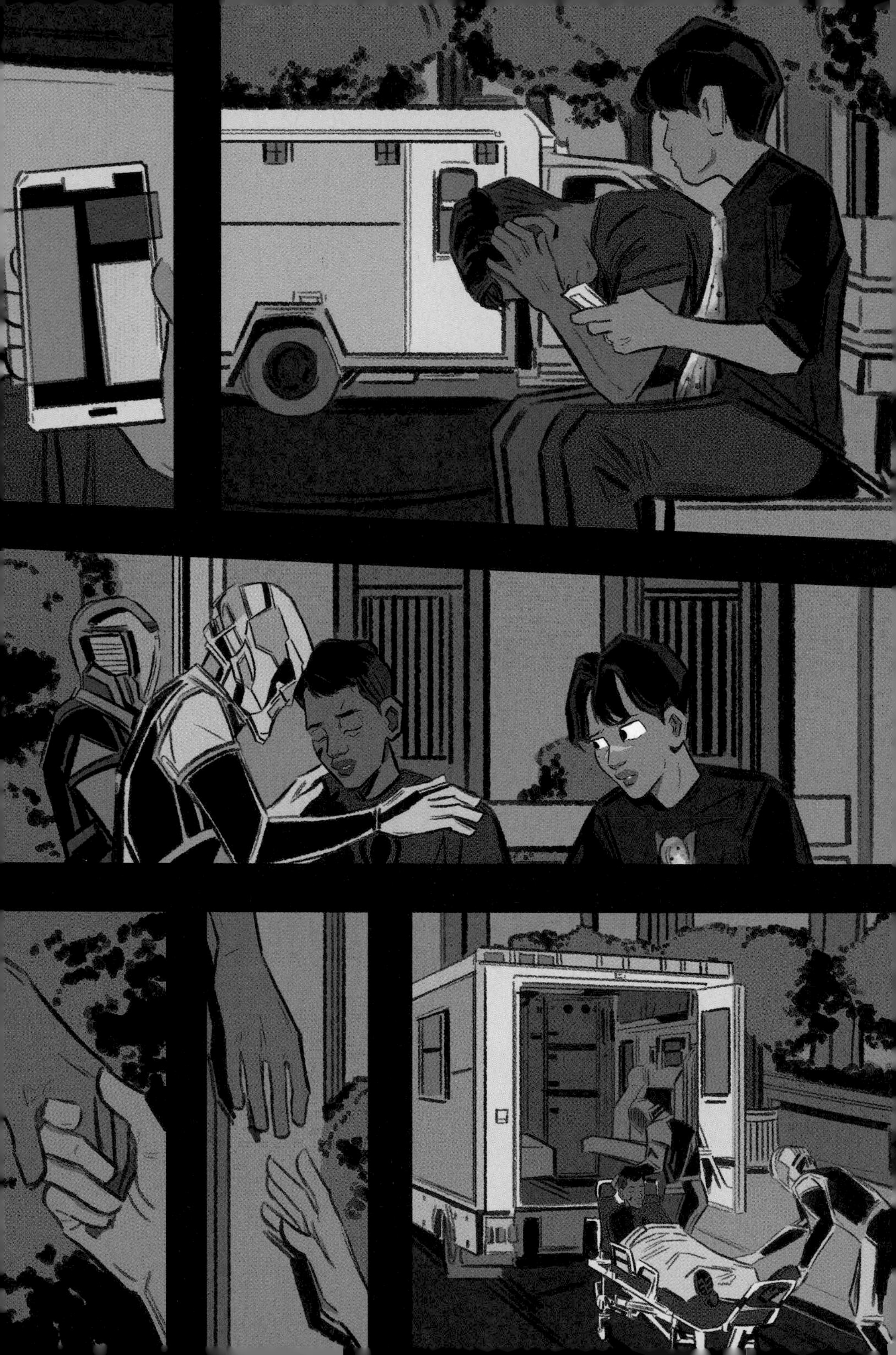

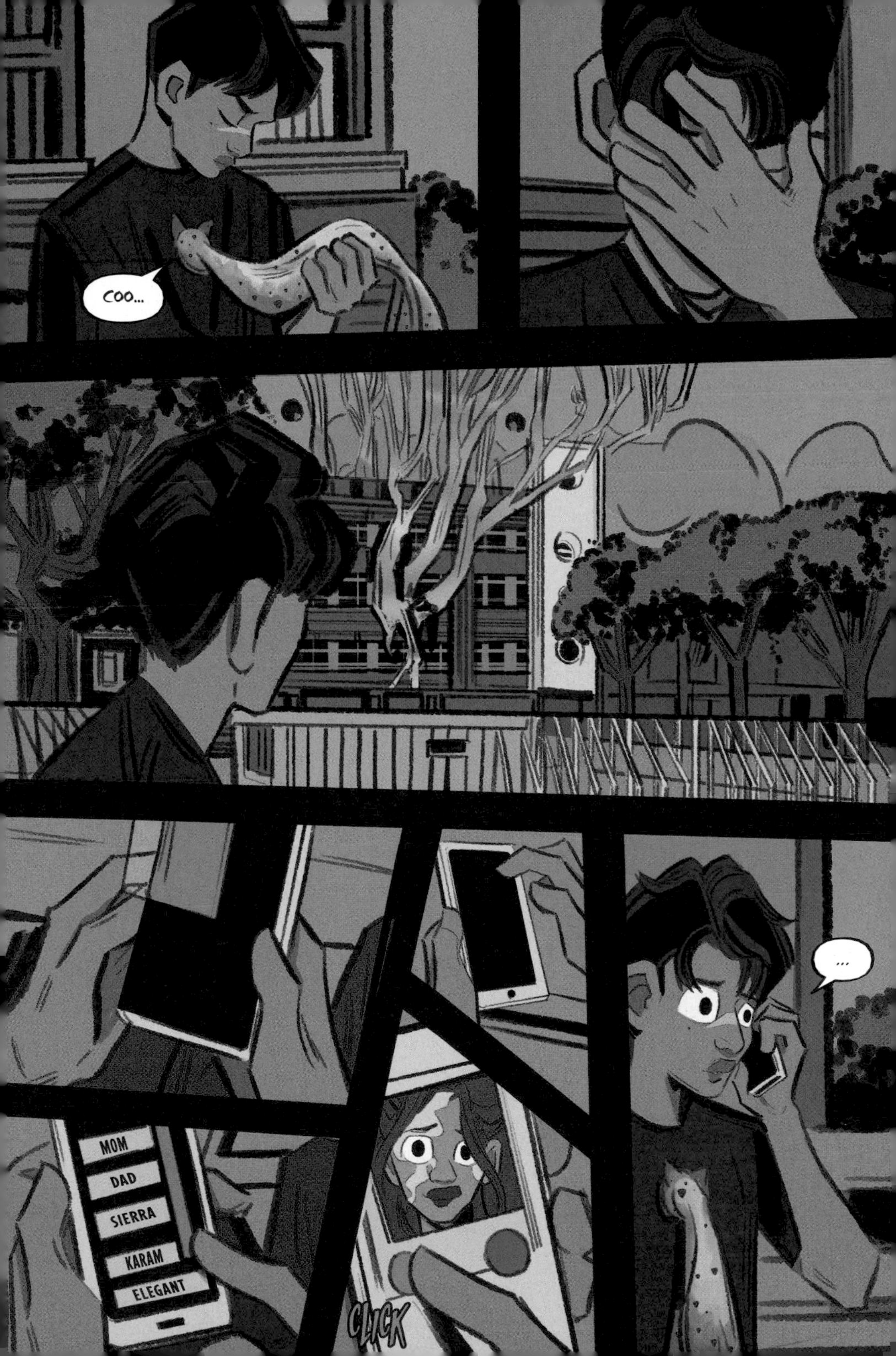
COO...
MOM
DAD
SIERRA
KARAM
ELEGANT
CLICK
...

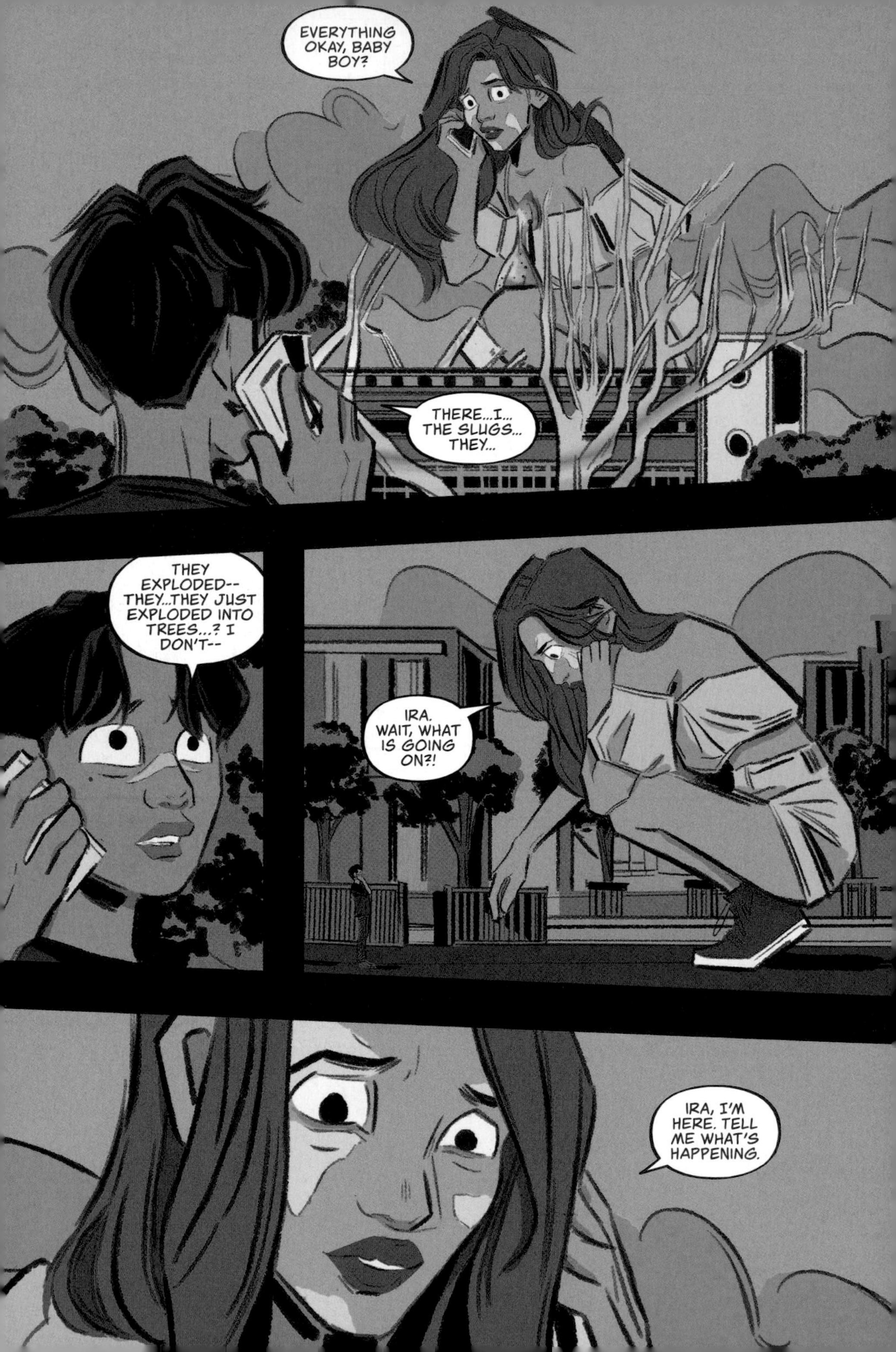
EVERYTHING OKAY, BABY BOY?
THERE...I... THE SLUGS... THEY...
THEY EXPLODED-- THEY...THEY JUST EXPLODED INTO TREES...? I DON'T--
IRA. WAIT, WHAT IS GOING ON?!
IRA, I'M HERE. TELL ME WHAT'S HAPPENING.

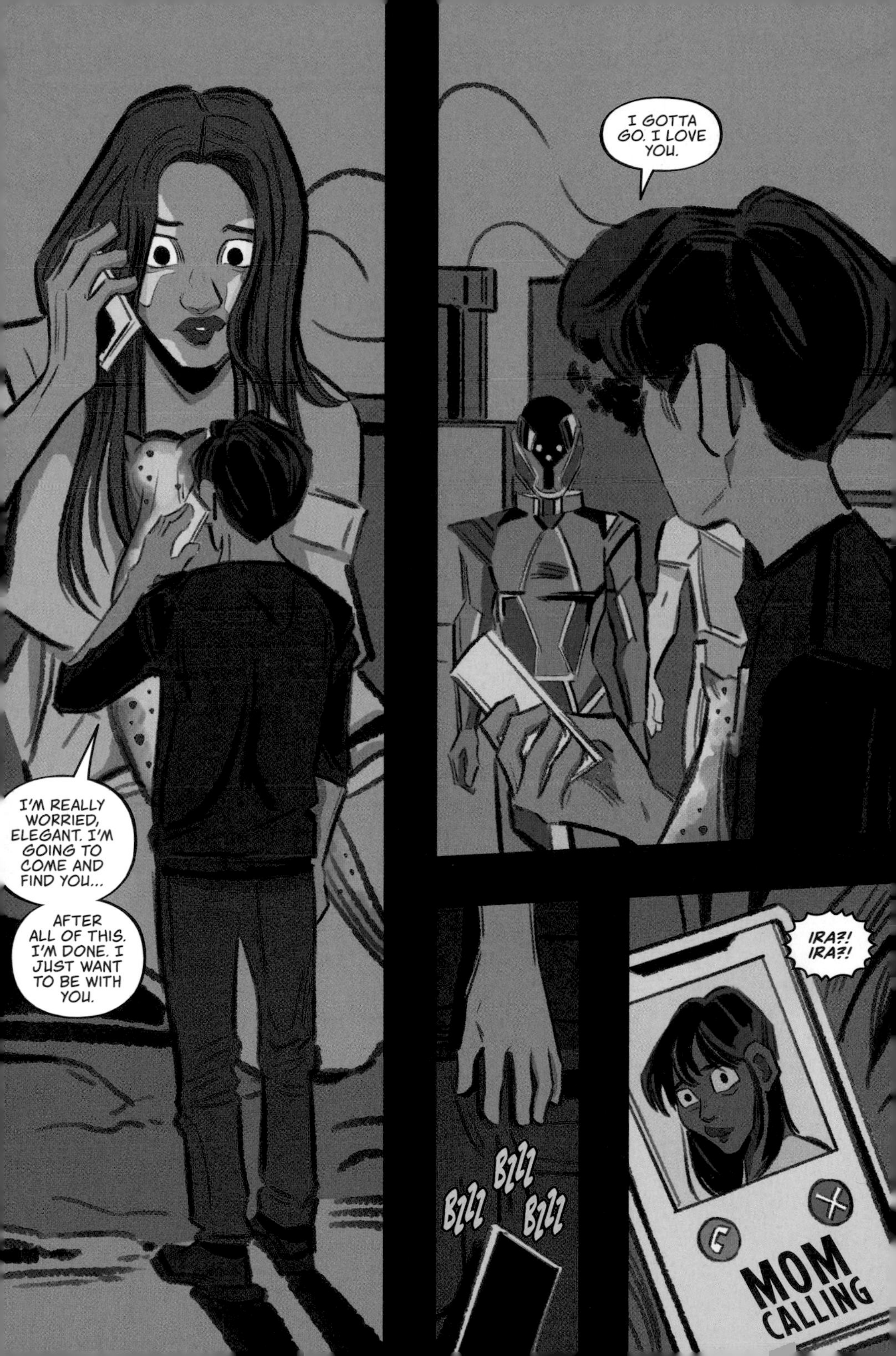
I'M REALLY WORRIED, ELEGANT. I'M GOING TO COME AND FIND YOU...
AFTER ALL OF THIS. I'M DONE. I JUST WANT TO BE WITH YOU.
I GOTTA GO. I LOVE YOU.
BZZZ
BZZZ
BZZZ
IRA?! IRA?!
MOM CALLING

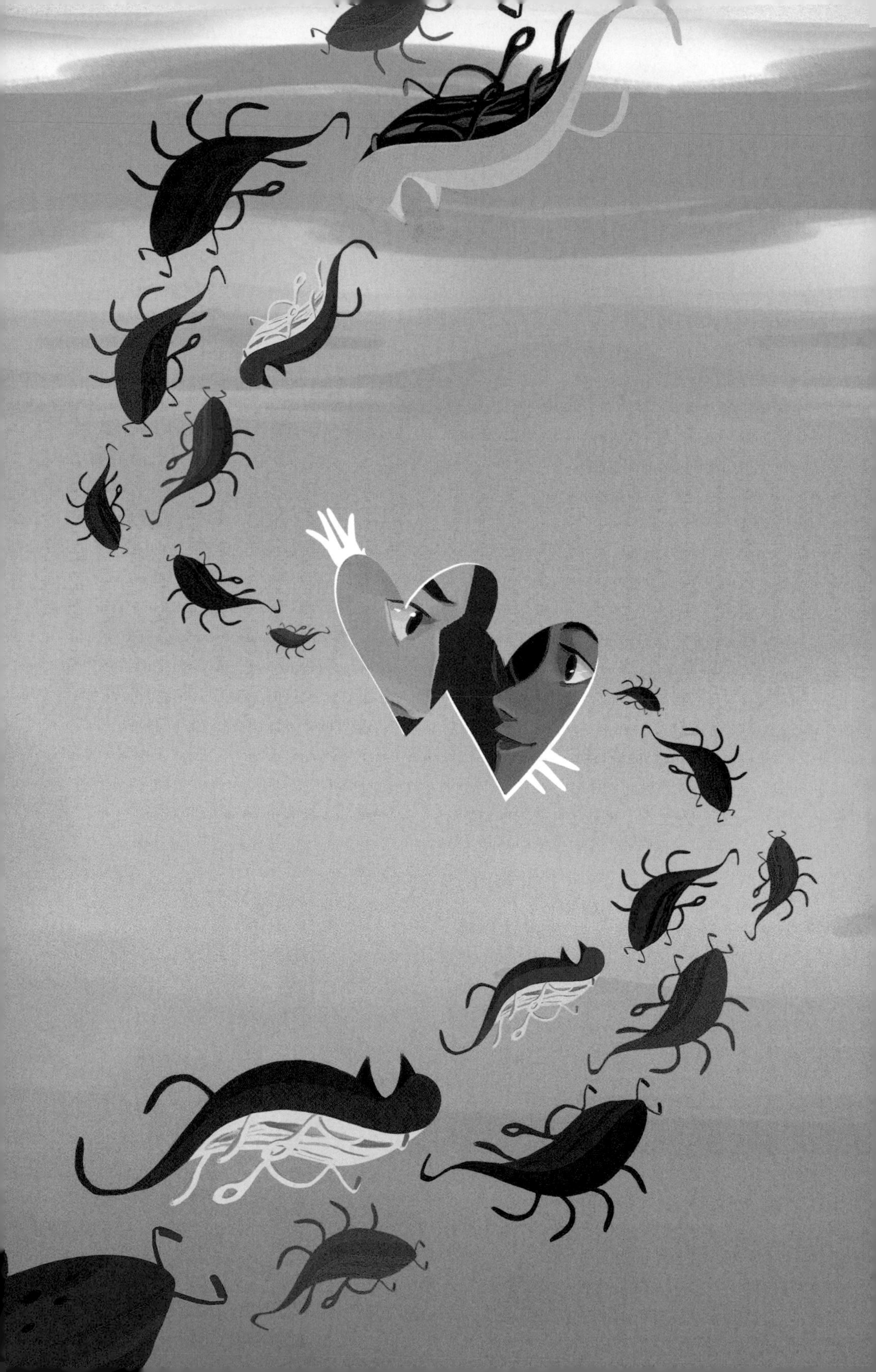

part seven

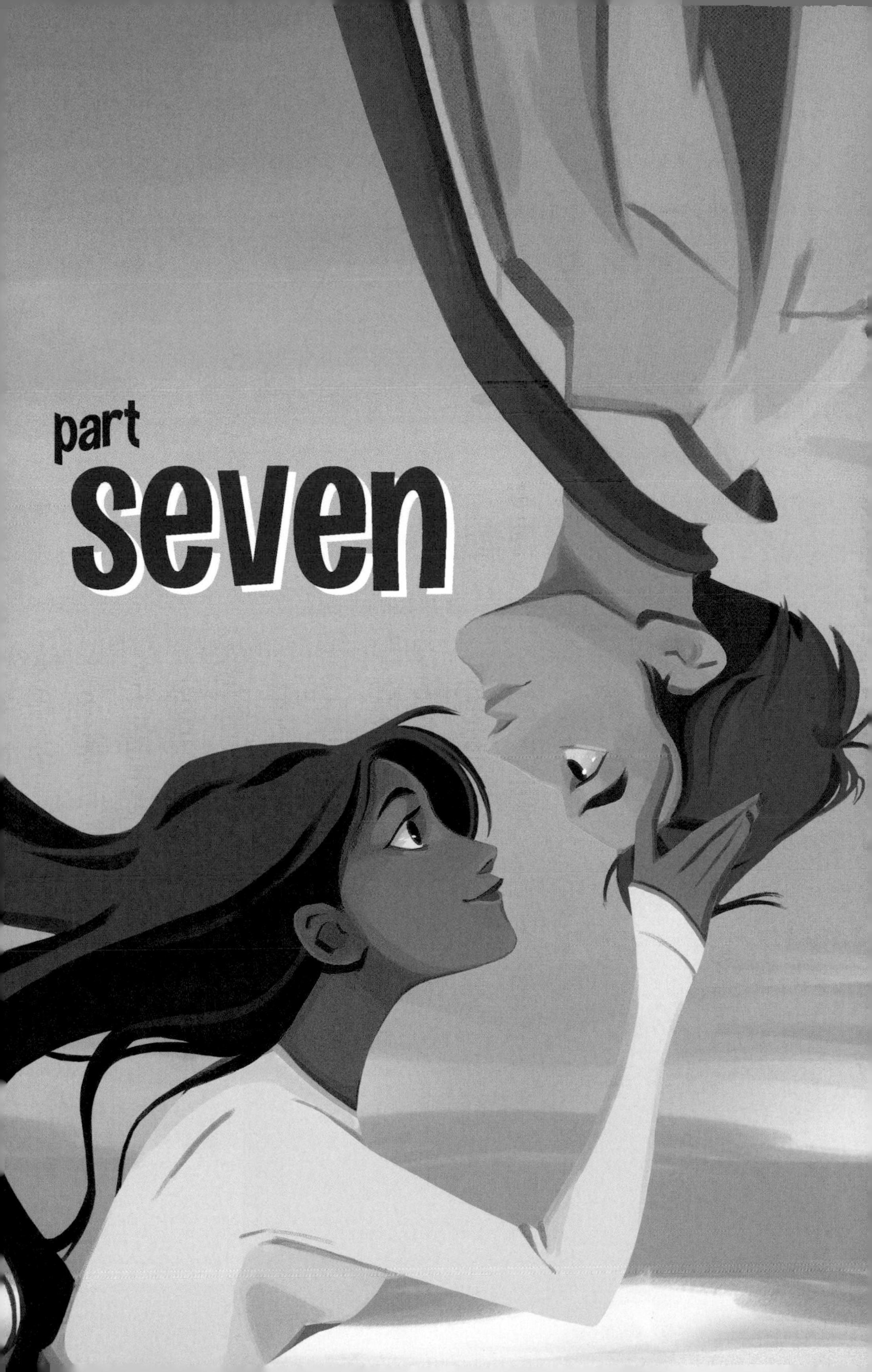

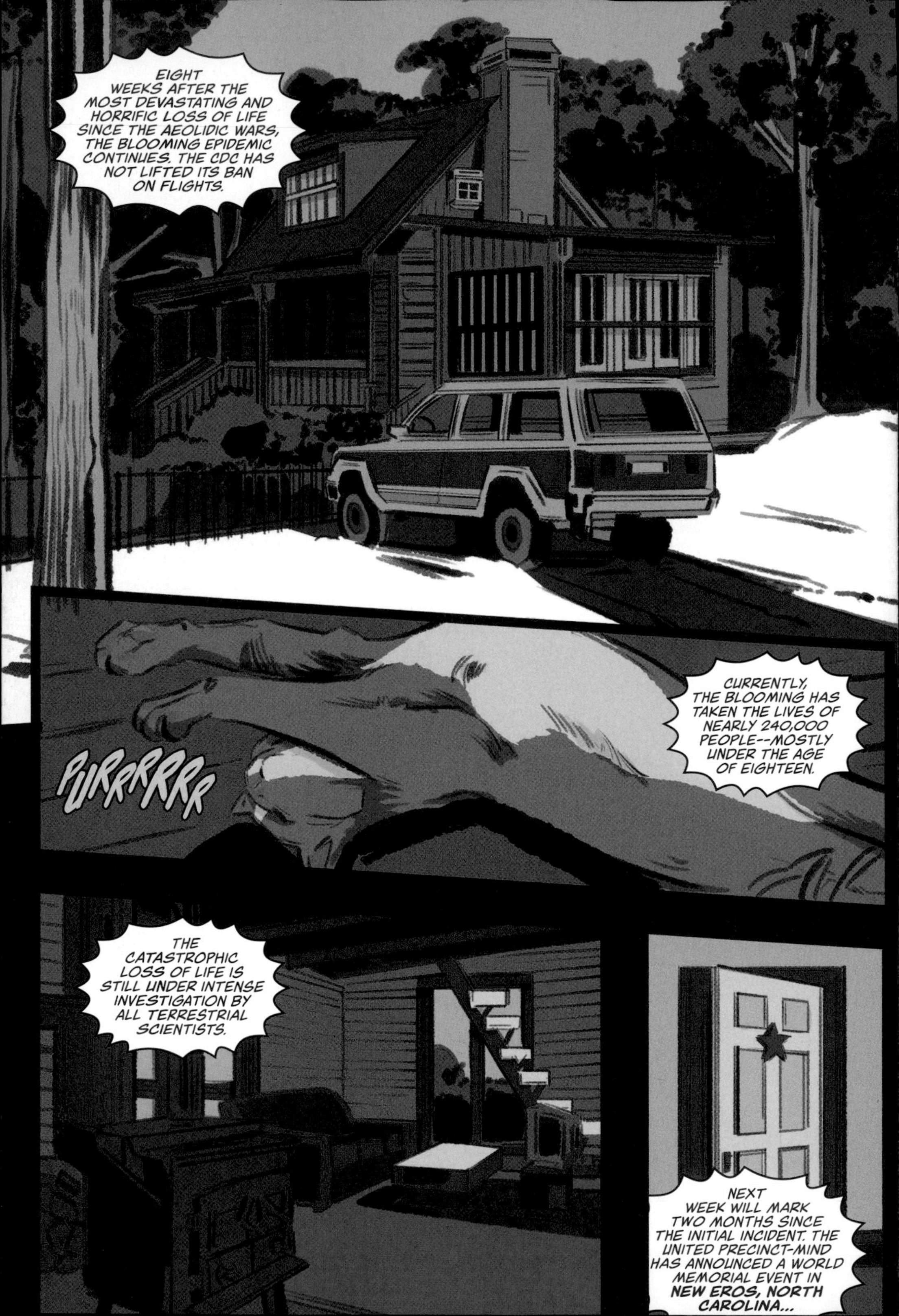
EIGHT WEEKS AFTER THE MOST DEVASTATING AND HORRIFIC LOSS OF LIFE SINCE THE AEOLIDIC WARS, THE BLOOMING EPIDEMIC CONTINUES. THE CDC HAS NOT LIFTED ITS BAN ON FLIGHTS.
CURRENTLY, THE BLOOMING HAS TAKEN THE LIVES OF NEARLY 240,000 PEOPLE--MOSTLY UNDER THE AGE OF EIGHTEEN.
PURRRRRR
THE CATASTROPHIC LOSS OF LIFE IS STILL UNDER INTENSE INVESTIGATION BY ALL TERRESTRIAL SCIENTISTS.
NEXT WEEK WILL MARK TWO MONTHS SINCE THE INITIAL INCIDENT. THE UNITED PRECINCT-MIND HAS ANNOUNCED A WORLD MEMORIAL EVENT IN **NEW EROS, NORTH CAROLINA...**

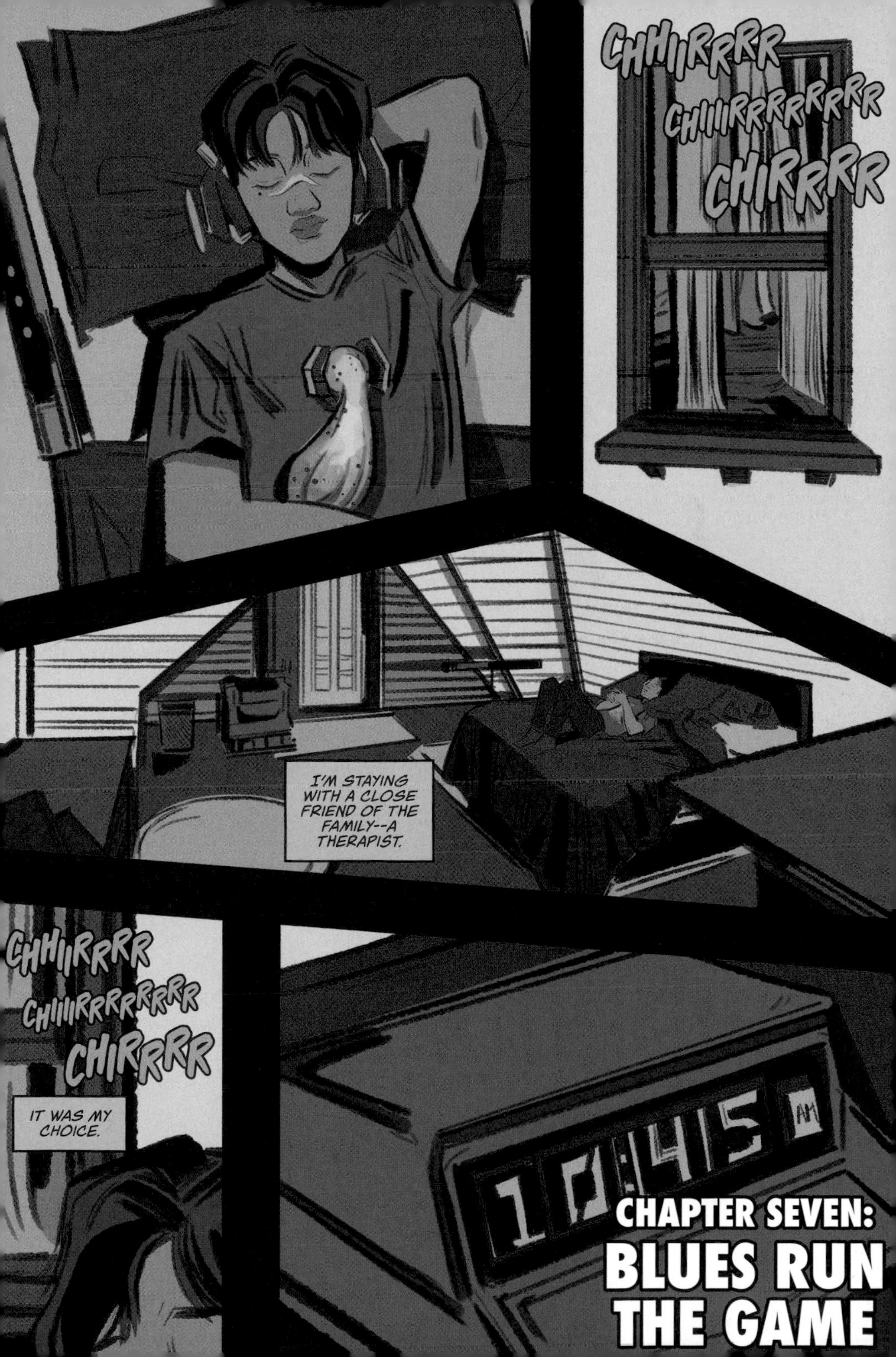
CHHIIRRRR
CHIIIIRRRRRRR
CHIRRRR
I'M STAYING WITH A CLOSE FRIEND OF THE FAMILY--A THERAPIST.
CHHIIRRRR
CHIIIIRRRRRRR
CHIRRRR
IT WAS MY CHOICE.
10:45 AM

CHAPTER SEVEN:
BLUES RUN THE GAME

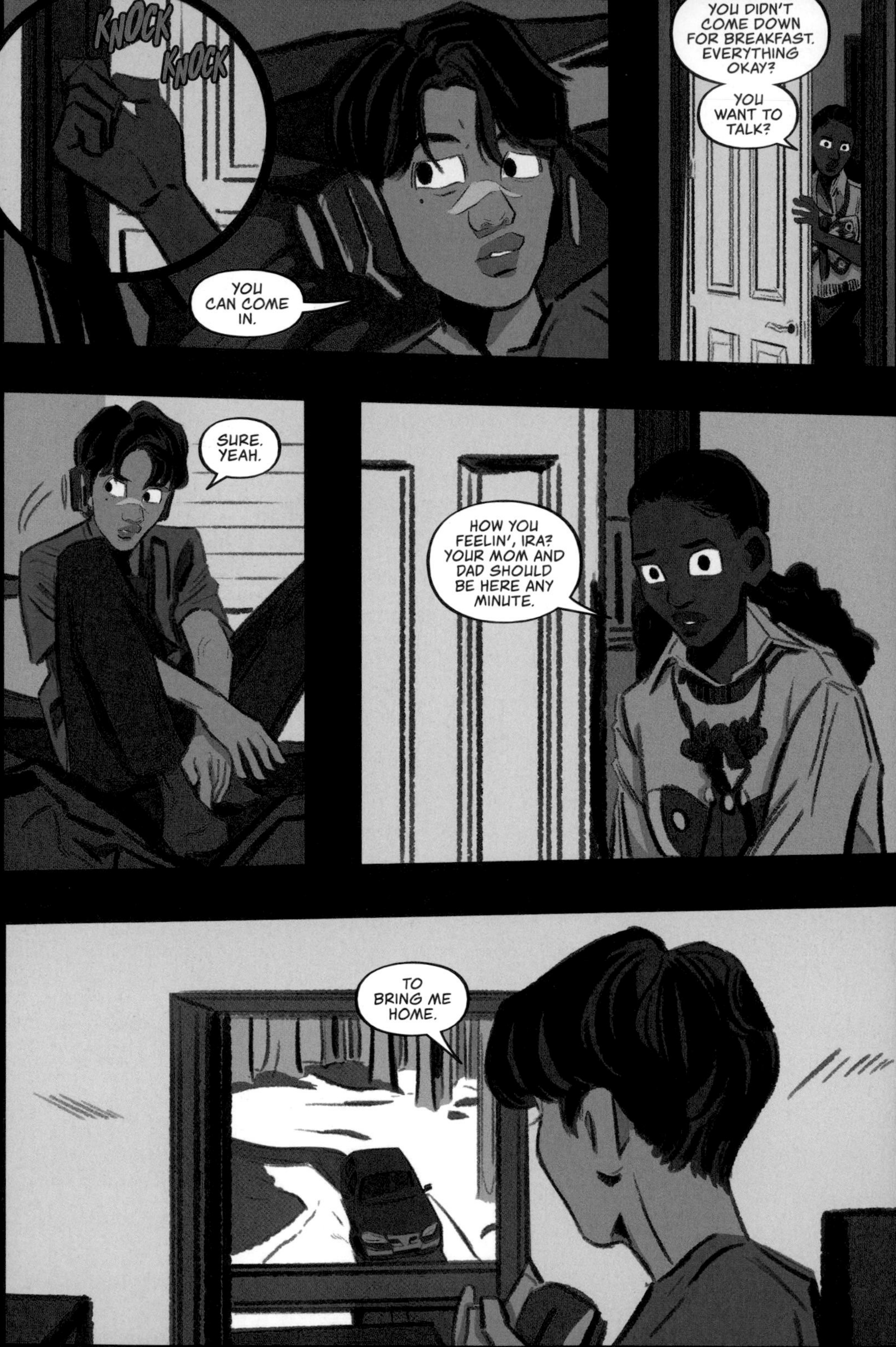
KNOCK KNOCK
YOU CAN COME IN.
YOU DIDN'T COME DOWN FOR BREAKFAST. EVERYTHING OKAY?
YOU WANT TO TALK?
SURE. YEAH.
HOW YOU FEELIN', IRA? YOUR MOM AND DAD SHOULD BE HERE ANY MINUTE.
TO BRING ME HOME.

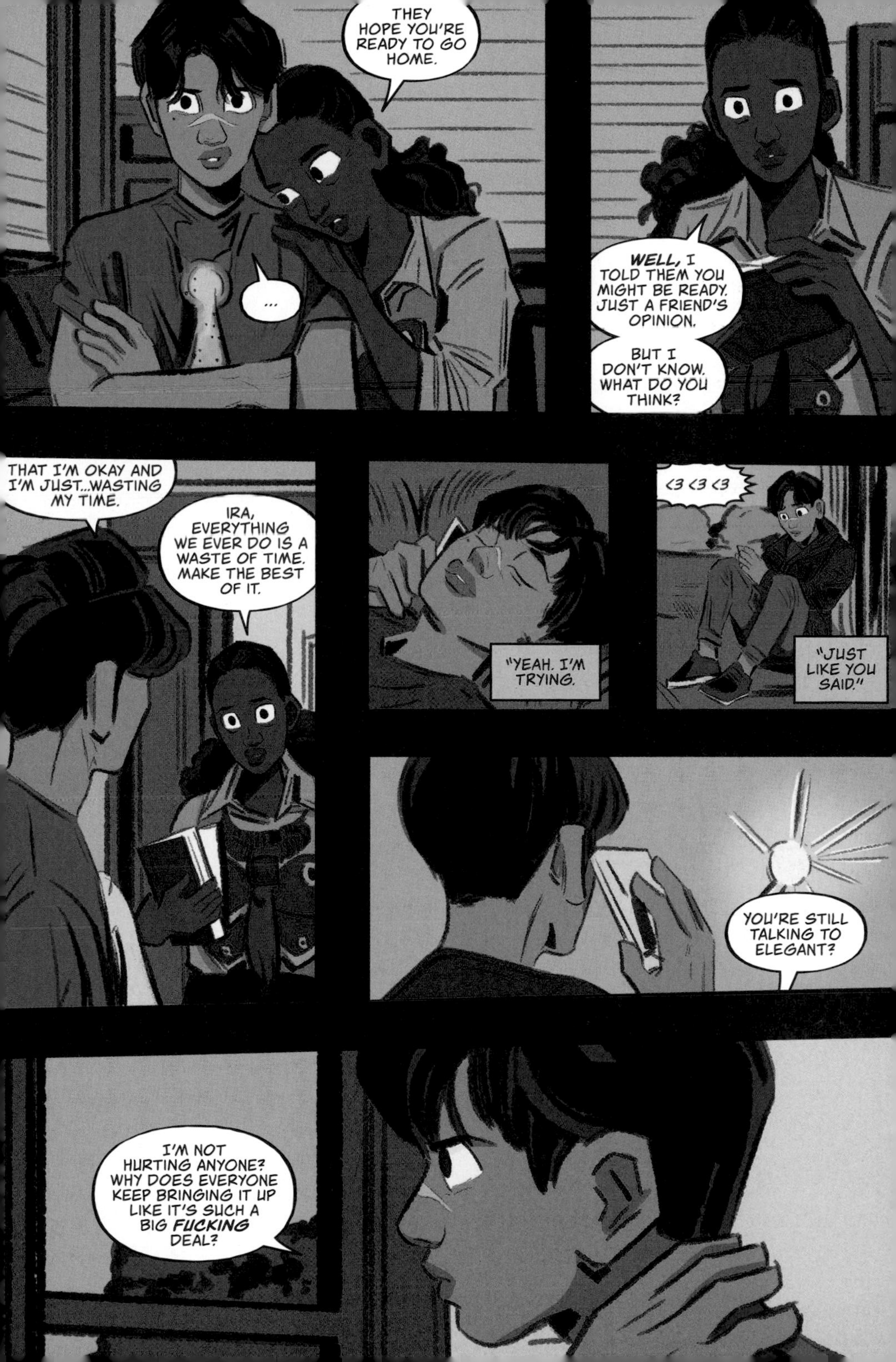
THEY HOPE YOU'RE READY TO GO HOME.
...
WELL, I TOLD THEM YOU MIGHT BE READY. JUST A FRIEND'S OPINION.
BUT I DON'T KNOW. WHAT DO YOU THINK?
THAT I'M OKAY AND I'M JUST...WASTING MY TIME.
IRA, EVERYTHING WE EVER DO IS A WASTE OF TIME. MAKE THE BEST OF IT.
"YEAH. I'M TRYING.
<3 <3 <3
"JUST LIKE YOU SAID."
YOU'RE STILL TALKING TO ELEGANT?
I'M NOT HURTING ANYONE? WHY DOES EVERYONE KEEP BRINGING IT UP LIKE IT'S SUCH A BIG *FUCKING* DEAL?

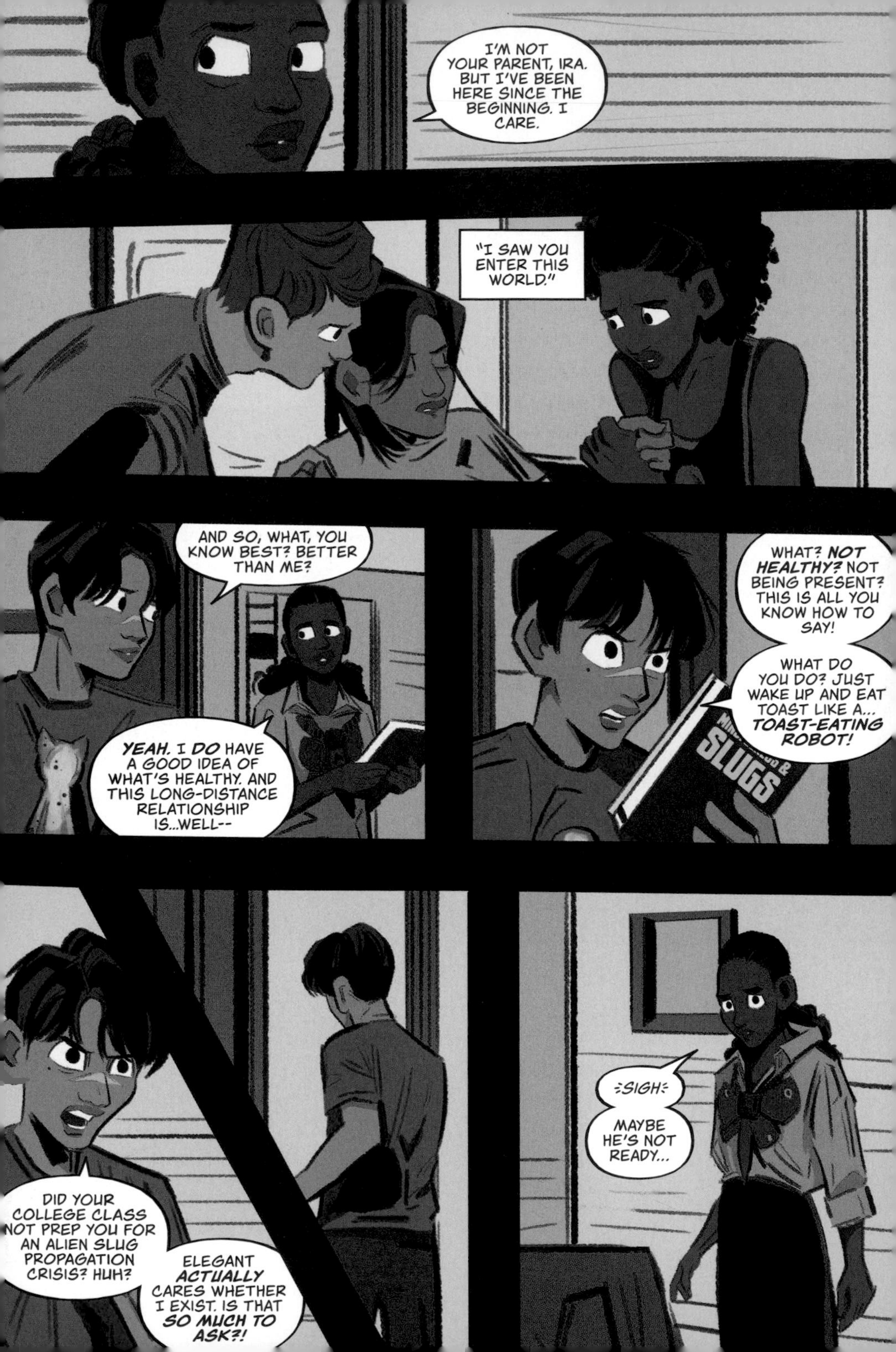
I'M NOT YOUR PARENT, IRA. BUT I'VE BEEN HERE SINCE THE BEGINNING. I CARE.
"I SAW YOU ENTER THIS WORLD."
AND SO, WHAT, YOU KNOW BEST? BETTER THAN ME?
YEAH. I ***DO*** HAVE A GOOD IDEA OF WHAT'S HEALTHY. AND THIS LONG-DISTANCE RELATIONSHIP IS...WELL--
WHAT? ***NOT HEALTHY?*** NOT BEING PRESENT? THIS IS ALL YOU KNOW HOW TO SAY!
WHAT DO YOU DO? JUST WAKE UP AND EAT TOAST LIKE A... ***TOAST-EATING ROBOT!***
SLUGS
DID YOUR COLLEGE CLASS NOT PREP YOU FOR AN ALIEN SLUG PROPAGATION CRISIS? HUH?
ELEGANT ***ACTUALLY*** CARES WHETHER I EXIST. IS THAT ***SO MUCH TO ASK?!***
SIGH
MAYBE HE'S NOT READY...

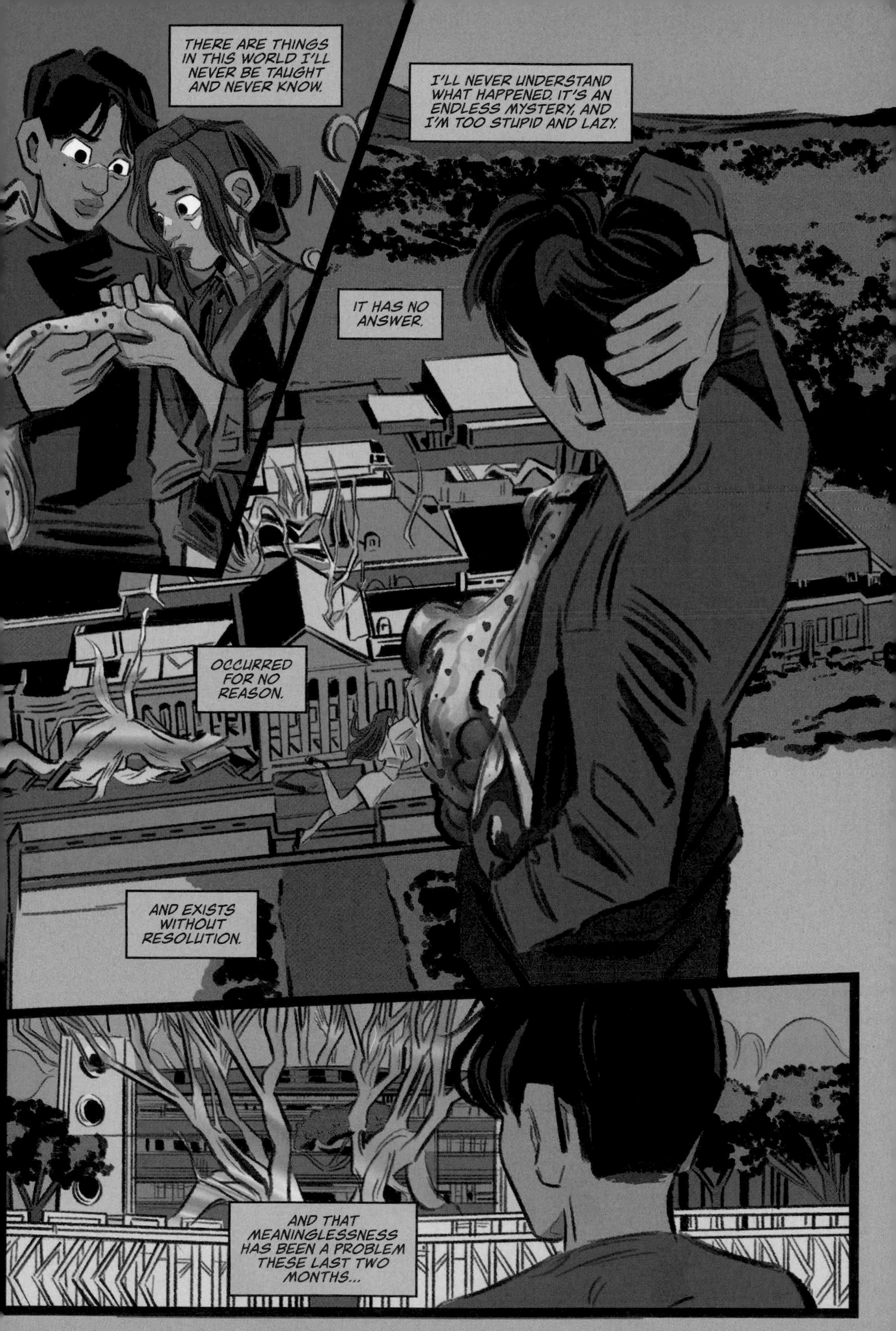
THERE ARE THINGS IN THIS WORLD I'LL NEVER BE TAUGHT AND NEVER KNOW.
I'LL NEVER UNDERSTAND WHAT HAPPENED. IT'S AN ENDLESS MYSTERY, AND I'M TOO STUPID AND LAZY.
IT HAS NO ANSWER.
OCCURRED FOR NO REASON.
AND EXISTS WITHOUT RESOLUTION.
AND THAT MEANINGLESSNESS HAS BEEN A PROBLEM THESE LAST TWO MONTHS...

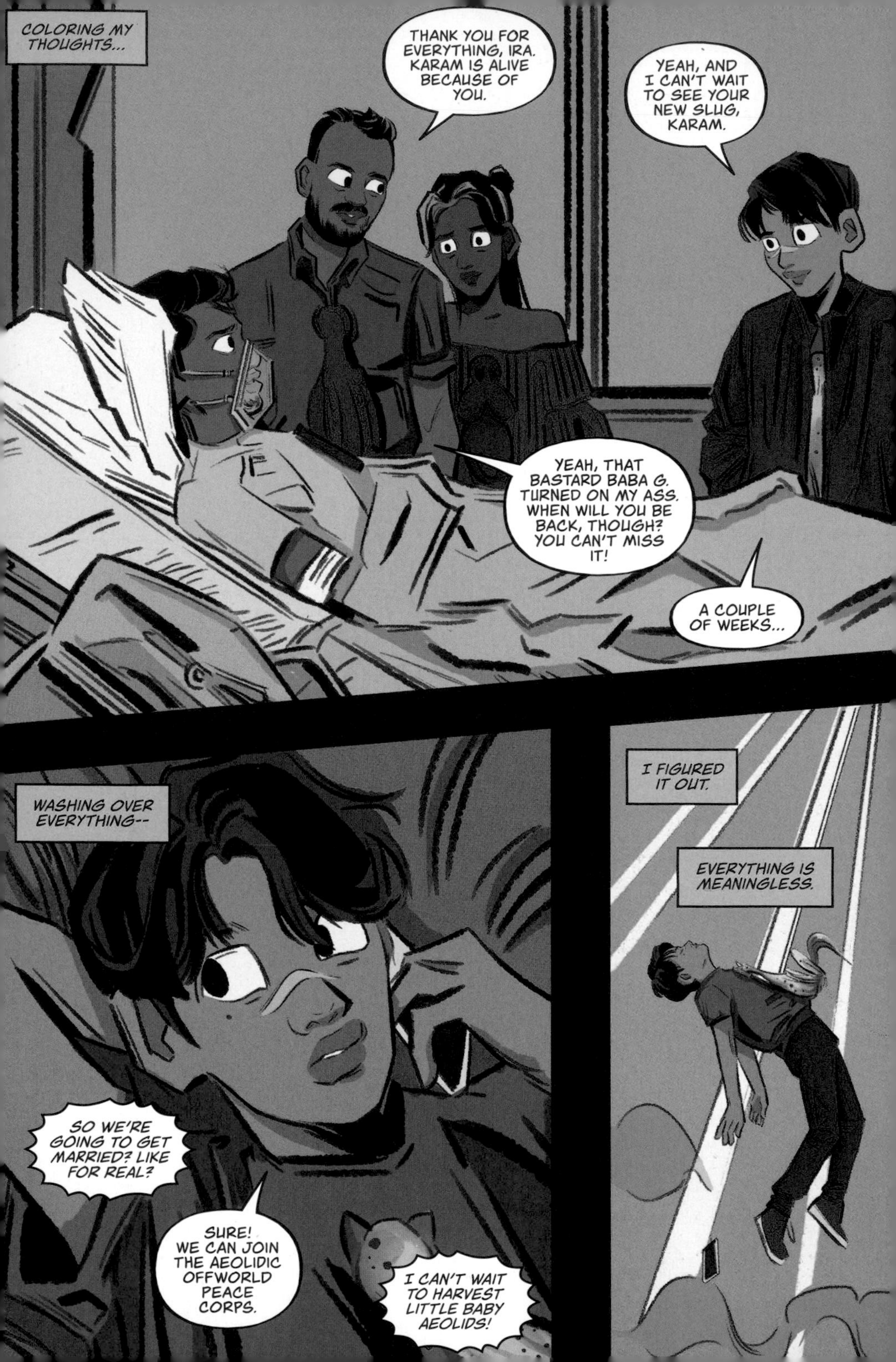
COLORING MY THOUGHTS...
THANK YOU FOR EVERYTHING, IRA. KARAM IS ALIVE BECAUSE OF YOU.
YEAH, AND I CAN'T WAIT TO SEE YOUR NEW SLUG, KARAM.
YEAH, THAT BASTARD BABA G. TURNED ON MY ASS. WHEN WILL YOU BE BACK, THOUGH? YOU CAN'T MISS IT!
A COUPLE OF WEEKS...
WASHING OVER EVERYTHING--
SO WE'RE GOING TO GET MARRIED? LIKE FOR REAL?
SURE! WE CAN JOIN THE AEOLIDIC OFFWORLD PEACE CORPS.
I CAN'T WAIT TO HARVEST LITTLE BABY AEOLIDS!
I FIGURED IT OUT.
EVERYTHING IS MEANINGLESS.

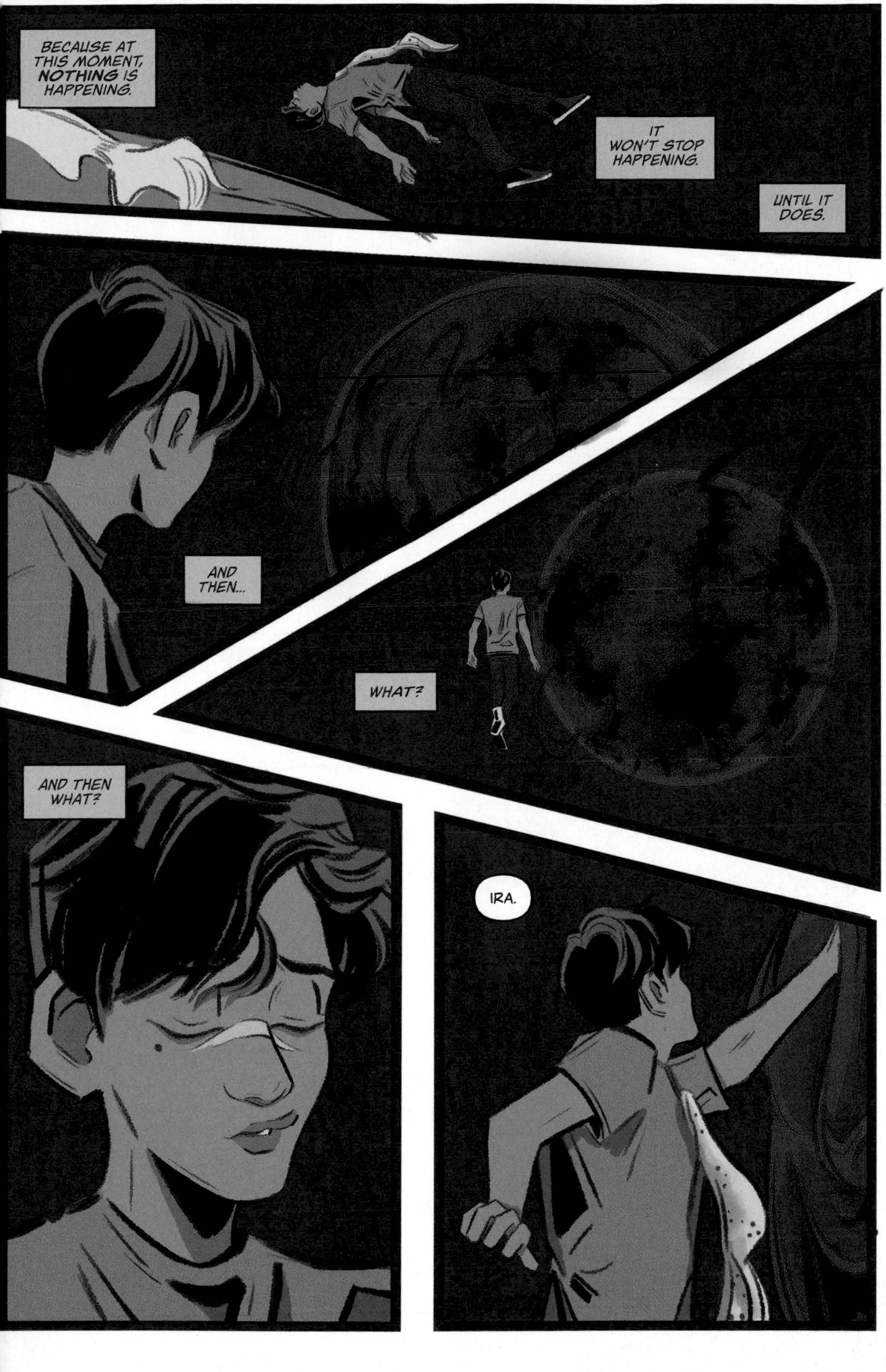
BECAUSE AT THIS MOMENT, NOTHING IS HAPPENING.
IT WON'T STOP HAPPENING.
UNTIL IT DOES.
AND THEN...
WHAT?
AND THEN WHAT?
IRA.

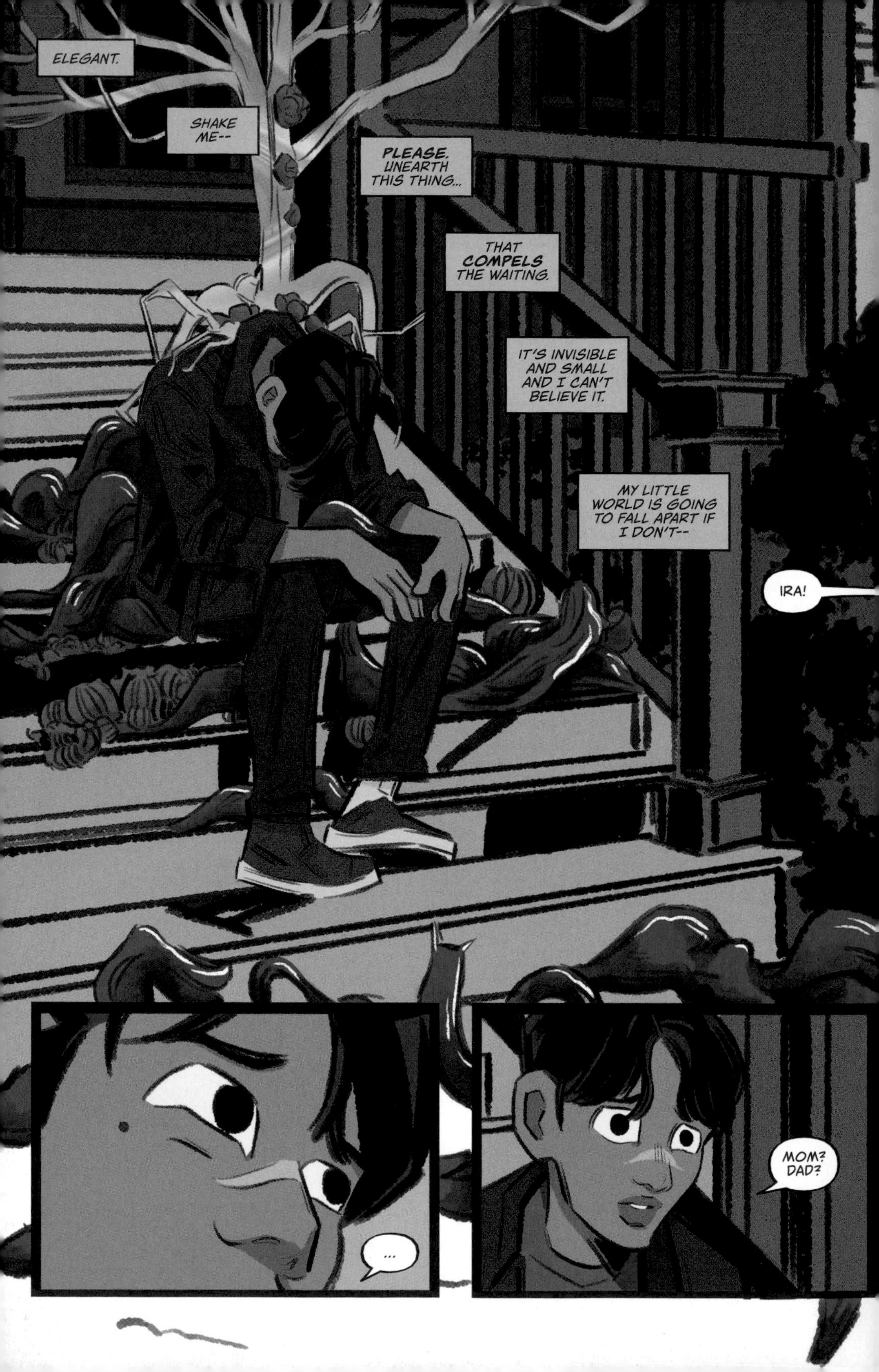
ELEGANT.
SHAKE ME--
PLEASE. UNEARTH THIS THING...
THAT COMPELS THE WAITING.
IT'S INVISIBLE AND SMALL AND I CAN'T BELIEVE IT.
MY LITTLE WORLD IS GOING TO FALL APART IF I DON'T--
IRA!
...
MOM? DAD?

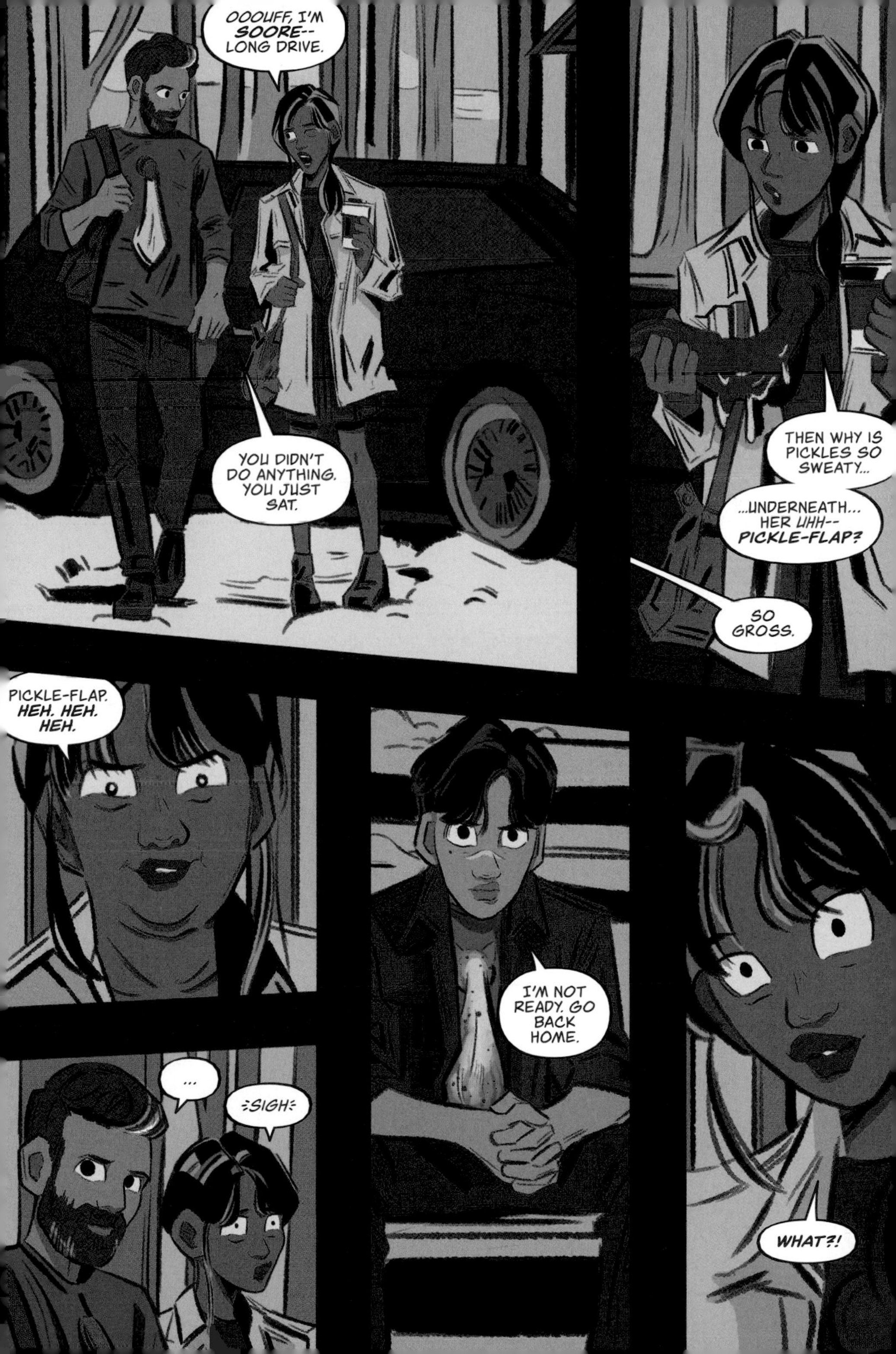
OOOUFF, I'M SOORE-- LONG DRIVE.
YOU DIDN'T DO ANYTHING. YOU JUST SAT.
THEN WHY IS PICKLES SO SWEATY...
...UNDERNEATH... HER UHH-- PICKLE-FLAP?
SO GROSS.
PICKLE-FLAP. HEH. HEH. HEH.
...
:SIGH:
I'M NOT READY. GO BACK HOME.
WHAT?!

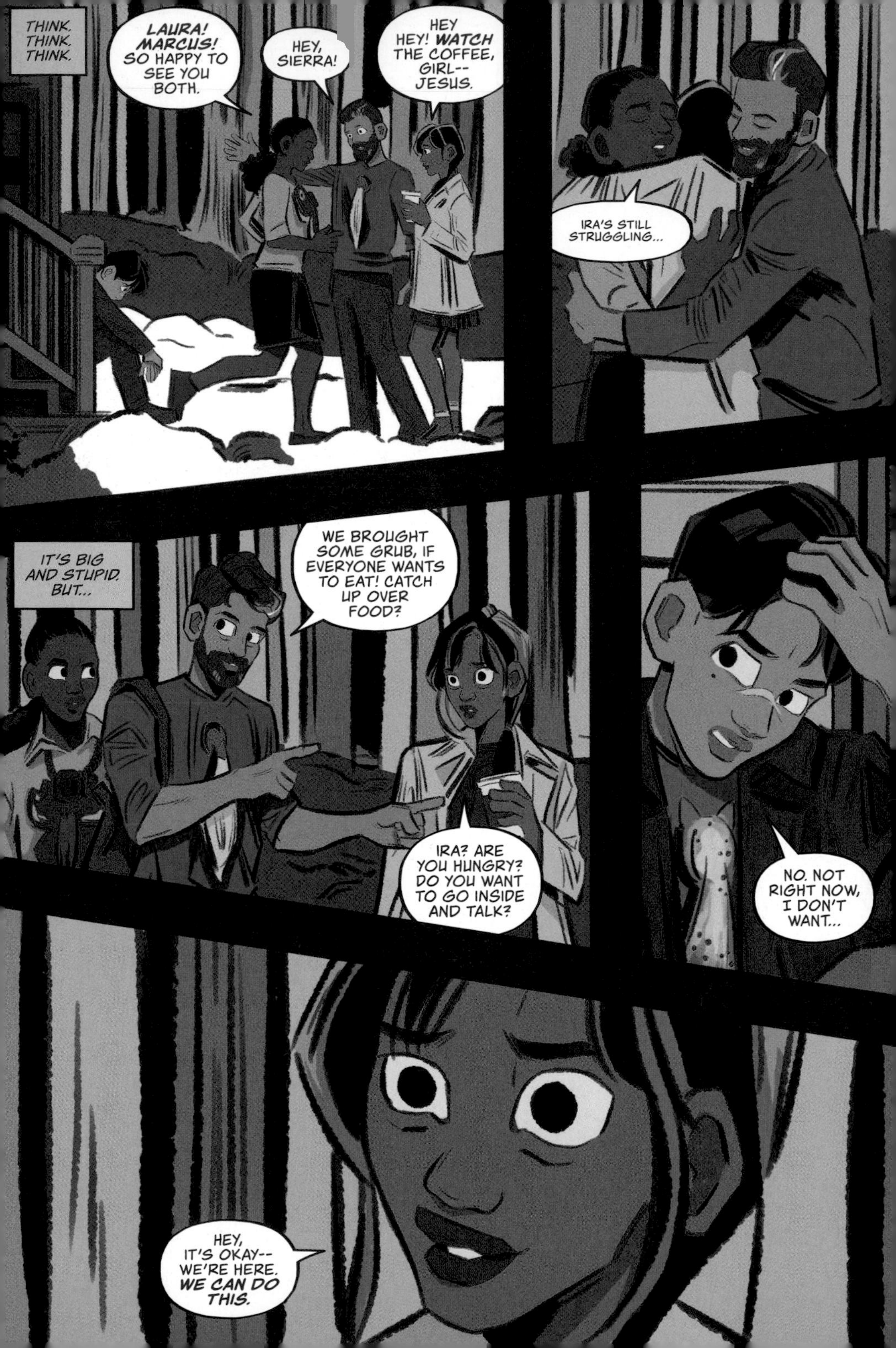
THINK. THINK. THINK.
LAURA! MARCUS! SO HAPPY TO SEE YOU BOTH.
HEY, SIERRA!
HEY HEY! *WATCH* THE COFFEE, GIRL-- JESUS.
IRA'S STILL STRUGGLING...
IT'S BIG AND STUPID. BUT...
WE BROUGHT SOME GRUB, IF EVERYONE WANTS TO EAT! CATCH UP OVER FOOD?
IRA? ARE YOU HUNGRY? DO YOU WANT TO GO INSIDE AND TALK?
NO. NOT RIGHT NOW, I DON'T WANT...
HEY, IT'S OKAY-- WE'RE HERE. *WE CAN DO THIS.*

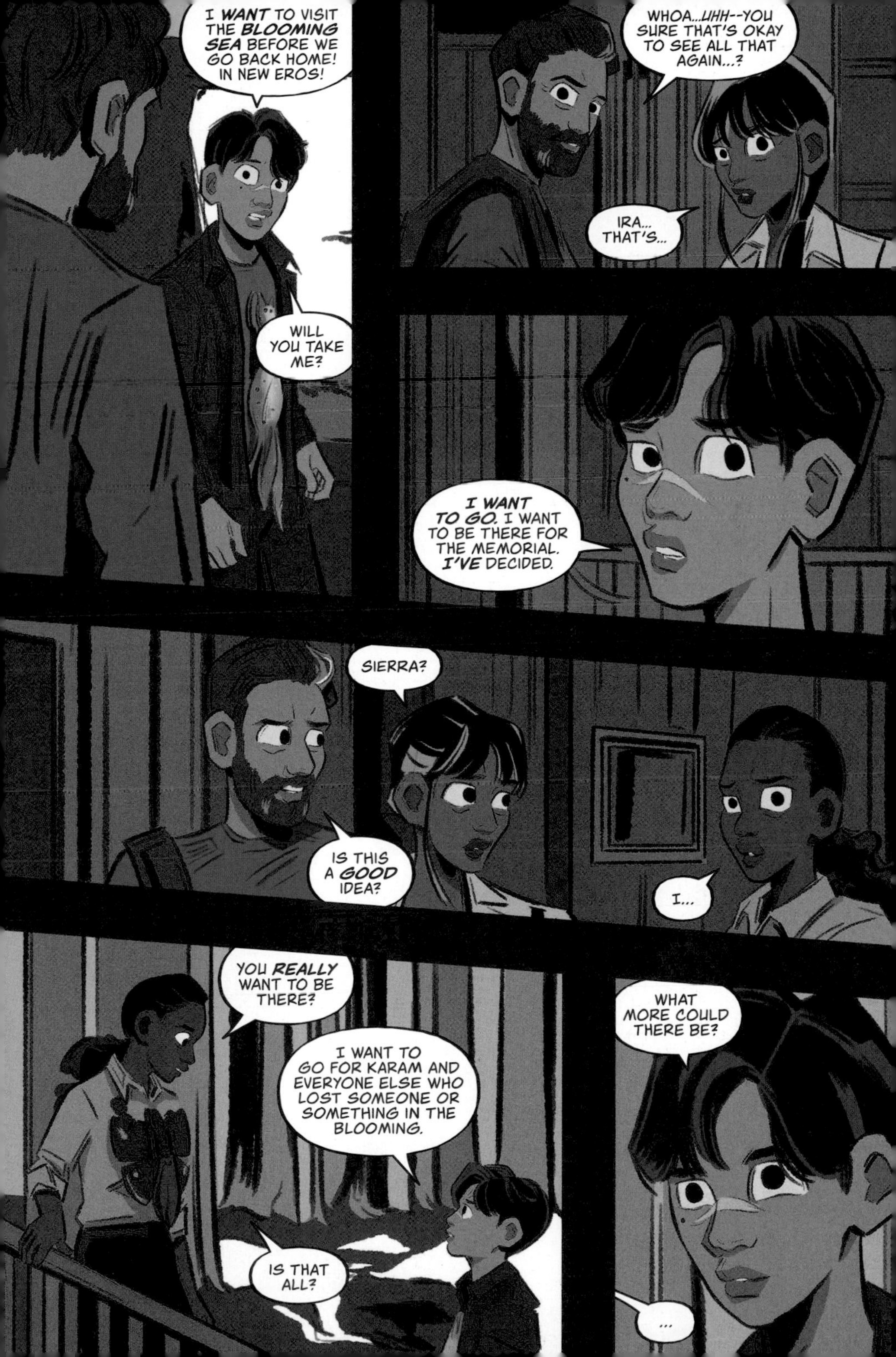
I WANT TO VISIT THE BLOOMING SEA BEFORE WE GO BACK HOME! IN NEW EROS!
WILL YOU TAKE ME?
WHOA...UHH--YOU SURE THAT'S OKAY TO SEE ALL THAT AGAIN...?
IRA... THAT'S...
I WANT TO GO. I WANT TO BE THERE FOR THE MEMORIAL. I'VE DECIDED.
SIERRA?
IS THIS A GOOD IDEA?
I...
YOU REALLY WANT TO BE THERE?
I WANT TO GO FOR KARAM AND EVERYONE ELSE WHO LOST SOMEONE OR SOMETHING IN THE BLOOMING.
IS THAT ALL?
WHAT MORE COULD THERE BE?
...

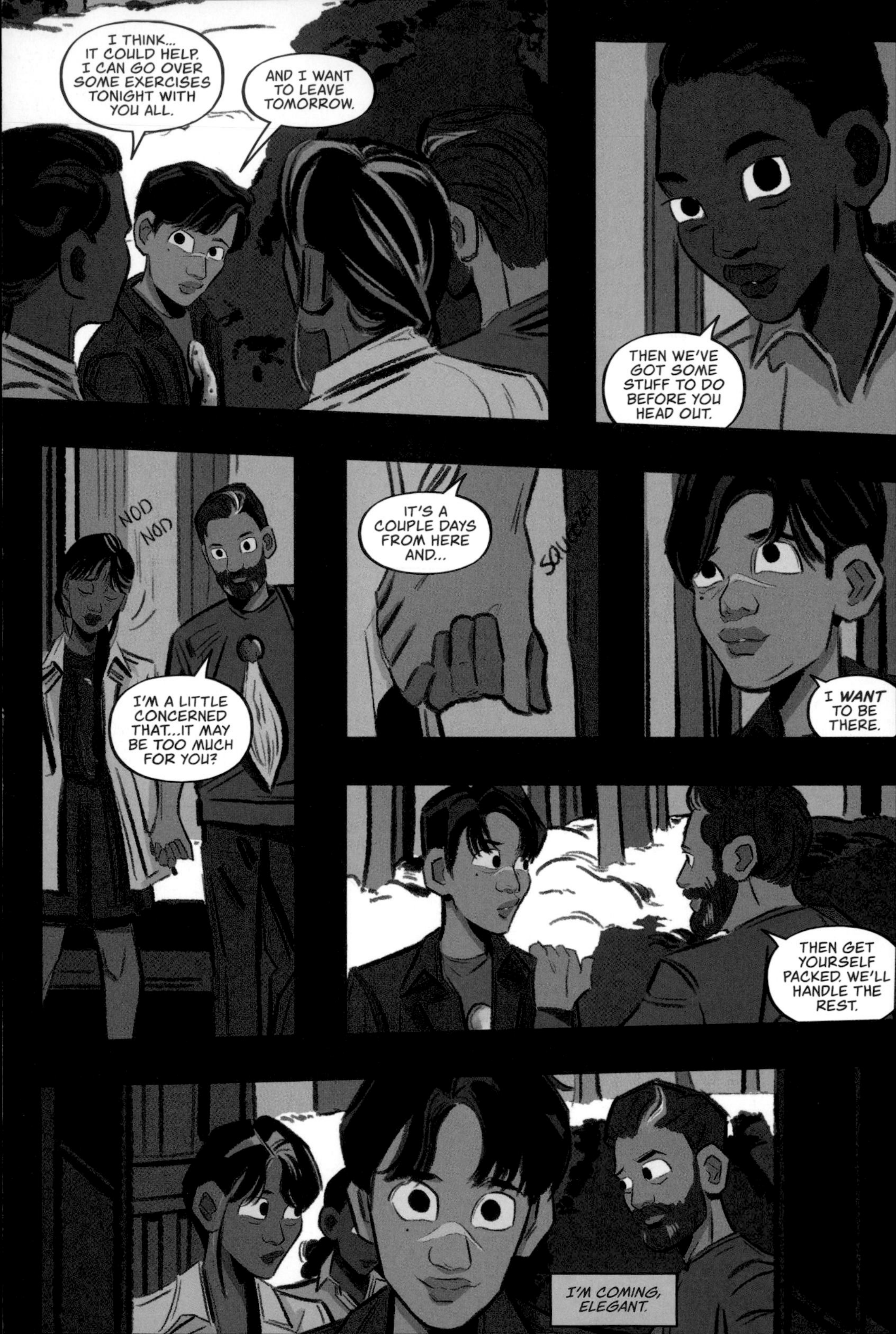
I THINK... IT COULD HELP. I CAN GO OVER SOME EXERCISES TONIGHT WITH YOU ALL.
AND I WANT TO LEAVE TOMORROW.
THEN WE'VE GOT SOME STUFF TO DO BEFORE YOU HEAD OUT.
NOD NOD
I'M A LITTLE CONCERNED THAT...IT MAY BE TOO MUCH FOR YOU?
IT'S A COUPLE DAYS FROM HERE AND...
I *WANT* TO BE THERE.
THEN GET YOURSELF PACKED. WE'LL HANDLE THE REST.
I'M COMING, ELEGANT.

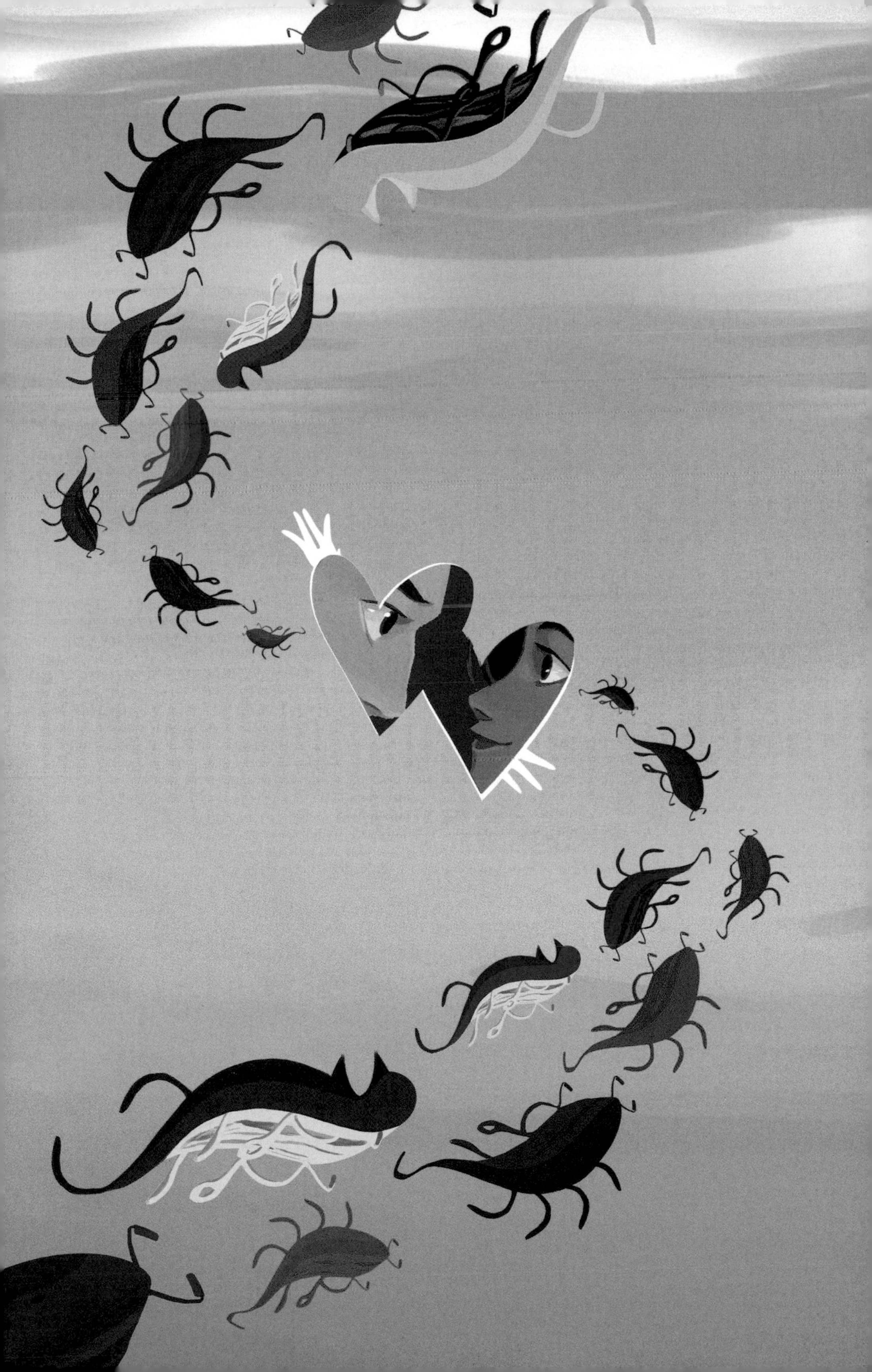

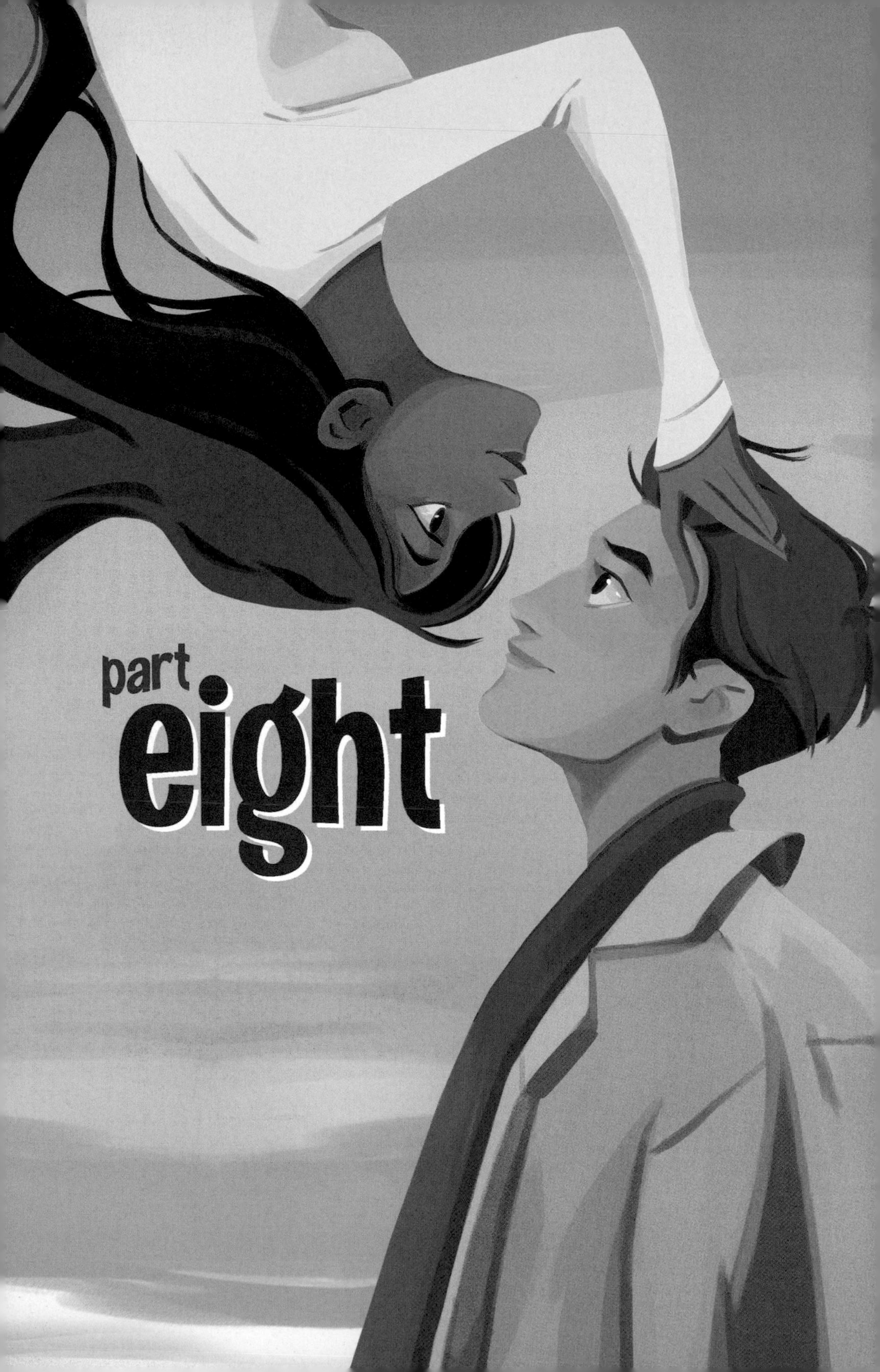
part
eight

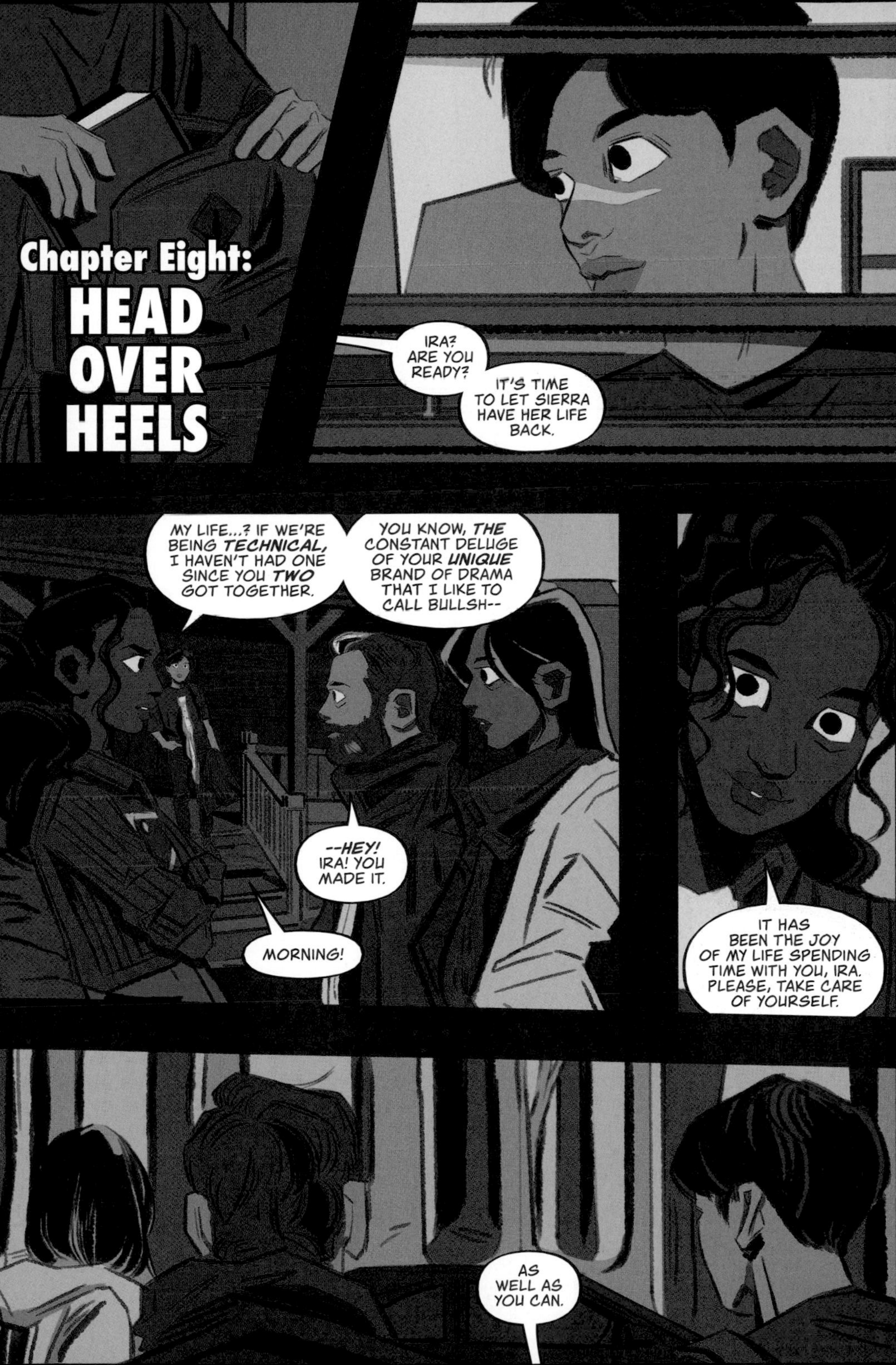
Chapter Eight:
HEAD OVER HEELS
IRA? ARE YOU READY?
IT'S TIME TO LET SIERRA HAVE HER LIFE BACK.
MY LIFE...? IF WE'RE BEING TECHNICAL, I HAVEN'T HAD ONE SINCE YOU TWO GOT TOGETHER.
YOU KNOW, THE CONSTANT DELUGE OF YOUR UNIQUE BRAND OF DRAMA THAT I LIKE TO CALL BULLSH--
--HEY! IRA! YOU MADE IT.
MORNING!
IT HAS BEEN THE JOY OF MY LIFE SPENDING TIME WITH YOU, IRA. PLEASE, TAKE CARE OF YOURSELF.
AS WELL AS YOU CAN.

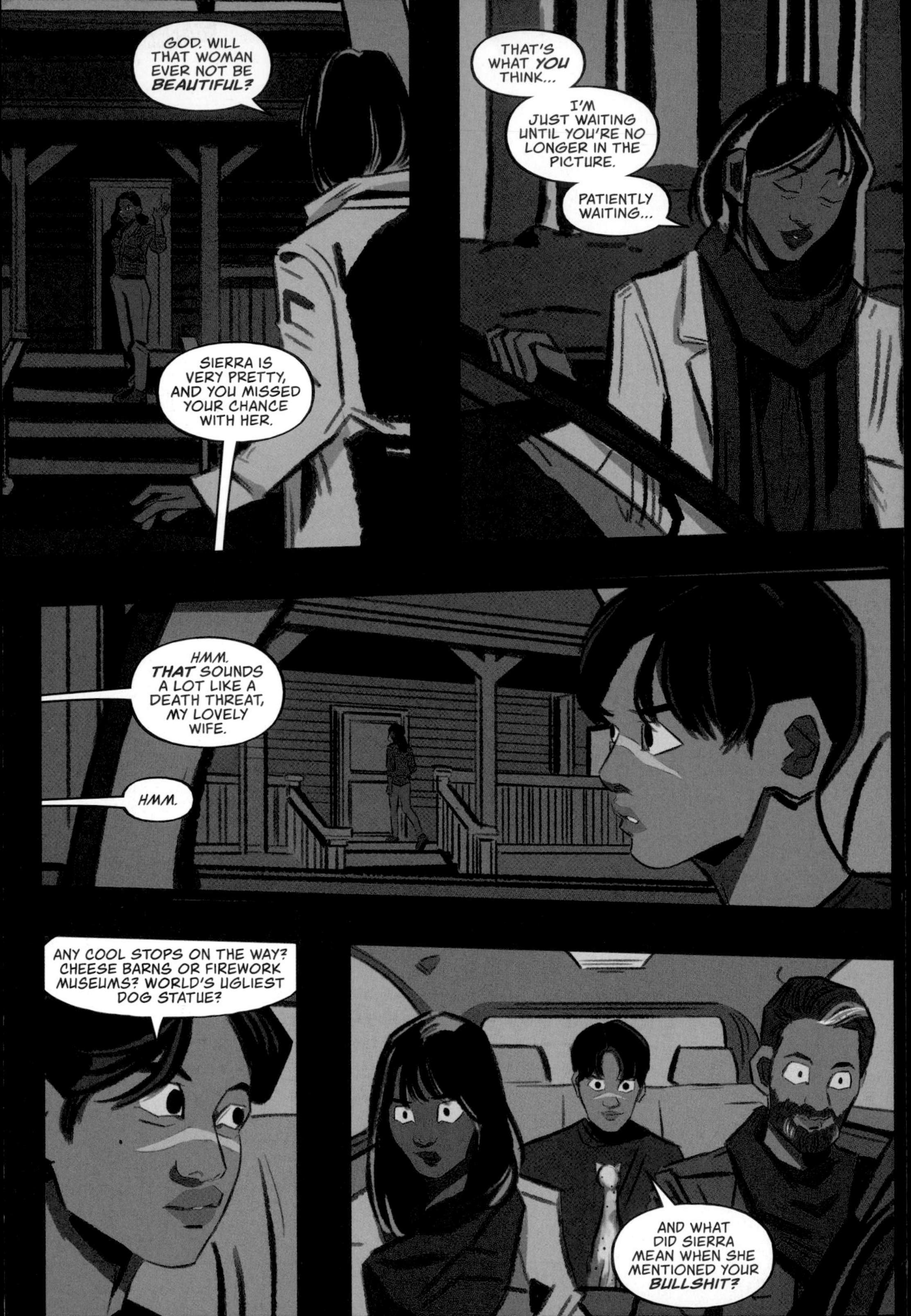
GOD. WILL THAT WOMAN EVER NOT BE *BEAUTIFUL?*
SIERRA IS VERY PRETTY, AND YOU MISSED YOUR CHANCE WITH HER.
THAT'S WHAT *YOU* THINK...
I'M JUST WAITING UNTIL YOU'RE NO LONGER IN THE PICTURE.
PATIENTLY WAITING...
HMM. ***THAT*** *SOUNDS A LOT LIKE A DEATH THREAT, MY LOVELY WIFE.*
HMM.
ANY COOL STOPS ON THE WAY? CHEESE BARNS OR FIREWORK MUSEUMS? WORLD'S UGLIEST DOG STATUE?
AND WHAT DID SIERRA MEAN WHEN SHE MENTIONED YOUR ***BULLSHIT?***

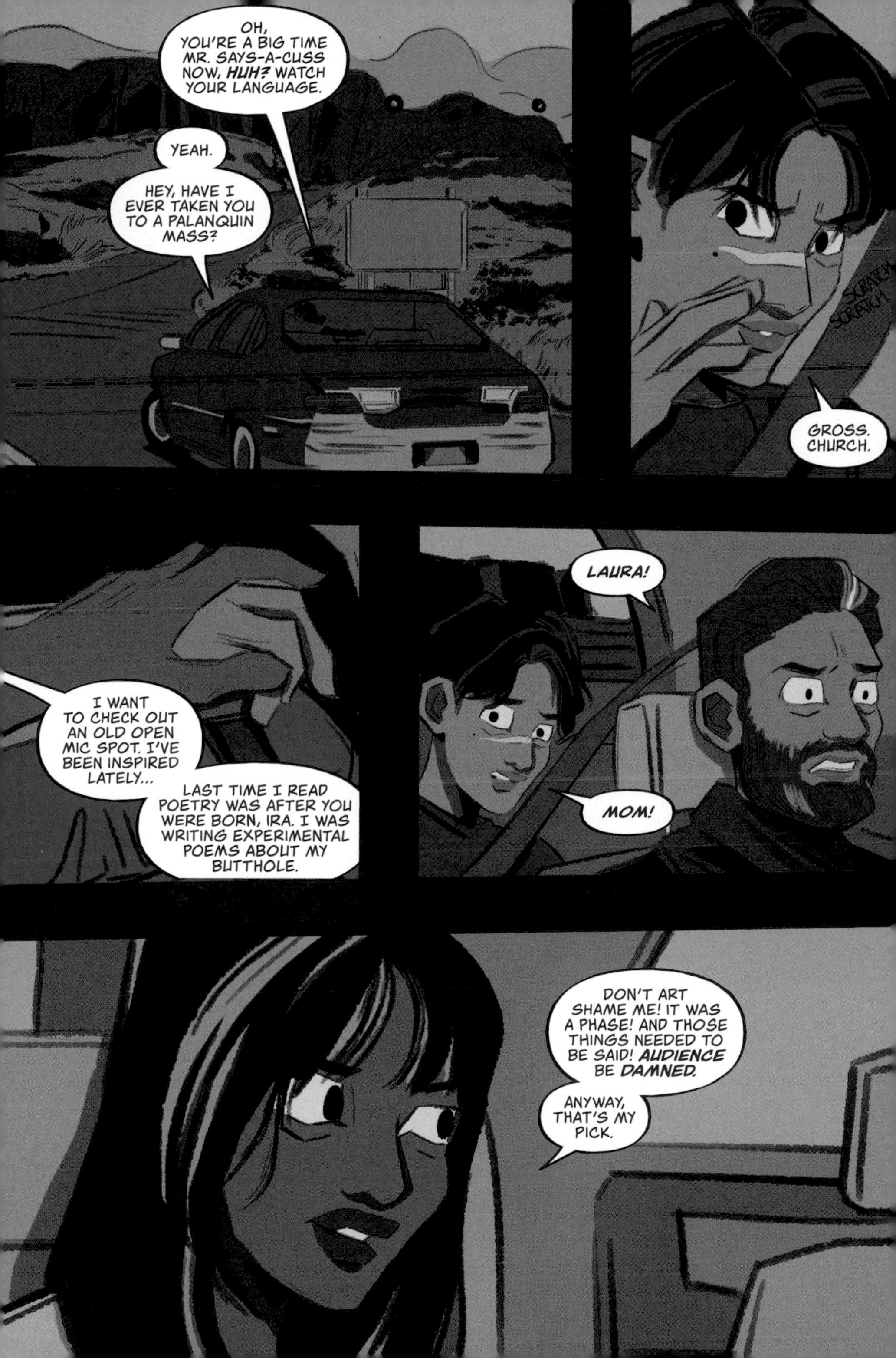
OH, YOU'RE A BIG TIME MR. SAYS-A-CUSS NOW, HUH? WATCH YOUR LANGUAGE.
YEAH.
HEY, HAVE I EVER TAKEN YOU TO A PALANQUIN MASS?
SCRATCH SCRATCH
GROSS. CHURCH.
I WANT TO CHECK OUT AN OLD OPEN MIC SPOT. I'VE BEEN INSPIRED LATELY...
LAST TIME I READ POETRY WAS AFTER YOU WERE BORN, IRA. I WAS WRITING EXPERIMENTAL POEMS ABOUT MY BUTTHOLE.
LAURA!
MOM!
DON'T ART SHAME ME! IT WAS A PHASE! AND THOSE THINGS NEEDED TO BE SAID! AUDIENCE BE DAMNED.
ANYWAY, THAT'S MY PICK.

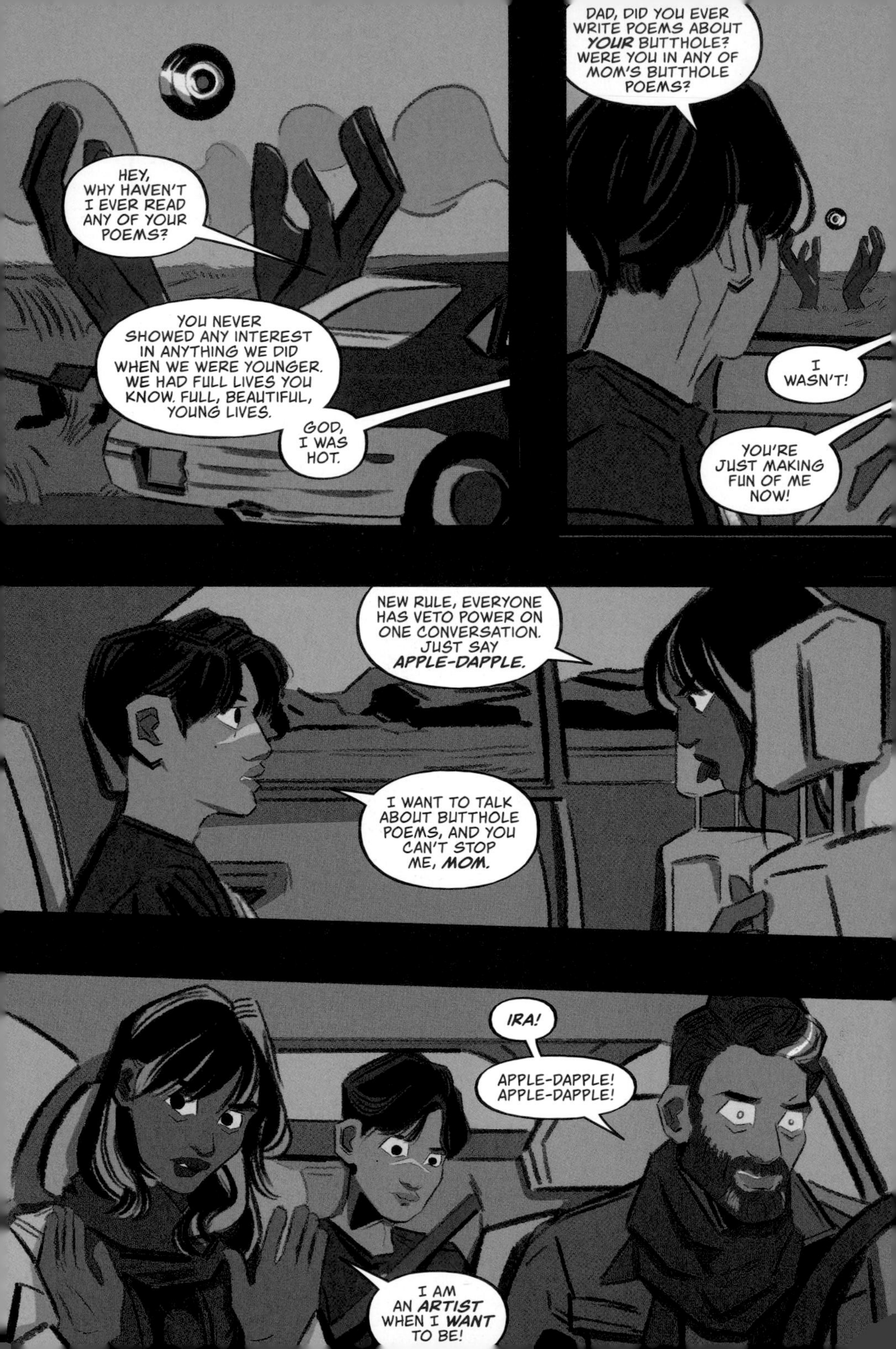
HEY, WHY HAVEN'T I EVER READ ANY OF YOUR POEMS?
YOU NEVER SHOWED ANY INTEREST IN ANYTHING WE DID WHEN WE WERE YOUNGER. WE HAD FULL LIVES YOU KNOW. FULL, BEAUTIFUL, YOUNG LIVES.
GOD, I WAS HOT.
DAD, DID YOU EVER WRITE POEMS ABOUT YOUR BUTTHOLE? WERE YOU IN ANY OF MOM'S BUTTHOLE POEMS?
I WASN'T!
YOU'RE JUST MAKING FUN OF ME NOW!
NEW RULE, EVERYONE HAS VETO POWER ON ONE CONVERSATION. JUST SAY APPLE-DAPPLE.
I WANT TO TALK ABOUT BUTTHOLE POEMS, AND YOU CAN'T STOP ME, MOM.
IRA!
APPLE-DAPPLE! APPLE-DAPPLE!
I AM AN ARTIST WHEN I WANT TO BE!

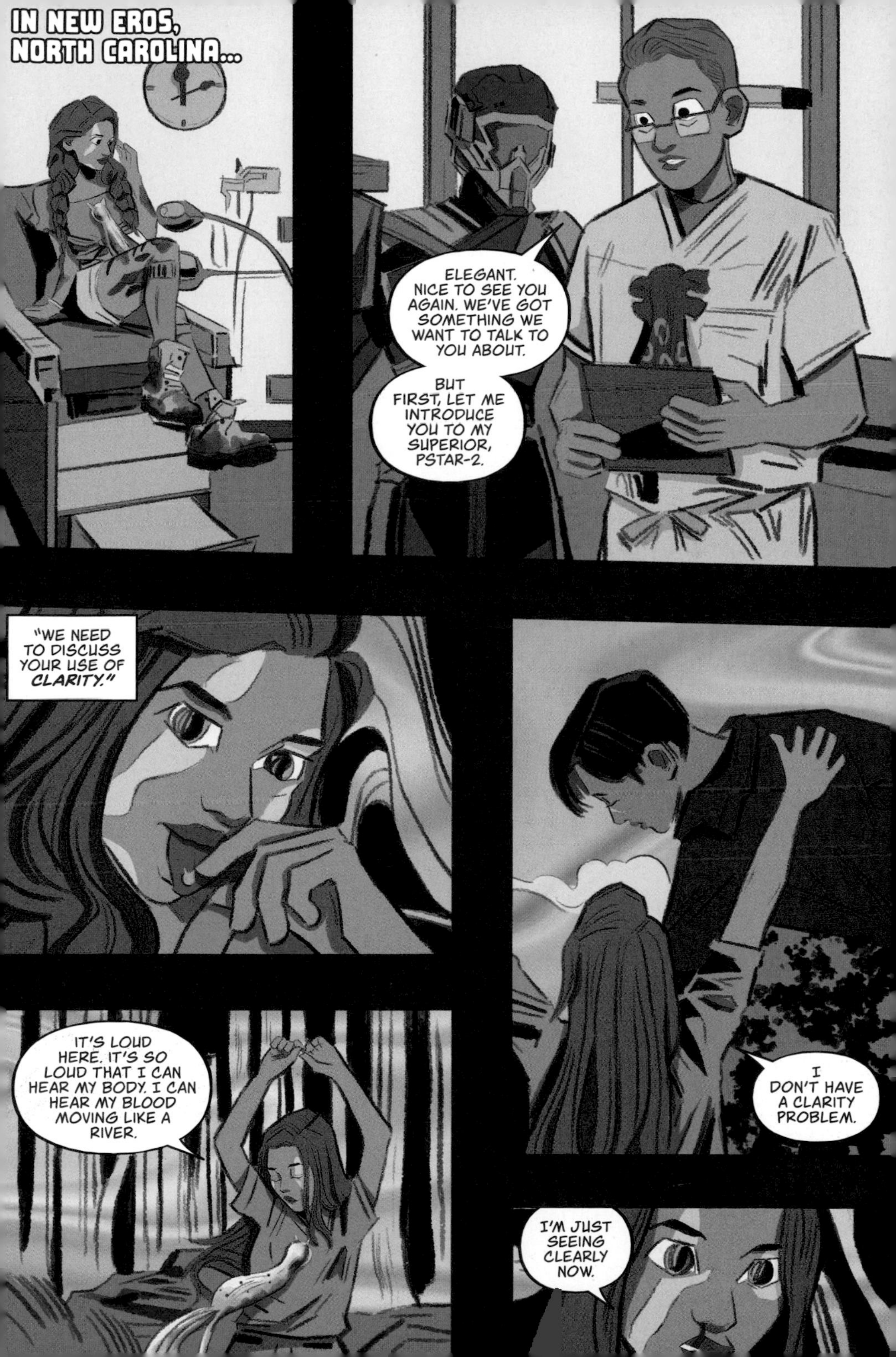
IN NEW EROS, NORTH CAROLINA...
ELEGANT. NICE TO SEE YOU AGAIN. WE'VE GOT SOMETHING WE WANT TO TALK TO YOU ABOUT.
BUT FIRST, LET ME INTRODUCE YOU TO MY SUPERIOR, PSTAR-2.
"WE NEED TO DISCUSS YOUR USE OF *CLARITY.*"
I DON'T HAVE A CLARITY PROBLEM.
IT'S LOUD HERE. IT'S SO LOUD THAT I CAN HEAR MY BODY. I CAN HEAR MY BLOOD MOVING LIKE A RIVER.
I'M JUST SEEING CLEARLY NOW.

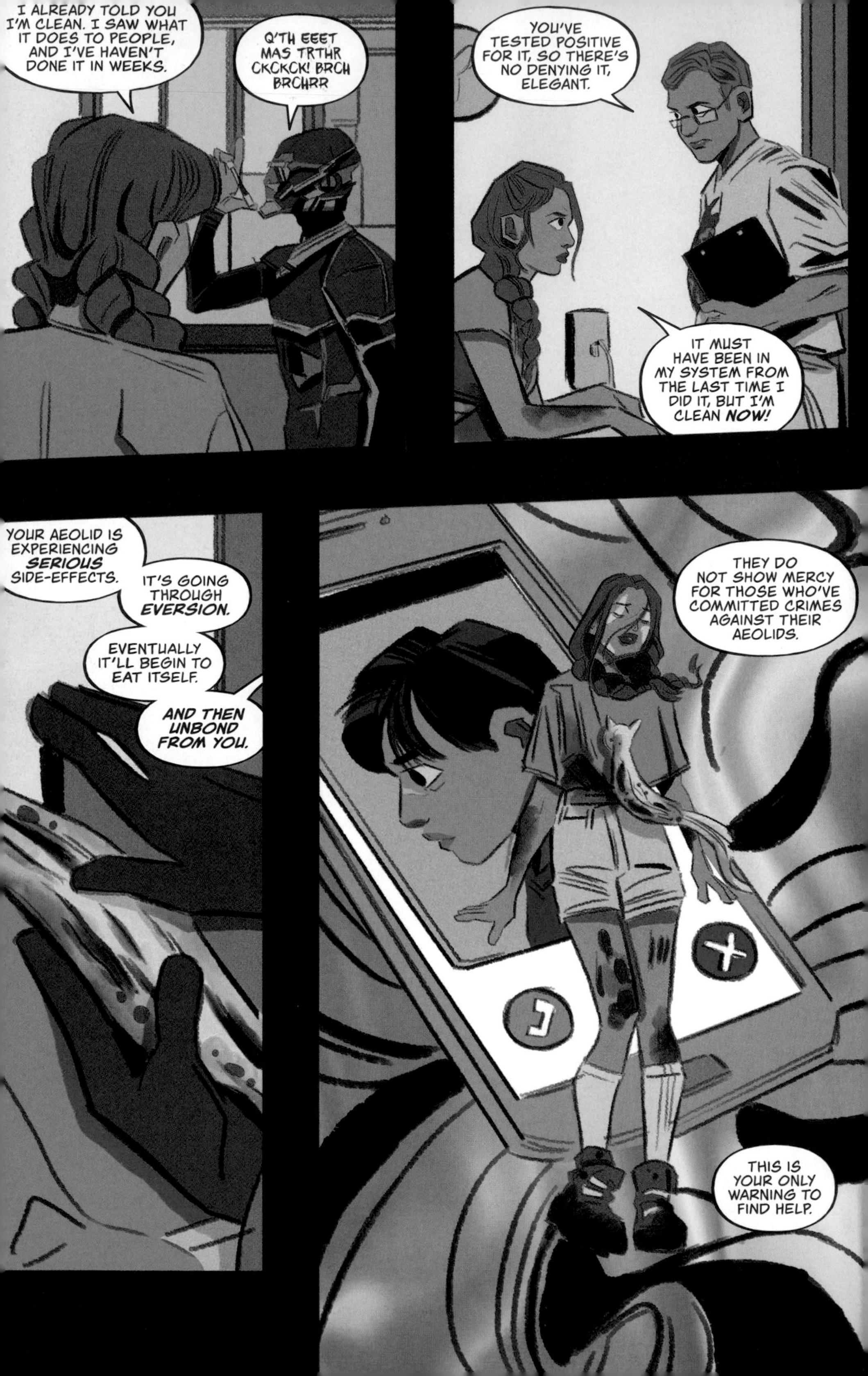

I ALREADY TOLD YOU I'M CLEAN. I SAW WHAT IT DOES TO PEOPLE, AND I'VE HAVEN'T DONE IT IN WEEKS.
Q'TH EEET MAS TRTHR CKCKCK! BRCH BRCHRR
YOU'VE TESTED POSITIVE FOR IT, SO THERE'S NO DENYING IT, ELEGANT.
IT MUST HAVE BEEN IN MY SYSTEM FROM THE LAST TIME I DID IT, BUT I'M CLEAN ***NOW!***
YOUR AEOLID IS EXPERIENCING ***SERIOUS*** SIDE-EFFECTS.
IT'S GOING THROUGH ***EVERSION.***
EVENTUALLY IT'LL BEGIN TO EAT ITSELF.
AND THEN UNBOND FROM YOU.
THEY DO NOT SHOW MERCY FOR THOSE WHO'VE COMMITTED CRIMES AGAINST THEIR AEOLIDS.
THIS IS YOUR ONLY WARNING TO FIND HELP.

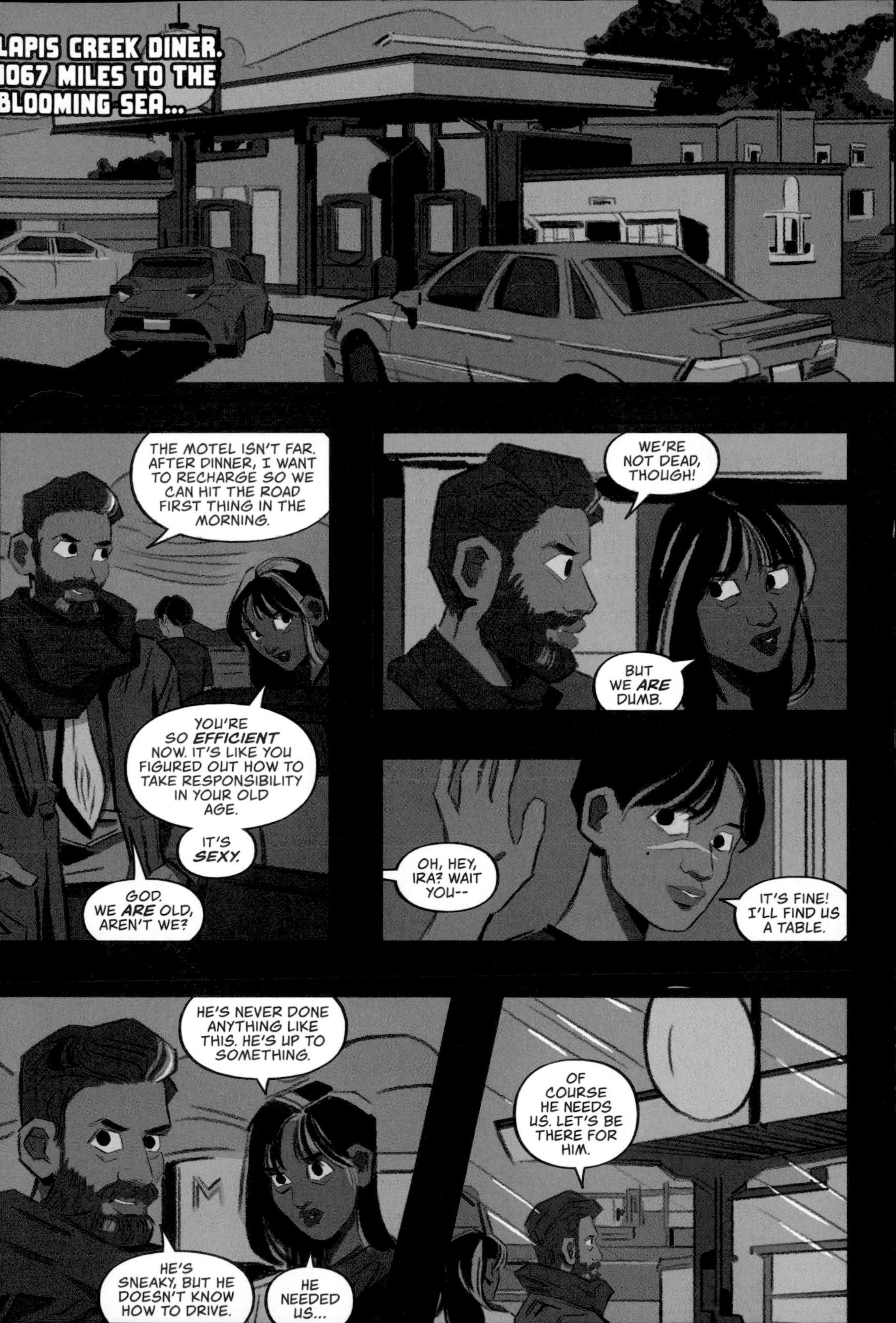
LAPIS CREEK DINER. 1067 MILES TO THE BLOOMING SEA...
THE MOTEL ISN'T FAR. AFTER DINNER, I WANT TO RECHARGE SO WE CAN HIT THE ROAD FIRST THING IN THE MORNING.
YOU'RE SO EFFICIENT NOW. IT'S LIKE YOU FIGURED OUT HOW TO TAKE RESPONSIBILITY IN YOUR OLD AGE.
IT'S SEXY.
GOD. WE ARE OLD, AREN'T WE?
WE'RE NOT DEAD, THOUGH!
BUT WE ARE DUMB.
OH, HEY, IRA? WAIT YOU--
IT'S FINE! I'LL FIND US A TABLE.
HE'S NEVER DONE ANYTHING LIKE THIS. HE'S UP TO SOMETHING.
OF COURSE HE NEEDS US. LET'S BE THERE FOR HIM.
HE'S SNEAKY, BUT HE DOESN'T KNOW HOW TO DRIVE.
HE NEEDED US...

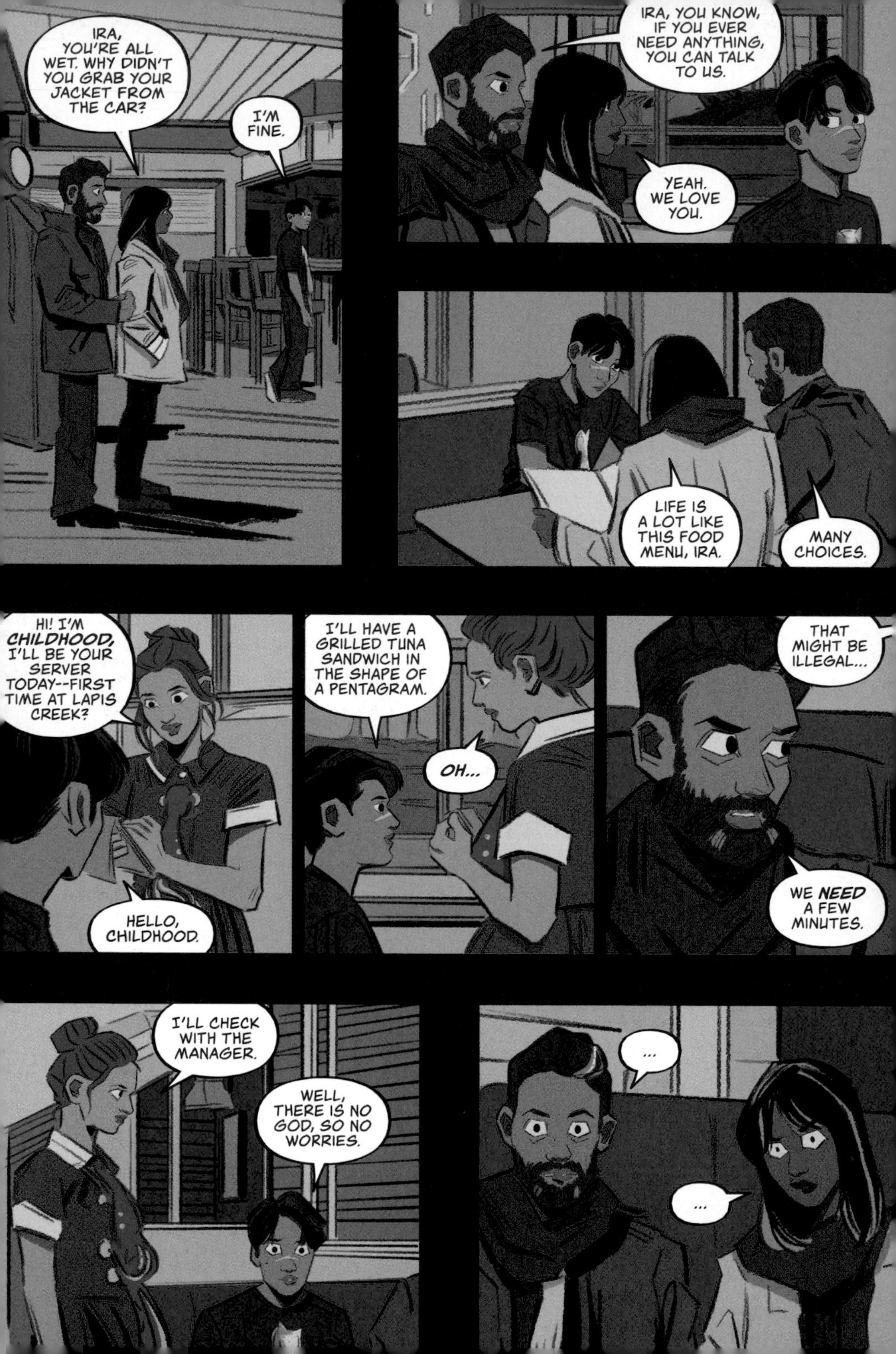
IRA, YOU'RE ALL WET. WHY DIDN'T YOU GRAB YOUR JACKET FROM THE CAR?
I'M FINE.
IRA, YOU KNOW, IF YOU EVER NEED ANYTHING, YOU CAN TALK TO US.
YEAH. WE LOVE YOU.
LIFE IS A LOT LIKE THIS FOOD MENU, IRA.
MANY CHOICES.
HI! I'M CHILDHOOD, I'LL BE YOUR SERVER TODAY--FIRST TIME AT LAPIS CREEK?
HELLO, CHILDHOOD.
I'LL HAVE A GRILLED TUNA SANDWICH IN THE SHAPE OF A PENTAGRAM.
OH...
THAT MIGHT BE ILLEGAL...
WE NEED A FEW MINUTES.
I'LL CHECK WITH THE MANAGER.
WELL, THERE IS NO GOD, SO NO WORRIES.
...
...

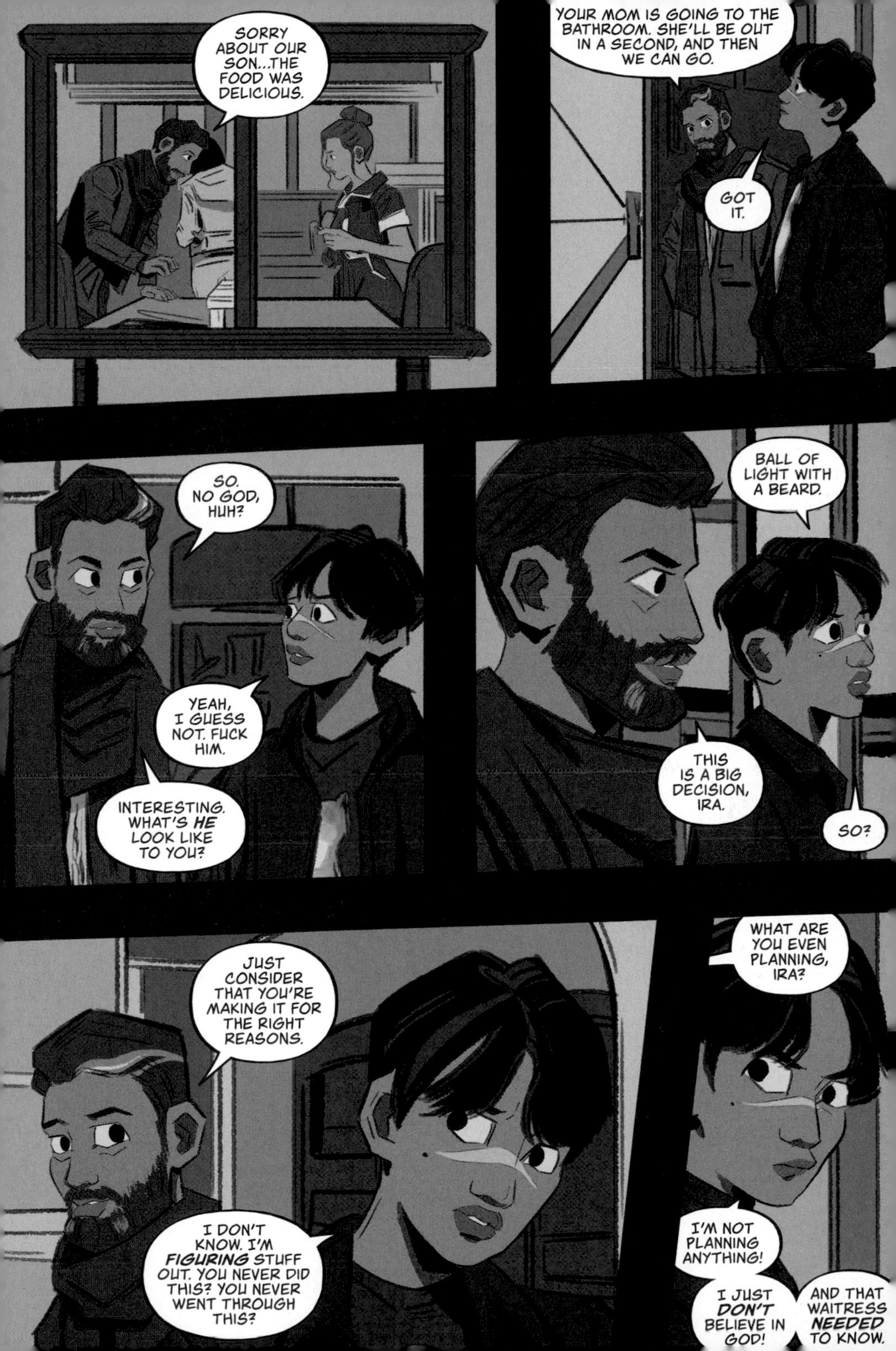
SORRY ABOUT OUR SON...THE FOOD WAS DELICIOUS.
YOUR MOM IS GOING TO THE BATHROOM. SHE'LL BE OUT IN A SECOND, AND THEN WE CAN GO.
GOT IT.
SO. NO GOD, HUH?
YEAH, I GUESS NOT. FUCK HIM.
INTERESTING. WHAT'S *HE* LOOK LIKE TO YOU?
BALL OF LIGHT WITH A BEARD.
THIS IS A BIG DECISION, IRA.
SO?
JUST CONSIDER THAT YOU'RE MAKING IT FOR THE RIGHT REASONS.
I DON'T KNOW. I'M *FIGURING* STUFF OUT. YOU NEVER DID THIS? YOU NEVER WENT THROUGH THIS?
WHAT ARE YOU EVEN PLANNING, IRA?
I'M NOT PLANNING ANYTHING!
I JUST *DON'T* BELIEVE IN GOD!
AND THAT WAITRESS *NEEDED* TO KNOW.

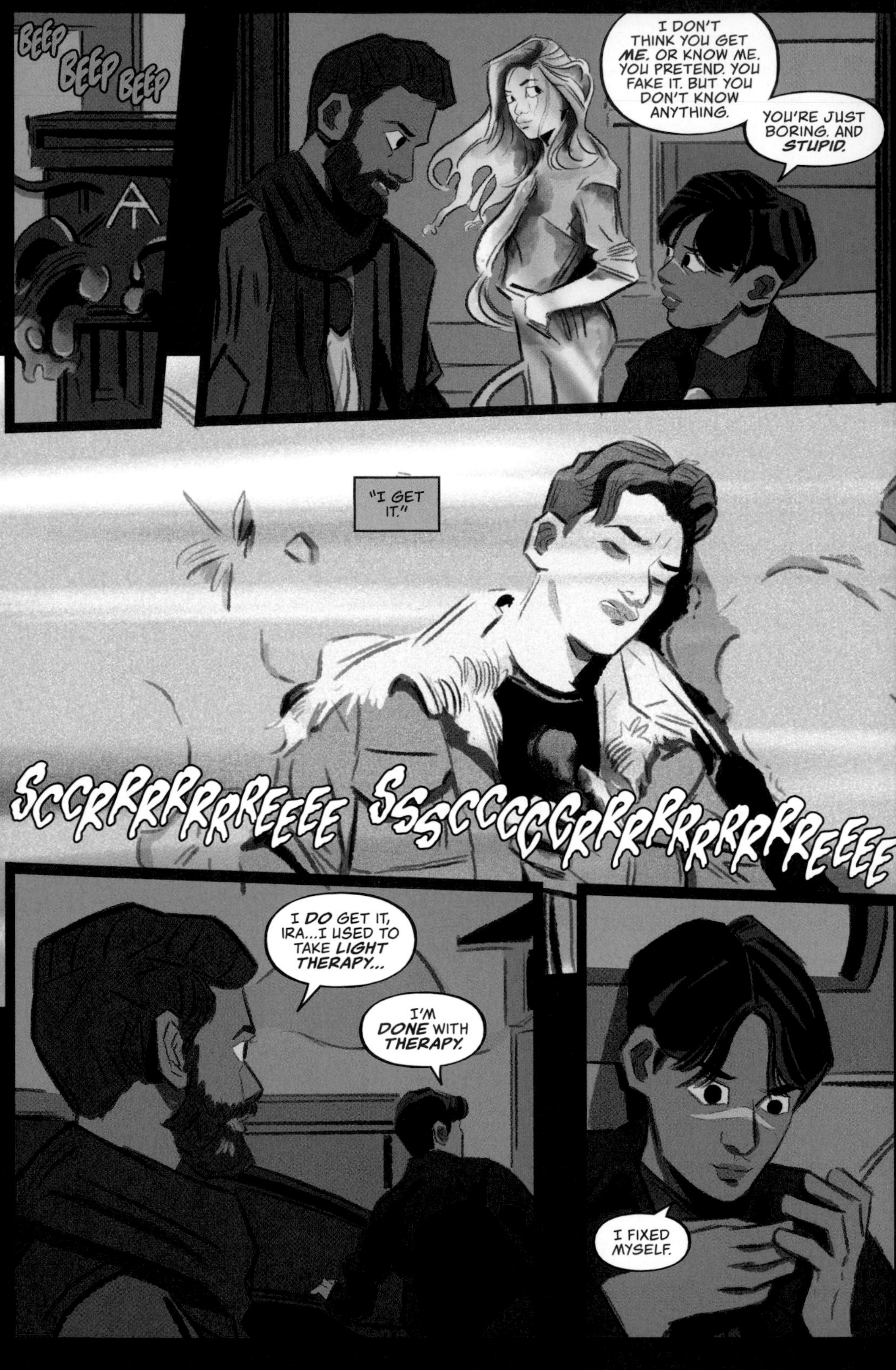
BEEP BEEP BEEP
I DON'T THINK YOU GET *ME*, OR KNOW ME. YOU PRETEND. YOU FAKE IT. BUT YOU DON'T KNOW ANYTHING.
YOU'RE JUST BORING. AND *STUPID*.
"I GET IT."
SCCRRRRRRREEEE SSSCCCCCGRRRRRRRRRREEEEE
I *DO* GET IT, IRA...I USED TO TAKE *LIGHT THERAPY*...
I'M *DONE* WITH *THERAPY*.
I FIXED MYSELF.

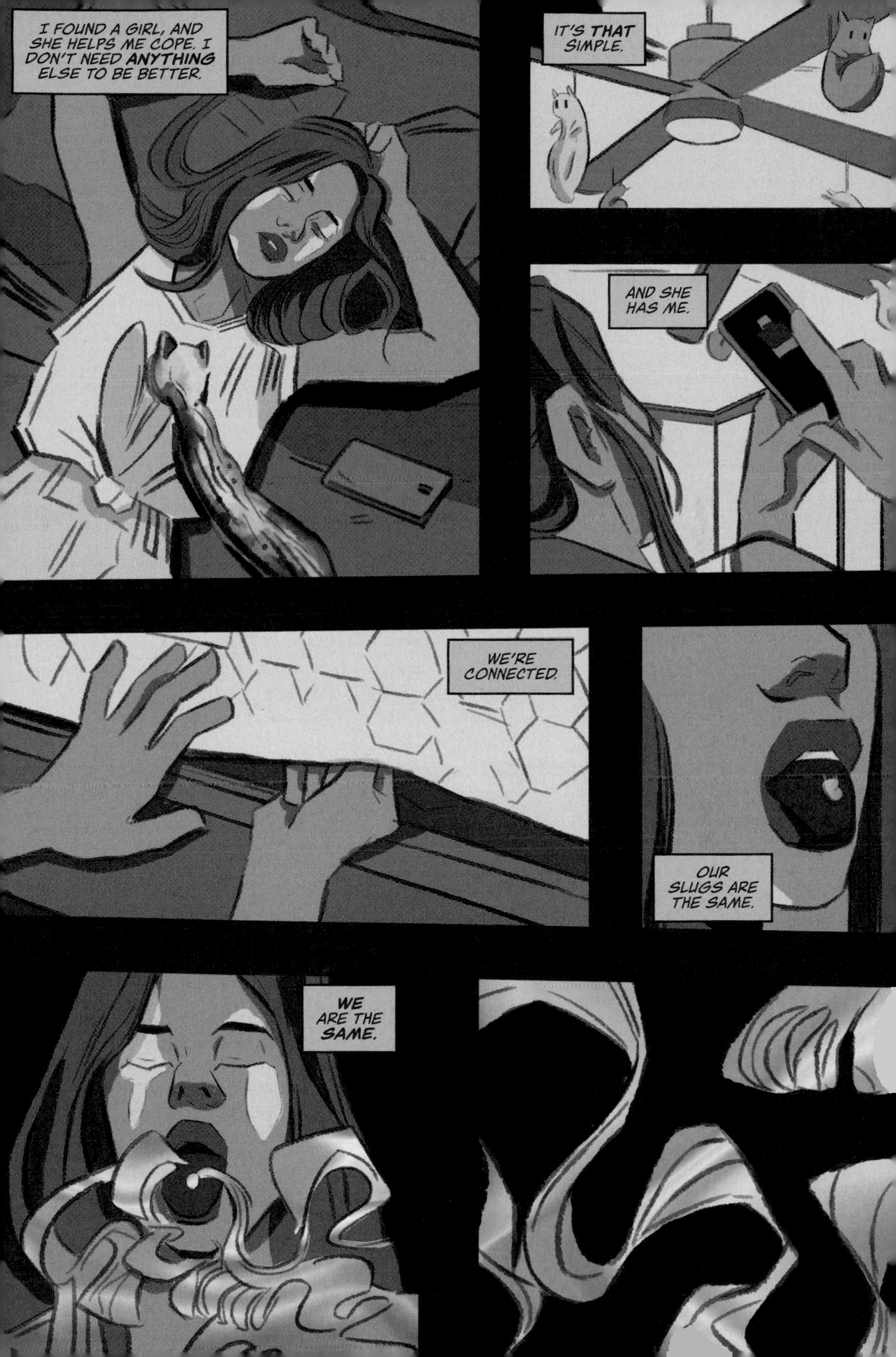
I FOUND A GIRL, AND SHE HELPS ME COPE. I DON'T NEED **ANYTHING** ELSE TO BE BETTER.
IT'S **THAT** SIMPLE.
AND SHE HAS ME.
WE'RE CONNECTED.
OUR SLUGS ARE THE SAME.
WE ARE THE **SAME.**

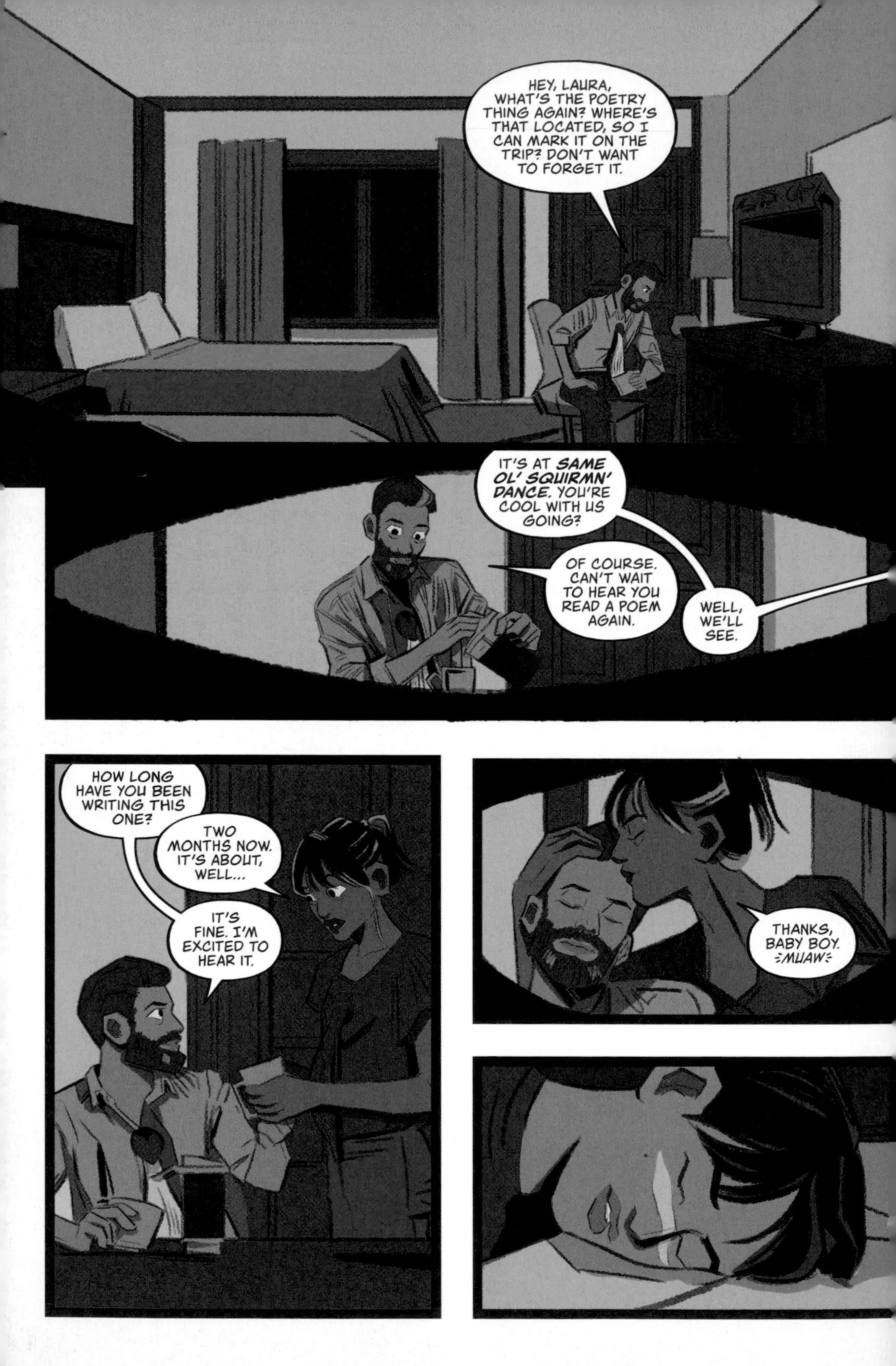
HEY, LAURA, WHAT'S THE POETRY THING AGAIN? WHERE'S THAT LOCATED, SO I CAN MARK IT ON THE TRIP? DON'T WANT TO FORGET IT.
IT'S AT **SAME OL' SQUIRMN' DANCE.** YOU'RE COOL WITH US GOING?
OF COURSE. CAN'T WAIT TO HEAR YOU READ A POEM AGAIN.
WELL, WE'LL SEE.
HOW LONG HAVE YOU BEEN WRITING THIS ONE?
TWO MONTHS NOW. IT'S ABOUT, WELL...
IT'S FINE. I'M EXCITED TO HEAR IT.
THANKS, BABY BOY.
MUAW

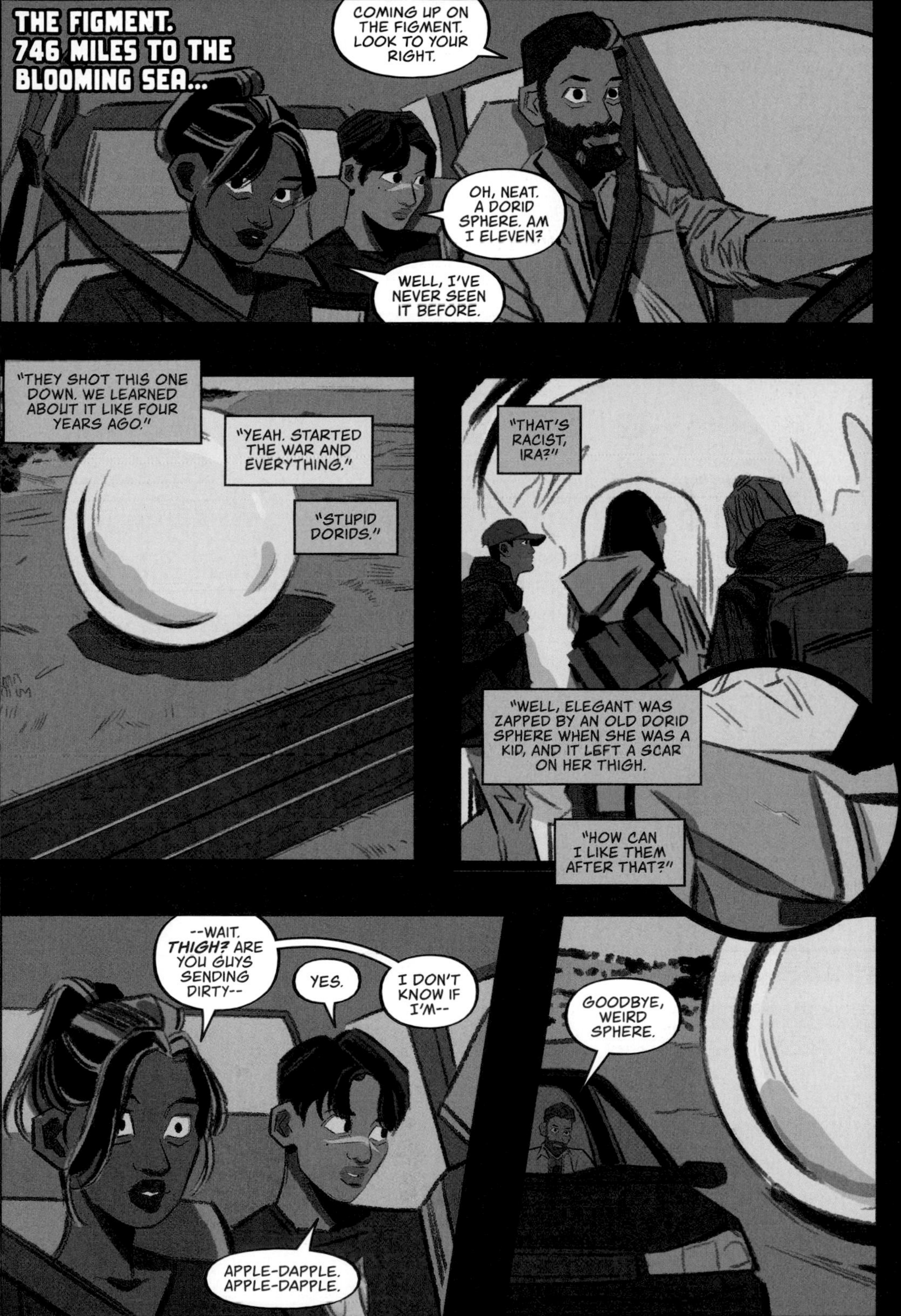
THE FIGMENT. 746 MILES TO THE BLOOMING SEA...
COMING UP ON THE FIGMENT. LOOK TO YOUR RIGHT.
OH, NEAT. A DORID SPHERE. AM I ELEVEN?
WELL, I'VE NEVER SEEN IT BEFORE.
"THEY SHOT THIS ONE DOWN. WE LEARNED ABOUT IT LIKE FOUR YEARS AGO."
"YEAH. STARTED THE WAR AND EVERYTHING."
"STUPID DORIDS."
"THAT'S RACIST, IRA?"
"WELL, ELEGANT WAS ZAPPED BY AN OLD DORID SPHERE WHEN SHE WAS A KID, AND IT LEFT A SCAR ON HER THIGH.
"HOW CAN I LIKE THEM AFTER THAT?"
--WAIT. THIGH? ARE YOU GUYS SENDING DIRTY--
YES.
I DON'T KNOW IF I'M--
APPLE-DAPPLE. APPLE-DAPPLE.
GOODBYE, WEIRD SPHERE.

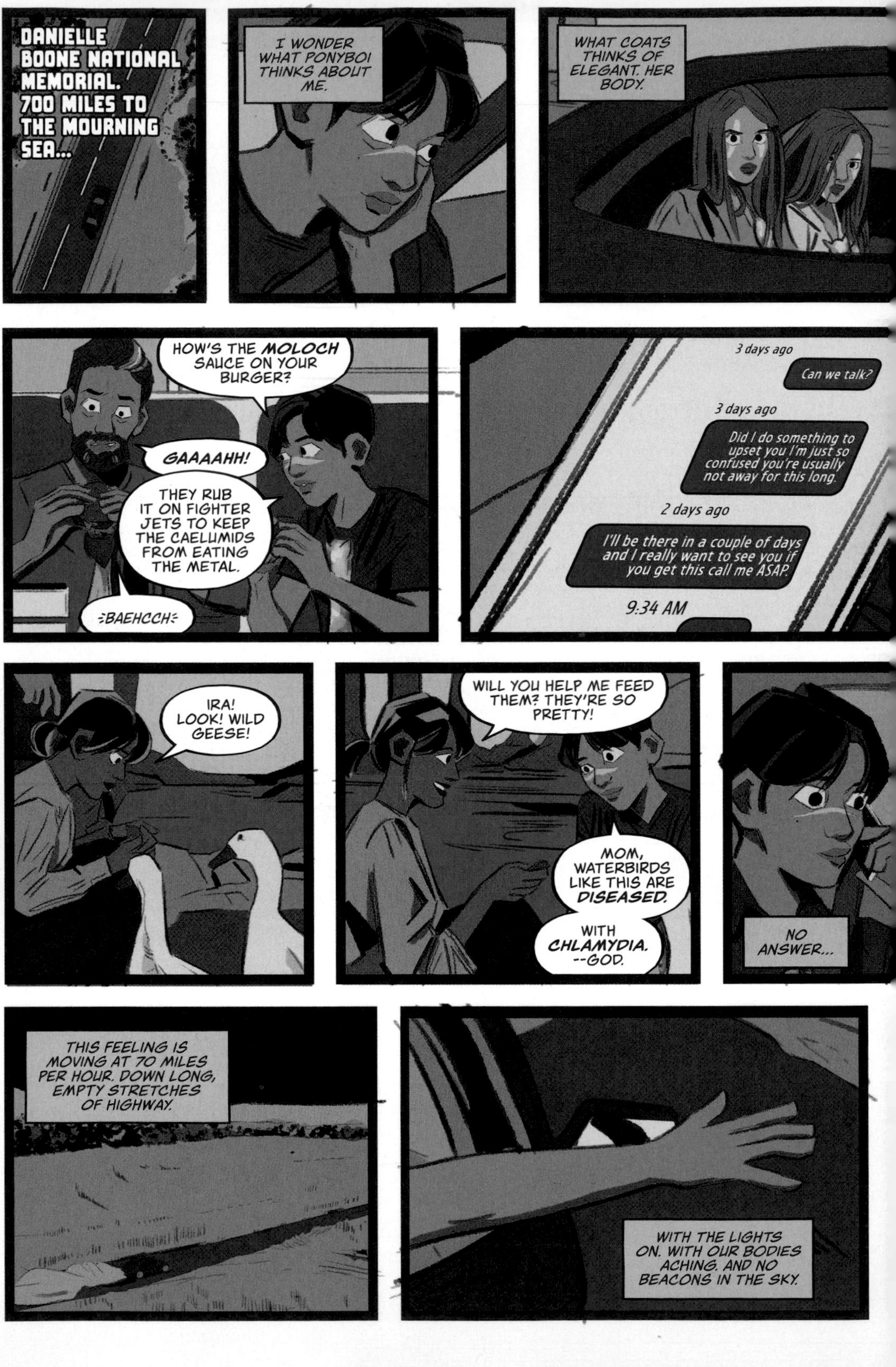
DANIELLE BOONE NATIONAL MEMORIAL. 700 MILES TO THE MOURNING SEA...
I WONDER WHAT PONYBOI THINKS ABOUT ME.
WHAT COATS THINKS OF ELEGANT. HER BODY.
HOW'S THE MOLOCH SAUCE ON YOUR BURGER?
GAAAAHH!
THEY RUB IT ON FIGHTER JETS TO KEEP THE CAELUMIDS FROM EATING THE METAL.
BAEHCCH
3 days ago
Can we talk?
3 days ago
Did I do something to upset you I'm just so confused you're usually not away for this long.
2 days ago
I'll be there in a couple of days and I really want to see you if you get this call me ASAP.
9:34 AM
IRA! LOOK! WILD GEESE!
WILL YOU HELP ME FEED THEM? THEY'RE SO PRETTY!
MOM, WATERBIRDS LIKE THIS ARE DISEASED.
WITH CHLAMYDIA. --GOD.
NO ANSWER...
THIS FEELING IS MOVING AT 70 MILES PER HOUR. DOWN LONG, EMPTY STRETCHES OF HIGHWAY.
WITH THE LIGHTS ON. WITH OUR BODIES ACHING. AND NO BEACONS IN THE SKY.

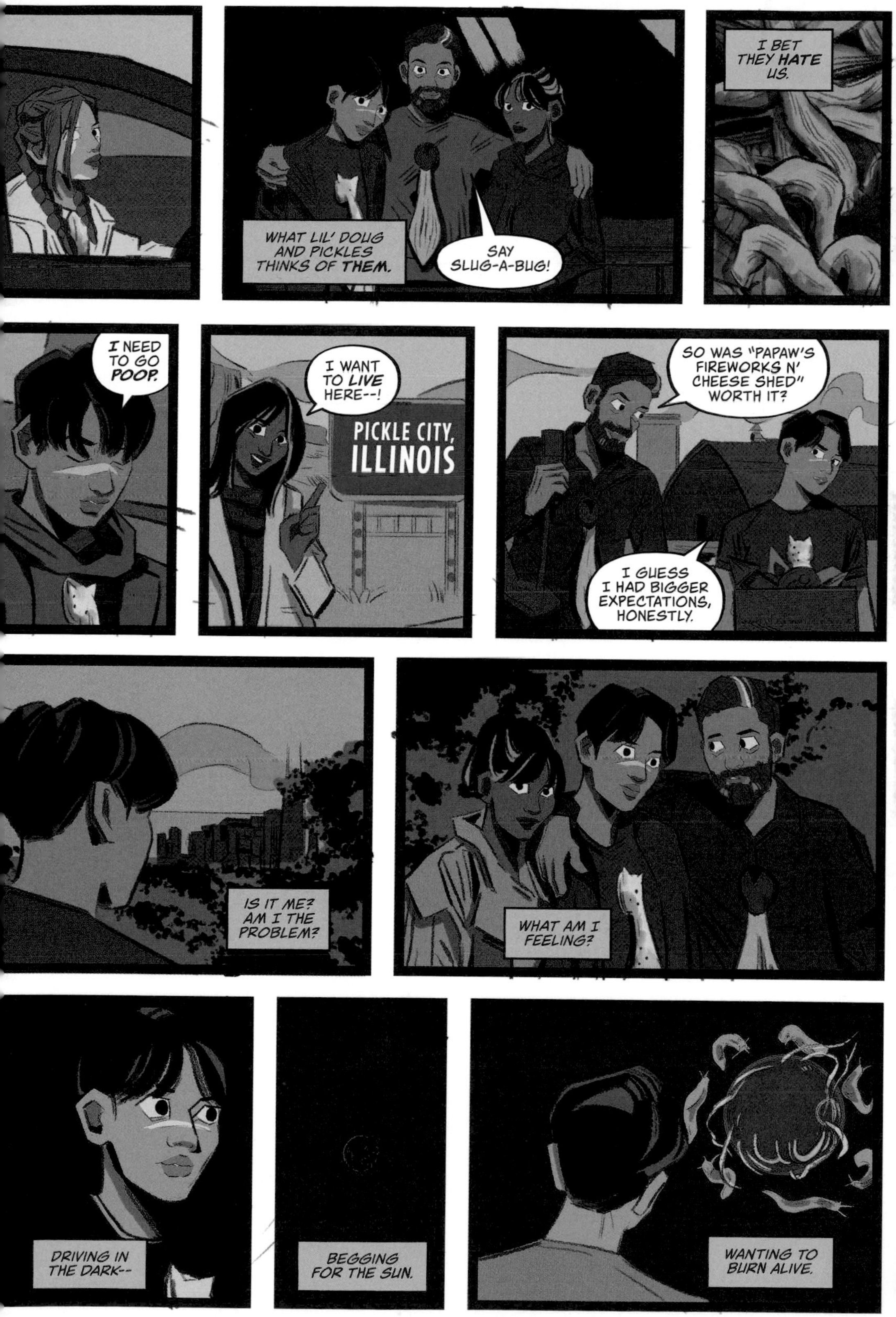
WHAT LIL' DOUG AND PICKLES THINKS OF THEM.
SAY SLUG-A-BUG!
I BET THEY HATE US.
I NEED TO GO POOP.
I WANT TO LIVE HERE--!
PICKLE CITY, ILLINOIS
SO WAS "PAPAW'S FIREWORKS N' CHEESE SHED" WORTH IT?
I GUESS I HAD BIGGER EXPECTATIONS, HONESTLY.
IS IT ME? AM I THE PROBLEM?
WHAT AM I FEELING?
DRIVING IN THE DARK--
BEGGING FOR THE SUN.
WANTING TO BURN ALIVE.

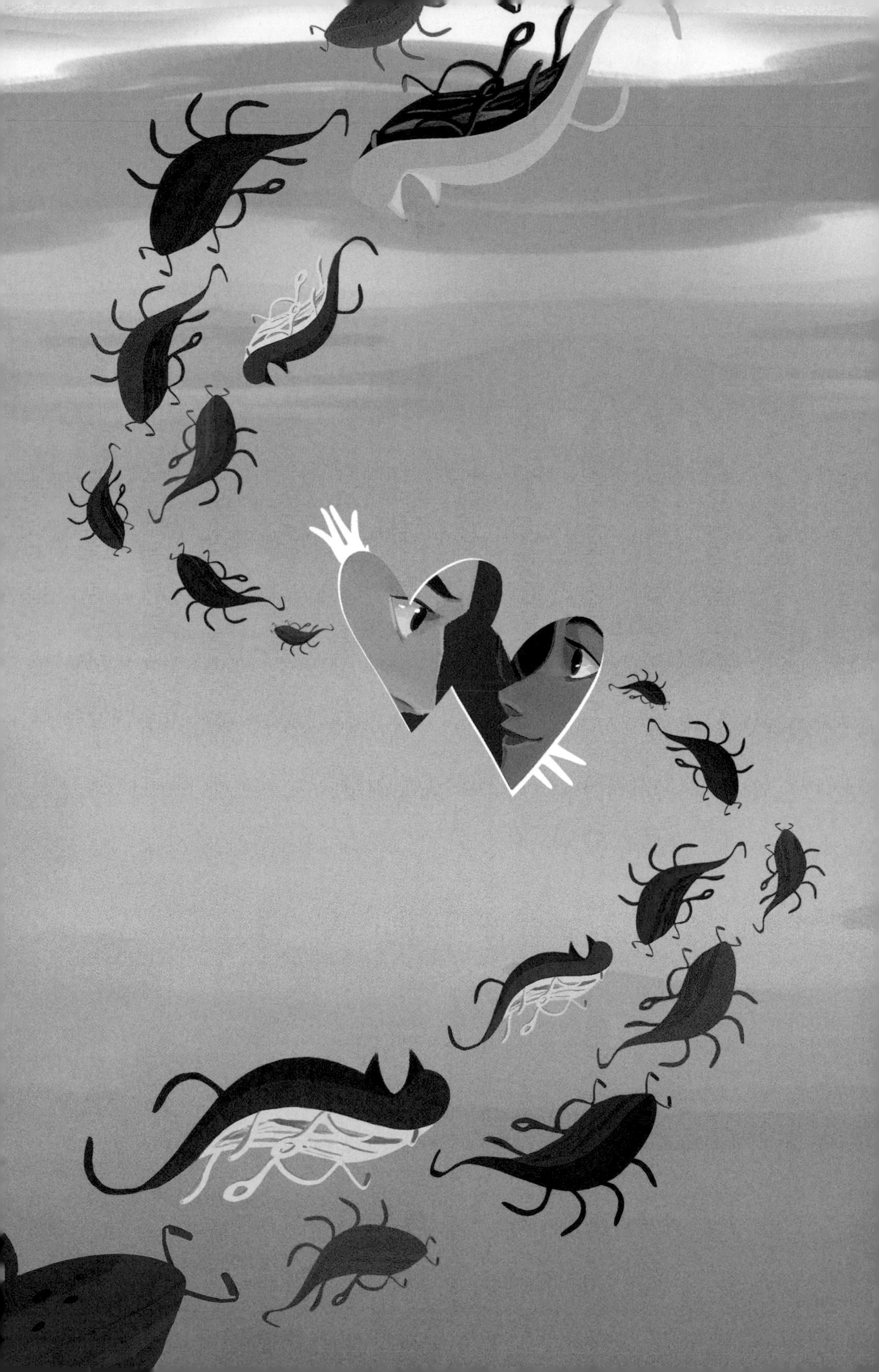

part nine

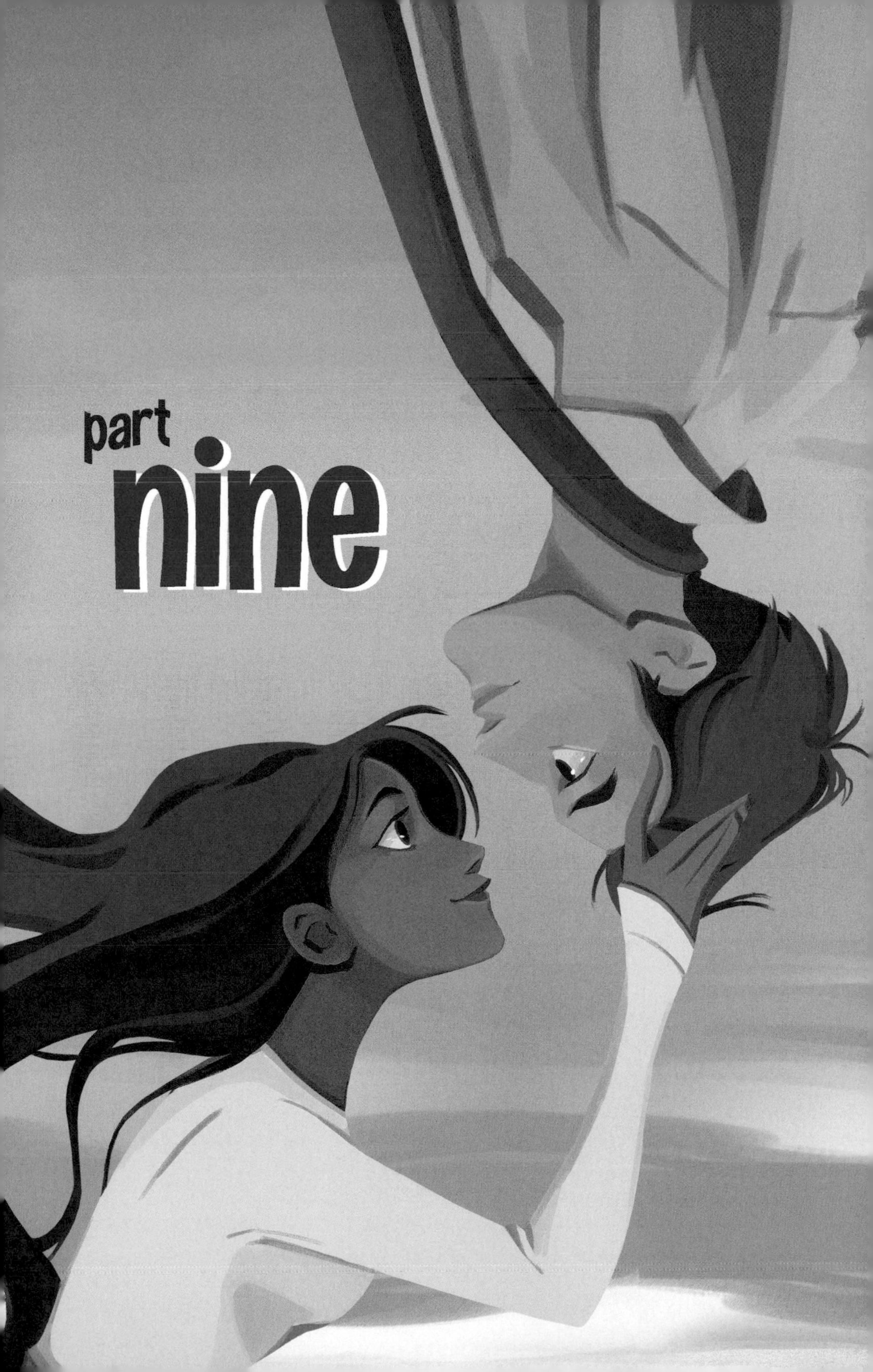

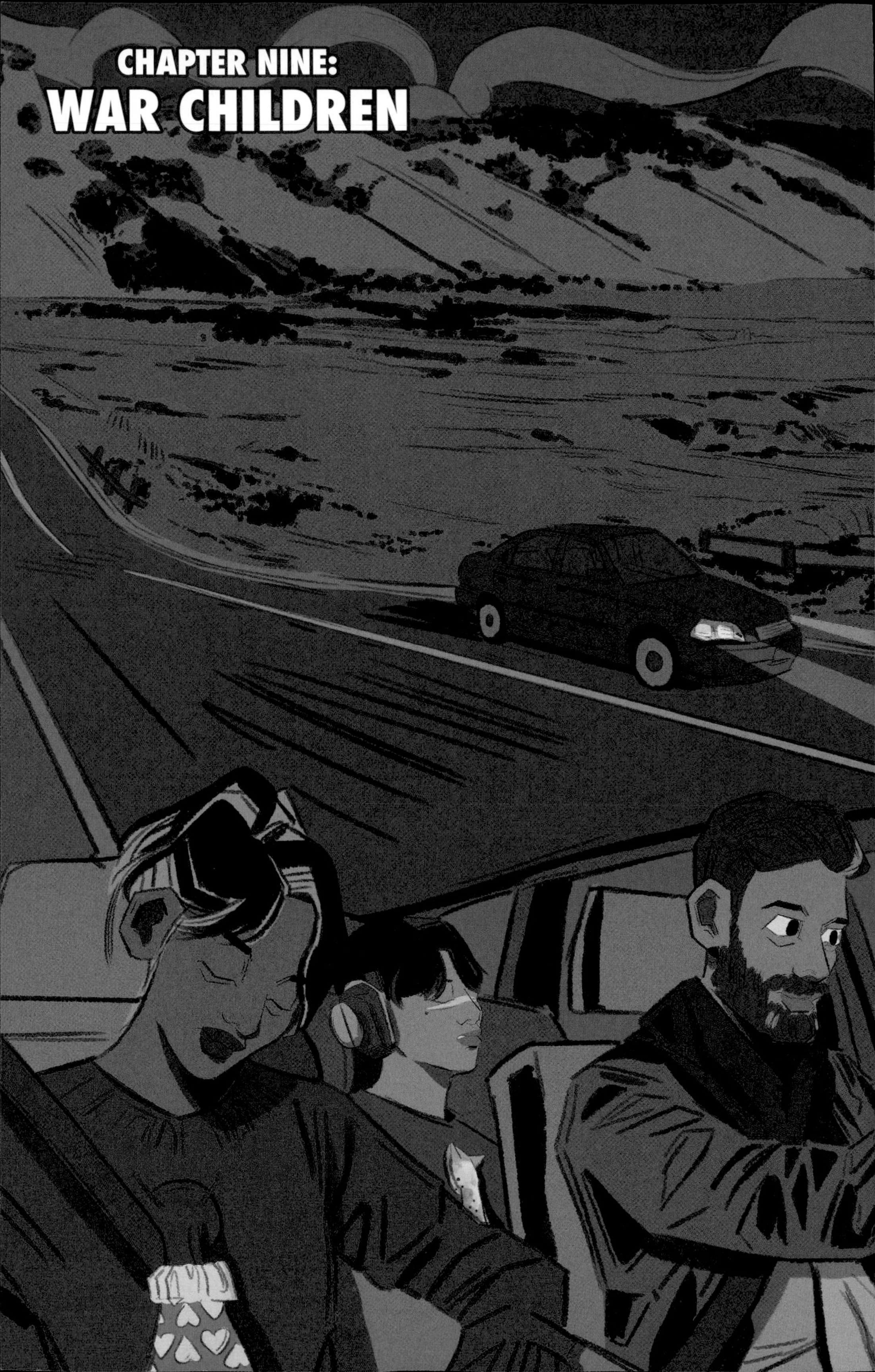
CHAPTER NINE:
WAR CHILDREN

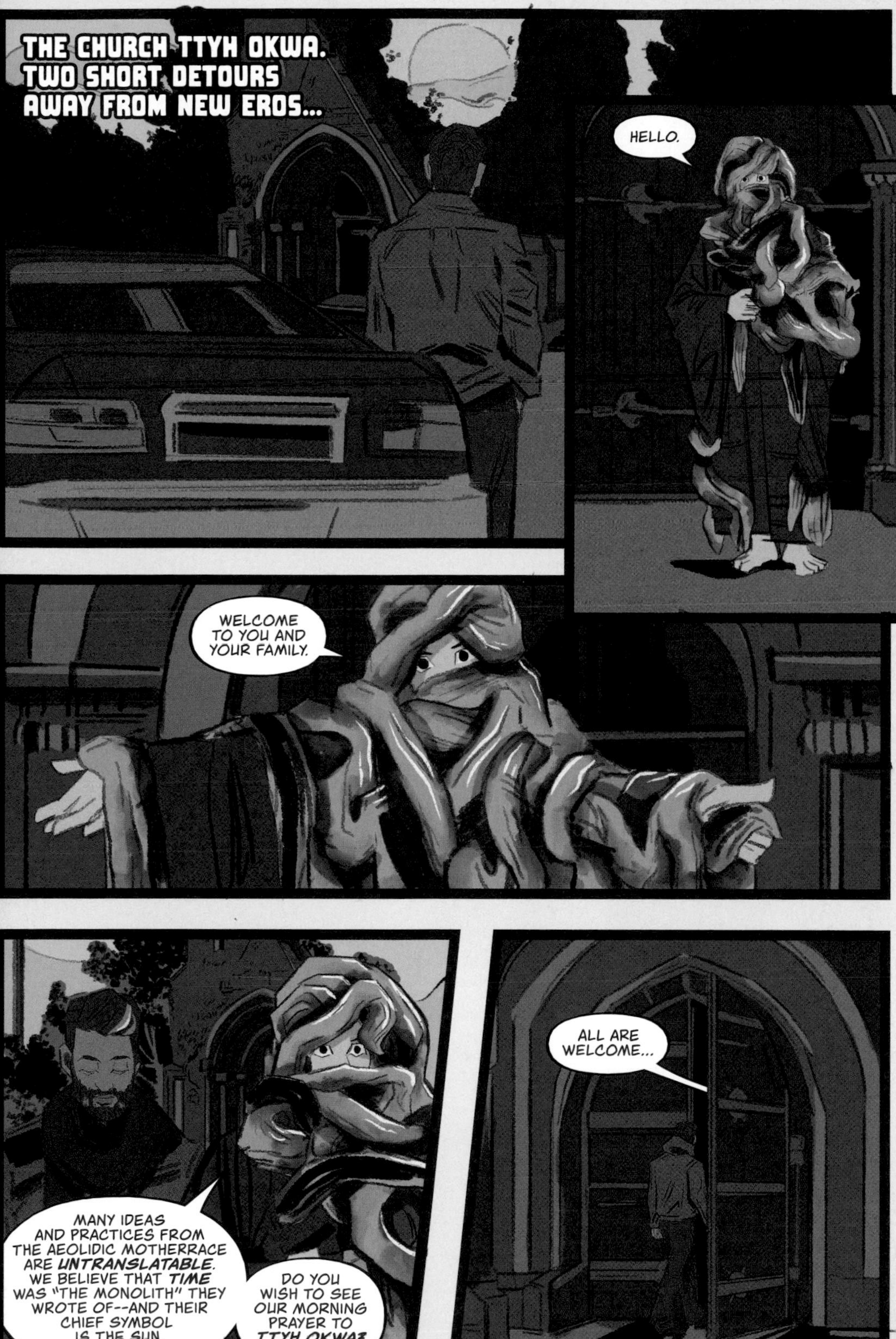
THE CHURCH TTYH OKWA. TWO SHORT DETOURS AWAY FROM NEW EROS...
HELLO.
WELCOME TO YOU AND YOUR FAMILY.
MANY IDEAS AND PRACTICES FROM THE AEOLIDIC MOTHERRACE ARE ***UNTRANSLATABLE***. WE BELIEVE THAT ***TIME*** WAS "THE MONOLITH" THEY WROTE OF--AND THEIR CHIEF SYMBOL IS THE SUN.
DO YOU WISH TO SEE OUR MORNING PRAYER TO ***TTYH OKWA?***
ALL ARE WELCOME...

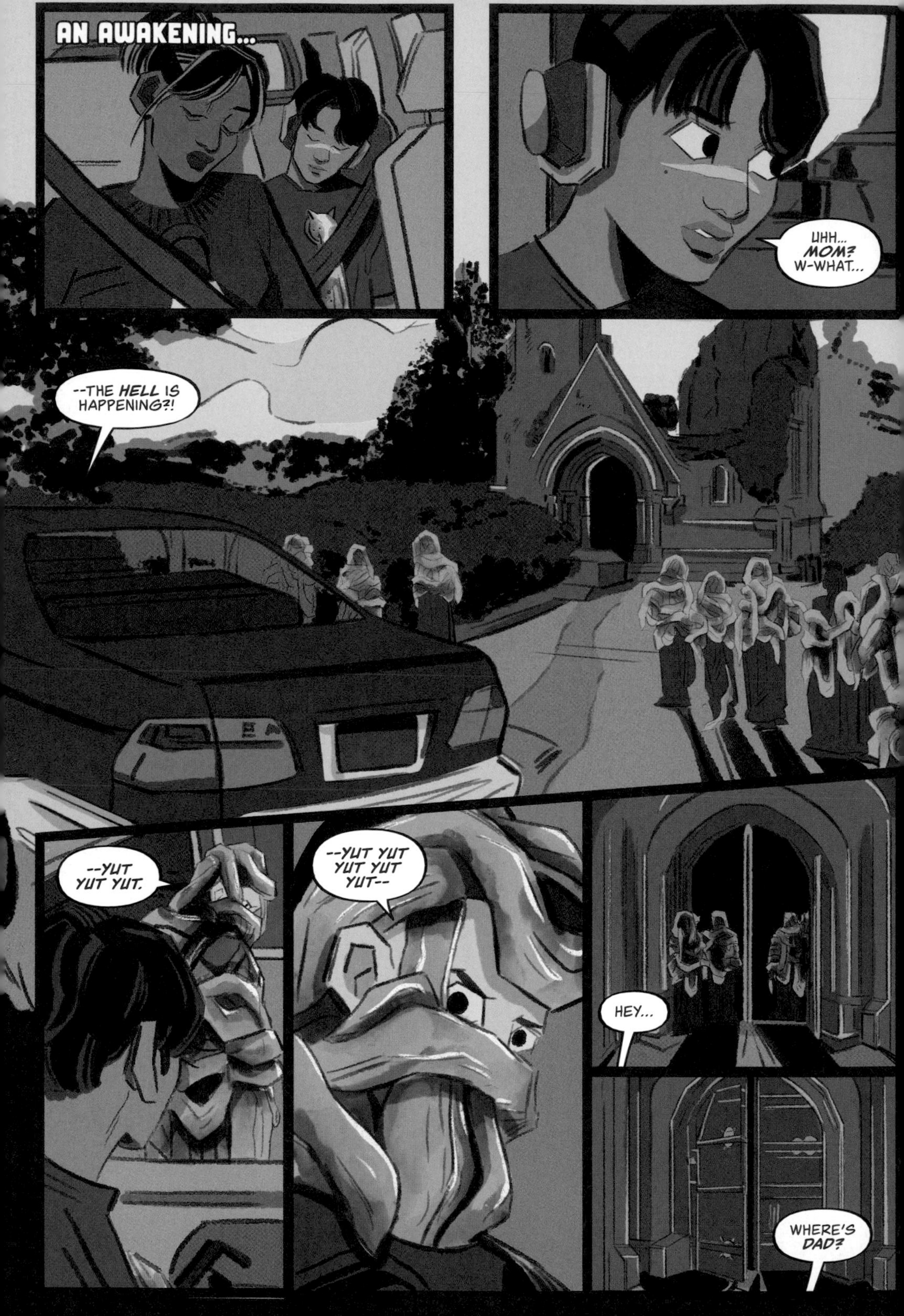
AN AWAKENING...
UHH... MOM? W-WHAT...
--THE HELL IS HAPPENING?!
--YUT YUT YUT.
--YUT YUT YUT YUT YUT--
HEY...
WHERE'S DAD?

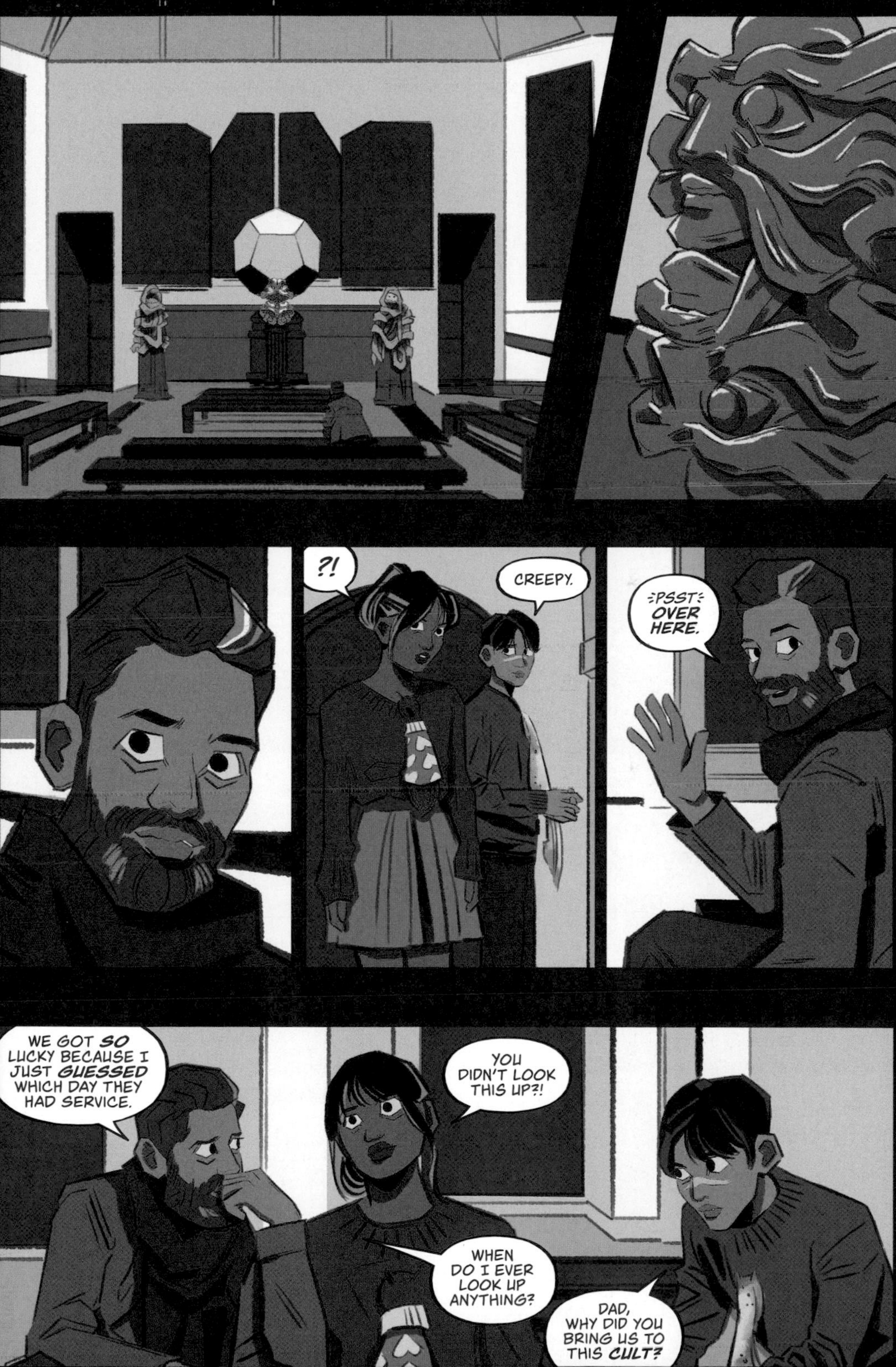
?!
CREEPY.
PSST
OVER HERE.
WE GOT SO LUCKY BECAUSE I JUST GUESSED WHICH DAY THEY HAD SERVICE.
YOU DIDN'T LOOK THIS UP?!
WHEN DO I EVER LOOK UP ANYTHING?
DAD, WHY DID YOU BRING US TO THIS CULT?

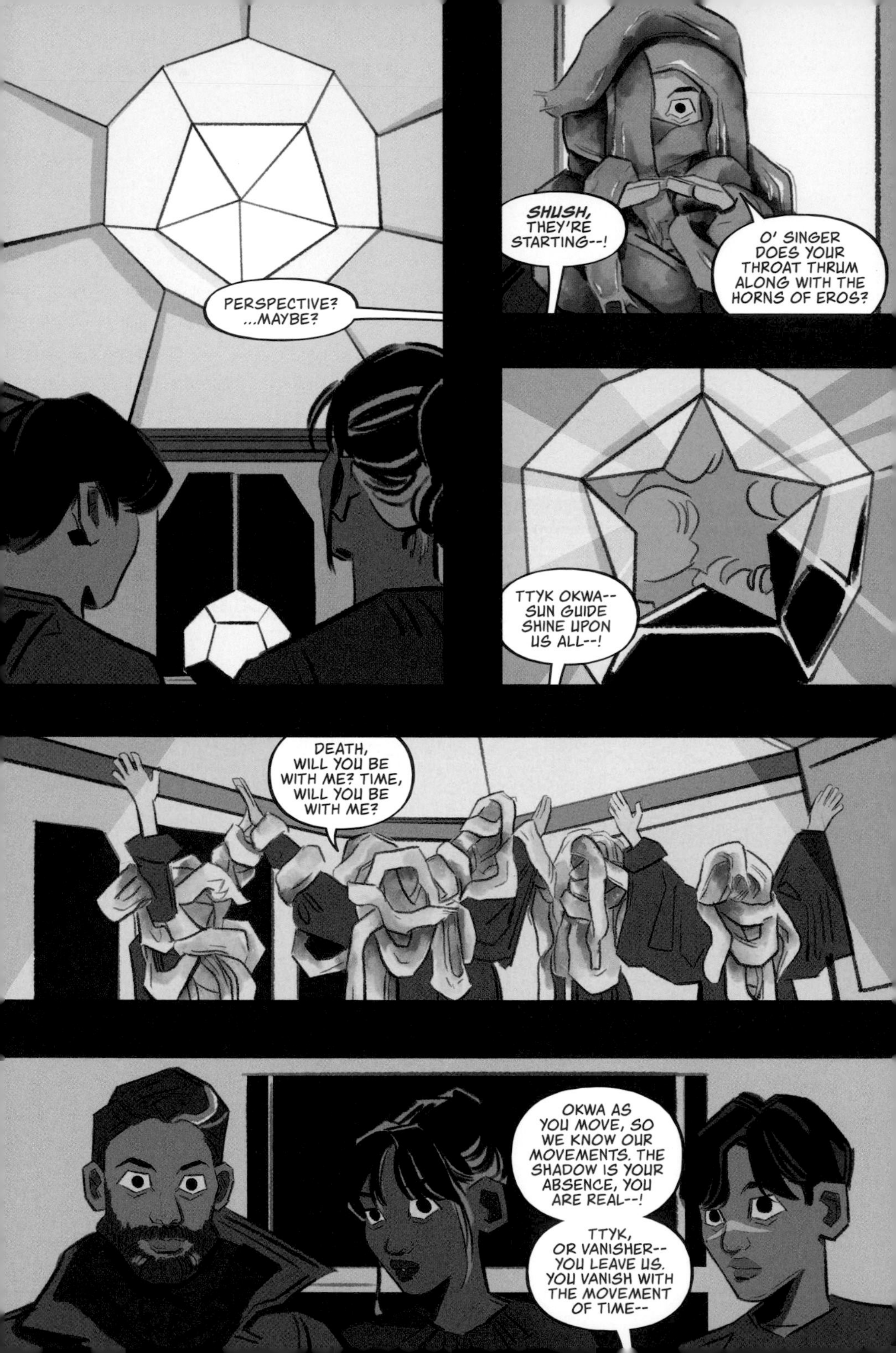
PERSPECTIVE? ...MAYBE?
SHUSH, THEY'RE STARTING--!
O' SINGER DOES YOUR THROAT THRUM ALONG WITH THE HORNS OF EROS?
TTYK OKWA-- SUN GUIDE SHINE UPON US ALL--!
DEATH, WILL YOU BE WITH ME? TIME, WILL YOU BE WITH ME?
OKWA AS YOU MOVE, SO WE KNOW OUR MOVEMENTS. THE SHADOW IS YOUR ABSENCE, YOU ARE REAL--!
TTYK, OR VANISHER-- YOU LEAVE US. YOU VANISH WITH THE MOVEMENT OF TIME--

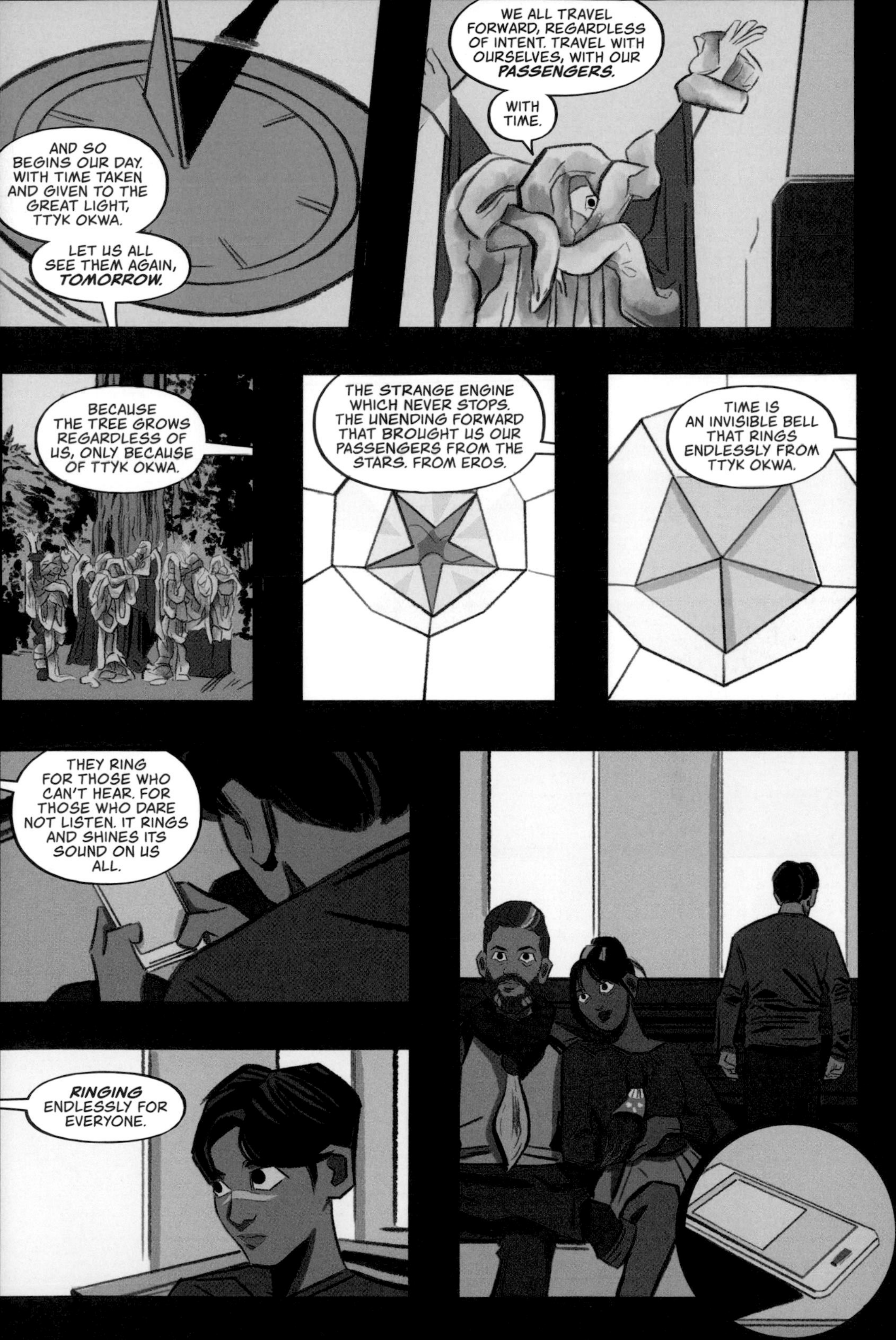
AND SO BEGINS OUR DAY. WITH TIME TAKEN AND GIVEN TO THE GREAT LIGHT, TTYK OKWA.
LET US ALL SEE THEM AGAIN, *TOMORROW.*
WE ALL TRAVEL FORWARD, REGARDLESS OF INTENT. TRAVEL WITH OURSELVES, WITH OUR *PASSENGERS.*
WITH TIME.
BECAUSE THE TREE GROWS REGARDLESS OF US, ONLY BECAUSE OF TTYK OKWA.
THE STRANGE ENGINE WHICH NEVER STOPS. THE UNENDING FORWARD THAT BROUGHT US OUR PASSENGERS FROM THE STARS. FROM EROS.
TIME IS AN INVISIBLE BELL THAT RINGS ENDLESSLY FROM TTYK OKWA.
THEY RING FOR THOSE WHO CAN'T HEAR. FOR THOSE WHO DARE NOT LISTEN. IT RINGS AND SHINES ITS SOUND ON US ALL.
RINGING ENDLESSLY FOR EVERYONE.

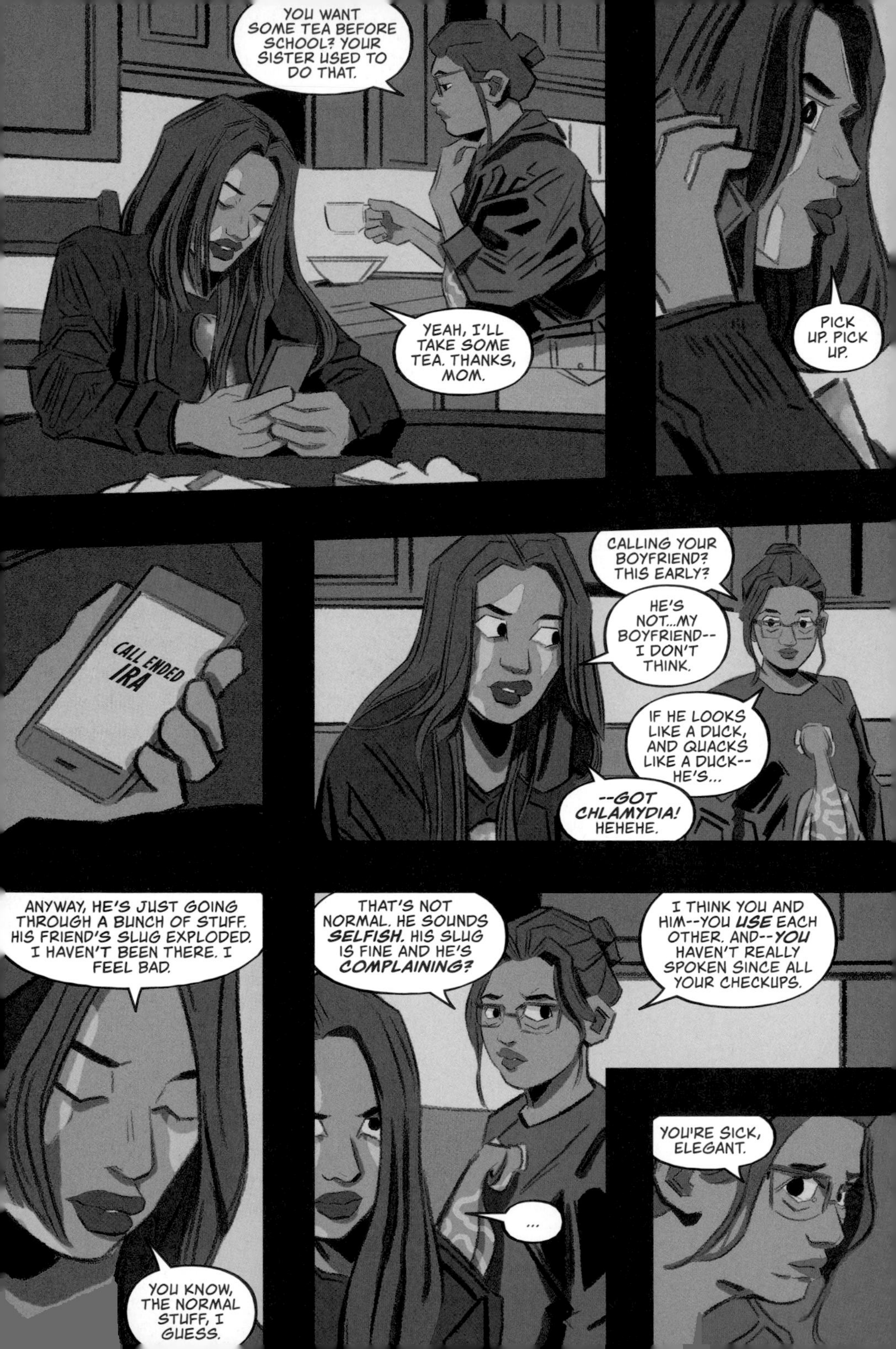
YOU WANT SOME TEA BEFORE SCHOOL? YOUR SISTER USED TO DO THAT.
YEAH, I'LL TAKE SOME TEA. THANKS, MOM.
PICK UP. PICK UP.
CALL ENDED
IRA
CALLING YOUR BOYFRIEND? THIS EARLY?
HE'S NOT...MY BOYFRIEND-- I DON'T THINK.
IF HE LOOKS LIKE A DUCK, AND QUACKS LIKE A DUCK-- HE'S...
--GOT CHLAMYDIA! HEHEHE.
ANYWAY, HE'S JUST GOING THROUGH A BUNCH OF STUFF. HIS FRIEND'S SLUG EXPLODED. I HAVEN'T BEEN THERE. I FEEL BAD.
YOU KNOW, THE NORMAL STUFF, I GUESS.
THAT'S NOT NORMAL. HE SOUNDS SELFISH. HIS SLUG IS FINE AND HE'S COMPLAINING?
...
I THINK YOU AND HIM--YOU USE EACH OTHER. AND--YOU HAVEN'T REALLY SPOKEN SINCE ALL YOUR CHECKUPS.
YOU'RE SICK, ELEGANT.

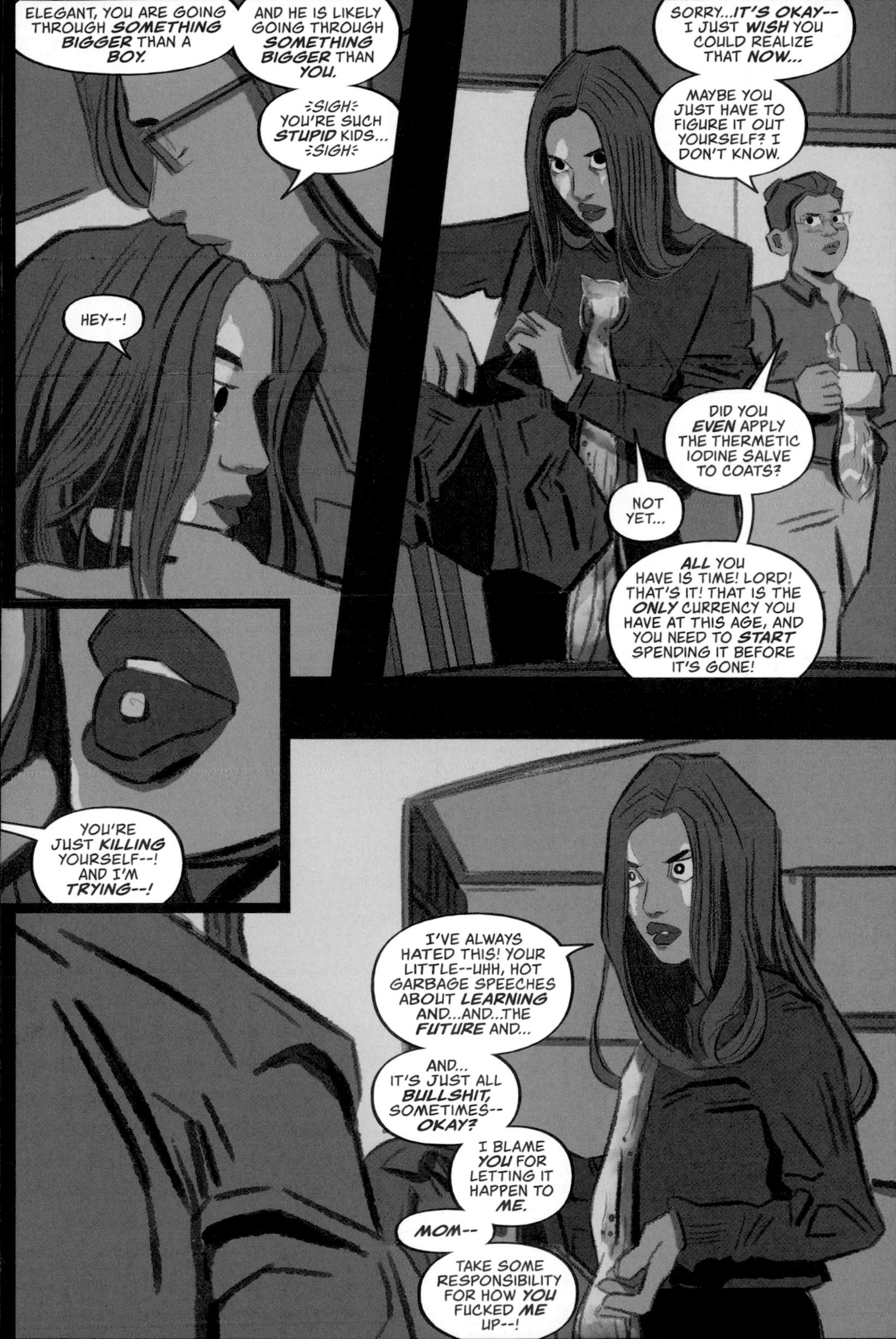
ELEGANT, YOU ARE GOING THROUGH SOMETHING BIGGER THAN A BOY.
AND HE IS LIKELY GOING THROUGH SOMETHING BIGGER THAN YOU.
=SIGH= YOU'RE SUCH STUPID KIDS... =SIGH=
HEY--!
SORRY...IT'S OKAY-- I JUST WISH YOU COULD REALIZE THAT NOW...
MAYBE YOU JUST HAVE TO FIGURE IT OUT YOURSELF? I DON'T KNOW.
DID YOU EVEN APPLY THE THERMETIC IODINE SALVE TO COATS?
NOT YET...
ALL YOU HAVE IS TIME! LORD! THAT'S IT! THAT IS THE ONLY CURRENCY YOU HAVE AT THIS AGE, AND YOU NEED TO START SPENDING IT BEFORE IT'S GONE!
YOU'RE JUST KILLING YOURSELF--! AND I'M TRYING--!
I'VE ALWAYS HATED THIS! YOUR LITTLE--UHH, HOT GARBAGE SPEECHES ABOUT LEARNING AND...AND...THE FUTURE AND...
AND... IT'S JUST ALL BULLSHIT, SOMETIMES-- OKAY?
I BLAME YOU FOR LETTING IT HAPPEN TO ME.
MOM--
TAKE SOME RESPONSIBILITY FOR HOW YOU FUCKED ME UP--!

I...

GULP!

I BLAME EVERYONE, OKAY? SO DON'T FEEL *SPECIAL* EITHER--

FOR, LIKE, LETTING IT BE THE *SAME*. YOU JUST PRETEND. YOU'RE NO *BETTER*.

NOTHING CHANGES. BECAUSE *THIS* MAKES YOU *FEEL* LIKE PART OF A BIGGER THING. LIKE YOU'RE *SAVING* ME?

YOU *FAILED* AT BEING A *CARETAKER* THE MOMENT YOU LET *ALIENS* PUT A GIANT *SLUG* ON MY BODY--!

IRA AND I WOULD HAVE *KILLED* THESE STUPID *FUCKIN'* THINGS BEFORE THEY LATCHED ONTO US!

I *HATE* YOU.

ELEGANT! I DON'T WANT YOU *TALKING* TO THAT BOY, ANYMORE--!

FUCK YOU!

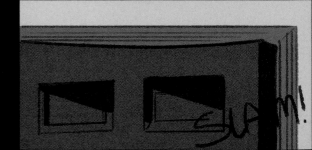

SLAM!

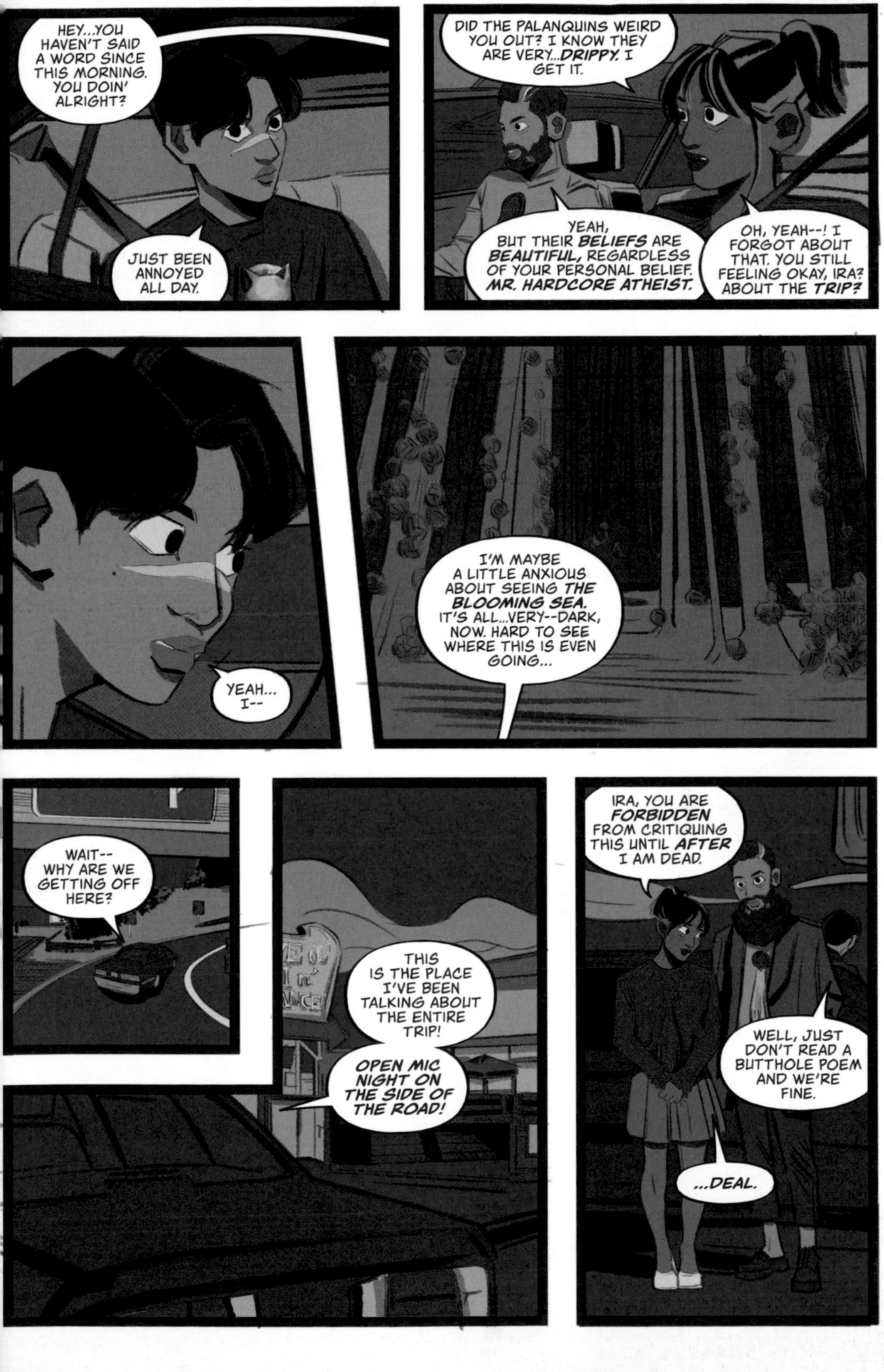
HEY...YOU HAVEN'T SAID A WORD SINCE THIS MORNING. YOU DOIN' ALRIGHT?
JUST BEEN ANNOYED ALL DAY.
DID THE PALANQUINS WEIRD YOU OUT? I KNOW THEY ARE VERY...DRIPPY. I GET IT.
YEAH, BUT THEIR BELIEFS ARE BEAUTIFUL, REGARDLESS OF YOUR PERSONAL BELIEF. MR. HARDCORE ATHEIST.
OH, YEAH--! I FORGOT ABOUT THAT. YOU STILL FEELING OKAY, IRA? ABOUT THE TRIP?
YEAH... I--
I'M MAYBE A LITTLE ANXIOUS ABOUT SEEING THE BLOOMING SEA. IT'S ALL...VERY--DARK, NOW. HARD TO SEE WHERE THIS IS EVEN GOING...
WAIT-- WHY ARE WE GETTING OFF HERE?
THIS IS THE PLACE I'VE BEEN TALKING ABOUT THE ENTIRE TRIP!
OPEN MIC NIGHT ON THE SIDE OF THE ROAD!
IRA, YOU ARE FORBIDDEN FROM CRITIQUING THIS UNTIL AFTER I AM DEAD.
WELL, JUST DON'T READ A BUTTHOLE POEM AND WE'RE FINE.
...DEAL.

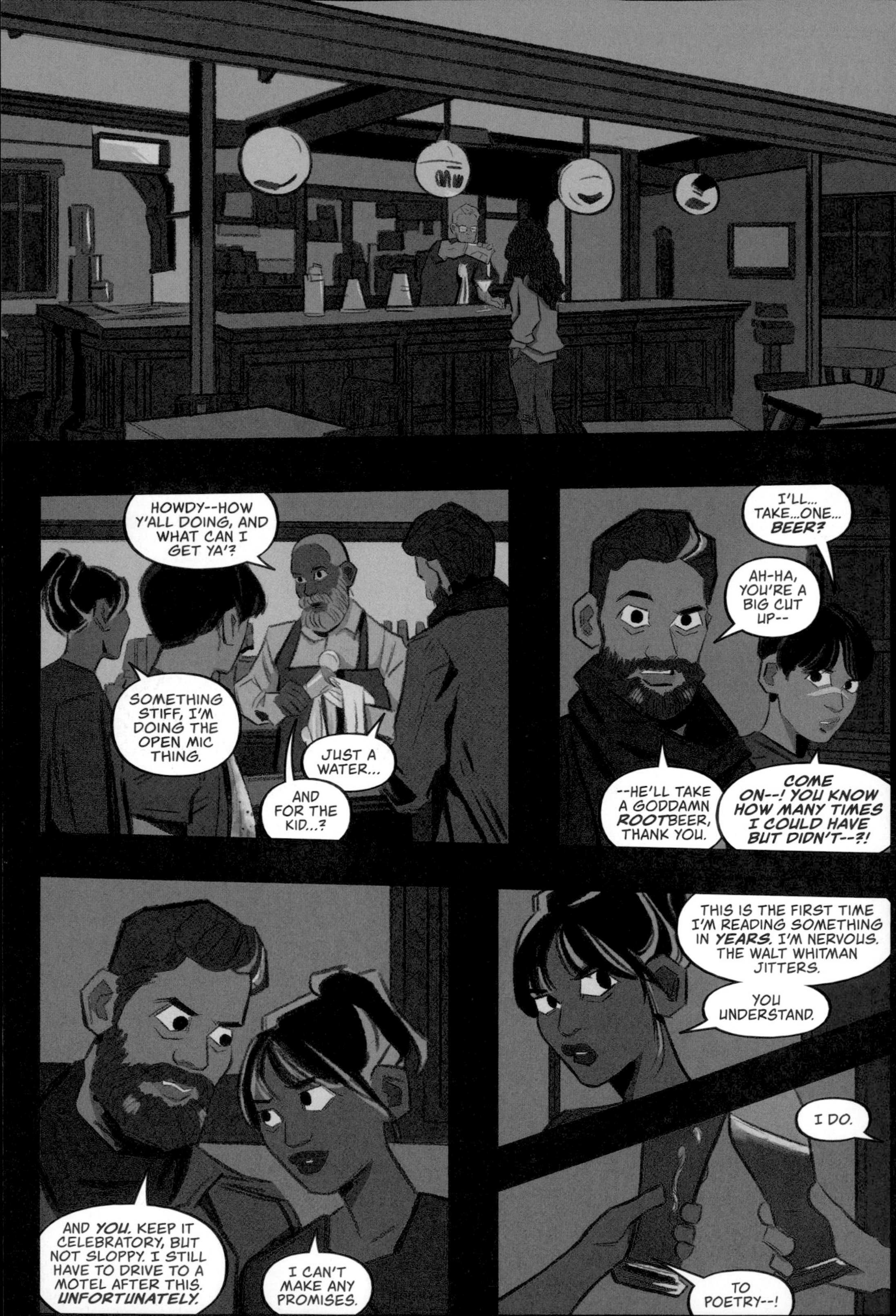
HOWDY--HOW Y'ALL DOING, AND WHAT CAN I GET YA'?
SOMETHING STIFF, I'M DOING THE OPEN MIC THING.
JUST A WATER...
AND FOR THE KID...?
I'LL... TAKE...ONE... BEER?
AH-HA, YOU'RE A BIG CUT UP--
--HE'LL TAKE A GODDAMN ROOTBEER, THANK YOU.
COME ON--! YOU KNOW HOW MANY TIMES I COULD HAVE BUT DIDN'T--?!
AND YOU. KEEP IT CELEBRATORY, BUT NOT SLOPPY. I STILL HAVE TO DRIVE TO A MOTEL AFTER THIS. UNFORTUNATELY.
I CAN'T MAKE ANY PROMISES.
THIS IS THE FIRST TIME I'M READING SOMETHING IN YEARS. I'M NERVOUS. THE WALT WHITMAN JITTERS.
YOU UNDERSTAND.
I DO.
TO POETRY--!

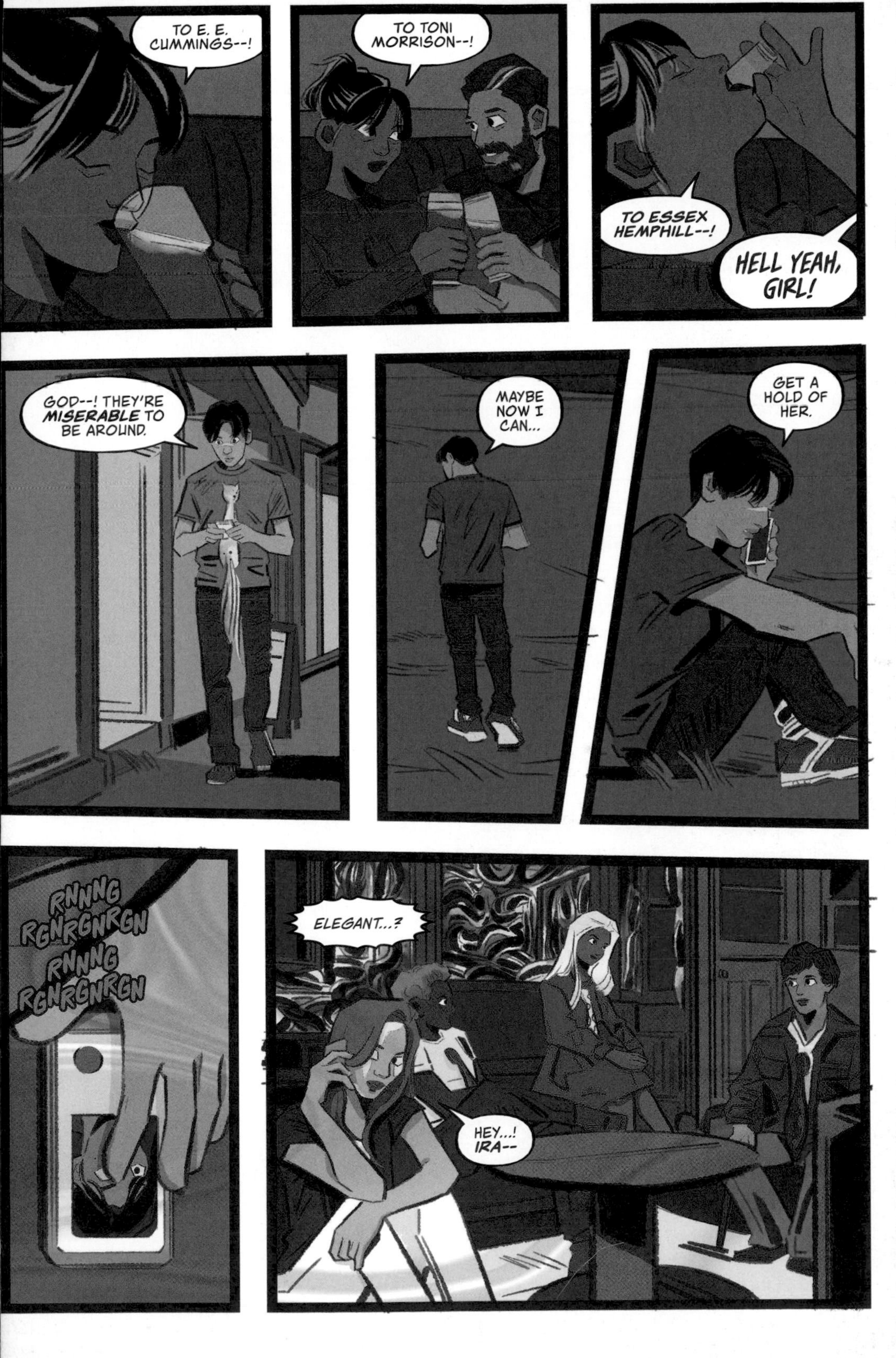
TO E. E. CUMMINGS--!
TO TONI MORRISON--!
TO ESSEX HEMPHILL--!
HELL YEAH, GIRL!
GOD--! THEY'RE MISERABLE TO BE AROUND.
MAYBE NOW I CAN...
GET A HOLD OF HER.
RNNNG RGNRGNRGN
RNNNG RGNRGNRGN
ELEGANT...?
HEY...! IRA--

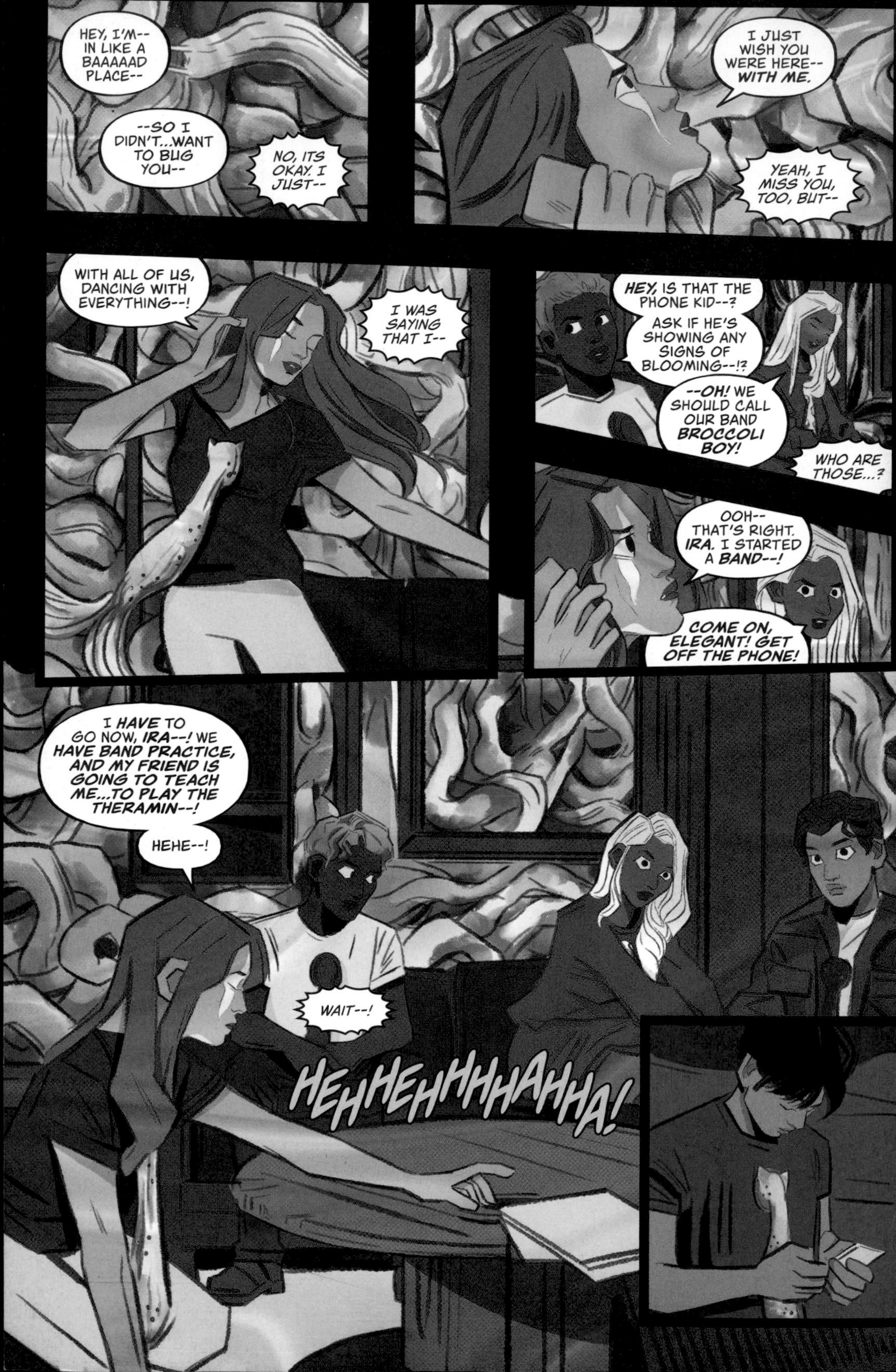
HEY, I'M-- IN LIKE A BAAAAAD PLACE--
--SO I DIDN'T...WANT TO BUG YOU--
NO, ITS OKAY. I JUST--
I JUST WISH YOU WERE HERE-- WITH ME.
YEAH, I MISS YOU, TOO, BUT--
WITH ALL OF US, DANCING WITH EVERYTHING--!
I WAS SAYING THAT I--
HEY, IS THAT THE PHONE KID--?
ASK IF HE'S SHOWING ANY SIGNS OF BLOOMING--!?
--OH! WE SHOULD CALL OUR BAND BROCCOLI BOY!
WHO ARE THOSE...?
OOH-- THAT'S RIGHT. IRA, I STARTED A BAND--!
COME ON, ELEGANT! GET OFF THE PHONE!
I HAVE TO GO NOW, IRA--! WE HAVE BAND PRACTICE, AND MY FRIEND IS GOING TO TEACH ME...TO PLAY THE THERAMIN--!
HEHE--!
WAIT--!
HEHHEHHHHAHHA!

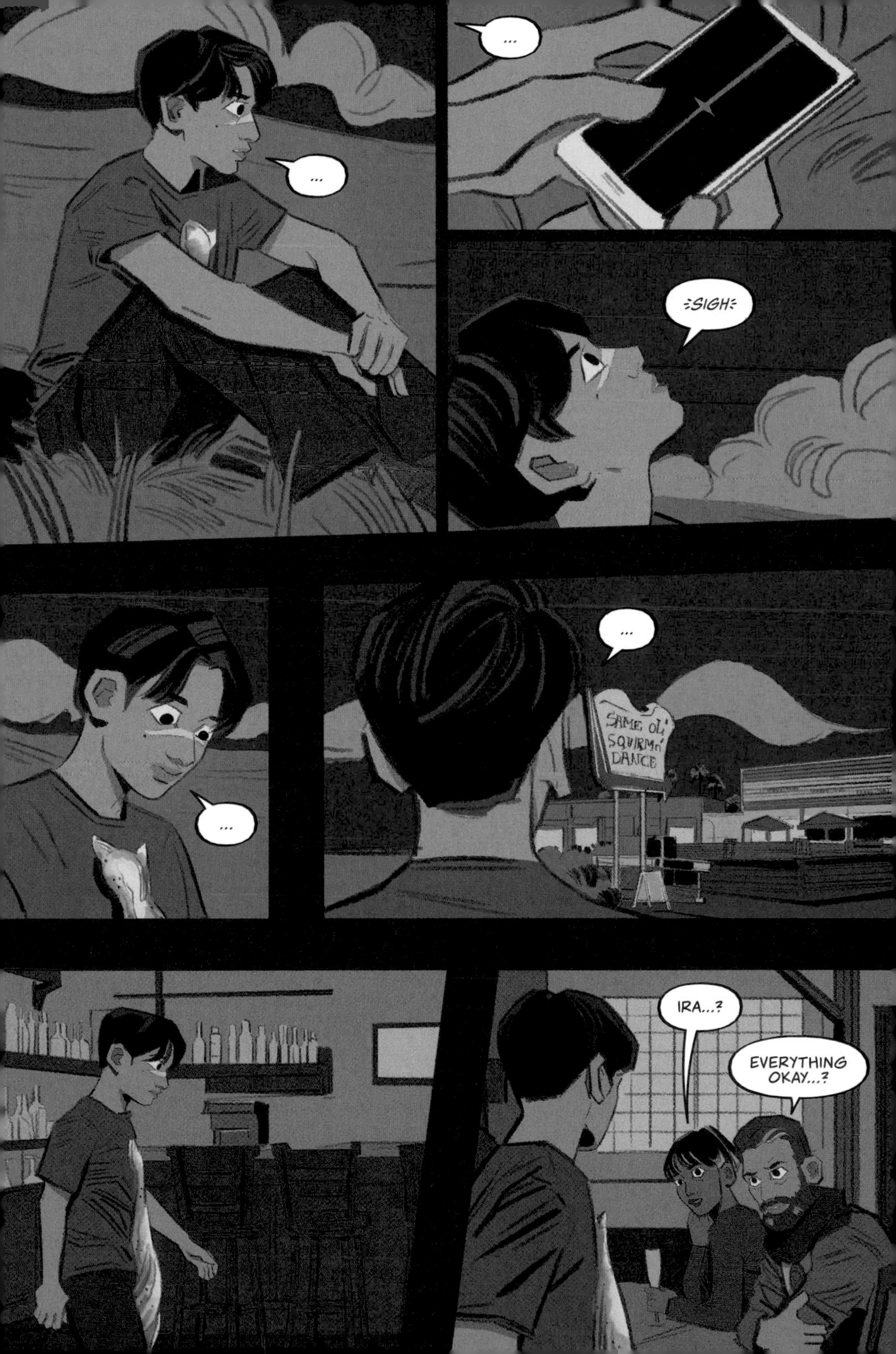
...
...
SIGH
...
...
SAME OL' SQUIRM n' DANCE
...
IRA...?
EVERYTHING OKAY...?

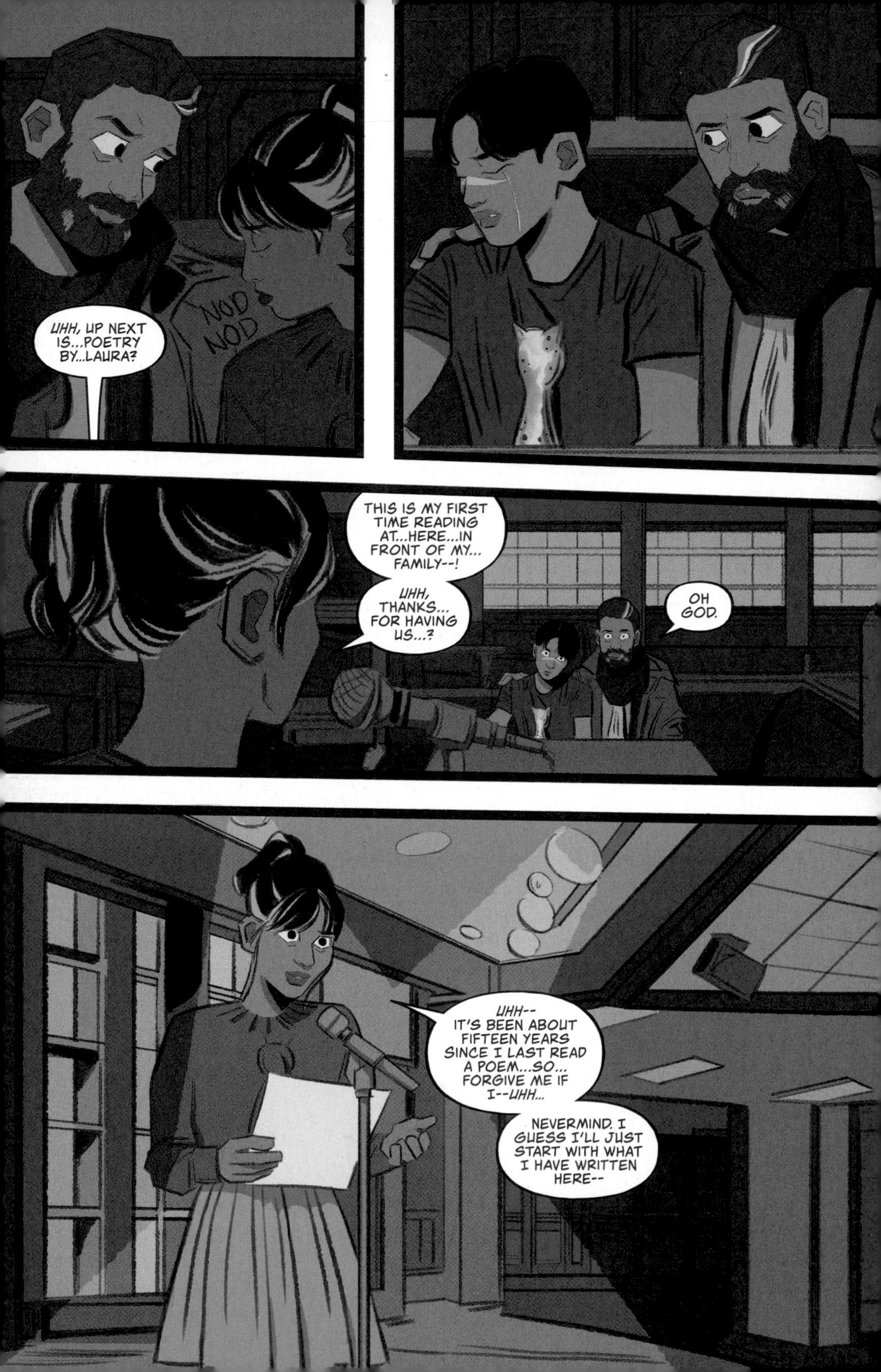
NOD NOD
UHH, UP NEXT IS...POETRY BY...LAURA?
THIS IS MY FIRST TIME READING AT...HERE...IN FRONT OF MY... FAMILY--!
UHH, THANKS... FOR HAVING US...?
OH GOD.
UHH-- IT'S BEEN ABOUT FIFTEEN YEARS SINCE I LAST READ A POEM...SO... FORGIVE ME IF I--UHH...
NEVERMIND. I GUESS I'LL JUST START WITH WHAT I HAVE WRITTEN HERE--

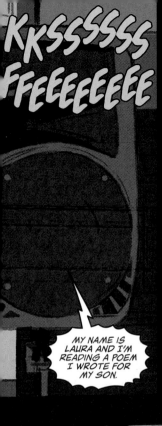

KKSSSSSS
FFEEEEEEEE

BRRRRR   RRRRRRRRR

MY NAME IS LAURA AND I'M READING A POEM I WROTE FOR MY SON.

IRA.

IT'S CALLED--

WARCHILD.

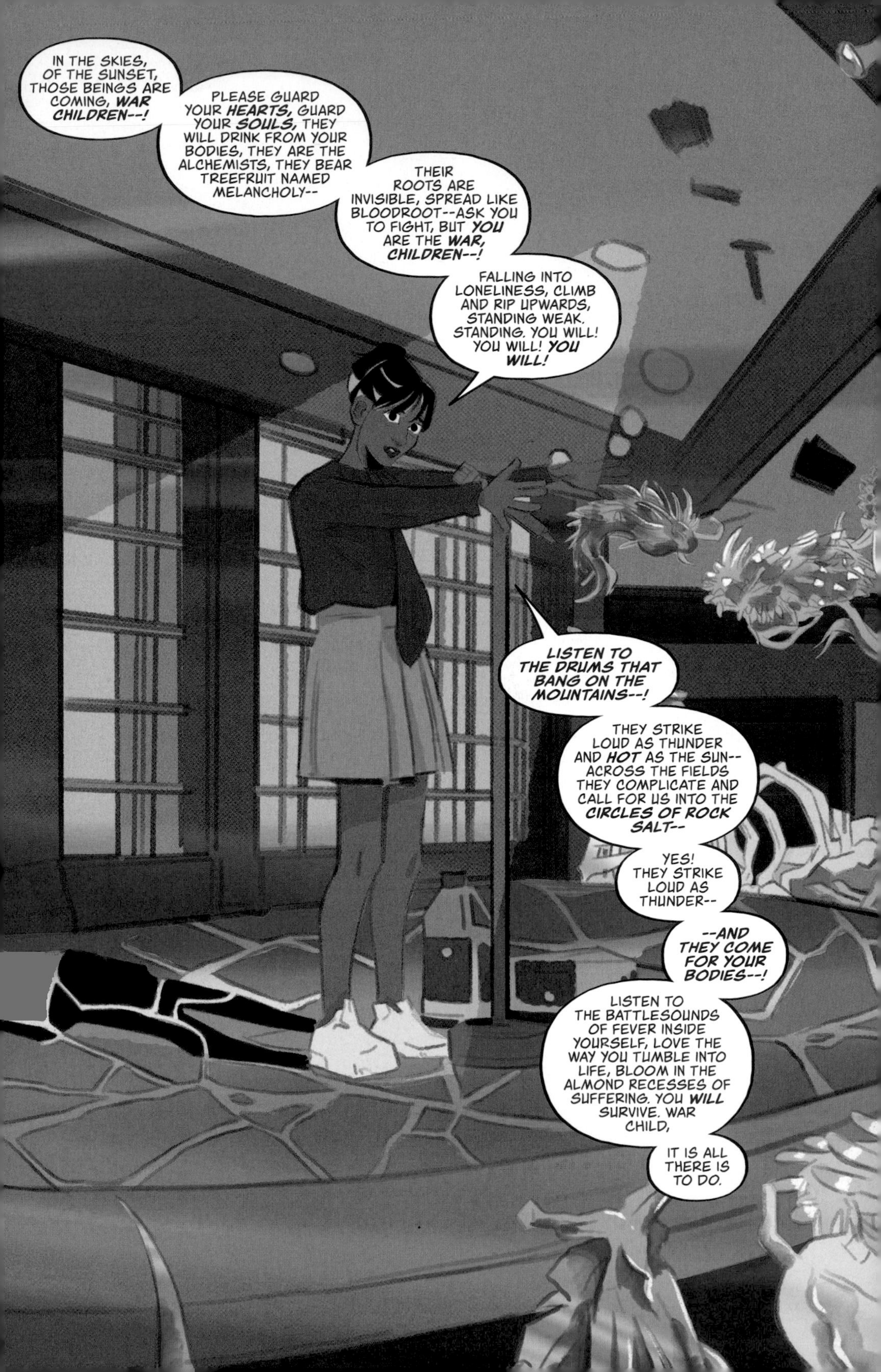
IN THE SKIES, OF THE SUNSET, THOSE BEINGS ARE COMING, WAR CHILDREN--!
PLEASE GUARD YOUR HEARTS, GUARD YOUR SOULS, THEY WILL DRINK FROM YOUR BODIES, THEY ARE THE ALCHEMISTS, THEY BEAR TREEFRUIT NAMED MELANCHOLY--
THEIR ROOTS ARE INVISIBLE, SPREAD LIKE BLOODROOT--ASK YOU TO FIGHT, BUT YOU ARE THE WAR, CHILDREN--!
FALLING INTO LONELINESS, CLIMB AND RIP UPWARDS, STANDING WEAK. STANDING. YOU WILL! YOU WILL! YOU WILL!
LISTEN TO THE DRUMS THAT BANG ON THE MOUNTAINS--!
THEY STRIKE LOUD AS THUNDER AND HOT AS THE SUN-- ACROSS THE FIELDS THEY COMPLICATE AND CALL FOR US INTO THE CIRCLES OF ROCK SALT--
YES! THEY STRIKE LOUD AS THUNDER--
--AND THEY COME FOR YOUR BODIES--!
LISTEN TO THE BATTLESOUNDS OF FEVER INSIDE YOURSELF, LOVE THE WAY YOU TUMBLE INTO LIFE, BLOOM IN THE ALMOND RECESSES OF SUFFERING. YOU WILL SURVIVE. WAR CHILD,
IT IS ALL THERE IS TO DO.

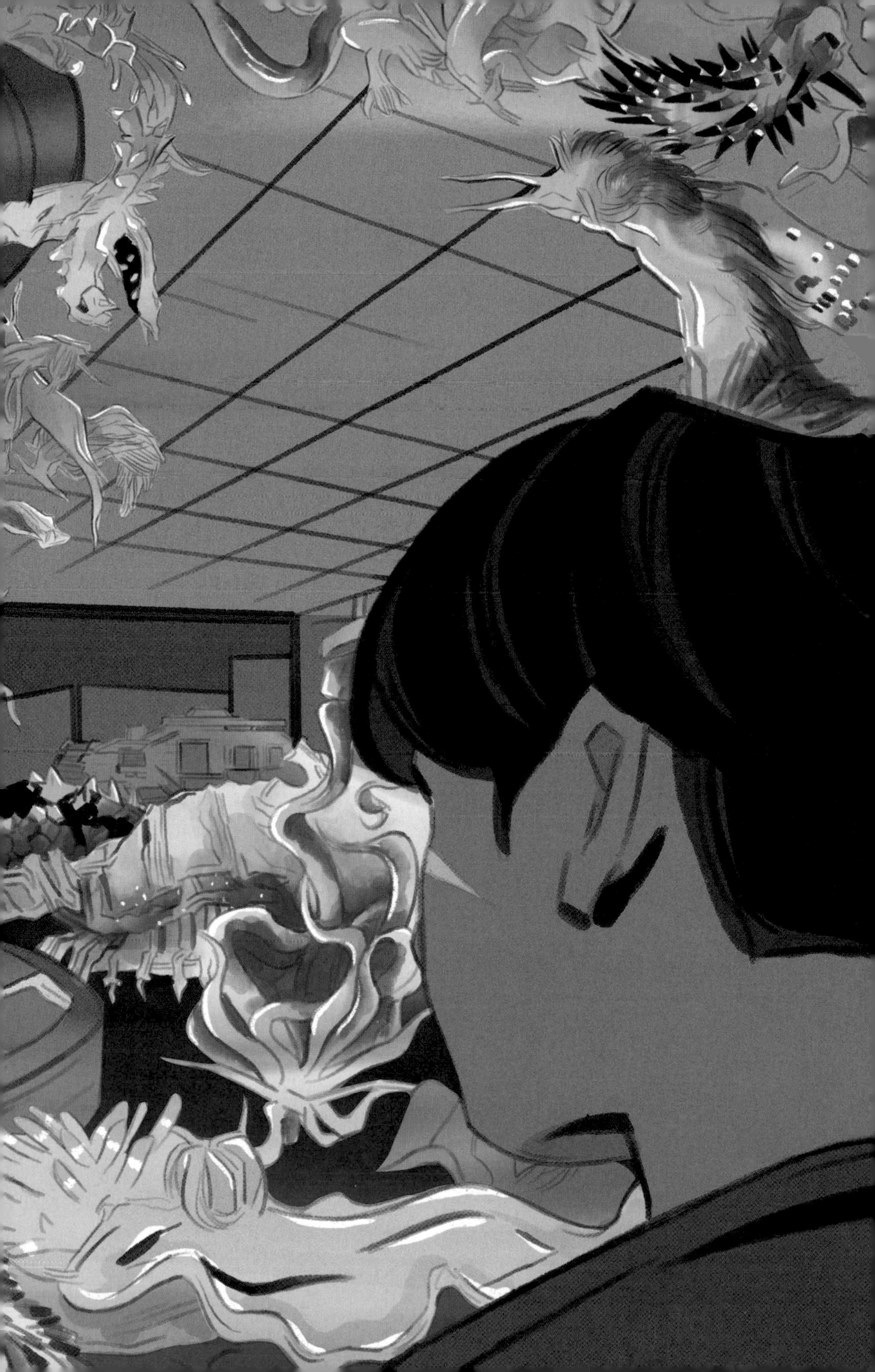

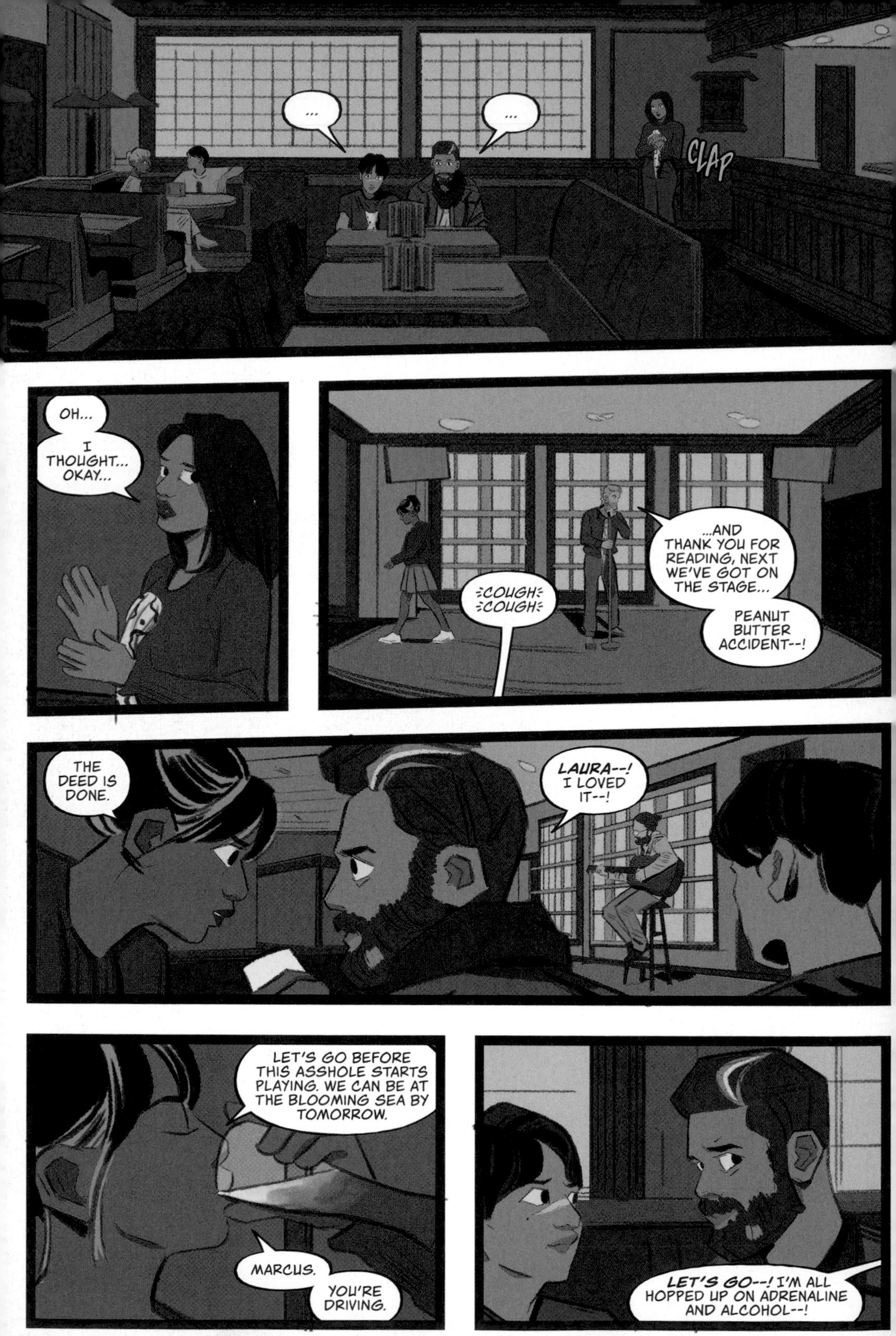

...
...
CLAP
OH...
I THOUGHT... OKAY...
...AND THANK YOU FOR READING, NEXT WE'VE GOT ON THE STAGE...
PEANUT BUTTER ACCIDENT--!
COUGH COUGH
THE DEED IS DONE.
LAURA--! I LOVED IT--!
LET'S GO BEFORE THIS ASSHOLE STARTS PLAYING. WE CAN BE AT THE BLOOMING SEA BY TOMORROW.
MARCUS.
YOU'RE DRIVING.
LET'S GO--! I'M ALL HOPPED UP ON ADRENALINE AND ALCOHOL--!

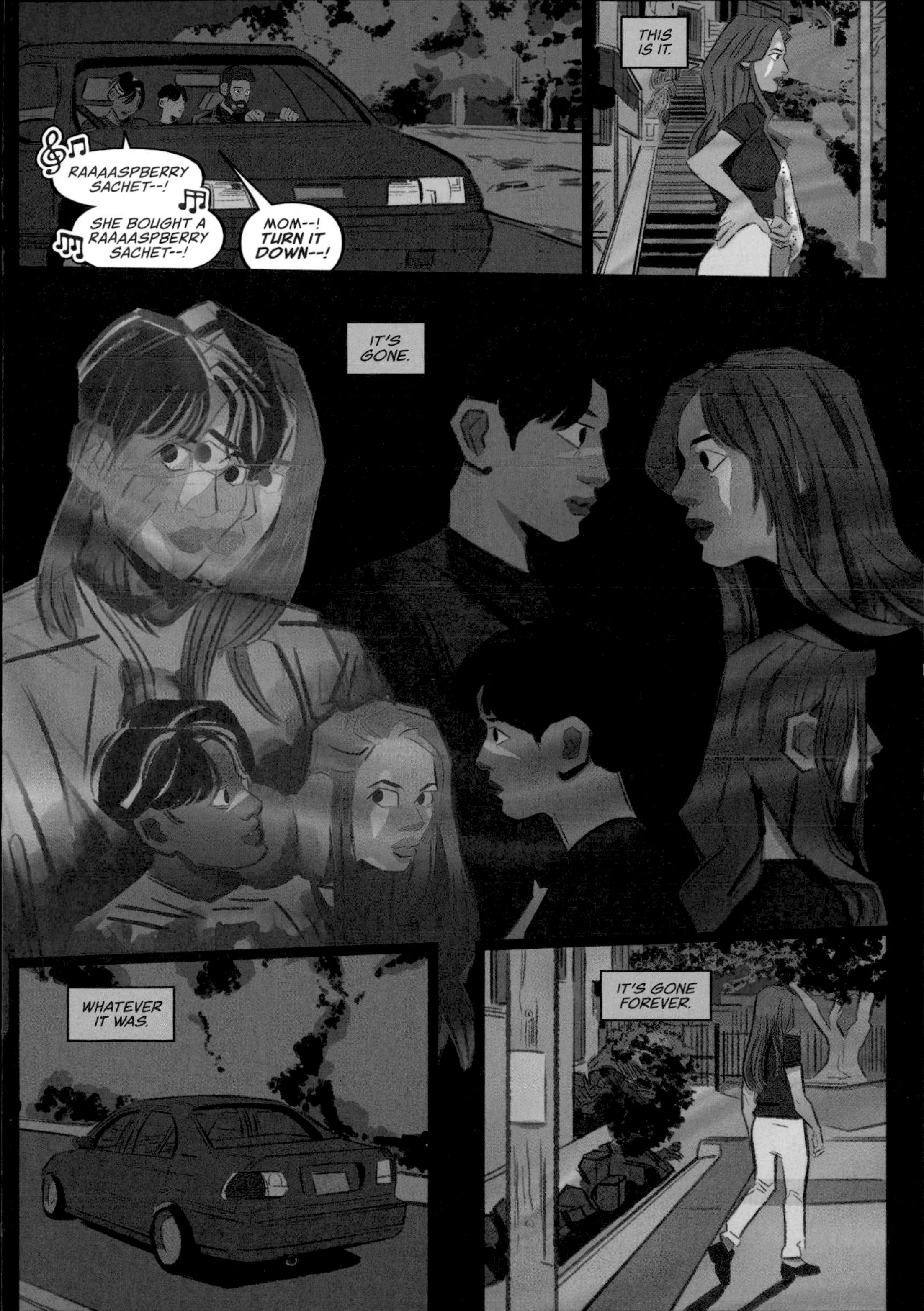
RAAAASPBERRY SACHET--!
SHE BOUGHT A RAAAASPBERRY SACHET--!
MOM--! TURN IT DOWN--!
THIS IS IT.
IT'S GONE.
WHATEVER IT WAS.
IT'S GONE FOREVER.

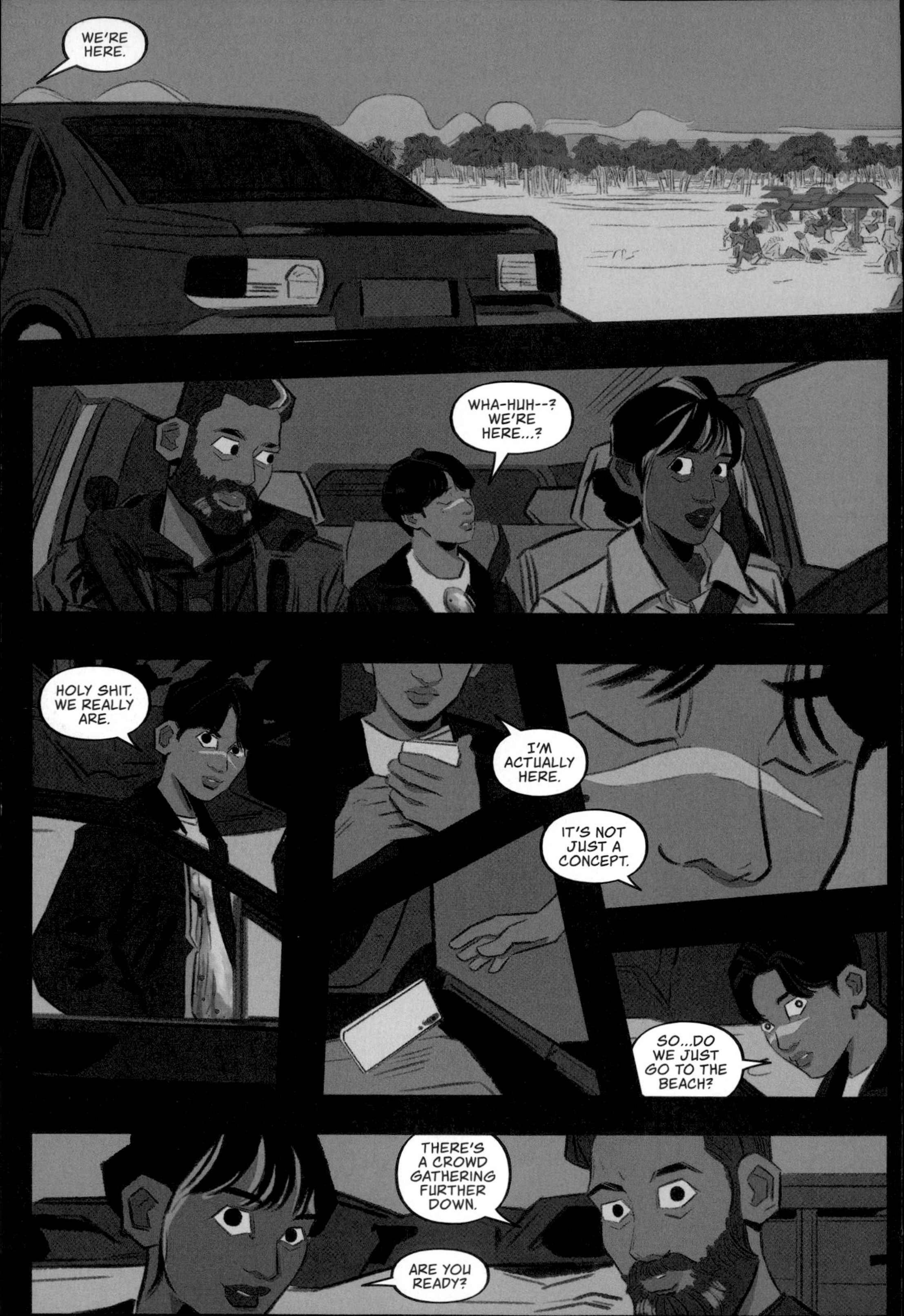
WE'RE HERE.
WHA-HUH--? WE'RE HERE...?
HOLY SHIT. WE REALLY ARE.
I'M ACTUALLY HERE.
IT'S NOT JUST A CONCEPT.
SO...DO WE JUST GO TO THE BEACH?
THERE'S A CROWD GATHERING FURTHER DOWN.
ARE YOU READY?

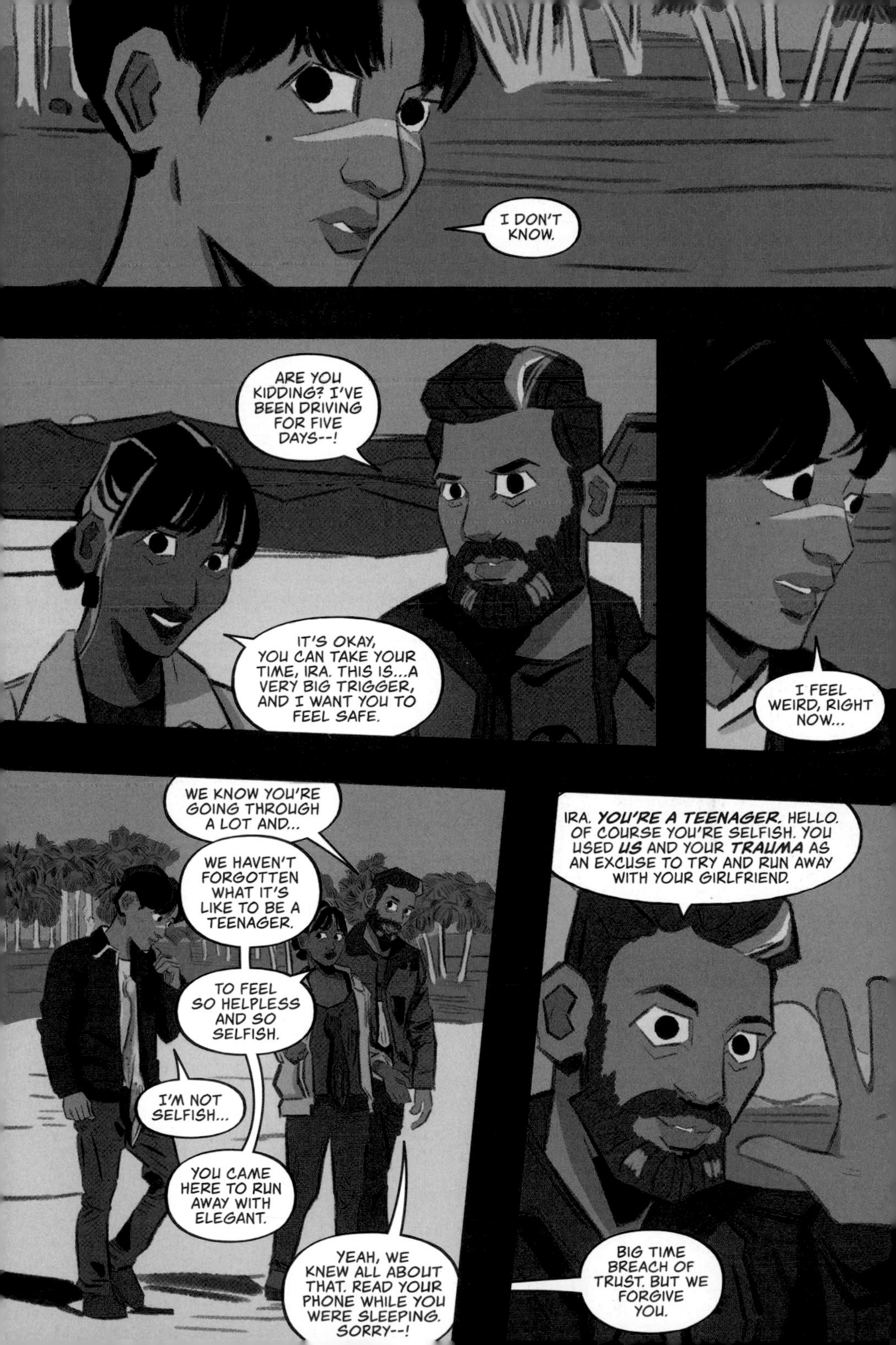
I DON'T KNOW.
ARE YOU KIDDING? I'VE BEEN DRIVING FOR FIVE DAYS--!
IT'S OKAY, YOU CAN TAKE YOUR TIME, IRA. THIS IS...A VERY BIG TRIGGER, AND I WANT YOU TO FEEL SAFE.
I FEEL WEIRD, RIGHT NOW...
WE KNOW YOU'RE GOING THROUGH A LOT AND...
WE HAVEN'T FORGOTTEN WHAT IT'S LIKE TO BE A TEENAGER.
TO FEEL SO HELPLESS AND SO SELFISH.
I'M NOT SELFISH...
YOU CAME HERE TO RUN AWAY WITH ELEGANT.
YEAH, WE KNEW ALL ABOUT THAT. READ YOUR PHONE WHILE YOU WERE SLEEPING. SORRY--!
IRA. ***YOU'RE A TEENAGER.*** HELLO. OF COURSE YOU'RE SELFISH. YOU USED ***US*** AND YOUR ***TRAUMA*** AS AN EXCUSE TO TRY AND RUN AWAY WITH YOUR GIRLFRIEND.
BIG TIME BREACH OF TRUST. BUT WE FORGIVE YOU.

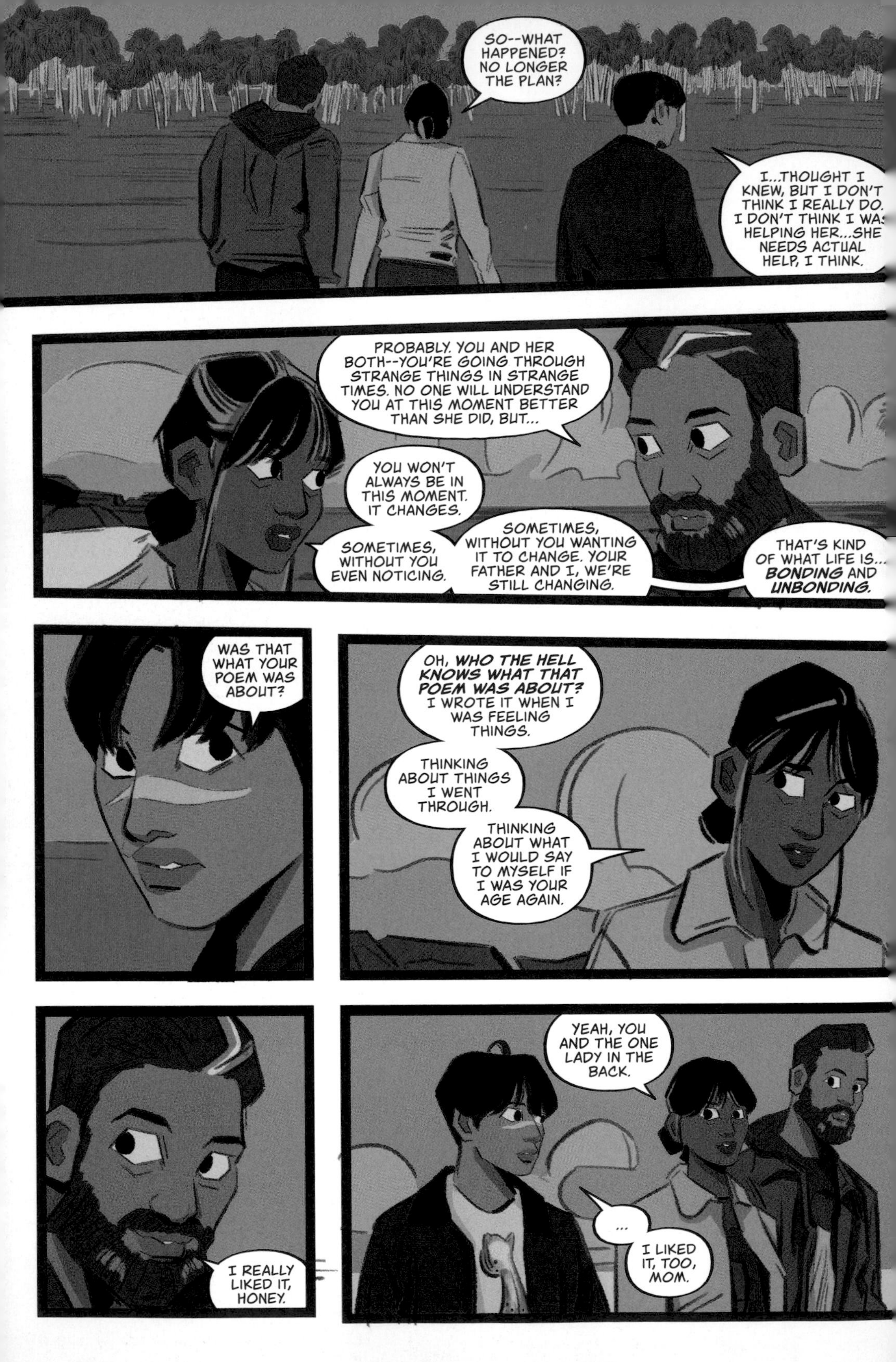
SO--WHAT HAPPENED? NO LONGER THE PLAN?
I...THOUGHT I KNEW, BUT I DON'T THINK I REALLY DO. I DON'T THINK I WAS HELPING HER...SHE NEEDS ACTUAL HELP, I THINK.
PROBABLY. YOU AND HER BOTH--YOU'RE GOING THROUGH STRANGE THINGS IN STRANGE TIMES. NO ONE WILL UNDERSTAND YOU AT THIS MOMENT BETTER THAN SHE DID, BUT...
YOU WON'T ALWAYS BE IN THIS MOMENT. IT CHANGES.
SOMETIMES, WITHOUT YOU EVEN NOTICING.
SOMETIMES, WITHOUT YOU WANTING IT TO CHANGE. YOUR FATHER AND I, WE'RE STILL CHANGING.
THAT'S KIND OF WHAT LIFE IS... ***BONDING*** AND ***UNBONDING.***
WAS THAT WHAT YOUR POEM WAS ABOUT?
OH, ***WHO THE HELL KNOWS WHAT THAT POEM WAS ABOUT?*** I WROTE IT WHEN I WAS FEELING THINGS.
THINKING ABOUT THINGS I WENT THROUGH.
THINKING ABOUT WHAT I WOULD SAY TO MYSELF IF I WAS YOUR AGE AGAIN.
I REALLY LIKED IT, HONEY.
YEAH, YOU AND THE ONE LADY IN THE BACK.
...
I LIKED IT, TOO, MOM.

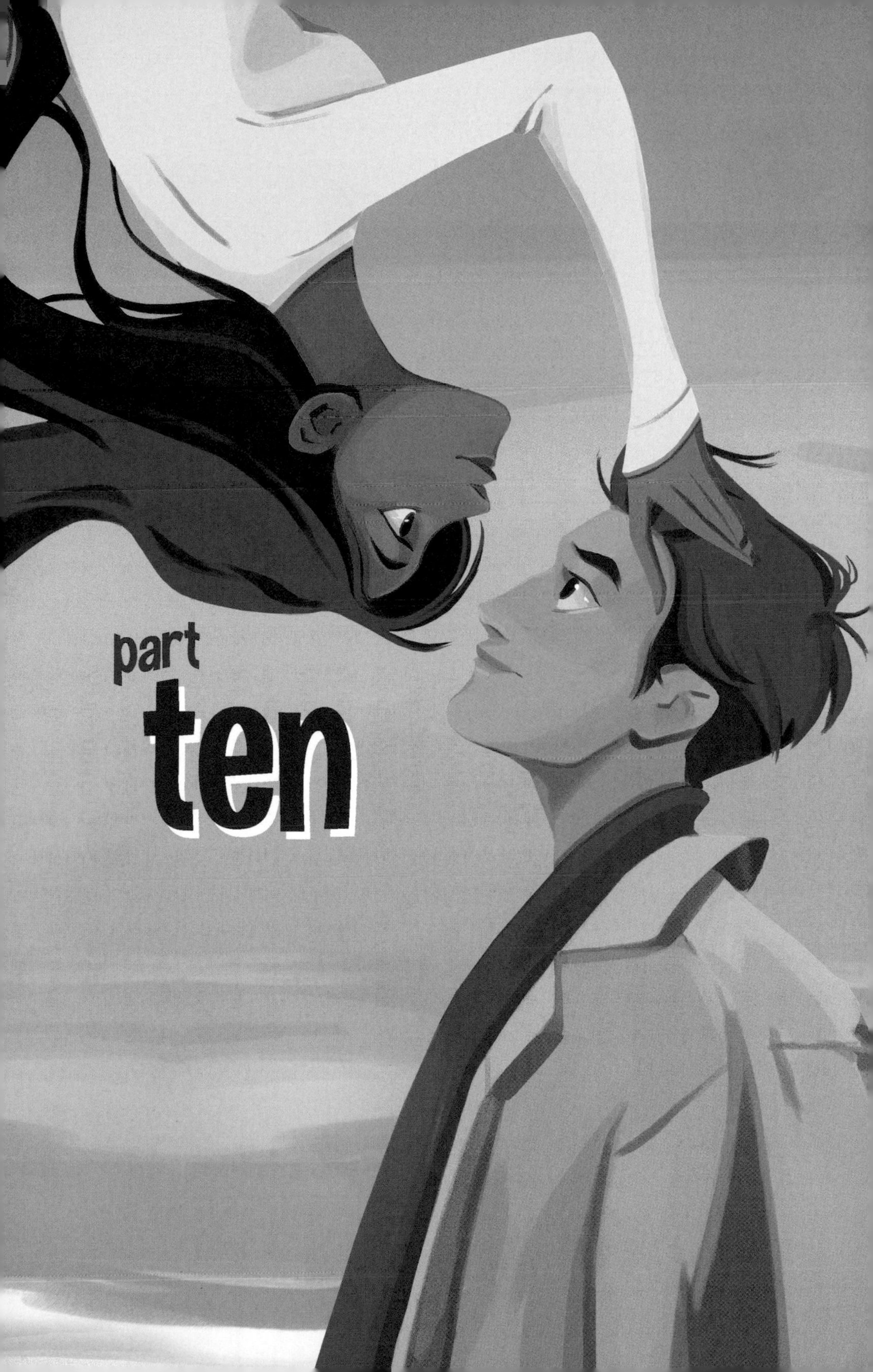
part
ten

Chapter Ten:
SEA OF LOVE

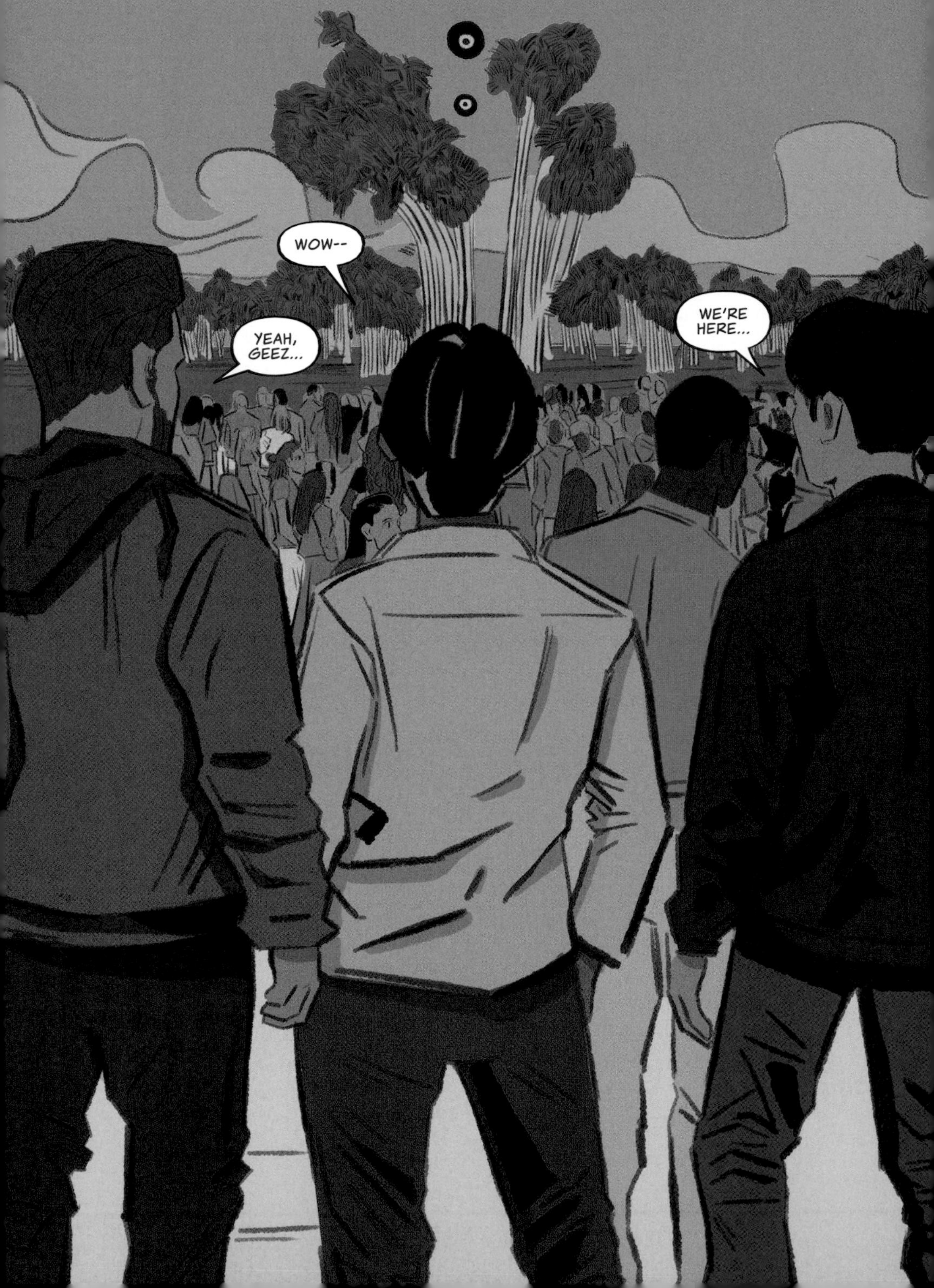
WOW--
YEAH, GEEZ...
WE'RE HERE...

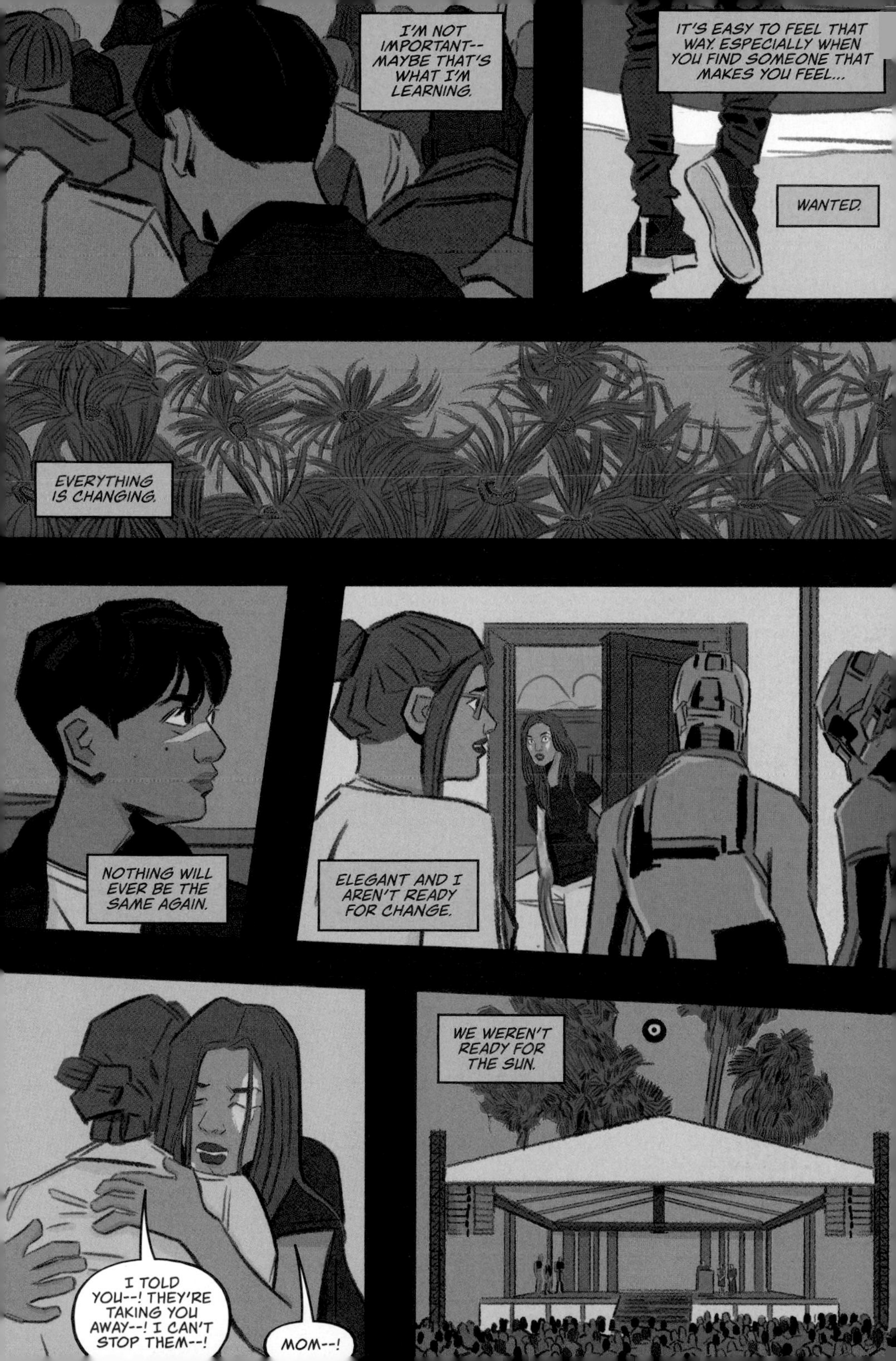
I'M NOT IMPORTANT-- MAYBE THAT'S WHAT I'M LEARNING.
IT'S EASY TO FEEL THAT WAY. ESPECIALLY WHEN YOU FIND SOMEONE THAT MAKES YOU FEEL...
WANTED.
EVERYTHING IS CHANGING.
NOTHING WILL EVER BE THE SAME AGAIN.
ELEGANT AND I AREN'T READY FOR CHANGE.
I TOLD YOU--! THEY'RE TAKING YOU AWAY--! I CAN'T STOP THEM--!
MOM--!
WE WEREN'T READY FOR THE SUN.

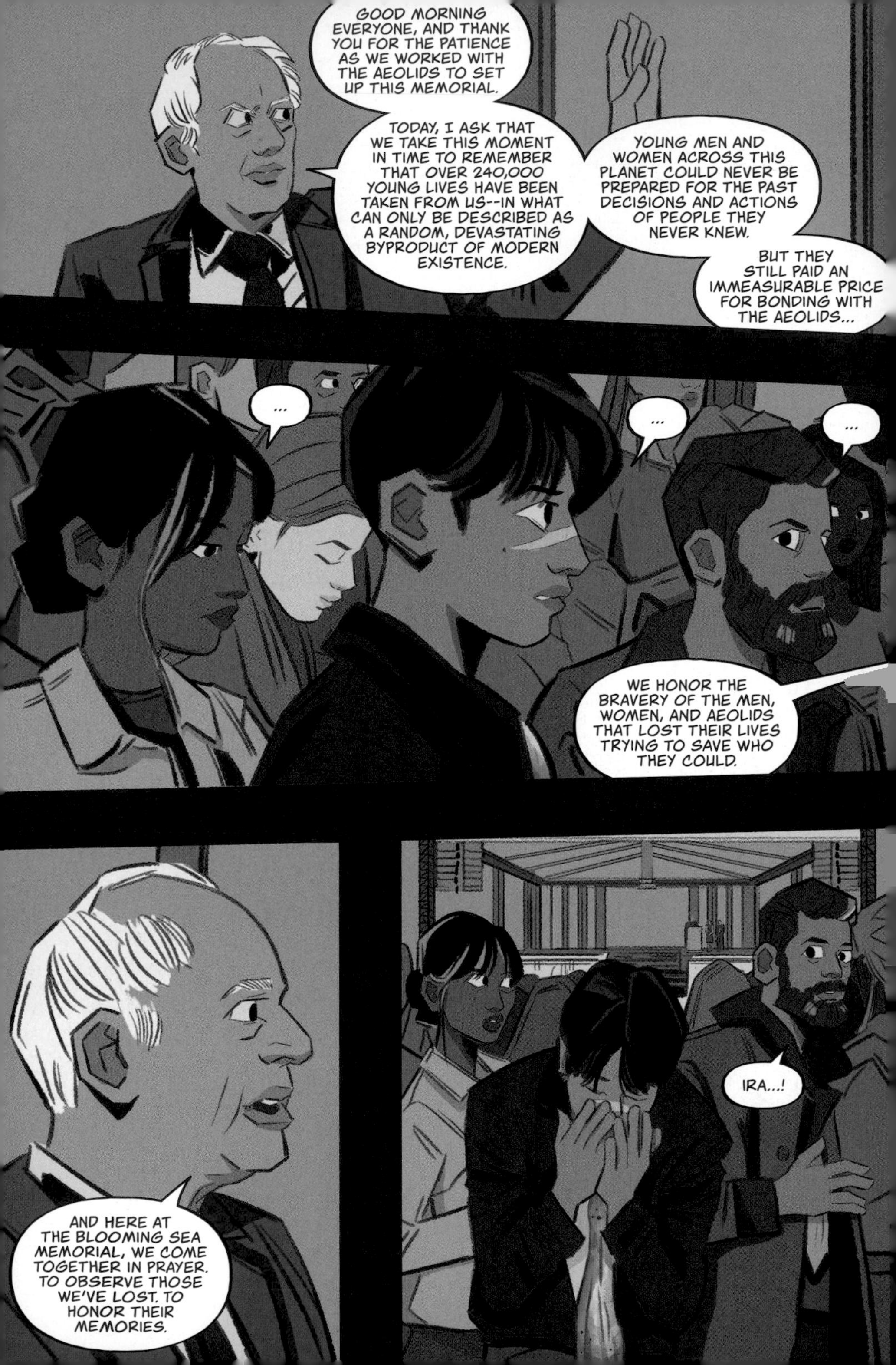
GOOD MORNING EVERYONE, AND THANK YOU FOR THE PATIENCE AS WE WORKED WITH THE AEOLIDS TO SET UP THIS MEMORIAL.
TODAY, I ASK THAT WE TAKE THIS MOMENT IN TIME TO REMEMBER THAT OVER 240,000 YOUNG LIVES HAVE BEEN TAKEN FROM US--IN WHAT CAN ONLY BE DESCRIBED AS A RANDOM, DEVASTATING BYPRODUCT OF MODERN EXISTENCE.
YOUNG MEN AND WOMEN ACROSS THIS PLANET COULD NEVER BE PREPARED FOR THE PAST DECISIONS AND ACTIONS OF PEOPLE THEY NEVER KNEW.
BUT THEY STILL PAID AN IMMEASURABLE PRICE FOR BONDING WITH THE AEOLIDS...
...
...
...
WE HONOR THE BRAVERY OF THE MEN, WOMEN, AND AEOLIDS THAT LOST THEIR LIVES TRYING TO SAVE WHO THEY COULD.
AND HERE AT THE BLOOMING SEA MEMORIAL, WE COME TOGETHER IN PRAYER. TO OBSERVE THOSE WE'VE LOST. TO HONOR THEIR MEMORIES.
IRA...!

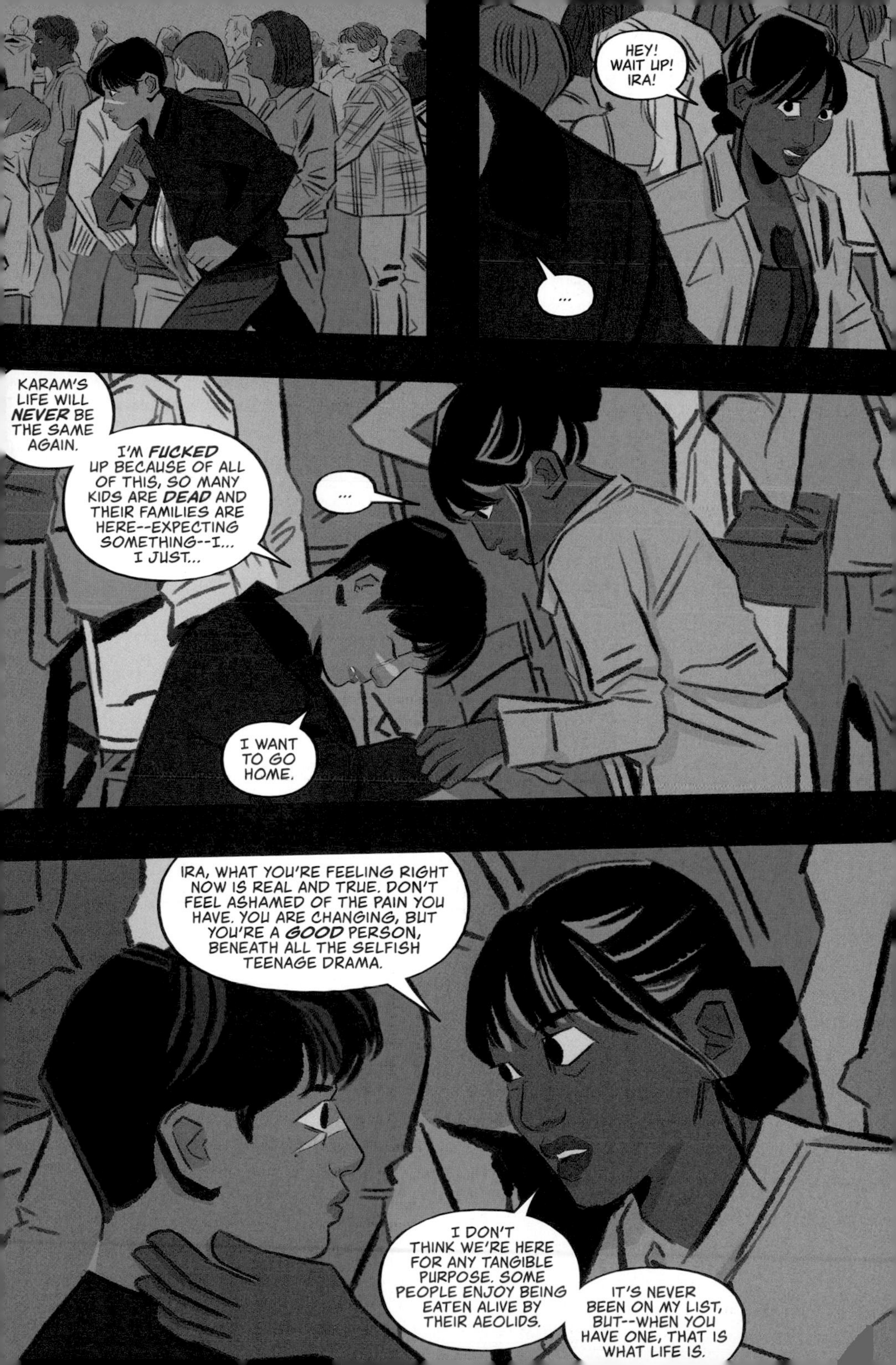
HEY! WAIT UP! IRA!
...
KARAM'S LIFE WILL NEVER BE THE SAME AGAIN.
I'M FUCKED UP BECAUSE OF ALL OF THIS, SO MANY KIDS ARE DEAD AND THEIR FAMILIES ARE HERE--EXPECTING SOMETHING--I... I JUST...
...
I WANT TO GO HOME.
IRA, WHAT YOU'RE FEELING RIGHT NOW IS REAL AND TRUE. DON'T FEEL ASHAMED OF THE PAIN YOU HAVE. YOU ARE CHANGING, BUT YOU'RE A GOOD PERSON, BENEATH ALL THE SELFISH TEENAGE DRAMA.
I DON'T THINK WE'RE HERE FOR ANY TANGIBLE PURPOSE. SOME PEOPLE ENJOY BEING EATEN ALIVE BY THEIR AEOLIDS.
IT'S NEVER BEEN ON MY LIST, BUT--WHEN YOU HAVE ONE, THAT IS WHAT LIFE IS.

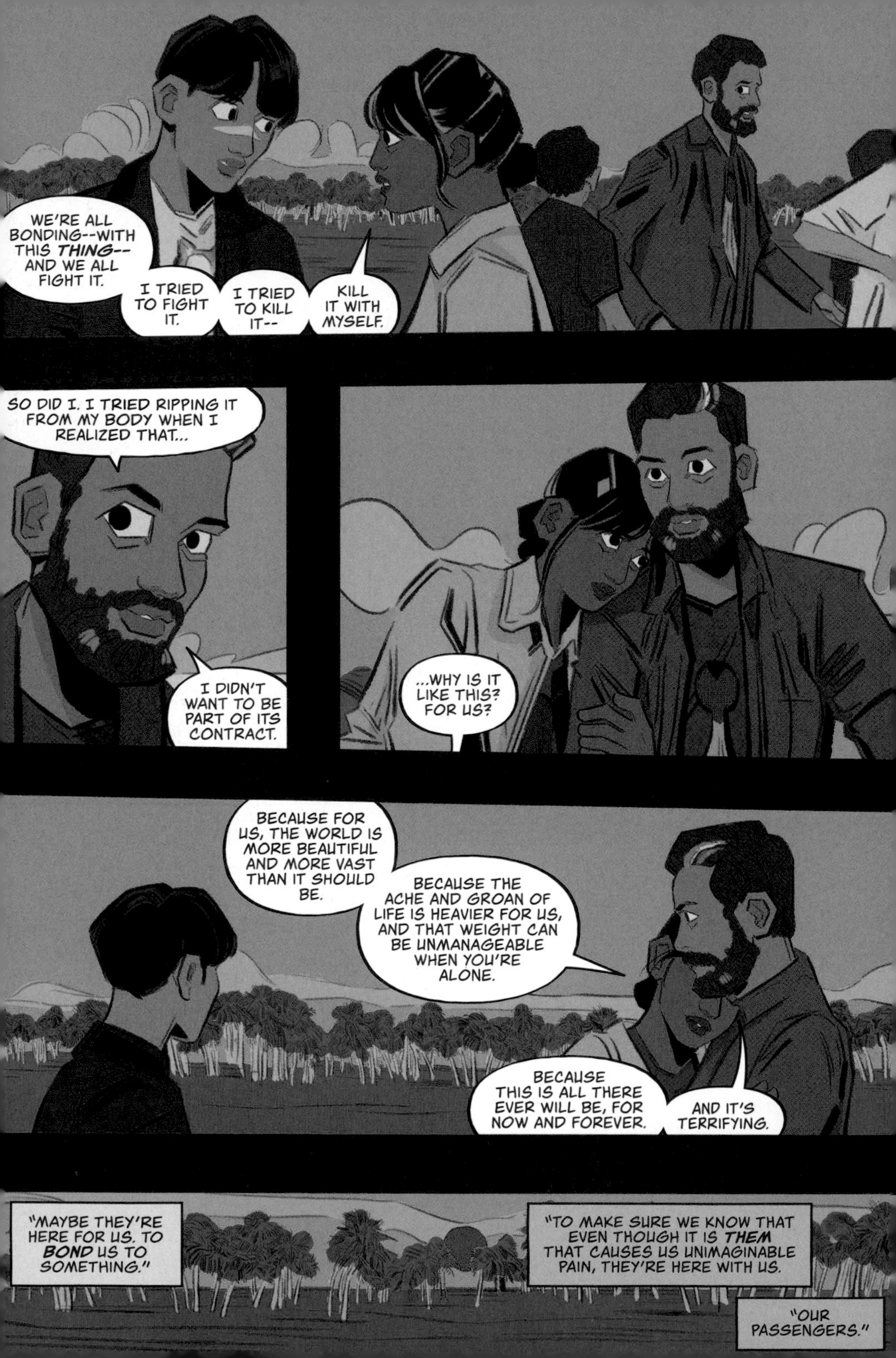
WE'RE ALL BONDING--WITH THIS *THING*-- AND WE ALL FIGHT IT.
I TRIED TO FIGHT IT.
I TRIED TO KILL IT--
KILL IT WITH MYSELF.
SO DID I. I TRIED RIPPING IT FROM MY BODY WHEN I REALIZED THAT...
I DIDN'T WANT TO BE PART OF ITS CONTRACT.
...WHY IS IT LIKE THIS? FOR US?
BECAUSE FOR US, THE WORLD IS MORE BEAUTIFUL AND MORE VAST THAN IT SHOULD BE.
BECAUSE THE ACHE AND GROAN OF LIFE IS HEAVIER FOR US, AND THAT WEIGHT CAN BE UNMANAGEABLE WHEN YOU'RE ALONE.
BECAUSE THIS IS ALL THERE EVER WILL BE, FOR NOW AND FOREVER.
AND IT'S TERRIFYING.
"MAYBE THEY'RE HERE FOR US. TO *BOND* US TO SOMETHING."
"TO MAKE SURE WE KNOW THAT EVEN THOUGH IT IS *THEM* THAT CAUSES US UNIMAGINABLE PAIN, THEY'RE HERE WITH US.
"OUR PASSENGERS."

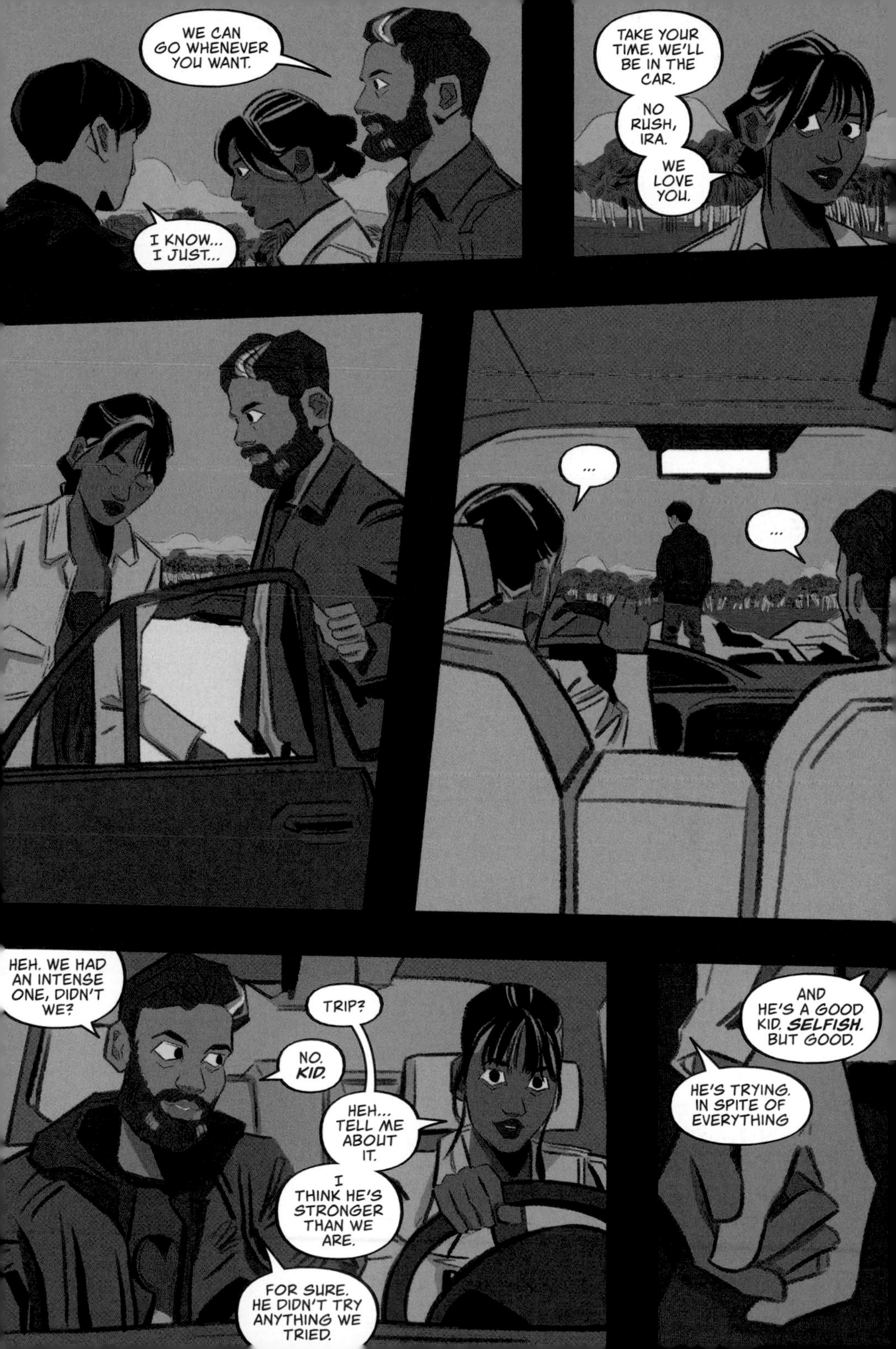
WE CAN GO WHENEVER YOU WANT.
I KNOW... I JUST...
TAKE YOUR TIME. WE'LL BE IN THE CAR.
NO RUSH, IRA.
WE LOVE YOU.
...
...
HEH. WE HAD AN INTENSE ONE, DIDN'T WE?
TRIP?
NO. KID.
HEH... TELL ME ABOUT IT.
I THINK HE'S STRONGER THAN WE ARE.
FOR SURE. HE DIDN'T TRY ANYTHING WE TRIED.
AND HE'S A GOOD KID. SELFISH. BUT GOOD.
HE'S TRYING. IN SPITE OF EVERYTHING

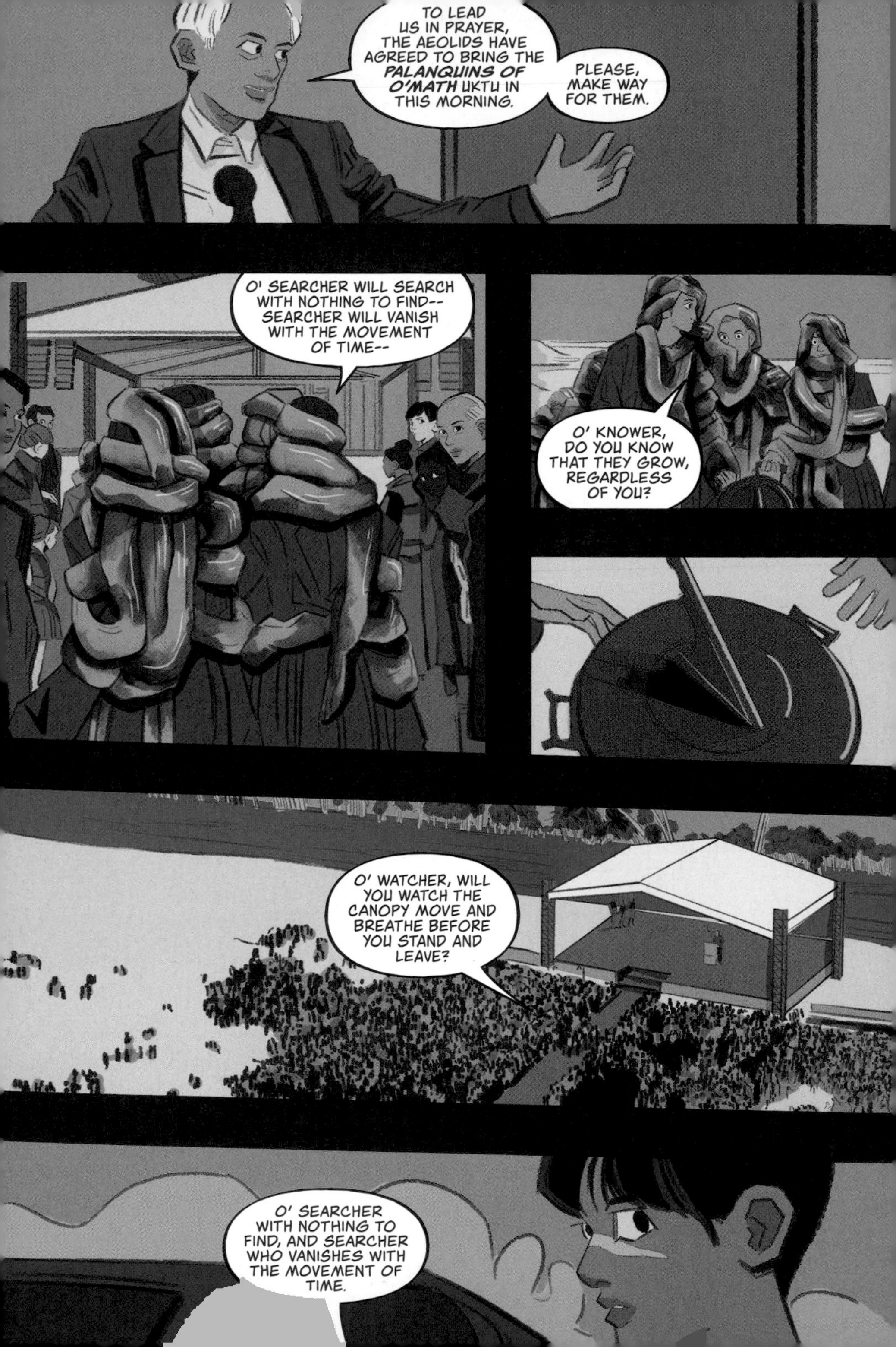
TO LEAD US IN PRAYER, THE AEOLIDS HAVE AGREED TO BRING THE PALANQUINS OF O'MATH UKTU IN THIS MORNING.
PLEASE, MAKE WAY FOR THEM.
O' SEARCHER WILL SEARCH WITH NOTHING TO FIND-- SEARCHER WILL VANISH WITH THE MOVEMENT OF TIME--
O' KNOWER, DO YOU KNOW THAT THEY GROW, REGARDLESS OF YOU?
O' WATCHER, WILL YOU WATCH THE CANOPY MOVE AND BREATHE BEFORE YOU STAND AND LEAVE?
O' SEARCHER WITH NOTHING TO FIND, AND SEARCHER WHO VANISHES WITH THE MOVEMENT OF TIME.

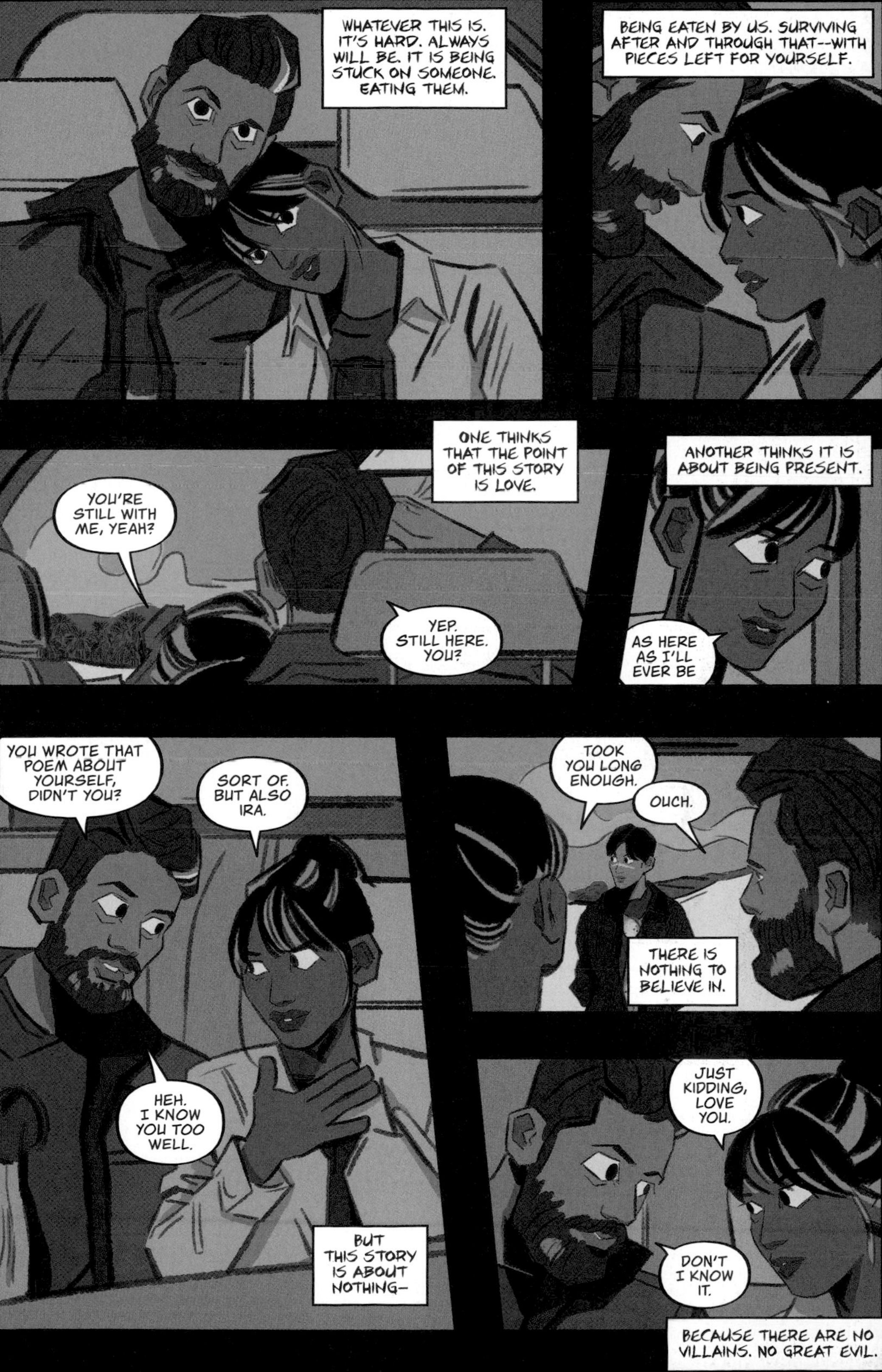

WHATEVER THIS IS. IT'S HARD. ALWAYS WILL BE. IT IS BEING STUCK ON SOMEONE. EATING THEM.
BEING EATEN BY US. SURVIVING AFTER AND THROUGH THAT--WITH PIECES LEFT FOR YOURSELF.
ONE THINKS THAT THE POINT OF THIS STORY IS LOVE.
YOU'RE STILL WITH ME, YEAH?
YEP. STILL HERE. YOU?
ANOTHER THINKS IT IS ABOUT BEING PRESENT.
AS HERE AS I'LL EVER BE
YOU WROTE THAT POEM ABOUT YOURSELF, DIDN'T YOU?
SORT OF. BUT ALSO IRA.
HEH. I KNOW YOU TOO WELL.
BUT THIS STORY IS ABOUT NOTHING-
TOOK YOU LONG ENOUGH.
OUCH.
THERE IS NOTHING TO BELIEVE IN.
JUST KIDDING, LOVE YOU.
DON'T I KNOW IT.
BECAUSE THERE ARE NO VILLAINS. NO GREAT EVIL.

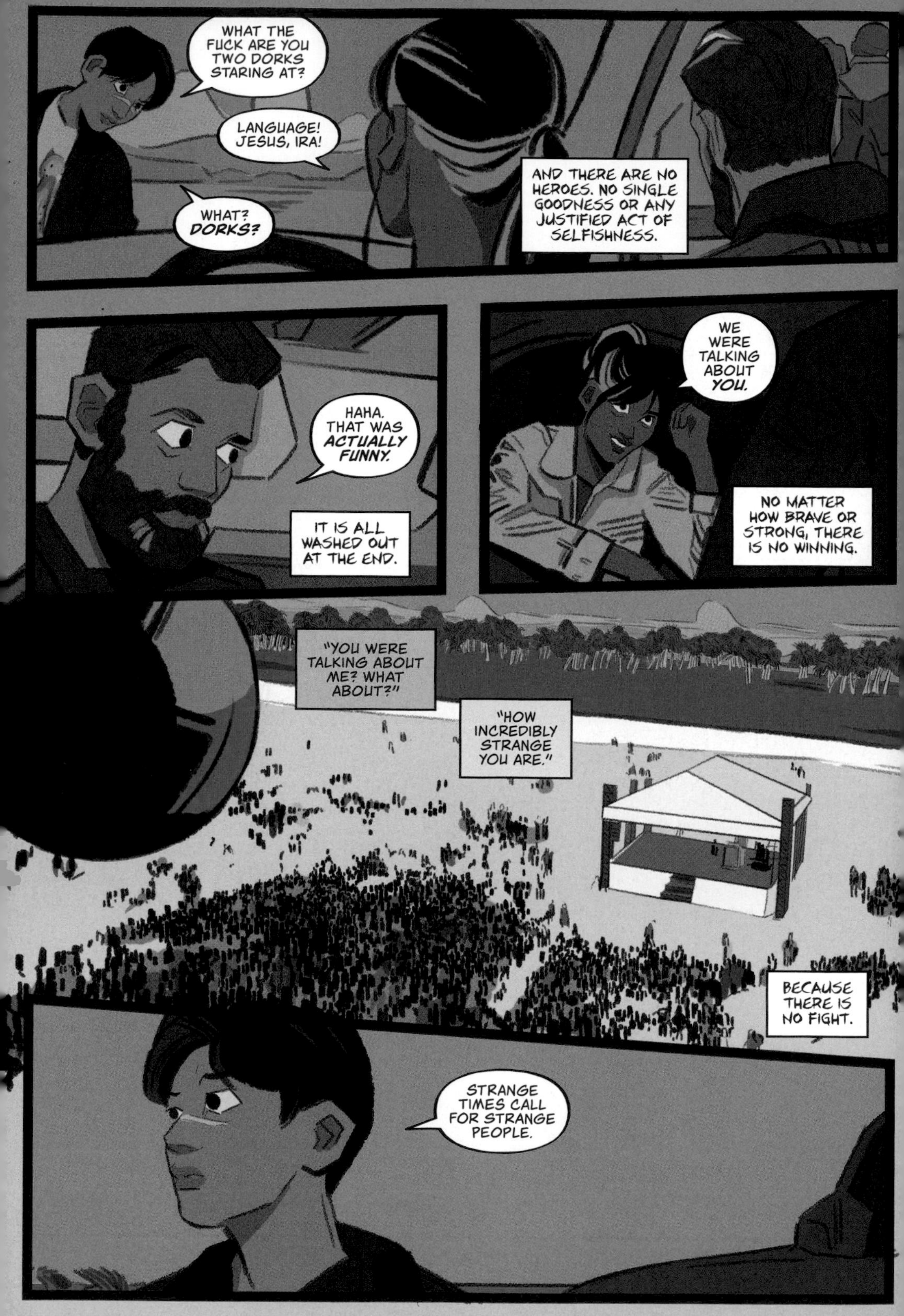
WHAT THE FUCK ARE YOU TWO DORKS STARING AT?
LANGUAGE! JESUS, IRA!
WHAT? DORKS?
AND THERE ARE NO HEROES. NO SINGLE GOODNESS OR ANY JUSTIFIED ACT OF SELFISHNESS.
HAHA. THAT WAS ACTUALLY FUNNY.
IT IS ALL WASHED OUT AT THE END.
WE WERE TALKING ABOUT YOU.
NO MATTER HOW BRAVE OR STRONG, THERE IS NO WINNING.
"YOU WERE TALKING ABOUT ME? WHAT ABOUT?"
"HOW INCREDIBLY STRANGE YOU ARE."
BECAUSE THERE IS NO FIGHT.
STRANGE TIMES CALL FOR STRANGE PEOPLE.

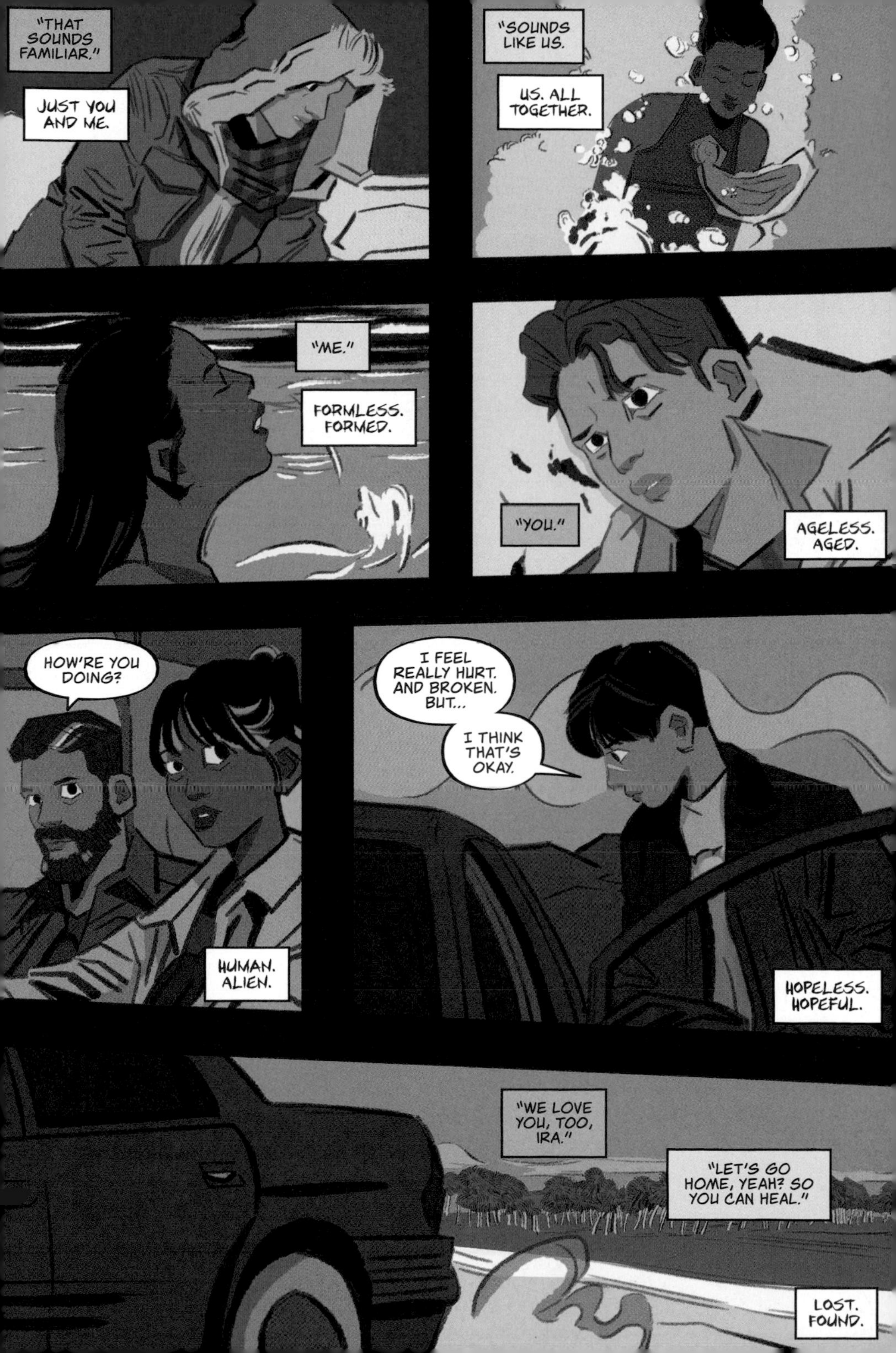
"THAT SOUNDS FAMILIAR."
JUST YOU AND ME.
"SOUNDS LIKE US.
US. ALL TOGETHER.
"ME."
FORMLESS. FORMED.
"YOU."
AGELESS. AGED.
HOW'RE YOU DOING?
HUMAN. ALIEN.
I FEEL REALLY HURT. AND BROKEN. BUT...
I THINK THAT'S OKAY.
HOPELESS. HOPEFUL.
"WE LOVE YOU, TOO, IRA."
"LET'S GO HOME, YEAH? SO YOU CAN HEAL."
LOST. FOUND.

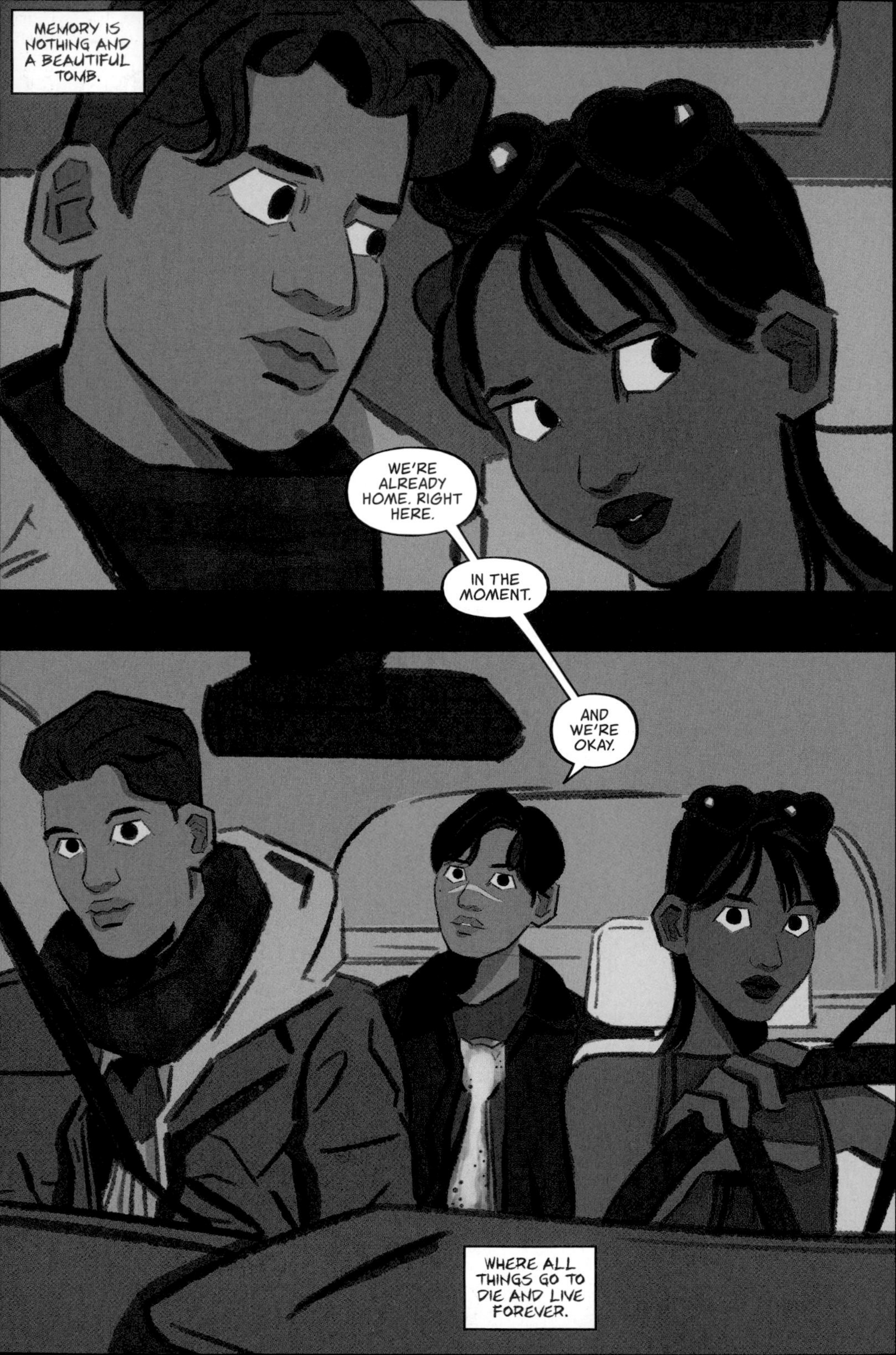
MEMORY IS NOTHING AND A BEAUTIFUL TOMB.
WE'RE ALREADY HOME. RIGHT HERE.
IN THE MOMENT.
AND WE'RE OKAY.
WHERE ALL THINGS GO TO DIE AND LIVE FOREVER.

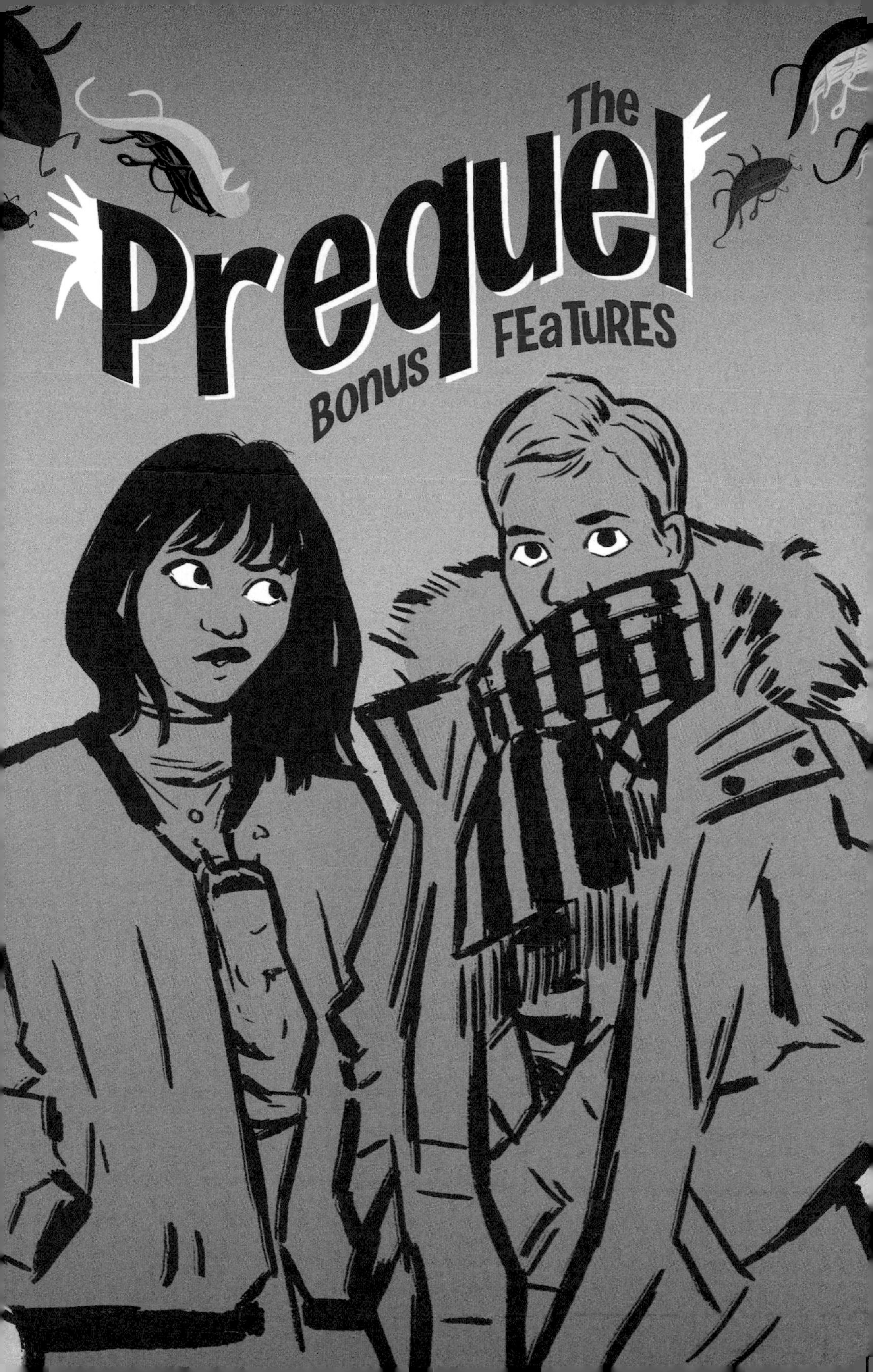
The
Prequel
Bonus Features

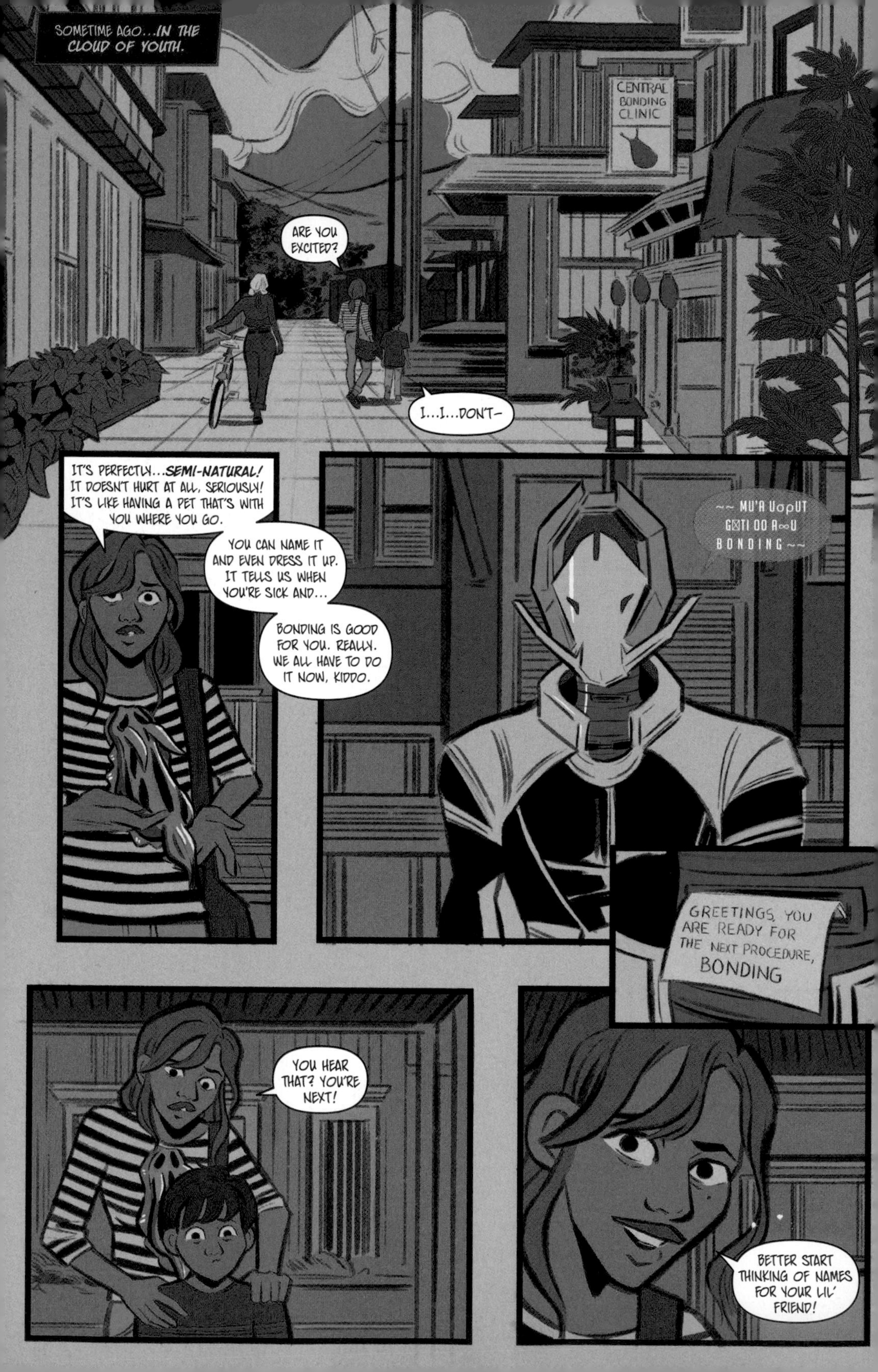
SOMETIME AGO...IN THE CLOUD OF YOUTH.
CENTRAL BONDING CLINIC
ARE YOU EXCITED?
I...I...DON'T-
IT'S PERFECTLY...SEMI-NATURAL! IT DOESN'T HURT AT ALL, SERIOUSLY! IT'S LIKE HAVING A PET THAT'S WITH YOU WHERE YOU GO.
YOU CAN NAME IT AND EVEN DRESS IT UP. IT TELLS US WHEN YOU'RE SICK AND...
BONDING IS GOOD FOR YOU. REALLY. WE ALL HAVE TO DO IT NOW, KIDDO.
BONDING
GREETINGS, YOU ARE READY FOR THE NEXT PROCEDURE, BONDING
YOU HEAR THAT? YOU'RE NEXT!
BETTER START THINKING OF NAMES FOR YOUR LIL' FRIEND!

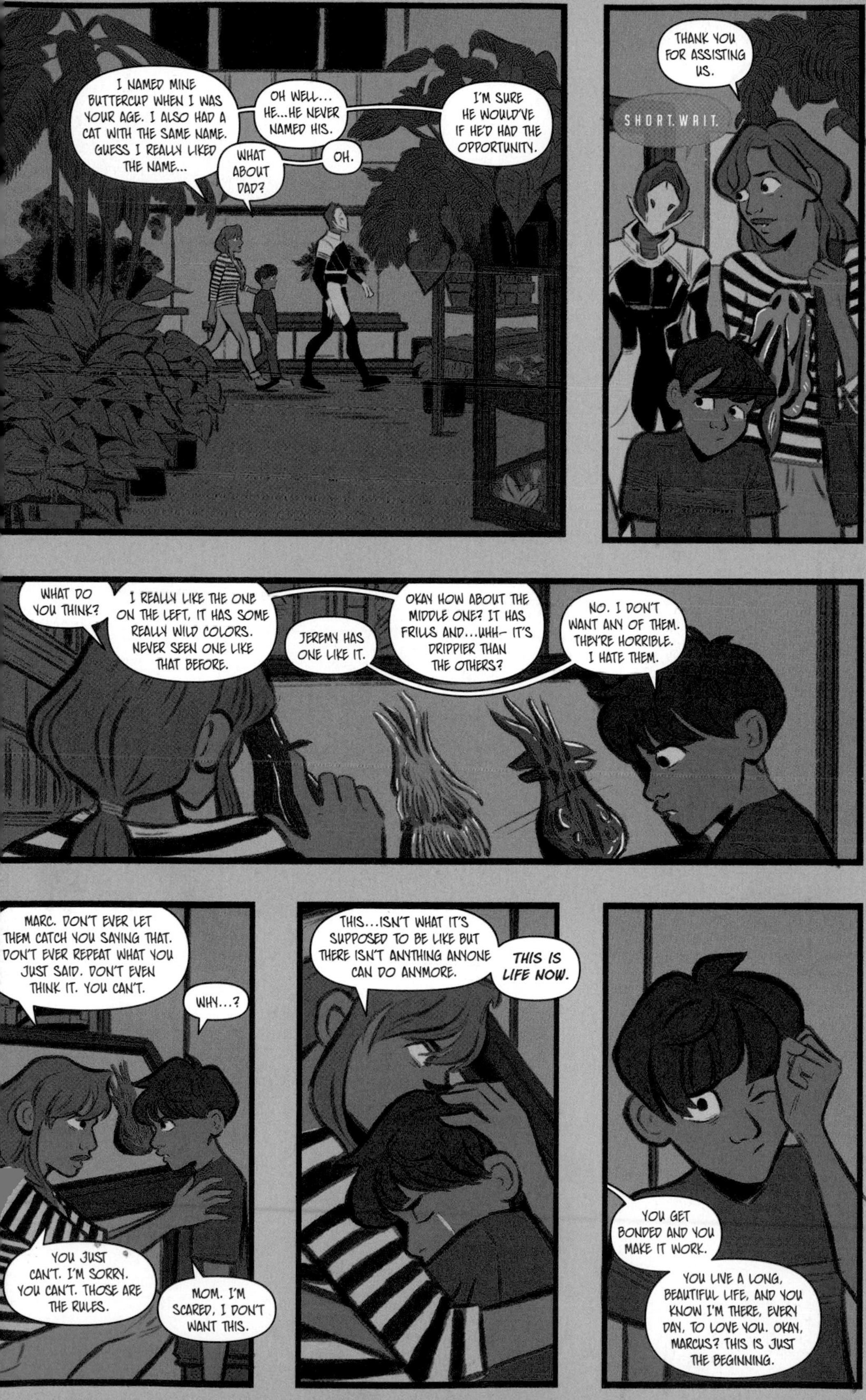
I NAMED MINE BUTTERCUP WHEN I WAS YOUR AGE. I ALSO HAD A CAT WITH THE SAME NAME. GUESS I REALLY LIKED THE NAME...
WHAT ABOUT DAD?
OH WELL... HE...HE NEVER NAMED HIS.
OH.
I'M SURE HE WOULD'VE IF HE'D HAD THE OPPORTUNITY.
THANK YOU FOR ASSISTING US.
SHORT. WAIT.
WHAT DO YOU THINK?
I REALLY LIKE THE ONE ON THE LEFT, IT HAS SOME REALLY WILD COLORS. NEVER SEEN ONE LIKE THAT BEFORE.
JEREMY HAS ONE LIKE IT.
OKAY HOW ABOUT THE MIDDLE ONE? IT HAS FRILLS AND...UHH– IT'S DRIPPIER THAN THE OTHERS?
NO. I DON'T WANT ANY OF THEM. THEY'RE HORRIBLE. I HATE THEM.
MARC. DON'T EVER LET THEM CATCH YOU SAYING THAT. DON'T EVER REPEAT WHAT YOU JUST SAID. DON'T EVEN THINK IT. YOU CAN'T.
WHY...?
YOU JUST CAN'T. I'M SORRY. YOU CAN'T. THOSE ARE THE RULES.
MOM. I'M SCARED, I DON'T WANT THIS.
THIS...ISN'T WHAT IT'S SUPPOSED TO BE LIKE BUT THERE ISN'T ANYTHING ANYONE CAN DO ANYMORE.
THIS IS LIFE NOW.
YOU GET BONDED AND YOU MAKE IT WORK.
YOU LIVE A LONG, BEAUTIFUL LIFE, AND YOU KNOW I'M THERE, EVERY DAY, TO LOVE YOU. OKAY, MARCUS? THIS IS JUST THE BEGINNING.

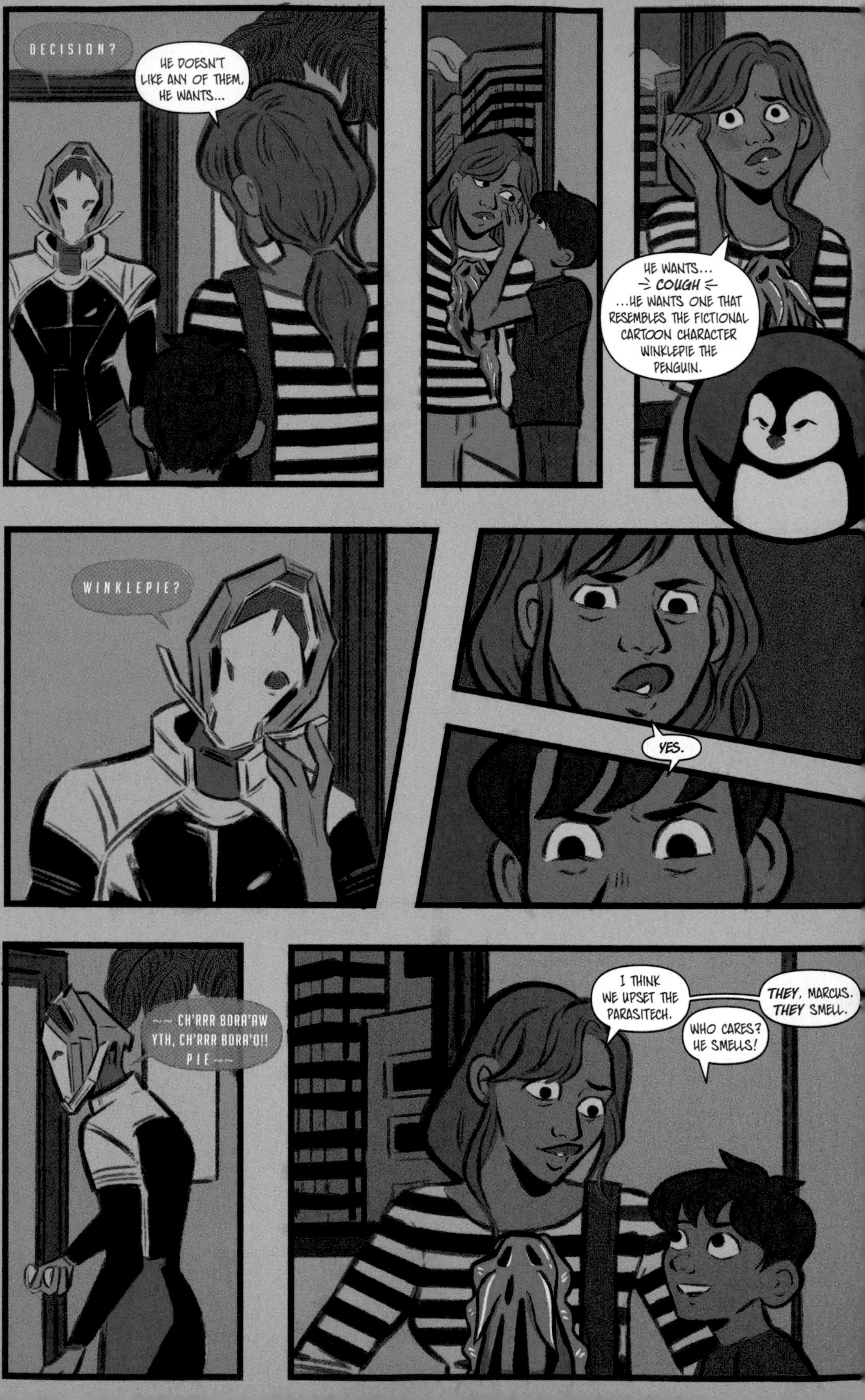
DECISION?
HE DOESN'T LIKE ANY OF THEM, HE WANTS...
HE WANTS... ⪢COUGH⪡ ...HE WANTS ONE THAT RESEMBLES THE FICTIONAL CARTOON CHARACTER WINKLEPIE THE PENGUIN.
WINKLEPIE?
YES.
~~ CH'RRR BORA'AW YTH, CH'RRR BORA'O!! PIE ~~
I THINK WE UPSET THE PARASITECH.
WHO CARES? HE SMELLS!
THEY, MARCUS. THEY SMELL.

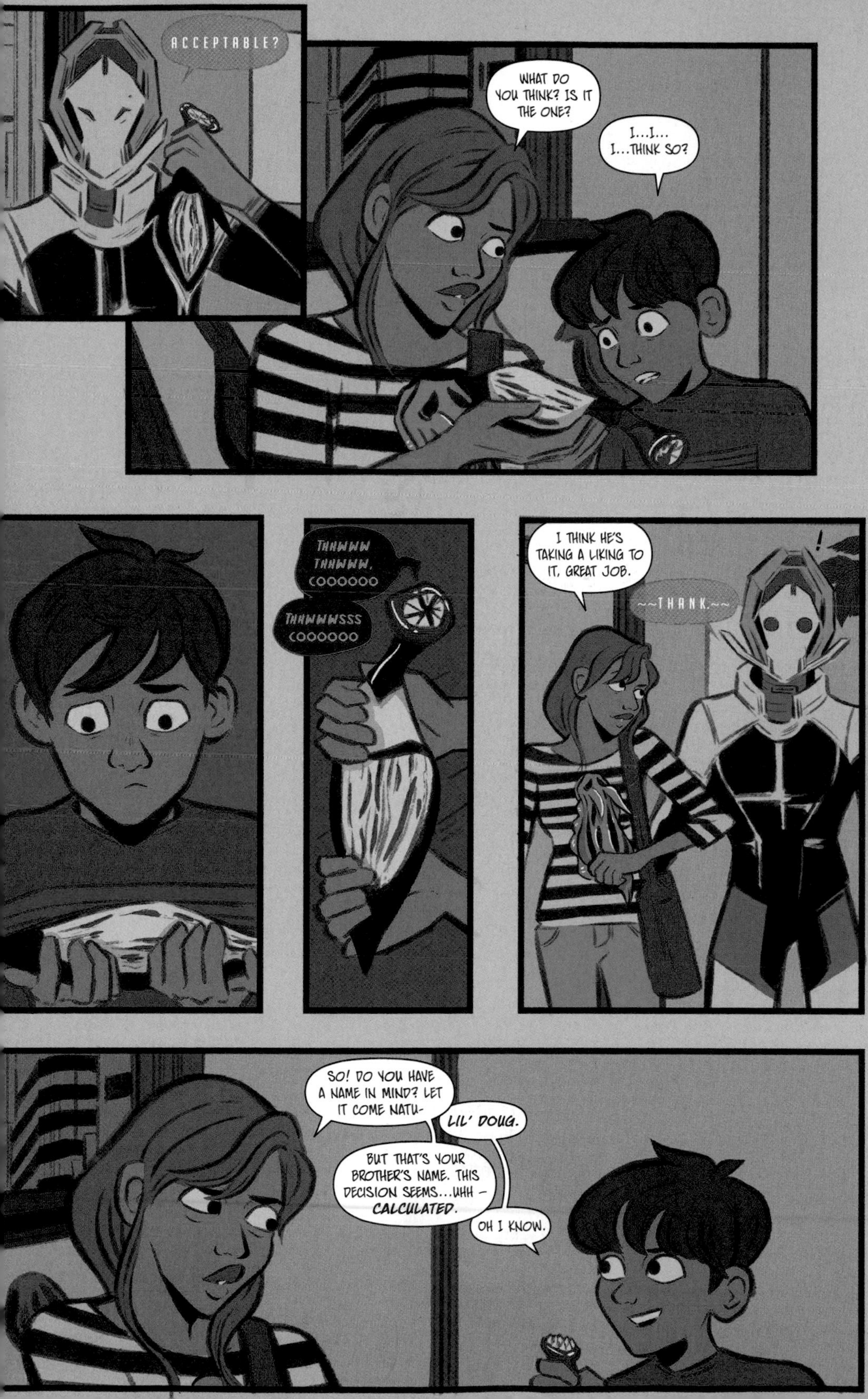

ACCEPTABLE?
WHAT DO YOU THINK? IS IT THE ONE?
I...I... I...THINK SO?
THHWWW THHWWW, COOOOOO
THHWWWSSS COOOOOO
I THINK HE'S TAKING A LIKING TO IT, GREAT JOB.
~~THANK.~~
!
SO! DO YOU HAVE A NAME IN MIND? LET IT COME NATU-
LIL' DOUG.
BUT THAT'S YOUR BROTHER'S NAME. THIS DECISION SEEMS...UHH – CALCULATED.
OH I KNOW.

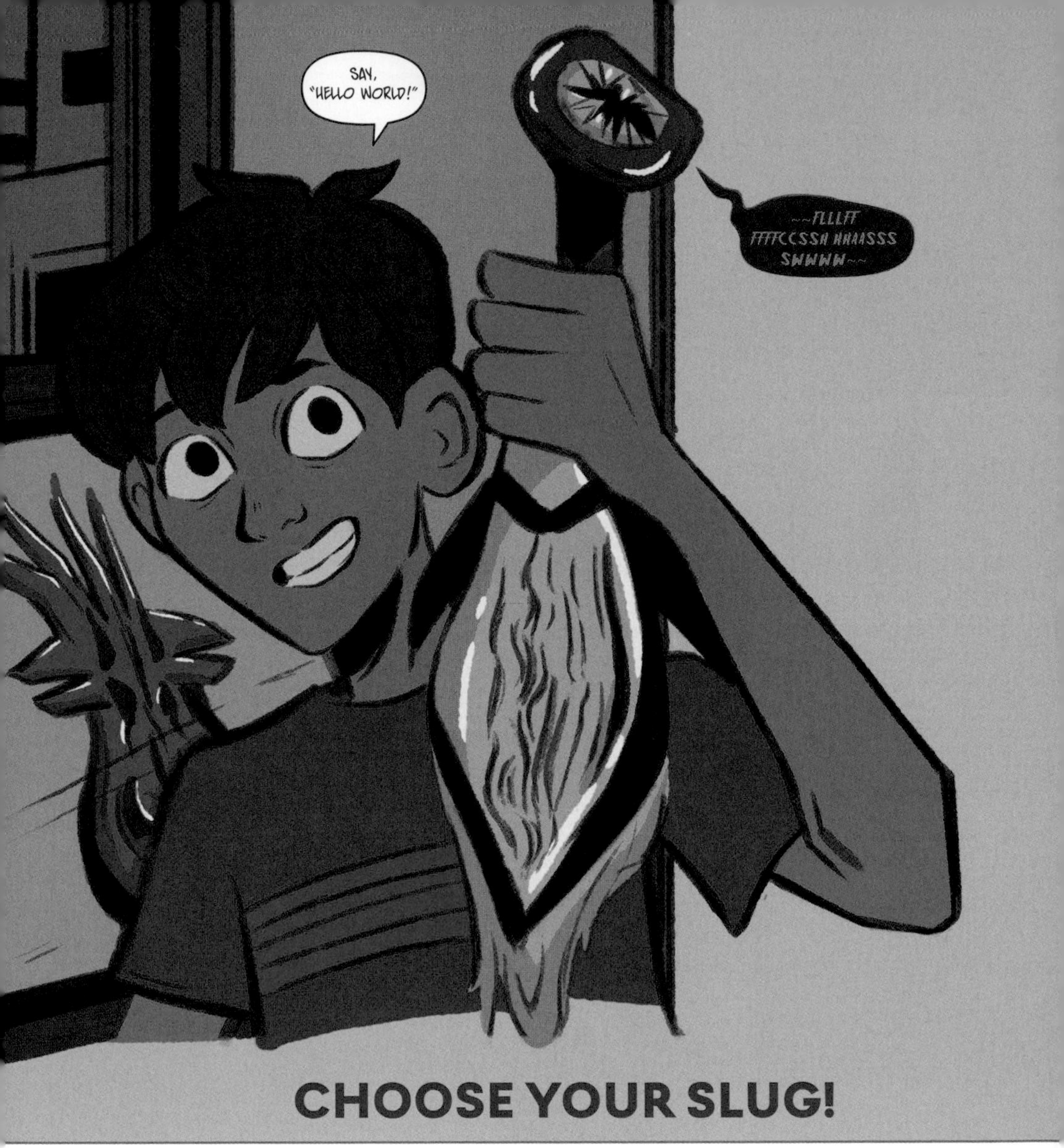
SAY, "HELLO WORLD!"
~~FLLLFF FFFFCCSSH HHAASSS SWWWW~~

CHOOSE YOUR SLUG!

A long time ago, when we had just started making *Bonding: A Love Story About People And Their Parasites* together, we created this prequel and invited readers to design their own slugs. Rather than letting our pages disappear forever, we thought we'd include them here in the final book! And, of course, we'd offer the invitation again. You probably don't want to tear the next page out (the original prequel was printed on a promo for just that purpose), but we're also not going to stop you. Your book, your rules. So, what'll you have?

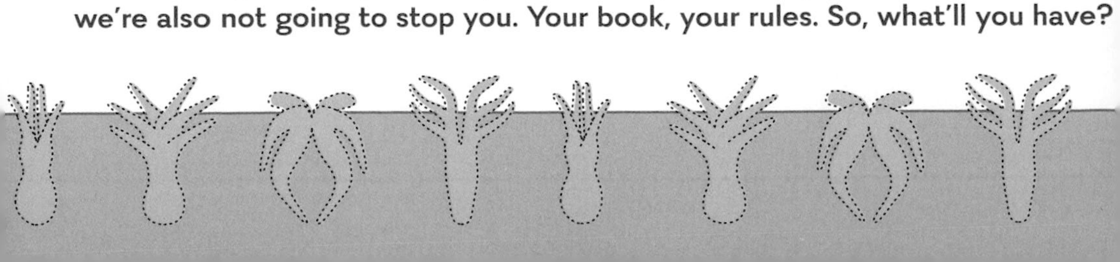

What's the Wiggle of Your Slug?

Use any of the templates below as inspiration to design your slug. Or get wacky and draw whatever you want. Slugs are weird. Be weird. Have fun.

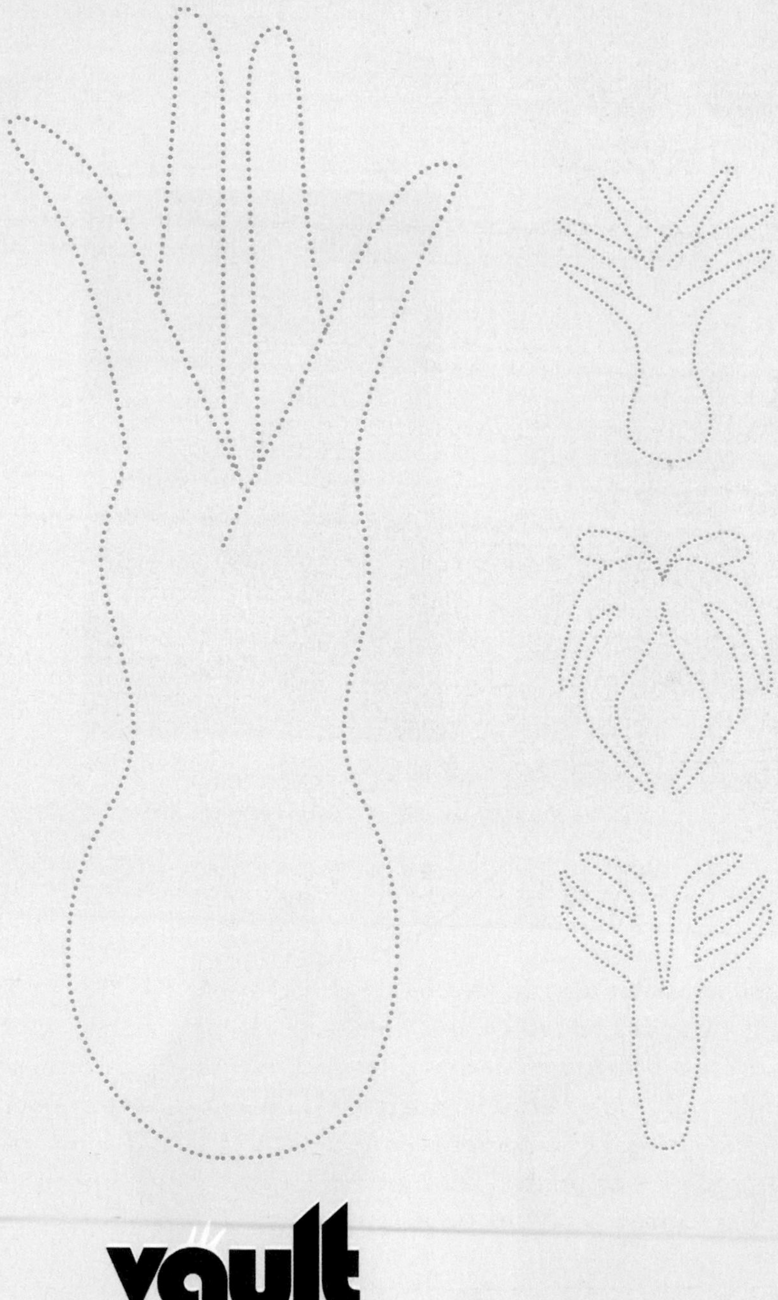

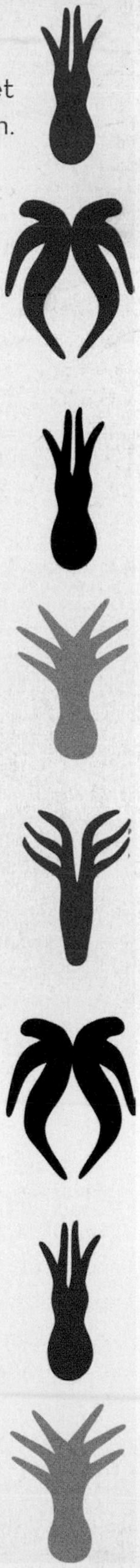

The Design Cover Process

BONDING
MATTHEW ER
ILY PEARSON

Bonding
So long as we're together...
MATTHEW ERMAN
EMILY PEARSON

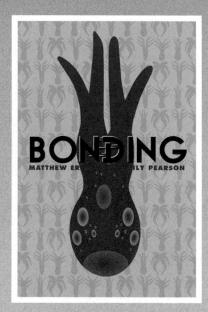

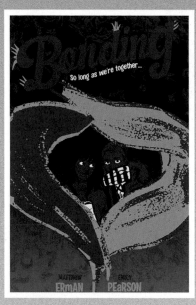

Discovering the cover composition and design required multiple iterations to properly convey the tone of a sci-fi romance.

Bonding
MATTHEW ERMAN EMILY PEARSON

BONDING
ERMAN • PEARSON • PINECONE • McCLEAN

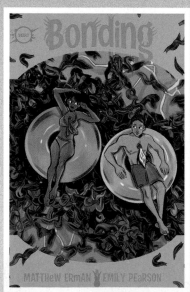

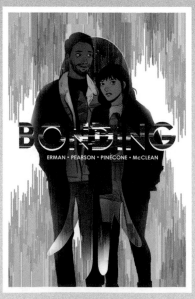

The Design Logo Process

The original logo design used for the prequel preview.

BONDING

The second iteration introducing the story's key element, the parasites.

Bonding

The basis of the final design involved a customized script-based font.

Bonding

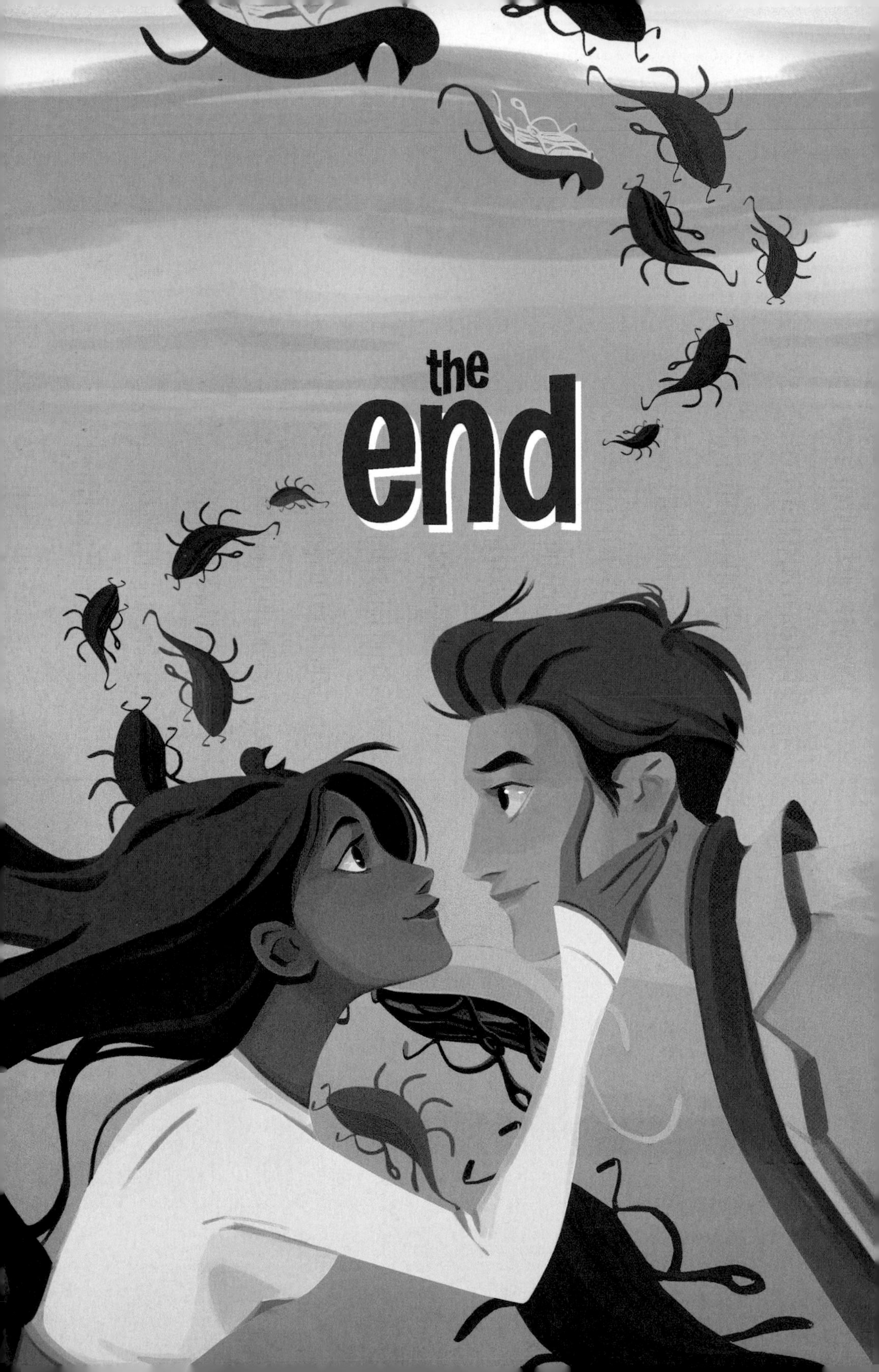

the
end